From Mobilization
to Revolution

CHARLES TILLY
The University of Michigan

From Mobilization
to Revolution

Addison-Wesley Publishing Company

Reading, Massachusetts
Menlo Park, California
London • Amsterdam
Don Mills, Ontario • Sydney

FOR LOUISE

with love, admiration,
and, sometimes, exasperation

Preface

My friends will recognize this book for what it is: stone soup. Like the down-and-out swindlers of the fable, I boiled up a pot of water, tossed in some pebbles, then invited passersby to add whatever soup makings they could spare. They added plenty. What's more, they performed a miracle: the stones became edible. Whether they actually became tasty as well, I leave you, the reader, to decide.

Several sections of the book first took shape as memoranda to a lively seminar in the now-defunct Center for Research on Conflict Resolution at the University of Michigan. Clint Fink, Bob Hefner, Bill Gamson, Joan Lind, Elizabeth Converse, and Dee Wernette provided fruitful feedback at that stage. Others emerged initially as informal written contributions to discussions with friends, students, and collaborators (the three categories are not, I am happy to note, mutually exclusive) at Michigan's Center for Research on Social Organization. Gamson, Lind, and Wernette again badgered me, now joined at different times by Bob Cole, Max Heirich, Louise Tilly, David Snyder, Frank Munger, Bruce Fireman, Bill Roy, and Ron Aminzade. Substantial portions of the book build on unpublished papers which circulated for years under the titles "From Mobilization to Political Conflict" and "Revolutions and Collective Violence." (One version of the latter paper eventually appeared in Fred I. Greenstein and Nelson Polsby, eds., *Handbook of Political Science*, volume III, also published by Addison-Wesley, 1975.) Anyone who looks closely at the soup will see some familiar ingredients floating around. Yet she or he will also see that I have chopped, blended, trimmed, and spiced the ingredients so that few of them remain in anything like their original condition.

About eighty people have given me reactions to the first draft of this book. Most, alas, were critical, although they tempered their criticism with the lame excuse that praise would do me no good. Ron Aminzade, Lynn Eden,

Bruce Fireman, Tony Oberschall, Bill Roy, Jan Smith, and Mike Useem provided especially searching reviews of my arguments. As a result, I have rewritten the entire manuscript, and expanded it from four chapters to eight. Louise Tilly, in contrast, was so busy with her own projects during the book's writing that she was unable to give the manuscript her customary devastating line-by-line review. I had to settle for her quick inspirations and peremptory challenges. Perhaps that works to my advantage. I can thank her for letting me get into print several months earlier, and blame her for any remaining errors and obscurities.

Sandra Ahrens, Anne Dolinka, Margaret Grillot, Pam Hume, Ruth Lewis, Mary Nensewitz, Rose Siri, Kathy Vargo, and Barbara White helped produce different versions of the manuscript, while Martha Guest and Bobbi Schweitzer gave me aid with bibliography. For recent research assistance in the studies of France and Britain on which this book draws repeatedly, I have a special debt to Priscilla Cheever, Leila Al-Imad, Elizabeth McDonald, Chantal Bancilhon, Mike Polen, and Bobbi Schweitzer.

Oh, yes: money. In recent years, the National Science Foundation has given generous support to the research which lies behind this book. I am grateful to Donald Ploch of the Foundation for his encouragement. A Guggenheim Fellowship and the Hudson Research Professorship of the University of Michigan gave me the leisure to write the first draft. And the joint support of the Ecole des Hautes Etudes en Sciences Sociales and the Maison des Sciences de l'Homme gave a great boost to my work in France.

A final note on stone soup. It's not good to the last drop. At the bottom of the pot, your ladle scrapes gravel. Even the miraculous ministrations and incantations of my friends did not dissolve all the rocks I started with. For the remainder I am doubly responsible: for having posed and answered questions badly; worse still, for having knowingly allowed bad questions and bad answers to remain. Why? Because halfway through the re-drafting I realized that soup was my life. There is the future: spooning out the minestrone, adding a pebble now and then, collecting recipes and complaints, trying to improve the taste and nutritional value, but never taking the pot off the fire. So long as friends are around, they won't lack for stone soup.

Ann Arbor, Michigan   Charles Tilly
January 1978

Contents

1
INTRODUCTION

2
THEORIES AND DESCRIPTIONS OF COLLECTIVE ACTION

7

REVOLUTION AND REBELLION

8

CONCLUSIONS AND NEW BEGINNINGS

APPENDIX 1

APPENDIX 2

APPENDIX 3

Figures

Tables

1
Introduction

THE STUFF OF COLLECTIVE ACTION

The year 1765 was a lively one in England, as it was in America. News coming in from the American colonies described the usual conficts: run-ins between smugglers and customs men, skirmishes of Indians with settlers, attempts of frontiersmen to take the law into their own hands. But the big news from America was the resistance to the British-imposed Stamp Act. The use of costly stamped paper for official transactions was supposed to begin on the first of November. Long before then, anonymous notices and determined crowds threatened anyone who showed signs of willingness to comply with the Stamp Act. In Boston and elsewhere, groups of citizens produced colorful street theater, complete with gallows, hand-lettered signs, and effigies of royal officials. Sometimes they sacked the houses or outbuildings of designated stamp agents and government officers. They succeeded in blocking the Act's application in the American colonies. With their allies in England, they obtained repeal in March 1766. That concerted resistance started ten years of nearly continuous struggle within the American colonies, and ended in a great struggle between the colonies and England. America was already on its way to revolution.

   In England, there was some sympathetic reaction to the American cause. For example, at the beginning of March 1766, " . . . a body of upwards of two hundred members of the house of Commons carried up the bill to the house of Peers, for repealing the American stamp-duty act; an instance of such a number going up with a single bill, has not been known in the memory of the oldest man" (*Annual Register 1766*: 72). Nevertheless, in 1765 and 1766 most of England's visible conflict concerned domestic issues. Tailors went on strike, weavers marched on Parliament to demand the exclusion of foreign competition, the sheriffs of London paraded to petition for government intervention against high food prices, countrymen seized and sold food at their own prices,

1

townsmen attacked the collectors appointed for England's own version of the Stamp Act.

That was not all. Near Ipswich, on the 12th of August:

> Several persons riotously assembed to pull down the house of industry, lately erected at Nacton . . . carried their boldness to such length that, neither the expostulations of the magistrates against the illegality of their design, which they openly avowed, the consequences of the riot proclamation act being read, which were explained to them, nor the appearance of a body of regular horse and foot, called in as part of the *posse comitatus,* seemed to make the least impression on them; nay, though the proclamation was then read to them with an audible voice, and they seemed to hear it with attention, not a man stirred (*Annual Register 1765*: 116–117).

On the contrary. As the troops readied themselves for the attack, the crowd of a hundred or so "fell upon both horses and men with such arms as they had, peasemakes, hedge-stakes, cudgels, etc., but in five minutes the affair was over." The soldiers arrested seven men as examples, and dispersed the rest.

Was that a riot? In the technical legal sense, it was: twelve or more people had, indeed, assembled with an apparent intent which local officials could reasonably regard as illegal; they had not dispersed within the hour the law allotted them from the time that the authorities had read the riot act. In the looser sense of frenzy, confusion or wanton destruction, however, the event does not qualify as a riot. Both sides apparently knew what they were doing, and did it as best they could. That was generally true of the many "disorders" reported in the *Annual Register* for 1765.

In the case of Nacton, the "house of industry" the crowd proposed to destroy was a recently built workhouse. Poor English villagers had for a long time drawn relief from their own parishes while living at home. The payments were miserable, but they assured survival. And the payments were a right. That was "outdoor relief." "Indoor relief" was now threatening to displace the older system. From the 1730s onward, many English local authorities responded to the increasing numbers of poor with two important innovations: locking up the poor to work under public supervision; combining the poor-law efforts of a number of adjacent parishes into a single administration. Parliamentary legislation had legalized both efforts. The building of workhouses for multiple parishes combined the two of them. It also permitted many parishes to reduce their relief payments and to ship their local paupers elsewhere. The poor fought indoor relief in the name of established rights.

In the 1750s, the landlords and parsons of the parishes near Ipswich, in Suffolk, caught the reform fever. Admiral Vernon donated a site on Nacton Heath for a new workhouse. A blue-ribbon committee supervised its construction. The Nacton House of Industry, a model of its kind, started enrolling paupers from a number of adjacent parishes in 1758. The parish poor went to work weaving sacks, making cordage, and spinning wool (Webb & Webb 1963: 127). By 1765, however, the elite supervision had slackened. It had proved difficult to find profitable work for the incarcerated paupers. The cooperating parishes, furthermore, had dumped into the poorhouse young and old, sick and well, regardless of their ability to work. Small wonder the poor people of Suffolk resisted the extension of the system.

The move against the Nacton poorhouse was one of many such conflicts in 1765. As *The Gentleman's Magazine* reported for the week before the Nacton confrontation:

> Some thousands of rioters assembled in the neighborhood of *Saxmundham* in *Suffolk*, and destroyed the industry-house, in which the poor were employed. Their pretence was to release the poor to assist in the harvest-work; but the fact was to defeat a late act of parliament, lately obtained for the relief of the poor of the hundreds of *Wilford*, and *Loes*, etc. In this riot, the military were called in, and several lost their lives before the rioters were dispersed (*The Gentleman's Magazine 1765*: 392).

At Saxmundham, not only the poor but also many of their less impoverished neighbors considered the new institution improper and intolerable.

During the second week of August 1765, in fact, much of Suffolk was alive with rebellion. A large crowd of people first gathered at Wickham Market, when the Directors of the Poor for Loes and Wilford Hundreds met to plan a new poorhouse; the crowd forced the Directors to sign a repudiation of their plan. For a week, the group went from workhouse to workhouse tearing the buildings down and demanding that the overseers commit themselves not to rebuild. They demanded "that the poor should be maintained as usual; that they should range at liberty and be their own masters" (Webb & Webb 1963: 141–142). Riots these were, in the legal sense of the word. They were clearly much more than that.

The confrontations at Nacton and Saxmundham acted out pervasive characteristics of eighteenth-century conflicts in Great Britain as a whole. While David Hume and Adam Smith worked out the relevant theories, ordinary Britons fought about who had the right to dispose of land, labor, capital, and commodities. Attacks on poorhouses, concerted resistance to enclosures, food riots, and a number of other common forms of eighteenth-century conflict all stated an implicit two-part theory: that the residents of a local community had a prior right to the resources produced by or contained within that community; that the community as such had a prior obligation to aid its weak and resourceless members. The right and the obligation should take priority over the interest of any particular individual and over any interest outside the community. It should even take priority over the interest of the Crown, or of the country as a whole. That was, in E. P. Thompson's terms, the ill-articulated but powerful theory of the "moral economy."

Meanwhile, many merchants, manufacturers, landlords, and local authorities favored another, newer, four-part theory: that all goods, including labor power, should be disposable property; that the individual property owner had the right, and to some extent the obligation, to use it to his own advantage; that the collective interest, as articulated by the state, had priority over parochial interests; that on the whole the collective interest will best be served by the rational, unconstrained pursuit of individual interests. C. B. Macpherson has called it the theory of "possessive individualism." The four-part theory is familiar nowadays. It expresses some founding principles of our own era. But in the eighteenth century the theory of possessive individualism was still new and contestable. To become dominant, it had to displace the rival theory of the "moral economy." Although they did not dream of saying it in those terms, the contestants at Nacton, Saxmundham, and many other places in eighteenth-century Britain were fighting the losing battle of the moral economy against the rise of possessive individualism.

Not that the fighters on either side were mere theorists, simple ideologues, hapless victims of shared delusions. Real interests were in play. The participants saw them more or less clearly. At two centuries' distance, we may find some of their pronouncements quaint, incomprehensible, or hopelessly romantic. In comfortable retrospect, we may question the means they used to forward their interests: scoff at tearing down poorhouses, anger at the use of troops against unarmed crowds. Yet in retrospect we also see that their actions followed a basic, visible logic. The more we learn about eighteenth-century changes in Great Britain, the clearer and more compelling that logic becomes.

The struggle did not simply pit different ways of thinking about the world against each other. Two modes of social organization locked in a battle to the death. The old mode vested power in land and locality. The new mode combined the expansion of capitalist property relations with the rise of the national state. Many other changes flowed from that fateful combination: larger-scale organizations, increasing commercialization, expanded communications, the growth of a proletariat, alterations of the very texture of daily life. The new mode won. The world of the moral economy dissolved. But when ordinary eighteenth-century Britons acted collectively at all, usually they acted against one feature or another of this new world. On the whole, they acted in defense of particular features of the moral economy.

The effort to understand the events of 1765 thus takes us in several very different directions. It requires some knowledge of the particular circumstances in which the participants found themselves: the problems they faced, the enemies before them, the means of action at their disposal, their definitions of what was happening. In eighteenth-century Britain, the magistrates' efforts to consolidate poor law administration, the vulnerability of the landless poor to swings in prices, the strength of a tradition involving local direct action against malefactors are all crucial. Understanding 1765 also calls for an analysis of the large-scale changes behind the conflicts of the moment; in the eighteenth century we can sort out little of the pattern of conflict until we detect the conjoint expansion of capitalism and rise of the state. It takes us, finally, to a general consideration of the ways that people act together in pursuit of shared interests. It takes us, that is, into the study of collective action.

STUDYING COLLECTIVE ACTION

The third inquiry—the study of collective action—is the chief concern of this book. I will often illustrate from specific historical circumstances and will frequently propose explanations involving state making, the expansion of capitalism, industrialization, or some other big structural change. But the pages to follow will concentrate on the general analysis of collective action.

The analysis of collective action is a risky adventure. For one thing, there are too many experts around. It is a bit like food, or sex, or speech. Almost all of us know enough about food, sex, and speech to survive in our own environments, and none of us likes to be told he is ignorant in any of these three regards. Yet from a scientific point of view, we all have lots to learn about all three. The same is true of collective action. Like the eighteenth-century people of Nacton, we all draw on a rich, concrete experience of acting on shared interests. Among us, furthermore, seasoned organizers are around to share—and even to lecture us on—the lessons of their practical experience. As with the student of food, or sex, or speech, the determined student of collective action runs the risk either of labeling the obvious or of urging hypotheses which common sense contradicts.

It is more delicate than that. Deep in every discussion of collective action stirs the lava of a volcanic eruption: collective action is about power and politics; it inevitably raises questions of right and wrong, justice and injustice, hope and hopelessness; the very setting of the problem is likely to include judgments about who has the right to act, and what good it does. Consider these words from a newspaper editorial (*Detroit Free Press* October 15, 1975):

> Present-day liberalism had its roots in the 19th century faith in the idea of human progress; that the lives of men could be made better by collective action. In its extreme form, it was always a naive faith, based on a naive view of human nature.

The 20th century has been a more tumultuous time, and it has meant considerable disillusionment with the idea of changing the human condition. Consider its multiple tragedies: Two world wars, the Great Depression, the often bewildering impact of technology on people, the aftereffects of colonialism and institutionalized racism, the growth in the concentration of wealth and influence, the H-bomb, the Cold War, the near-breakdown of many cities.

("Heavy stuff, that Collective Action!" said the note inked on the editorial when someone tacked it on our research group's bulletin board.) In some sense, *every* position one takes on the desirability, feasibility, or effectiveness of collective action is a political position. The tone of later discussions in this book is generally hostile to the collective action of governments and favorable to the collective action of ordinary people; that, too, is a political stance.

These risks provide, alas, a strong temptation to dress up the topic in fancy, obscure terminology and fearsome abstract models. Yet plain talk also has its disadvantages: people often respond more to the overtones and undertones than to the solid information. Without some standardization of terms and some effort at abstraction we run the further risk of bogging down in more and more fastidious description of the details of particular actions. We must find the balance point between imprecision and obscurantism.

Another risk results from the fact that collective action straddles a divide which ordinarily separates one major kind of social analysis from another. That is the divide between causal and purposive explanation (see Coleman 1973: 1–5). We may choose to consider the action of an individual or of a group as the resultant of forces external to the individual or group; those external forces supposedly *cause* the behavior. In this case, we are likely to think we have a good explanation when a careful look at the actor's situation permits us to deduce more or less accurately how the actor will behave.

Alternatively, we may consider the individual or group to be making choices according to some set of rules, implicit or explicit; that approach is *purposive*. Then we are likely to think we have a sound explanation when we can impute to the actor a rule which leads logically to most or all of the choices we observe the actor making. In the realm of collective action, it is hard to build causal models which give serious attention to the interests, grievances, and aspirations of the actors. It is also hard to build purposive models which specify the constraints limiting the pursuit of interests, grievances, and aspirations.

So why not try a synthesis? Why not combine causal models of constraints with purposive models of choices among available courses of action? The synthesis is surprisingly difficult to achieve. Before this book is over, we will have spent a good deal of time oscillating between the two alternatives, and trying to draw them together.

THE COMPONENTS OF COLLECTIVE ACTION

The analysis of collective action has five big components: interest, organization, mobilization, opportunity, and collective action itself. The *interests* which concern us most are the gains and losses resulting from a group's interaction with other groups. Later on we will have to worry about what constitutes a relevant group, and how to identify or measure real, durable interests.

The *organization* which concerns us most is that aspect of a group's structure which most directly affects its capacity to act on its interests. Clearly one of the problems is to determine which features of organization *do* make a difference. Is it possible, for example, that how committed members are makes little difference to the form and intensity of their collective action? Is it possible that the neatness of an organization's division of labor matters greatly?

Mobilization is the process by which a group acquires collective control over the resources needed for action. Those resources may be labor power, goods, weapons, votes, and any number of other things, just so long as they are usable in acting on shared interests. Sometimes a group such as a community has a complex internal structure, but few pooled resources. Sometimes it is rich in resources, but the resources are all under individual control. The analysis of mobilization deals with the ways that groups acquire resources and make them available for collective action.

Opportunity concerns the relationship between a group and the world around it. Changes in the relationship sometimes threaten the group's interests. They sometimes provide new chances to act on those interests. The trouble with studying opportunity is that it is hard to reconstruct the opportunities realistically available to the group at the time. Knowledge of later outcomes makes it too easy to second-guess a group's action, or inaction. We can minimize that disadvantage by looking only at contemporary collective action or by concentrating on situations in which the opportunities are rigorously defined and strictly limited. But then we lose our ability to follow large-scale changes, in their real complexity, over considerable periods of time.

Collective action consists of people's acting together in pursuit of common interests. Collective action results from changing combinations of interests, organization, mobilization, and opportunity. The most persistent problem we will face in analyzing collective action is its lack of sharp edges: people vary continuously from intensive involvement to passive compliance, interests vary from quite individual to nearly universal. Toward the end of this book, we will pursue that complexity into the analysis of revolutionary processes. Our chief effort, then, will flow along the lines going from organization to mobilization to collective action to revolution. Especially from mobilization to revolution.

In dealing with each of these problems, the analyses which follow make serious, debatable choices. With respect to interests, they give priority to economic and political life. They favor a group's own articulation of its interest over the assumptions of contemporary observers and over our own retrospective judgment as to what would have been best for the group. With respect to organization, they focus on relatively well-defined groups. They therefore neglect two fascinating sorts of questions: how new groups oriented to new world-views come into being, and under what conditions ill-defined sets of people, such as passersby or friendship networks, become important collective actors. In regard to mobilization, they stress the factors of production—land, labor, capital, technology—and neglect the possibility that attitudes are more important resources for collective action than any of these. On the side of opportunity, the analyses in this book stress political opportunity, coalition, repression, and relations among governments and well-defined contenders for power over those governments. When it comes to collective action as such, most of the concrete discussion deals with contentious gatherings: publicly visible assemblies in which conflicting interests are clearly in play.

GROUPS, EVENTS, AND MOVEMENTS

We find our subject matter in the overlaps of three intersecting areas. Sometimes we are interested in a particular population in its own terms. For example, we want to know what was happening to poor people in eighteenth-century Suffolk. Sometimes we are chiefly concerned with a set of beliefs. For instance, we want to follow the rise and fall of ideas about the proper treatment of the poor and incompetent. Sometimes certain kinds of action attract our attention; we might want to understand the conditions in which people take the law into their own hands. The study of collective action ordinarily requires us to deal with at least two of these areas at once. We could diagram the situation as in Figure 1-1.

We can take groups as our basic units for the study of collective action. Then we typically start with a population which has some common structure and shared beliefs. We are likely to accent those actions which we think result from that combination of structure and beliefs. We pay relatively little attention to other versions of the same beliefs or to other actions of the same kind. Histories of the working class often take this form: much attention to changes in living conditions, work, and internal organization; plenty of material on beliefs and outlook; analysis of those actions which appear to express the character of the working-class population and its beliefs.

We can also take events as our starting point. We begin with a particular revolution, ceremony or confrontation. Or we begin with a class of events:

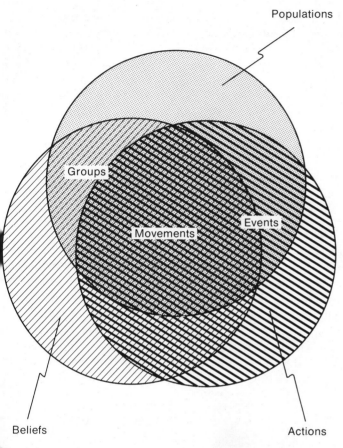

Fig. 1-1
Units in the study of collective action

attacks on poorhouses, demonstrations, revolutions in general. In either case, we become concerned about populations and beliefs to the extent that they are involved directly in the events. Analyses of "collective behavior" commonly take this tack. At their abstract extreme, they strive for general laws governing all actions of certain kinds of populations: large crowds, for example, or people hit by disaster.

The notion of a "movement" is more complicated than the ideas of groups and events. By a social movement we often mean a group of people identified by their attachment to some particular set of beliefs. In that case, the population in question can change drastically, but so long as some group of people is still working with the same beliefs, we consider the movement to survive. Thus the Women's Movement survives major changes in composition and internal organization. But movement also commonly means action. People writing histories of the women's movement are quite likely to include past heroines who were quite different in beliefs and personal characteristics from current activists, just so long as their actions were similar or had similar effects. The fact that population, belief, and action do not always change together causes serious problems for students of social movements. When they diverge, should we follow the beliefs, whatever populations and actions they become associated with? Should we follow the population, whatever beliefs and actions it adopts? Should we follow the action, regardless of who does it and with what ideas?

WHAT YOU WILL FIND HERE

This book will generally avoid the analysis of social movements as such. Nevertheless, plenty of material other people have analyzed under that heading will come into the discussion. We will alternate between groups and events as our starting points for the analysis of collective action. Sometimes we will begin by asking what peasants are up to, and how that helps us understand rural collective action. Sometimes we will begin by asking what food riots are about, and how that helps us understand the collective action of poor people. Sometimes we will try to start both places at once, searching for connections between food riots and peasant social life, or between some other class of events and some other kind of social group.

From Mobilization to Revolution offers both a partial synthesis and a proposal for further inquiry. As a result, it does not contain a sustained analysis of a single body of evidence. The illustrations and findings run from brawls to strikes to revolutions. At one point or another, the discussion ranges over much of the world. Most of the material, however, comes from the experiences of Western Europe and North America over the last few centuries. That focus gives us much opportunity to consider state making, the expansion of capitalism, industrialization, urbanization, electoral politics, and formally organized interest groups. All of them have figured importantly in the modern European and American experiences with collective action.

The focus on the modern West also costs us something. It gives us little chance to think about collective action in the absence of a strong state, about people whose social relations are organized mainly around kinship, about exotic movements such as Melanesian cargo cults. The conclusions may, at best, apply only to the modern urban-industrial world. Still, making sense of collective action in that world is a big enough task for one book.

The remaining chapters follow a simple plan. Chapter 2 catalogs competing theories of collective action in order to lay out the choices before us and to
identify the major disagreements and uncertainties. Chapter 3 presents and
illustrates a simple set of concepts and models for the analysis of collective action, then works out their implications for the ways groups acquire the ability
to act; that chapter dwells on interests, organization, and mobilization.
Chapter 4 adds opportunity to the analysis; it dwells on conflict, repression,
and struggles for power. Chapter 5 closes in on the specific forms of collective
action: how they vary, how they relate to each other, and how they alter
under the impact of industrialization, state making, and other big social
changes. Chapter 6 closes in on violent collective action while Chapter 7
applies the general line of reasoning to rebellions and revolutions. Chapter 8
then sums up conclusions, and inventories new problems encountered along
the way.

2
Theories and Descriptions of Collective Action

MARX ON 1848

Well over a century ago, Karl Marx set out his analysis of the French Revolution of 1848 and of the internal struggles which engaged France for the next four years. To Marx, the revolution was the work of a temporary coalition among the Parisian proletariat, the petty bourgeoisie, and an enlightened fragment of the bourgeoisie. Among the many segments of the population with intense grievances against the existing state of affairs, these were the ones who combined a high degree of internal communication, a consciousness of common interests, and a collective vision, however fleeting, of future transformations which could improve their lot.

Although each group had its own communications structure, its own interests and its own vision, in Marx's analysis the crisis of 1846–47 drove them together and made the regime vulnerable. Thus they joined in toppling the regime, as a miserable but incoherent peasantry sat by, as the bourgeois of finance and big industry wrung their hands, as the great landlords looked for their own ways to profit by the destruction of a regime which had shunted them aside.

The class base of each participant limited its revolutionary vision and checked its activity. The class bases of the revolutionary coalition as a whole, Marx thought, condemned it to default on the promises of spring 1848. Despite the extension of the revolutionary coalition to proletarians and bourgeois in a few advanced centers outside of Paris, the revolutionary leadership compromised. It failed to expand its program or its power. The coalition began to disintegrate as the workers and the bourgeois within it headed separate ways. A conservative coalition of landlords and bourgeois formed with passive support from the more comfortable segments of the peasantry. Thus began the process which led to Louis Napoleon's *coup d'état* and the establishment of an empire, an empire devoted to canceling the gains of the

12

evolution and ensuring against its recurrence. Marx's account contained a good deal more—not least the relentless wit he trained on the individual personalities of 1848—but these are the main lines of the analysis.

Twelve decades of historical work have identified some gaps and errors in Marx's analysis. For one example, Marx did not see that many French workers were already sympathetic to Bonaparte in 1848. For another, he neither appreciated the extent of the armed resistance to the 1851 coup nor recognized the considerable involvement of landowning peasants in that insurrection. Yet the arguments Marx stated in *The Eighteenth Brumaire of Louis Bonaparte* and *The Class Struggles in France* have stood the passage of time rather well. In his book-length confrontation of Marx's account with the Second Republic scholars have come to know, Roger Price offers many a cavil and not a few nuances, but ends up in basic agreement. The broad lines of Marx's analysis have survived more than a hundred years of historical criticism.*

Few interpretations of historical events last as long as a century. Some endure because scholars lose interest in the events, others because they fit prevailing prejudices and doctrines, the remaining few because they explain what happened better than their available competitors do. Although the rise of Marxist doctrines and political movements has undoubtedly promoted the acceptance of Marx's historical analyses as well, it has also directed criticism and new research to his main arguments. That they have survived testifies to their explanatory power.

If that is so, we might pay attention to Marx's mode of analysis. Implicitly, Marx divided the entire population into social classes based on their relationships to the prevailing means of production. Explicitly, he identified the major visible actors in the politics of the time with their class bases, offering judgments of their basic interests, conscious aspirations, articulated grievances, and collective readiness for action. Classes act, or fail to act. In general, individuals and institutions act on behalf of particular social classes. There is an important exception: in analyzing Louis Napoleon's seizure of power, Marx allowed that those who run the state may act, at least for a while, in their own political interest without reference to their class base.) In analyzing readiness to act, Marx attached great importance to the ease and durability of communications within the class, to the visible presence of a class enemy. When Marx's political actors acted, they did so out of common interests, mutual awareness, and internal organization.

For a determined attempt to review and revise Marx's arguments concerning the determinants of worker militancy, which concludes with a more extensive restatement than Price finds necessary for 1848, see J. A. Banks's *Marxist Sociology in Action.*

As compared with other analysts of the same events, Marx attached little importance to generalized tension, momentary impulses, or personal disorganization. While he saw the Lumpenproletariat as liable to crime and disorder, he also saw a world of difference between brawling and making revolutions. If you want to analyze major conflicts, we hear him telling us, identify the major classes and interests which emerge from the organization of production. Catalogue the resulting conflicts of interest. Examine each class you have enumerated in terms of its preparedness to act on its interests. Work out the class bases of the chief institutions and leaders involved in the conflict. Watch out for crises which make the dominant classes vulnerable, and expect the organized underclasses to strike. There is much more to it, but those are Marx's essential instructions.

We are dealing with a theory of collective action: of the conditions in which people act together in pursuit of common ends. Marx's theory of collective action is debatable. It is not self-evident that social classes and their representatives are the principal actors in politics. It is not necessarily true that prior organization strongly affects a group's readiness to act. It can easily be maintained, contrary to Marx, that participants in mass movements tend to ignore their own true interests. The Marxian theory emphasizes the collective rationality of political action.

Nowadays, Marx's theory sounds familiar. In some ways it seems obvious. Yet in the nineteenth century, it broke decisively with the prevailing accounts of mass action. Other theories treated "the people" as incapable of continuous, calculating pursuit of their collective interests, as responding mainly to impulses—good impulses or bad—and to manipulation by elites. Today the Marxian view again has important competitors. The condescending nineteenth-century view of mass action has remained popular with critics of democracy. It has lingered on in academic analyses of "mass society." And that theory, too, has rivals.

Among professional students of politics, at least three additional lines of argument have acquired eloquent advocates. We can identify the lines loosely with three other nineteenth-century and early twentieth-century figures: Emile Durkheim, John Stuart Mill, and Max Weber. Figure 2–1 sketches out the general logic of Marxian, Durkheimian, Millian, and Weberian analyses. The Marxian analysis, as we have just seen, generally traces collective action back to solidarity within groups and conflicts of interest between groups, considers the solidarity and the conflicts of interest to reinforce each other, and bases both of them on the organization of production. Durkheim treated collective action as a relatively direct response to processes of integration and disintegration in whole societies. As the diagram suggests, his followers have developed rather different explanations of routine and nonroutine collective action. The nonroutine forms, according to Durkheimians, grow from the discontent and

MARXIAN

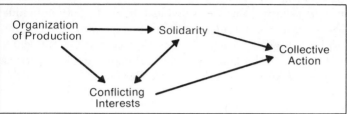

DURKHEIMIAN

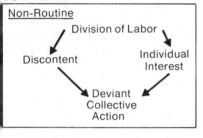
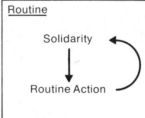

MILLIAN

WEBERIAN

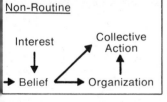
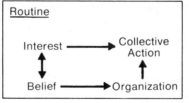

Fig. 2–1
Competing analyses of collective action

pursuit of individual interests produced by disintegration of the division of labor; under conditions of routine integration, on the other hand, solidarity leads to collective action, which in its turn reinforces solidarity. Mill rooted collective action in the strictly calculating pursuit of individual interest. The distinctive approach of Millians, as the diagram indicates, is the analysis of the various decision rules which translate individual interests into individual action and which aggregate individual actions into collective action. Max Weber, finally, portrayed collective action as the outgrowth of commitment to certain systems of belief. Weberians, like Durkheimians, tend to propose different explanations for routine and nonroutine collective action. In the non-routine forms the shared beliefs of the group have a strong, direct impact on the group's collective action, while as action routinizes two things happen: organization grows up to mediate between the beliefs and the action, and group interests play a larger and more direct role in collective action.

Marx, Durkheim, Mill, and Weber had distinctively different views of the world, and bequeathed to their heirs significantly different analyses of collective action. Let us review characteristic analyses in the Durkheimian, Millian, and Weberian traditions before returning to the Marxian line of argument.

DURKHEIM

Durkheim crystallized a widespread nineteenth-century view of what industrialization was doing to the world. He fashioned it into a set of arguments which have remained dominant in sociology, especially American sociology, up to our own time. As Talcott Parsons put it:

> . . . it was the problem of the integration of the social system, of what holds societies together, which was the most persistent preoccupation of Durkheim's career. In the situation of the time, one could not have chosen a more strategic focus for contributing to sociological theory. Moreover, the work Durkheim did in this field can be said to have been nothing short of epoch-making; he did not stand entirely alone, but his work was far more sharply focused and deeply penetrating than that of any other author of his time (Parsons 1960: 118).

In *The Division of Labor in Society* and in *Suicide*, Durkheim laid out a view of something called a "society" differentiating unsteadily in response to a variety of pressures. Speaking abstractly, Durkheim summed up those pressures as a growth in the volume and density of society. Speaking concretely, he discussed occupational changes.

The pressures emphatically included the internal logic of industrialization. On the very first page of *Division of Labor*, Durkheim tells us:

> We need have no further illusions about the tendencies of modern industry: it advances steadily towards powerful machines, towards great concentrations of forces and capital, and consequently to the extreme division of labor. Occupations are infinitely separated and specialized, not only inside the factories, but each product is itself a specialty dependent upon others (Durkheim 1933: 39).

The "society," according to Durkheim, exerts its control over individuals via their participation in a shared consciousness. As Durkheim puts it, "The totality of beliefs and sentiments common to average citizens of the same society forms a determinate system which has its own life; one may call it the collective or common conscience" (Durkheim 1933: 79). The advancing division of labor, he says, threatens the shared consciousness based on the essential similarity of individuals, and thereby threatens the primacy of the needs and demands of the society as a whole over the impulses and interests of the individual. A new shared consciousness based on interdependence and common fate is both problematic and slow to emerge. Into the gap between the level of differentiation and the level of shared consciousness moves *anomie*.

To be precise, *anomie* is Durkheim's name for that gap between the degree of differentiation and the extent of regulation of social relations; from it he derives a set of undesirable results: individual disorientation, destructive social life, extensive conflict. His concrete examples again come almost entirely from the industrial world. They are the economic crash, the conflict between management and labor, the separation of work and family life, and so on through the standard concerns of nineteenth-century reformers.

In *Suicide,* Durkheim sketches the consequences of a rapid growth in power and wealth:

> Time is required for the public conscience to reclassify men and things. So long as the social forces thus freed have not regained equilibrium, their respective values are unknown and so all regulation is lacking for a time . . . Consequently, there is no restraint upon aspirations . . . With increased prosperity desires increase. At the very moment when traditional rules have lost their authority, the richer prize offered these appetites stimulates them and makes them more exigent and impatient of control. The state of de-regulation or anomy is thus further heightened by passions being less disciplined, precisely when they need more disciplining (Durkheim 1951: 253).

We begin to see that Durkheim not only propounded a theory of social change, but also proposed a theory of collective action.

In fact, he proposed two or three of each. When it comes to the link between large-scale social change and collective action, we find Durkheim distinguishing sharply between the orderly pursuit of shared interests which occurs when the division of labor is not outrunning the shared consciousness, and the free-for-all which results for *anomie*. Later, in *The Elementary Forms of the Religious Life*, we find Durkheim analyzing the solidarity-producing consequences of ritualized, approved forms of collective action. In an amazingly anthropomorphic passage, he says:

When a society is going through circumstances which sadden, perplex or irritate it, it exercises a pressure over its members, to make them bear witness by significant acts, to their sorrow, perplexity or anger. It imposes upon them the duty of weeping, groaning or inflicting wounds upon themselves or others for these collective manifestations, and the moral communion which they show and strengthen, restore to the group the energy which circumstances threaten to take away from it, and thus they enable it to become settled (Durkheim 1961: 459).

The basic Durkheimian idea presents a society strained by a continuous struggle between forces of disintegration (notably rapid differentiation) and forces of integration (notably new or renewed commitment to shared beliefs). From the basic notion Durkheim derives models of three different kinds of collective action: let us call them routine, anomic, and restorative.

We might sum up Durkheim's analysis of collective action in a simple diagram (Fig. 2–2). The shaded area above the diagonal is safe; there, the development of shared belief is equal to or greater than the stress imposed by differentiation and other calamities. The area below the diagonal is dangerous; there, differentiation outstrips the extent of shared belief. Routine collective action goes on in the safe area, and renews shared belief routinely. Anomic collective action increases as the society slides down from the diagonal, and perpetuates itself by shaking shared beliefs even more than they were already shaken. Restorative collective action occurs near the diagonal, and moves the society back into the safe area. Although the language is a little odd, the argument is very familiar.

Durkheim's theory, in contrast to Marx's, leads us to expect anomic and restorative collective action to rise as differentiation accelerates. It leads us to anticipate finding the populations newly created or displaced by differentiation at the center of collective action. It predicts a close association among suicide, crime, violence, and nonroutine collective action. In the twentieth century, most theories for collective behavior embody some version of the Durkheimian argument. Indeed, the standard analyses of industrialization, urbanization, deviance, social control, social disorganization, and collective behavior which emerged in the twentieth century all bore the Durkheimian stamp.

THE DURKHEIMIAN TRADITION

To see this clearly, we need only examine an influential book from the 1960s: Samuel Huntington's *Political Order in Changing Societies.* Huntington argues that the extensive domestic conflict in developing countries after World War II resulted from the fact that political institutions

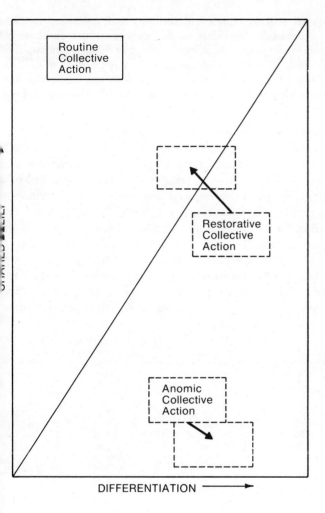

Fig. 2–2
Durkheim's analysis of collective action

developed only slowly, while rapid social change both placed new strain on existing political institutions and promoted the participation of new, demanding groups in political life. Concretely:

> Social and economic change—urbanization, increases in literacy and education, industrialization, mass media expansion—extend political consciousness, multiply political demands, broaden political participation. These changes

undermine traditional sources of political authority and traditional political institutions; they enormously complicate the problems of creating new bases of political association and new political institutions combining legitimacy and effectiveness. The rates of social mobilization and the expansion of political participation are high; the rates of political organization and institutionalization are low. The result is political instability and disorder (Huntington 1968: 5)

The larger the discrepancy between institutionalization and modernization, the greater the disorder. At the extreme lies revolution: "The political essence of revolution is the rapid expansion of political consciousness and the rapid mobilization of new groups into politics at a speed which makes it impossible for existing political institutions to assimilate them" (Huntington 1968: 266).

In this formulation, either a speedup of institutionalization or a slowdown of modernization will decrease the amount of disorder. But if political institutions are very rigid, they will inhibit essential social change. Schematically, Huntington's analysis takes the pattern of Fig. 2-3. Furthermore, the argument describes different paths through these possibilities, depending on the pace of social change (see Fig. 2-4). Slow social change,

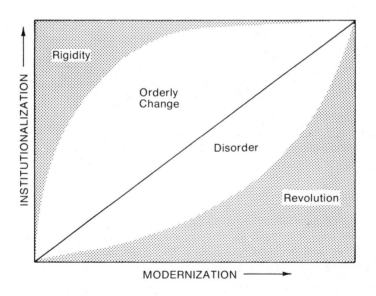

Fig. 2-3
Huntington's basic argument

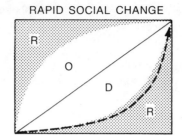

SLOW SOCIAL CHANGE   RAPID SOCIAL CHANGE

Fig. 2-4
Trajectories of slow and rapid social change in Huntington's
argument

then, is likely to be orderly throughout its course. Rapid social change
brings a likelihood of disorder, and a possibility of revolution. The
similarity to Durkheim is impressive. Institutionalization takes the place of
Durkheim's shared beliefs, modernization the place of Durkheim's differentiation. Huntington's model is much more clearly political than Durkheim's.
On one side of Huntington's argument, the capacity of political institutions
(not of society in general) to handle new demands becomes crucial. On the
other, the political mobilization of new groups and the production of new
political problems are the chief means by which modernization incites disorder. Yet Durkheim could not have disagreed very vociferously; at most
he would have insisted on the importance of nonpolitical restraints,
especially religion, ritual, and occupational organization. The Durkheimian
argument is very much alive. (For an empirical evaluation of one part of
Huntington's argument—casting doubt on rapid mobilization as a major
source of political disorder—see Przeworski 1975.)

Another version from the 1960s appears in Chalmers Johnson's *Revolutionary Change*. Johnson identifies three clusters of causes for revolution:

1   A disequilibrated social system, especially one with power deflation: "the
    fact that during a period of change the integration of a system depends
    increasingly upon the maintenance and deployment of force by the occu-
    pants of the formal authority statuses" (Johnson 1966: 90).

2   Inability of authorities to develop policies which maintain the confidence
    of ordinary people.

3   Events, often fortuitous, which deprive the elite of their means of
    enforcing conformity, or which lead revolutionary groups to believe they
    can deprive the elite of those means.

Johnson then links these very general phenomena to individual behavior through the sequence:

Rapid change
  Systemic disequilibrium
    Overtaxing of existing means of homeostatic and purposive response to change
    Individual disorientation
      Panic–anxiety–shame–guilt–depression, etc.
      Formation of movements of protest

True to his Durkheimian heritage, he proposes the suicide rate as a prime index of disequilibrium.

The Durkheimian kernel in Johnson's scheme has around it a husk of post Durkheimian words and ideas. Johnson's analysis of revolution differs from Huntington's in several important regards. It is even more strictly political than Huntington's. The pivotal variable is the authority of the established elite. Yet the central idea treats disorder as the outcome of a process in which social change weakens the controls and attachments which under more stable conditions hold people in their places.

Let us take a third recent example: Ted Gurr's *Why Men Rebel.* Gurr seeks to provide a general explanation of "political violence." Political violence includes all collective attacks on major political actors—especially agents of the state—within a particular community. Instead of elaborating a theory of how political communities operate, however, Gurr concentrates on experiences which happen to individuals and then cumulate into mass action.

Gurr's central arguments concern a psychological process. Individuals anger when they sense a large gap between what they get and what they deserve. That can happen through a decline in what they get, or a rise in what they feel they deserve. Given the chance, angry people rebel. When many people go through that same experience of increasing Relative Deprivation plus widening opportunity for rebellion at the same time, political violence generalizes. Gurr once summarized the argument in this way:

$$\begin{array}{l}\text{Magnitude of}\\ \text{political}\\ \text{violence}\end{array} \quad = \quad \text{RD} + (\text{RD} \times \text{JUST} \times \text{BALANCE}) + \varepsilon$$

"where RD is the scope and intensity of relative deprivation (discontent) in a population; JUST is the scope and intensity of beliefs in that population about the justifiability and utility of engaging in overt strife; BALANCE refers to the balance of organization and coercive capacities between dissidents and regimes; and ε is an error term" (Gurr & Duval 1973: 137). Similar ideas have often emerged in the analysis of American ghetto rebellions, of Latin American palace coups, and of the French Revolution. We saw part of the argument formulated in Durkheim's treatment of suicide. Gurr has explicated the logic of this line of analysis and developed means of measuring a number of the variables involved—although not, as it happens, to measure RD and JUST directly.

Gurr complements his argument with an analysis of 1100 "strife events" which occurred in 114 states or colonies from 1961 through 1965. In the first round of analysis, Gurr takes the results as confirming the influence of some of the variables which presumably produce RD, some variables measuring behavior which presumably reflect JUST and, especially, a cluster of variables outside the core theory: Social and Structural Facilitation. A later formulation contains much less psychology. In the new set of models, the major predictors to the magnitude of political violence represent " 'cleavages' and discriminatory inequalities . . . relative impoverishment and foreign economic exploitation . . . short-term declines in economic conditions . . . regime imposition of new political sanctions . . . historical persistance of dissident-initiated conflicts . . . level of economic development . . . external intervention on behalf of dissidents" (Gurr & Duval 1973: 138–139). These variables do appear to account jointly for a good deal of the international variation in major domestic conflicts from 1961 through 1965. In this reformulation, however, the Durkheimian tint has almost bleached away. To the extent that the models embody a central argument, the argument accentuates the principal actors' interests and capacity to act.

The standard Durkheimian arguments, as we have seen, select heavily from among the determinants of collective action—organization, mobilization, opportunity, and interests. On the whole, they neglect the analysis of organization and mobilization in favor of a view of collective action as a resultant of interest plus opportunity. The prevalent version of interest, furthermore, is attitudinal: the motivations, anxieties, and needs of individuals. Opportunity, in the Durkheimian line, consists mainly of the presence or absence of social controls over the expression of those motivations, anxieties, and needs.

If we take Durkheimian arguments seriously, we will expect to find sharp discontinuity between routine and nonroutine collective action; their causes, content, and consequences will all differ significantly. We will hypothesize that the faster and more extensive the social change, the more widespread the anomic and restorative forms of collective action; concretely, we will expect rapid industrialization or urbanization to produce exceptionally high levels of conflict and protest. We will suppose that individual disorder and collective protest are closely tied to each other, and sometimes indistinguishable. We will argue that the more coherent and compelling a group's beliefs, the less likely it is to engage in disorderly behavior. We will imagine that shifts in individual dissatisfactions and anxieties are the strongest and most reliable predictors of collective contention.

Some version of the Durkheimian formulation has been the dominant explanation of collective action—especially contentious and nonroutine collective action—for close to a century. It still appeals to many people today. Nevertheless, even in America, Durkheim's analysis has never quite squeezed out its major rivals: arguments in the traditions of Mill, Weber, and Marx.

MILL AND THE UTILITARIANS

John Stuart Mill represents the treatment of collective action as a strictly calculating pursuit of individual interest. Among the English Utilitarians, we find the individual acquiescing in a set of binding political arrangements (a state, the rules of the game, or some system of cooperation) at the expense of some personal short-run interests, in order to ensure the pursuit of those interests in the long run. As Buchanan and Tullock say of Mill's most distinguished predecessor:

> Hume recognized, of course, that *were it possible*, the individual's own interest would best be served by the adhering to the conventional rules of all other persons but himself while remaining free to violate these rules. However, precisely because such rules are *socially* derived, they must apply generally. Hence each individual must recognize that, were he to be free to violate convention, others must be similarly free, and as compared with this chaotic state of affairs, he will rationally choose to accept restrictions on his own behavior (Buchanan & Tullock 1962: 315).

The key analytic questions concern the determinants of individual decisions, the collective consequences of alternative decision rules, and the interaction between the two.

Mill and the Utilitarians are imperfect exemplars of the relevant twentieth-century line of argument. Their account of collective action dealt almost exclusively with the state. It gave almost no attention either to the striving of groups between the individual and the state as a determinant of political decisions or to the explanation of the behavior of the groups themselves. "The individualism of the utilitarians, their explanation of social phenomena by a human psychology supposedly prior to society," comments John Plamenatz (1949: 158), "also made them indifferent to social classes. They conceived of society as composed of a number of competing individuals and not of rival groups."

For John Stuart Mill, it would be more accurate to say he *feared* class action than to say he ignored it. In a chapter of his *Representative Government* titled "Of the Infirmities And Dangers to Which Representative Government Is Liable," Mill wrote "If we consider as a class, politically speaking, any number of persons who have the same sinister interest—that is, whose direct and apparent interest points toward the same description of bad measures; the desirable object would be that no class, and no combination of classes likely to combine, should be able to exercise a preponderant influence in the government" (Mill 1950: 342). (The term "sinister interest" comes from Bentham.) At some points in his political career, Mill feared the class action of landowners; at others, of landless laborers (Duncan 1973: chapter 6). But at all points he considered it natural and inevitable that a class given an opportunity to act on a particular narrow interest would do so. The task of government—and of a theory of representative government—was to forestall that opportunity, to make likely action on the common interest of the entire population.

Mill's liberal solution and his cautious optimism foreshadowed those of twentieth-century pluralists:

> The reason why, in any tolerably constituted society, justice and the general interest mostly in the end carry their point, is that the separate and selfish interests of mankind are almost always divided: some are interested in what is wrong, but some, also, have their private interest on the side of what is right; and those who are governed by higher considerations, though too few and weak to prevail against the whole of the others, usually after sufficient discussion and agitation become strong enough to turn the balance in favour of the body of private interests which is on the same side with them (Mill 1950: 343).

A good constitution and a valid theory of political obligation, thought Mill, would facilitate that outcome.

By contrast with Mill, twentieth-century theorists of individual interests show relatively little interest in the general problem of political obligation. Instead, they show much interest in two other problems: the consequences of alternative decision rules and the causes and effects of different forms of interest-group politics. Yet Mill is a useful symbol for a line of argument which leads us to expect collective action to fluctuate largely as a consequence of changing decision rules and the changing costs of accomplishing various individual interests.

COLLECTIVE CHOICE

The clearest contemporary expressions of this view appear in models of *collective choice*: the determinants of alternative outcomes in situations in which two or more parties make choices affecting the outcomes. In a sense, all of microeconomics deals with collective choice. Microeconomic models have been the best developed and most popular in the field. Nonetheless, political scientists, psychologists, sociologists, logicians, statisticians, and mathemati-

cians have all accompanied the economists in their search. Game theory, some
forms of voting analysis, some approaches to formal organization, many
treatments of public goods, and a few analyses of power illustrate the relevant
work within this tradition (for a careful review, see Taylor 1975).

James Coleman's general treatise on collective choice offers the following
examples of applications: a simple legislature, realization of interests as a function of their concentration, paying the cost of a public facility, formation of a
constitution, patterns of influence in informal groups, exchange between
representatives and constituents, a parliamentary system, money as power in
legislative issues, committee structure in a legislature, a simple bureaucratic
structure (Coleman 1973: 96–126). In all these cases, Coleman works with
some version of a basic equation:

$$v_i = \sum_j x_{ji} \sum_k v_k\, c_{kj}$$

in which v_i is the value of a given event within an array of k possible events,
$\sum_j x_{ji}$ is the sum over j actors of individual interests in that event, v_k is the value
to an individual actor of a particular event, and c_{kj} is the control actor j has
over event k.

In example 6, the exchange between a representative and his constituents,
Coleman assumes a representative who is totally interested in reelection and
six blocs of voters who have no interest in the outcome of the election as such
but have varying interests with respect to a half-dozen different legislative
actions, as well as varying degrees of control over the election's outcome. He is
able to show good theoretical grounds for expecting the legislator to follow the
constituency where there is consensus. Less obviously, he gives grounds for
attributing greater chances of success to the actor whose interests are
concentrated in few legislative actions and/or allied with the interests of other
actors (Coleman 1973: 115–117).

Coleman has extended the same sort of inquiry to the structure of society
as a whole. He puts together two crucial observations: *first*, in their very
nature corporate actors each attend to a narrower range of interests than
natural persons do; that is their rationale, part of the secret of their success;
second, in our own age an enormously increasing share of important resources
has been coming under the control of corporate actors. Consequence: " . .
among the variety of interests that men have, those interests that have been
successfully collected to create corporate actors are the interests that dominate
the society" (Coleman 1974: 49). We are no longer dealing with the
consequences of decision rules in any simple sense. Yet the problem is very
similar. Coleman is still analyzing how the method of aggregating interests
affects the realization of those interests—whatever those interests are. Under

the conditions Coleman describes, an increasing share of collective action, and especially of collective action that changes things, is carried on by, within, or against corporate actors. Millian analysis identifies a situation which Mill would have abhorred.

Albert Hirschman supplies a complement to Coleman's analysis. In the very title of *Exit, Voice, and Loyalty*, he identifies the three main responses the members or clients of a corporate actor may give to its declining performance. The constituents of a corrupt state may, at a price, vote with their feet; they may *exit*. They may *voice* their dissatisfaction more or less aggressively; that response, too, will have its price. Or they may wait out the bad times in hopes of better—remain *loyal*. Loyalty, too, has a price: enduring the substandard performance. All three responses cost something. The analytic problem is to specify the trade-offs among exit, voice, and loyalty, and to see how the trade-offs vary.

For the analysis of collective action, Hirschman's formulation improves greatly on a simple analogy with a price system. In a simple price system, the inefficient firm faces the loss of its customers to its competitors, but no other sanction. The model of a simple price system often applies poorly to collective action, since the costs of exit are frequently too high. When the government is corrupt, most actors have to choose between stating their opposition and suffering in silence, between voice and loyalty. However, Hirschman argues, voice is at its most effective when exit is possible (and therefore a realistic threat) but not so easy that people rush away as soon as performance declines. Voice then carries the threat of exit. A modicum of loyalty—of reluctance to leave—strengthens the corrective effect of voice. Hirschman clarifies the strategic choices for collective action in a world of giant corporate actors.

Hirschman's analysis steers us into the world of *collective goods*, as well as of collective action. A collective good is " . . . any good such that, if any person X_i in a group X_1 . . . X_i . . . X_n consumes it, it cannot feasibly be withheld from the others in that group" (Olson 1965: 14). Examples are a smog-free environment and military defense. Mancur Olson treats collective action, in essence, as the effort to produce collective goods. That permits him to apply the economic theory of public goods to a new domain: the actions of labor unions, interest groups, and similar organizations. One result is Olson's serious challenge to a common assumption: that the existence and activity of such organizations flows naturally from the rational pursuit of shared interests.

In most circumstances, according to Olson's analysis, the average group member's estimated additional return from participation in the effort will be less than the cost of the effort itself. If collective action does occur, then, its explanation must lie outside the rational self-interest of the average participant. One likely candidate which Olson identifies is the provision of selective incentives other than the outcome of the collective action to particular members of the group. Another is coercion, which is the negative counterpart of selective incentives. It is also possible that people are acting irrationally—but then we must explain why.

Many other students of collective action have tried to pick up the problem where Olson left it. Some criticize Olson's analysis. Some try to refine and qualify it. Some go back to the classic political idea of a government (or another organization with powers of compulsion) which overrides individual interests to serve the common good; in that case, it does not matter whether the coercive organization came into being through a deliberate prior agreement, a conquest, a deception, or something else.

Other people have tried to identify aspects of rationality which Olson neglected. One promising suggestion separates (1) the average participant's return from collective action from (2) the possible return to the political entrepreneur who organizes an action. As Frohlich, Oppenheimer, and Young (1971: 6) put it, collective goods "will be supplied when someone finds it profitable to set up an organization (or make use of some existing organization), collect resources, and supply the goods in question." The entrepreneur arranges for the supply of the collective good in return for donations, extortions, purchases, and taxes. If the sum of donations, extortions, purchases, and taxes is smaller than the value of the collective good to all recipients, yet larger than the entrepreneur's cost in supplying it, the collective action serves the interest of the entrepreneur as well as the collective interest.

Frohlich, Oppenheimer, and Young work out the theoretical implications of such an approach in microeconomic language. The theory leads to some interesting hypotheses concerning collective action. For example:

> "The more a political leader depends upon donations, the more wary he will be of collective goods that are durable or have high initial costs of supply."

> "A political entrepreneur will diversify his activities more and more into the provision of private goods as the size of his overall operation increases . . . "

> "If his chances of victory are near zero, an opposition leader will differentiate his program sharply from that of the incumbent leader, and/or plan his actions to maximize the surplus he can obtain from remaining in opposition."

> "Competitors operating under a decision rule will place a higher premium on firm commitments on the part of their supporters than those who do not."

> "Whenever a competitor makes a definite promise to supply a collective good in exchange for contributions from a given supporter or group of supporters, he will try to hide this fact from as many people as possible." (Frohlich, Oppenheimer, and Young 1971: 139–141.)

Thus the tactical situation of political entrepreneurs becomes a major part of the explanation of the form and intensity of collective action. As in most Millian work, the interests in question are given and fixed. Yet the analysis permits both uncertainty and strategic interaction concerning alternative courses of collective action.

The same emphasis on the incentives and tactical problems of political entrepreneurs appears in the recent work of John McCarthy and Mayer Zald. Looking at American social movements, McCarthy and Zald observe the rise of professionally staffed movement organizations such as Common Cause and the National Council of Senior Citizens for Health Care through Social Security. Reflection on such organizations leads them to two criticisms of classic analyses of social movements: (1) their strong emphasis on grievances and states of mind as opposed to organizational and tactical problems; (2) their assumption of an identity among the aggrieved population, the support for a movement, and the sources of leadership or activism. Against the "classic model" they argue that all movement organizations, whatever the grievances to which they respond, face the common, pressing problems of acquiring enough resources to do their work. In a similar environment, the common problems tend to produce common solutions, such as the professionalization of the staff and the turning to people outside the aggrieved population for support. The common solutions, in turn, produce their own problems—for example, real conflicts among the interests of the movement organization as such, the interests of the outsiders who provide major support for the organization, and the interests for whose benefit the organization presumably first arose. If we are a long way from Mill's concern with the conditions for good government, we are a *very* long way from Durkheim's anomic individuals. The analysis is still essentially Millian; it tends to take the interests for granted, and to emphasize the causes and effects of different means of action on those interests.

STRATEGIC INTERACTION

We have followed the path from John Stuart Mill which leads to social movements via collective choice and collective goods. There are other, less trodden, paths, which could take us to the same destination. The most important ones pass through the study of strategic interaction: bargaining, warmaking, game-playing, and the like. Here we tend to take both the interests and the organization of our actors as given, and to concentrate on tactics and strategy as functions of varying opportunities and of varying information about those opportunities.

Implicitly, most studies of strategic interaction begin with some version of the following scheme:

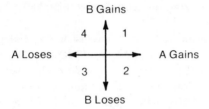

In the simple two-party interaction with a single outcome, an end point anywhere in quadrant 2 means that A gains while B loses, an end point in quadrant 3 means that both lose, and so on. The possible outcomes of a zero-sum interaction will fall into a straight line:

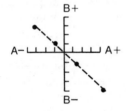

And we can describe some extreme types of interaction by placing boundaries around all possible outcomes:

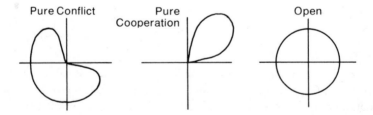

In the pure-conflict case, no possible outcome provides gains for both parties. In the pure-cooperation case, the worst that can happen is that neither gains. In the open case, all four quadrants are available.

The same diagram serves to trace the path of a strategic interaction through a series of intermediate outcomes (see Fig. 2–5). In this instance adapted from Kenneth Boulding's *Conflict and Defense*, p. 50), the short-ighted interest of each party is to arm against the other, and the short-sighted quilibrium has both worse off because of arming. The dotted line represents he possibility of a longer-sighted, more advantageous equilibrium through lisarmament.

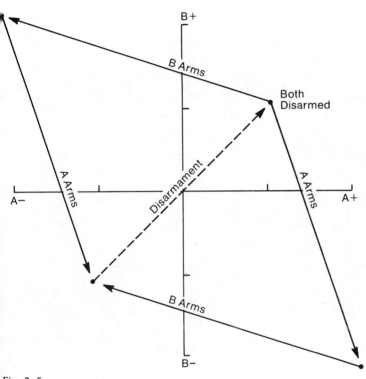

Fig. 2–5
The hypothetical course of a strategic interaction

In its many variants, this approach clarifies the analysis of outcomes and paths to outcomes. As in studies of collective choice, the analyst typically manipulates the relevant incentives, information, decision rules, and available strategies. He does not attempt to explain how and why incentives, information, decision rules, and available strategies vary. That is generally true, for example, of the theory of games. It is "a general framework for the analysis of interactions among several agents who are mutually interdependent . . . and whose interests are to some degree conflicting" (Kramer and Hertzberg 1975:

379). Game theorists typically organize their analyses around a *payoff matrix*. In an elementary version, we have two sharpshooting pirates, Hook and Blackbeard, duelling over a thousand-dollar chest of gold. Neither one ever misses his mark, both fire at once, but their old pistols fail one time out of two. The survivor, if any, takes the gold; if both survive, they split the treasure evenly. The payoff matrix looks like Fig. 2–6.

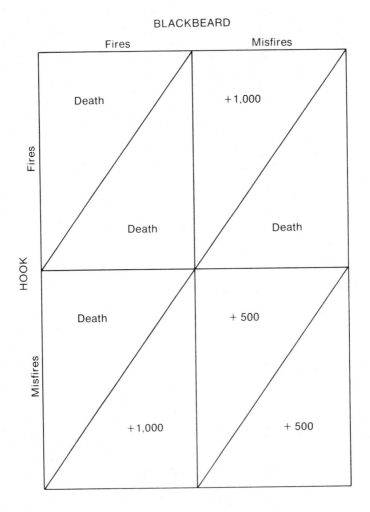

Fig. 2–6
A simple payoff matrix for two pirates

(In each case, the payoff to Hook lies above the diagonal, the payoff to Blackbeard below the diagonal.) Left in this form, the duel is not much of a game. Each pirate has two chances in four of dying, one chance of gaining a thousand dollars, and one chance of gaining 500. If each values his own life at a thousand dollars, in the instant before firing each pirate should estimate his probable gain as

$$\frac{1000 + 500 - 1000 - 1000}{4} = -125 \text{ dollars.}$$

Not very encouraging. Without a chance to run away, to bargain, or to cheat, nevertheless, the size of that estimate will not affect Hook's or Blackbeard's behavior.

To convert this confrontation into an interesting *game*, we must give each pirate a choice of strategies, and introduce some uncertainty about which strategy each will choose. We can do that by (a) giving each pirate the choice between firing, as before, or trying to run off with the chest while the other pirate is loading his gun, (b) noticing that one is a slower runner, the other a worse shot. One plausible matrix resulting from those changes is Fig. 2–7. Overall, "grab and run" is a more favorable strategy for either pirate. But if Hook is sure that Blackbeard will "grab and run," he may be tempted to fire. If Blackbeard is sure that Hook will run, he will be inclined to "grab and run" himself; Hook, being faster, is more likely to escape with the loot, but there is some chance Blackbeard will get there first, a good chance that they will split the treasure, and no chance that either will die.

This fanciful illustration makes the essential point: a game-theoretical analysis portrays a strategic interaction as the outcome of one or more well-defined, deliberate decisions on the part of each of the participants. The decision is a function of the outcomes each participant considers likely to follow from the various possible combinations of his own action and the action of the other participants. So far, the applications of game theory to the analysis of collective action have been indirect. At its best, game theory helps us understand the strategic problems of collective actors, and helps us see how the available means of interaction limit the possibilities of realizing the best interests of any particular actor, or of all actors together.

Analyses of bargaining likewise concentrate on outcomes and paths to outcomes. Ashenfelter and Johnson, for example, analyze strike activity. They begin with a three-party bargaining model which involves a firm, its workers, and the workers' union leadership. The strike, in that model, is a consequence of the firm's unreadiness to accede to wage demands prior to open conflict,

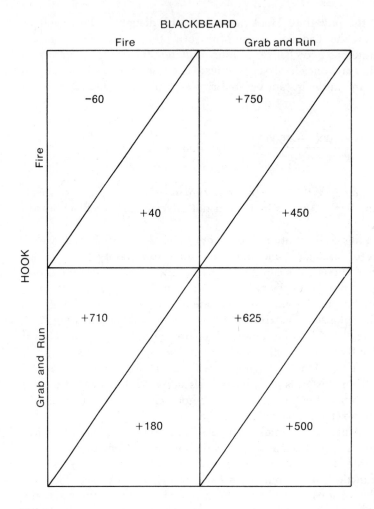

Fig. 2-7
The two-pirate payoff matrix with uncertainty

which in turn depends in part on the discrepancy between what the workers want and what the union leaders think they can get. The firm-level model therefore incorporates a series of conditions (the size of wage increase acceptable to the workers, the speed at which the workers' expectations decline during a strike, and so on) which predict to that unreadiness.

For lack of evidence to test their models at the level of the firm, Ashenfelter and Johnson make some plausible inferences to determinants of strike activity at a larger scale. At the level of the labor force as a whole, they build models involving unemployment levels, previous changes in real wages, and corporate profits. Estimating their principal equations on numbers of strikes reported quarterly in the United States from January 1952 through June 1967, they achieve a good fit to the observed time series. They conclude that strike activity is, in fact, mainly a function of the tightness of the labor market and of previous rates of change in real wages (Ashenfelter and Johnson 1969: 47). (All the substantial work done so far points to a general tendency for strike activity in contemporary western countries to rise in good times and to decline in bad.) In both the small-scale model they formulate and the large-scale model they estimate, Ashenfelter and Johnson portray strike activity as one outcome of a coherent bargaining process in which all parties watch closely their opportunities to act on their interests. The formulation differs from those of game theory, but the tone of the analysis is still resolutely Millian.

MILL AND PSEUDO-MILL

At the edge of the Millian tradition stand a number of quantitative analyses of conflict and collective action. We might better call them pseudo-Millian. They resemble the work of collective-choice and collective-goods theorists in that the models and estimating procedures typically take an econometric form. They are pseudo-Millian because of their theoretical content, or lack of it. Some (like Ted Gurr's earlier work) attempt to estimate essentially attitudinal models in an econometric style. Some (like Gurr's reformulation of his initial argument) are eclectic efforts to assemble individually plausible variables into equations which state their joint effects and interrelations. In either case, we find relatively little of the Millian concern with the effects of alternative decision rules in the context of fixed interests and changing opportunities to act on those interests.

Douglas Hibbs's cross-national study of "mass political violence" exemplifies the best in pseudo-Millian analyses. Hibbs analyzes counts of riots, armed attacks, political strikes, assassinations, deaths from political violence, and antigovernment demonstrations in 108 countries summed for two adjacent decades: 1948–57 and 1958–67. Via factor analysis, Hibbs combines these diverse events into two dimensions: Collective Protest and Internal War. Then he combs the existing literature for proposed predictors of these variables, cautiously working them into causal models. One of Hibbs's diagrams of the estimated causal relationships (expressed here as standardized regression coefficients) appears in Fig. 2–8. The diagram indicates, among other things, that the negative sanctions (censorship, restrictions on political activity) imposed

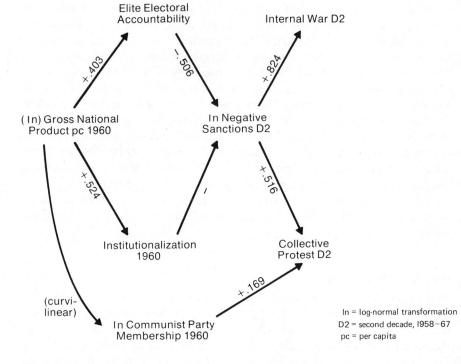

Fig. 2-8
One of Douglas Hibbs's causal models of political violence

by the government during the second decade predicted strongly to the country's level of internal war and of collective protest, while the membership of the national Communist Party in 1960 predicted weakly to the level of collective protest during the second decade.

Hibbs's work is representative in that it formulates and tests general arguments by means of comparisons of aggregated measures for considerable numbers of whole countries. It does not examine variation within countries, among groups, or from one time period to another; it does not treat the determinants of particular events or deal with their internal development. With the expanded use of computers, multivariate statistical analysis, and international data banks in the 1960s, a large number of studies in the same style appeared. Hibbs's study summarizes and improves upon the entire lot.

As compared with Durkheimian work, Millian analyses of collective action have regularly involved careful formalization and statistical estimation of their arguments. Where Durkheimians postulate two or three rather distinct types of collective action arising out of different patterns of social change, Millians tend to think of all collective action as expressing the same fundamental rationality. The price of these advantages has been some loss of richness, some concentration on situations in which the choices and interests are exceptionally clear, some tendency to emphasize variables which are easy to quantify. So far we have a good deal of rigor, but no models of revolution so suggestive as those of Huntington or Johnson. The Millian emphasis on the rational pursuit of interests is a welcome antidote to notions of crowd action as impulsive and irrational. Yet so far the followers of Mill have not given us much insight into the way those interests arise and change. They have not said much about the way people define, articulate, and organize their interests. For further ideas on those questions, we may turn to the tradition of Max Weber.

WEBER

In Max Weber's treatment, groups commit themselves to collective definitions of the world and of themselves. The definitions incorporate goals, entail standards of behavior, and include justifications for the power of authorities. Constituted authorities act on behalf of the groups. Sometimes the authorities act on the basis of their traditional roles, sometimes on the basis of their rational-legal designation as agents for the group, sometimes on the basis of their extraordinary personal character—their charisma. Which of these bases the group adopts strongly affects its organization and its fate. Whether in traditional, charismatic, or rational-legal form, however, the justifications all constrain the authorities' actions. In Weber's account, the structure and action of the group as a whole spring largely from the initial commitment to a particular kind of belief system. Beliefs have their own logic and force.

Weber offered his fullest account of the origins of the fundamental beliefs in his discussions of charisma: the divine gift of grace and its secular equivalents. According to Weber, religious and ideological virtuosos are continually formulating new definitions of the world and of themselves. Only a few, however, attract anyone besides their inventors. In those few cases, a group of followers commit themselves both to the belief system and to an acknowledgment of the charisma—the exceptional moral qualities—of the leaders, objects, and rituals consecrated by those beliefs.

Where many more people, for whatever reason, find that the new definitions of the world provide more coherent answers to the problem of meaning they face than do the old definitions already available to them, they join and the group expands. Then the group as a whole faces the problem of the "routinization of charisma." (Weber's German for routinization is *Veralltäglichung*—literally the "everydaying" of the charisma in question—which states dramatically the process of turning something extraordinary into something ordinary, into something understood and controllable.) The routinization of charisma involves reconciliation of the beliefs with the exigencies of organization, development of reliable means for distinguishing true and false versions of the beliefs, provision for succession to the leadership.

Weber sees six main mechanisms by which charismatic groups solve the problem of succession (Weber 1972: 143–144):

1 A search for another charismatic leader of the same type.
2 Revelation through some procedure honored by the group.
3 The old leader's personal designation of a successor, with the group's approval.
4 Ritual designation by the body of surviving leaders.
5 Reliance on kinship, with the idea that charisma is inheritable.
6 Transfer of charisma to the organization, therefore to its officials and rituals.

The choice among these strategies then limits what the group can do next. But all the choices require the creation of a certain amount of organizational structure, with its own momentum and its own exigencies. If the group survives that process, we have another durable collective actor operating under the direction of its own constituted authorities.

Weber's discussion of the "everydaying" of charisma fits neatly into his general theory of social change. Weber portrays traditional authority as a sort of equilibrium into which social life tends to fall if no strenuous disruption occurs. But two opposing sources of disruption are always possible: the power of rationality and the power of charisma. Each represents the force of a coherent idea, of a pure principle, when applied to history.

Bureaucratic rationalization, says Weber, "can be a revolutionary force of the first rank against tradition, and often has been. But it revolutionizes by means of techniques . . . from outside, things and arrangements first" (Weber 1972: 657). The rational rearrangement of the environment eventually transforms people and their world views. Charisma, in Weber's analysis, works in exactly the opposite way: first transforming the inner life, then leading people to transform their worlds. "It is in this purely empirical and value-free sense the supremely and specifically 'creative' force in history" (Weber 1972: 658). As Francesco Alberoni points out, in Weber's view "Charisma does not grow from bureaucracy, but counterpoises itself to bureaucracy; it appears as something gratuitous, miraculous, irrational" (Alberoni 1968: 15).

As Alberoni also points out, Weber's theorizing stops at exactly that point. Weber gives us a dramatic, compelling sense of social change as a product of the irruption of charisma into history and of the diffusion of rationalization through history. He provides a sense of the historical power of a movement oriented to a coherent idea. Yet he offers no theory of the circumstances under which charismatic movements arise. His giant comparison of civilizations gives us a heroic historical analysis of the way one rationalizing movement—that of modern western Europe—developed, but no manageable general scheme for the explanation of rationalizing movements. As a result, Weber's followers have had to complement their Weberian treatments of the life-courses of movements with non-Weberian explanations of why people formed and joined the movements in the first place.

Nevertheless, Weber's formulation agrees with Durkheim's in suggesting that rapid social change (hence, presumably greater likelihood that existing beliefs will become inadequate as guides to routine social life) will produce widespread nonroutine collective action. Then Weber goes his own way in implying that there are really two main categories of collective actors, those oriented to deviant beliefs and those oriented to beliefs which have won general acceptance; routinization and diffusion turn one into the other. By extension, the Weberian theory also suggests that commitment to a group is an incentive, rather than a barrier, to participation in collective action—including nonroutine collective action. Today, political analysts commonly invoke essentially Weberian explanations of the collective actions of national states and complex organizations. They are less likely to apply Weber to the actions of crowds, political movements or revolutionary groups.

SOCIAL MOVEMENTS

Studies of collective action within the Weberian tradition have commonly employed the framework of the *social movement*. In his brief conceptual work on the subject, Paul Wilkinson defines a social movement as:

> . . . a deliberate collective endeavour to promote change in any direction and by any means, not excluding violence, illegality, revolution or withdrawal into 'utopian' community . . . A social movement must evince a minimal degree of organization, though this may range from a loose, informal or partial level of organization to the highly institutionalized and bureaucratized movement and the corporate group . . . A social movement's commitment to change and the *raison d'être* of its organization are founded upon the conscious volition, normative commitment to the movement's aims or beliefs, and active participation on the part of the followers or members (Wilkinson 1971: 27).

This definition, although clearer than most of those one encounters on a tour through the literature of social movements, conveys the usual meaning of the term. The underlying conception reflects that of Weber: a group of people somehow orient themselves to the same belief system and act together to promote change on the basis of the common orientation. Thus the standard questions become: How do such systems of beliefs arise and acquire followings? How do they constrain their adherents? How do they and the groups which form around them change, routinize, disappear?

We are not surprised, then, to find Michael Useem beginning his discussion of the Resistance, the American movement of the 1960s against military conscription, with these words:

> The formation of a protest movement is generally contingent on the preexistence of a group of people united around a set of political principles dealing with a solution to a social problem. Some protests erupt spontaneously and reflect little conscious effort by a politicized leadership. But many movements, the Resistance included, are instituted only after a lengthy maturation process in which a substantial number of people come to view a new protest program as valid and realistic (Useem 1973: 37).

Given that beginning, Useem's own inquiry into American draft resistance proceeds logically: the character of campus discontent, conscription as a reality and as an issue, the base and process of recruitment to the movement, organizational problems and transformations of the movement, political outcomes of movement actions. For example, Useem points out the great importance of the fragile student draft deferment as a stimulus to joining the movement. For another, he analyzes the significance of temporary coalitions between Resistance and other protest groups seeking substantially different goals; in his view, the decay of coalitions with such groups as SDS accelerated the decline of Resistance as a movement.

Useem's agenda is classic. We find it directing studies of revolutionary movements, religious movements, ethnic movements, movements of reform. Useem himself has applied the same scheme to a wide variety of American protest movements. He ends that survey with two major complaints about existing analytical schemes: (1) although they provide a reasonable grip on the internal development of a movement once it has begun, they contain no serious explanation of the genesis of protest movements; (2) their accounts of the process by which such movements mobilize for action are quite unsatisfactory. "Attention must be directed," concludes Useem, "at the conflicts within major institutional systems in America, both as sources of protest and also for the role they play in shaping the program, organization, and growth of the movement. Since many types of collective behavior and social movements do not share such roots, attempts to develop a single theory for explaining a full range of collective phenomena are bound to overlook factors that play a role in protest, but not other types of, movements" (Useem 1975: 51).

Anyone who runs through the many writings on American social movements will notice, in fact, a good deal of agreement about the characteristic life histories of movements and widespread disagreement about why and how movements arise in the first place. Joseph Gusfield's *Symbolic Crusade*, a thoughtful analysis of the American Temperance movement, distinguishes among three types of movement: class, status, and expressive. The class movement, according to Gusfield, organizes instrumentally around some specific interest of its public. The status movement orients itself toward the enhancement or maintenance of the group's prestige. Expressive movements "are marked by goalless behavior or by pursuit of goals which are unrelated to the discontents from which the movement had its source" (Gusfield 1966: 23). In all three cases the character of the public and the character of the goal provide the major explanations of the movement's content.

Temperance, in Gusfield's view, is largely a status movement; it arose as a defense of old elites against their declining prestige. In the twentieth century:

> The polarization of the middle classes into abstainers and moderate drinkers is part of a wider process of cultural change in which traditional values of the old middle class are under attack by new components of the middle stratum. In this process of change, Temperance is coming to take on new symbolic properties as a vehicle of status protest (Gusfield 1966: 139).

Gusfield sees post-Prohibition Temperance as coalescing with a new fundamentalism against self-indulgent, morally lax, consumption-oriented modernism—and thus expressing the status anxieties of the old middle class in the twentieth century.

Roberta Ash embeds her own brief discussion of Temperance in a survey of nineteenth-century middle-class movements. They were more or less interchangeable, she says, but Temperance mingled "a desire to ameliorate the lot of workers, to destroy a less genteel life style and perhaps unconsciously express frustration at the loss of political power . . ." (Ash 1972: 136). The characterization differs somewhat from Gusfield's, but the basic procedure is the same: account for the movement's genesis and content by means of the structural situation in which the adherents find themselves at the start. In her general analysis of social movements in America, Ash portrays changes in the organization of production as producing new structural problems for different social groups; when ideologically legitimate means for acting on those problems are not available, the groups tend to create social movements for the solutions of their problems. She eventually comes to the conclusion that the "status politics" which are so important to Gusfield's analysis actually turn out to be class politics, misdirected or in disguise.

The analyses of Gusfield and Ash are only loosely Weberian. They accept the Weberian idea of a social movement with its own rationale, momentum, and life history. Yet they do not assign such a compelling power to the idea around which the movement organizes in the first place, and they expend much of their effort in tracing the correspondences between the social situations of the actors and the contents of the movements they form or join. Furthermore, Ash self-consciously adopts Marxian ideas concerning the origins of structural change. Yet in identifying the social movement as a coherent object of study and in treating its formation as a break with legitimate, routine social life, both Ash and Gusfield align themselves with Max Weber.

The Weberian tradition has been rich in inspiration for case studies and poor in inspiration for further theorizing. In both regards it differs from the Durkheimian and Millian traditions: both of them have stimulated reformulation after reformulation, but have proved very hard to apply to individual, concrete cases. Alberoni and Useem have already identified the problem for us. Weber left almost untouched the analysis of the genesis and mobilization of charismatic movements. At the same time, he taught that such movements had their own logic, and represented a sharp break with routine, legitimate social life. The assumptions of autonomy and separateness make it awkward for the student of a movement to fill the gap in Weber's analysis by appealing to the everyday interests of the participants.

Nevertheless, students of social movements who were serious about origins and mobilization have normally gone outside the Weberian framework for their explanations. Ash turns to an unexpected combination: neo-Marxism and the work of Edward Shils. Useem's proposal to study "institutional contradictions" is Marxist in inspiration. Anthony Oberschall's general work on *Social Conflict and Social Movements* essentially breaks the subject into three parts: (1) an analysis of social conflict, which is quite eclectic in its theoretical origins; (2) an analysis of the mobilization of conflict groups, which relies especially on the Millian framework of Mancur Olson; (3) an analysis of the life histories of conflict groups, which resembles classic treatments of social movements. In Oberschall's analyses, the strong emphasis on real interests and strategic problems with regard to social conflict and mobilization wars against the autonomy and separateness inherent in the idea of a "movement." In this case, the interests and strategy win; the notion of a social movement as anything more than a set of mobilized conflict groups collapses.

So why bother with Weber? Because Weber and the Weberians have pursued several problems in collective action more persistently and effectively than have the followers of Durkheim and Mill. People *do* sometimes group around distinctive definitions of the world and of themselves: why and how? There *is* something about the growth of Temperance or Abolitionism that neither an analysis of whole social classes nor a study of specific associations exhausts: what it it? A group's conception of its aims and rights *does* inform its action and influence its very readiness to act: can't we take that into account? Weber left us an important agenda.

MARXIAN ANALYSES SINCE MARX

The classic Marxist analysis derives shared interests from common positions in the organization of production, changes in interest from shifts in the organization of production. Any set of people in a common relationship to the means of production form a class, but classes vary greatly in internal structure and common consciousness. Shared aims and beliefs emerge from shared interests, as mediated by a class's internal structure and its relationship to other classes. Collective action likewise results from shared interests, as mediated by internal structure, relationship to other classes, and common consciousness. Thus the broad logic follows the pattern presented in Fig. 2–9.

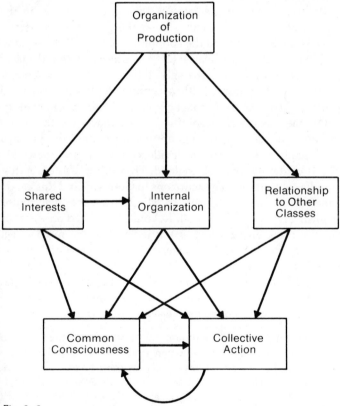

Fig. 2–9
The simple Marxist model of collective action

Marxian analysts since Marx have varied considerably in the relative weight and autonomy they have assigned to these variables. They have also varied in how much they have recognized other significant actors than social classes: states, ethnic groups, religious movements, and so on. The stricter the Marxism, the less significance attributed to these other actors. By a strict standard, many people in the Marxian tradition do not qualify as Marxists at all. Nonetheless, they stand out from the followers of Durkheim, Mill, and Weber by insisting on the priority of material interests and by following the general logic of Marx's explanation of collective action. Although there are strictly contemporary examples, two of the most useful illustrations for our purposes are the historical syntheses of Barrington Moore, Jr., and Eric Wolf.

The complex web of Moore's *Social Origins of Dictatorship and Democracy* hangs on two pegs: (1) the idea that the class coalitions involved in the great modernizing revolutions—hence the character of those revolutions—have depended especially on the fates of the agrarian classes in the course of the commercialization of agriculture and the growth of the state, with the liquidation of the peasantry and the cooptation of the aristocracy and gentry, for example, being crucial in England; (2) the further idea that the class coalition making the revolution has strongly influenced the subsequent political organization of that country, with a coalition of bureaucrats and landlords, for instance, tending to produce fascism. Thus parliamentary democracy becomes the historically specific consequence of the early emergence of agrarian capitalism in certain countries, a circumstance perhaps never to be repeated again. Moore provides evidence for his twin theses via extended comparisons of the histories of England, France, the United States, China, Japan, and India, plus numerous excursions to Germany and Russia.

Revolution takes on an interesting role in Moore's scheme. The major revolution—the English Civil War, the French Revolution, and so on—acts as a crucial switch in the track along which a particular country moves. Yet revolution dissolves as a phenomenon *sui generis*, for it becomes simply the maximum moment of conflicts which endure long before and long after the transfer of power; indeed, the case of Germany shows that the fundamental transfers of power which occupy the center of Moore's analysis can occur without any revolution at all in the conventional sense of the word:

> The notion that a violent popular revolution is somehow necessary in order to sweep away "feudal" obstacles to industrialization is pure nonsense, as the course of German and Japanese history demonstrates. On the other hand, the political consequences from dismounting the old order from above are decidedly different. As they proceeded with conservative modernization, these semiparliamentary governments tried to preserve as much of the original social structure as they could, fitting large sections into the new building wherever possible. The results

had some resemblance to present-day Victorian houses with modern electrical kitchens but insufficient bathrooms and leaky pipes hidden decorously behind newly plastered walls. Ultimately the makeshifts collapsed (Moore 1966: 438).

We find ourselves at the opposite pole from Chalmers Johnson's "disequilibration" and "dysfunction." In Moore's analysis, the major conflicts which occur—including the revolutions themselves—are part of the very logic of the political systems they shake apart.

The second case in point is Eric Wolf's *Peasant Wars of the Twentieth Century*. Wolf takes on the revolutions of Mexico, Russia, China, Viet Nam, Algeria, and Cuba. He extracts from them important lessons about the response of peasants the world over to being drawn into the capitalist world economy. Even less concerned to lay out an explicit theoretical structure than Moore, Wolf nevertheless builds a powerful analysis of the structural foundations of peasant life, the precise ways in which the expansion of national and international markets shakes those foundations, the conditions under which peasants resist the threat with force, and the circumstances under which that resistance (however reactionary its inception) serves revolutionary ends.

The most general argument is simple and telling:

> The major aim of the peasant is subsistence and social status gained within a narrow range of social relationships. Peasants are thus unlike cultivators, who participate fully in the market and who commit themselves to a status game set within a wide social network. To ensure continuity upon the land and sustenance for his household, the peasant most often keeps the market at arm's length, for unlimited involvement in the market threatens his hold on his source of livelihood. He thus cleaves to traditional arrangement which guarantee his access to land and to the labor of kin and neighbors . . . Perhaps it is precisely when the peasant can no longer rely on his accustomed institutional context to reduce his risks, but when alternative institutions are either too chaotic or too restrictive to guarantee a viable commitment to new ways, that the psychological, economic, social and political tensions all mount toward peasant rebellion and involvement in revolution (Wolf 1969: xiv–xv).

From that springboard, Wolf leaps to a close examination of the experience of the peasantry in each of his countries, to scrutiny of the conditions under which each of the revolutions in question broke out, and to comparative analyses of the determinants of the considerably different forms of involvement of these various peasant populations in their national movements.

Some common features emerge: the crucial role of the middle peasants, rather than the rural proletarians or the *kulaki*; the influence of alliances with disaffected intellectuals; the initially defensive and inward-looking character of all the peasant rebellions; the frequent occurrence of a deadlock of weak contenders for power, ultimately favorable to well-organized central groups allied with military power; the final inability of peasants to accomplish their political ends, however successful their rebellions in the short run, in the absence of strong alliances with determined and organized nonpeasants.

Wolf's sense of the variables involved will probably contribute more to our understanding of political conflict than his enumeration of the constants. He shows very effectively (in a line of argument similar to Moore's) that the coalitions formed by rebellious peasants strongly affect whether their actions go beyond the immediate redress of grievances; that where commercialization has proceeded so far as to dissolve the traditional organization of the peasant community, rebellion does not occur (contrary to the mass-society notion that atomized and anguished people make ideal rebels); that a center-outward pattern of rebellion, as in Russia, China, and Viet Nam, favors the expanded power of a single party, as opposed to an army and/or a national bourgeoisie.

THE COLLECTIVE HISTORY OF COLLECTIVE ACTION

Both Barrington Moore and Eric Wolf are nonhistorians who turned to history for evidence-concern processes going on in the contemporary world. They have plenty of companions within the historical profession. Among recent historians of collective action, Marxian thinking has prevailed. Georges Lefebvre, the great, long-lived historian of the French Revolution, provided much of the inspiration, if not much of the techniques. He forwarded the idea of multiple, semiautonomous revolutions converging into a single Revolution. He demonstrated that the semiautonomous revolutions—especially the peasant revolution—were accessible to study from the bottom up. But he did not systematize the study of the populations involved.

Albert Soboul did. Soboul has no doubt been Lefebvre's most influential heir in both regards. His 1958 thesis, *Les sans-culottes parisiens en l'an II*, shone a torchlight on faces previously deep in shadow: the faces of the day-to-day activists of the Parisian sections. (The "sections" were essentially neighborhood governments and political associations.) It did so mainly through the straightforward but extremely demanding analysis of the papers of the sections themselves, and the painstaking reconstitution of their membership.

At about the same time, Richard Cobb was carrying out a close study of the composition and characteristics of the volunteer Revolutionary Armies which played such a crucial role in the early years of the Revolution. Kåre Tønnesson was following the Parisian sans-culottes through the Year III, George Rudé was analyzing the composition of the revolutionary crowds on the great *Journées*, Adeline Daumard, Louis Chevalier and François Furet were closely scrutinizing the changing composition and wealth of the Parisian population from the late eighteenth century to 1848, and Rémi Gossez was applying many of the same microscopic procedures to the Revolution of 1848. These historians varied greatly in preconceptions, techniques and subject matter. What brought them together, with dozens of their compatriots, as exponents of a new brand of history is the deliberate accumulation of uniform dossiers on numerous ordinary individuals in order to produce solid information on collective characteristics not readily visible in the experiences of any one of them. The solid information was often numerical, although the quantification involved was ordinarily elementary.

The adoption of this sort of "collective history" did not guarantee success. It could have been a terrible waste of time. Indeed, it *should* have been a waste of time, if old theories about the blind spontaneity of the masses were correct. As it turned out, however, collective history yielded great returns when applied to French political conflicts. Historians now understand how wide and deep was the political mobilization of ordinary Frenchmen in 1789 and 1848, how coherent the action of the so-called mob, how sharp the rifts within the coalition which made the Revolution of 1789 had become by 1793. The Marxist approach to the study of French political conflicts gained new strength, both because Marxists were more inclined than others to take up the close study of the "little people" which this sort of collective history involved, and because the Marxist tradition provided more powerful means of analyzing major divisions within the population than its rivals did.

Outside of France, the greatest impact of collective history on the study of collective action appeared in England. England has its own tradition of collective biography, exemplified by the parliamentary analyses of Lewis Namier. In the field of collective action, however, the distinctive English contribution did not consist of formal individual-by-individual analysis of participants. It was the application of the logic of collective biography to *events*, complemented by the identification and analysis of evidence concerning the character, outlook, and behavior of ordinary participants in major conflicts and movements. As a prime example of the first we have Hobsbawm and Rudé's *Captain Swing;* the book reports a thorough systematic study of the many local conflicts comprising the Swing Rebellion, the great agricultural laborers' revolt of 1830. As the dominant work of the second type we have E. P. Thompson's *The Making of the English Working Class,* a richly documented portrayal of workers' struggles from the period of the French Revolution to the beginning of Chartism.

A recent English example combines the Hobsbawm-Rudé and Thompson approaches. John Foster's *Class Struggle and the Industrial Revolution* traces the development of class consciousness and working-class collective action in three industrial towns—Oldham, Northampton, and South Shields—during the first half of the nineteenth century. Several features of Foster's study are extraordinary. He is meticulous and self-conscious in his theorizing; he carefully spells out the empirical implications of an essentially Leninist argument: a labor aristocracy forms and serves for a time as a vanguard of class-conscious collective action, but is eventually split, its fragments coopted or isolated in the capitalist counterattack. Foster is equally meticulous in assembling and presenting his evidence; it includes close analyses of marriage patterns, collective biographies of working-class activists, and treatments of changes in the labor force. Finally, Foster devotes great attention to the opponents and exploiters of the workers: the local bourgeoisie. Indeed, one of Foster's most illuminating discussions treats the bourgeois adoption of rigorous religious practice as a means of taming and shaming the workers.

It is no accident that solid Marxist analyses abound in European historical work and are rare in studies of contemporary America. There are two basic reasons. The first is simply that Marxism has remained a lively, evolving body of thought in Europe while sometimes fossilizing and sometimes having to hide underground in America. The second is that Marxist ideas are most adequately developed in regard to the experience Marx himself treated most fully: the conflicts surrounding the growth of capitalism in Europe. The Marxist scholar's task is to adapt to other settings a model which is already well fitted to the European historical experience.

Among the determinants of collective action, Marxists have generally given great attention to interests and organization, have sometimes dealt with mobilization, but have generally neglected opportunity. As compared with Durkheimian, Millian, and Weberian analyses, the Marxian treatment of collective action stresses the ubiquity of conflict, the importance of interests rooted in the organization or production, the influence of specific forms of organization on the character and intensity of collective action. Marxists have not paid as much attention as Weberians have to the implications of prevalent belief systems, or to the processes by which movements rise and fall. They have not matched the Millians in precise modeling of decision-making processes. There is, however, no obvious analytic ground on which the Durkheimians have the advantage over the Marxians.

That will be the general attitude of the analyses to follow: doggedly anti-Durkheimian, resolutely pro-Marxian, but sometimes indulgent to Weber and sometimes reliant on Mill. Good Durkheimians will find little comfort in my arguments or in such evidence as I present: no support in either regard for uprooted masses as makers of revolutions, rapid social change as a generator of anomic collective action, and so on. Orthodox Marxists will find themselves somewhat more at home than the Durkheimians, but will still find much to disagree with—notably the considerable importance attached to political processes and to interests which are not obviously and directly based on class conflict. Followers of Weber will despair at the virtual absence of charisma and at my avoidance of the social movement as a unit of analysis; at least they will gloat over the concessions made to shared conceptions of rights and obligations as bases of collective action. Millians will reject much of the discussion as imprecise and unparsimonious, yet they should find familiar the efforts to analyze the strategic problems of collective actors.

OUR TASK

If we try to adjudicate among the theories of collective action I have somewhat arbitrarily identified with Marx, Mill, Durkheim, and Weber, we find ourselves in a frustrating situation. The situation, alas, is common in the social sciences. The theories at hand clearly lead in different directions. Yet in many areas they are too incomplete or too imprecisely specified to permit either clear confrontations with other theories or decisive testing against the facts. Where they are well specified, furthermore, it often turns out that they are talking about different things: theories of collective choice apply to situations in which the alternatives are limited and well defined, theories of collective behavior refer to what happens when the standard choices are suspended, and so forth.

In Kenneth Boulding's terms, theories in the tradition of Mill deal mainly with exchange systems (those in which the incentive for one person or group to act is the desirable return someone else will give them in response). Durkheimian theories deal mainly with integration systems (those in which the incentive is a sense of common fate or identity). Weber's line emphasizes threat systems (those in which the incentive is an undesirable response another group will visit on the actor if he fails to act in a certain way). The Marxian line of thinking deals mainly with threats and exchange, although integration *within* groups—especially within classes—becomes an important condition for effective action by those groups.

We can criticize the available theories on logical grounds, appraise their fruitfulness in generating hypotheses, explanations, and research strategies, examine how well they work in their own fields of application, and assess the fidelity or effectiveness with which their advocates employ them. In their present stage of development, however, we cannot devise a set of general tests which will convincingly establish their relative validity.

Nevertheless, the accumulating literature of collective action offers an inviting terrain for theoretical exploration. My plan here is to draw on it in proposing general concepts and hypotheses for the study—contemporary or historical—of concrete cases of collective action. We return to some of the problems posed, but not resolved, by Marx's analyses of nineteenth-century political conflicts: how do big structural changes affect the prevailing patterns of collective action? Among the big changes, I want especially to inquire into the effects of urbanization, industrialization, state making, and the expansion of capitalism. Among prevailing patterns of collective action, I would particularly like to know what kinds of groups gain or lose the capacity to act together effectively, and how the forms of action themselves change.

In this abstract formulation, the problems look like a desert: huge, dry, and forbidding. Happily, all real deserts contain oases; so does this one. Some of the specific questions which follow from the abstract problem are engaging and important. Some are even answerable: Is it true that the political participation of ordinary people greatly increases with urbanization, industrialization, and the growth of national states? Is it true that repression can work only for a while, because sooner or later people become so frustrated they snatch at any chance to rebel? Why has the anti-tax rebellion, once the most common occasion for large-scale popular violence in western countries, almost disappeared? In our own time, why have strikes and demonstrations become so frequent? Is there a tendency for political life to become less and less turbulent, more and more routinized, as a country gets older and richer? To what extent (and when) are social classes the chief political actors? Our questions run the whole range of political processes from the mobilization of groups for action to the working out of revolution.

The pages to follow will not lay out firm answers to these questions. Their purpose is more limited. They lay out a set of concepts which apply across this wide range of problems; they thereby help identify the connections among the problems. The following chapters state some general arguments concerning the political processes involved, and illustrate the arguments with a number of different concrete cases. Now and then they pause to sum up the existing evidence on some major controversy concerning collective action.

The illustrations and the evidence deal mainly with discontinuous, contentious collective action: strikes, demonstrations, and tax rebellions rather than workaday ward politics. That is no accident. The Marxian tradition on which I rely has dealt most fully and effectively with situations of open conflict. My own empirical work has concentrated on conflict rather than consensus. At a number of points later in the book I argue and illustrate the great continuity between open conflict and routine contention for power. Still, the relative weakness of the evidence concerning everyday, routinized, peaceful collective action will leave open the possibility that Weber and Durkheim were right: that there really is a separate realm of contentious, extraordinary collective action which requires a separate mode of explanation. I do not think so. But the skeptical reader may prefer to treat what follows as an analysis of discontinuous, contentious collective action, and to reserve judgment about the rest.

The remainder of this book proposes strategies for the study of mobilization, repression, struggles for power, and related processes. It returns repeatedly to the problems of observing and measuring the political processes reliably, because those problems of observation and measurement have been handled thoughtlessly in the past. In passing—but only in passing—the following discussion comments on previous work concerning collective action, conflict, and revolution. Our main concern is with the work that has yet to be done.

3

Interests Organization, and Mobilization

THE ELEMENTARY MODELS

To get anywhere at all, we will have to hew out rough models of interaction among groups, and of a single group's collective action. At first chop, the model of interaction is quite static. Let us call it our *polity model*. Its elements are a population, a government, one or more contenders, a polity, and one or more coalitions. We define a population of interest to us by any means we please. Within that population we search for one or more of the following:

> *Government:* an organization which controls the principal concentrated means of coercion within the population.
>
> *Contender:* any group which, during some specified period, applies pooled resources to influence the government. Contenders include *challengers* and *members of the polity*. A *member* is any contender which has routine, low-cost access to resources controlled by the government; *challenger* is any other contender.
>
> *Polity:* consists of the collective action of the members and the government.
>
> *Coalition:* a tendency of a set of contenders and/or governments to coordinate their collective action.

Figure 3–1 presents these elements schematically.

To apply the polity model to an actual population, we have a choice of starting points. We can identify a government, then identify the population over which that government exercises (or claims) control; the great bulk of political analysis starts that way, and within political analysis national states are the most common points of reference. We can, however, start by identifying a population, then identify all governments exercising control within that population and/or designate one such government as the point of reference.

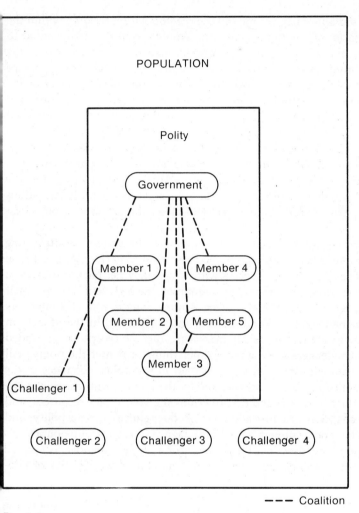

POPULATION

Polity

Government

Member 1   Member 4

Member 2   Member 5

Member 3

Challenger 1

Challenger 2   Challenger 3   Challenger 4

— — — Coalition

Fig. 3-1
The polity model

In the first approach, we might take the U.S.S.R. as our point of departure, and then interest ourselves in all populations over which the U.S.S.R.
exercises jurisdiction. The criteria we use for "government" and "jurisdiction"
will clearly determine how large a population will fall into our analysis: by a
weak criterion much of Asia and Eastern Europe would qualify; by a strong
criterion, given the federal structure of the U.S.S.R., we could end up with
nothing but the central bureaucracies.

In the second approach, we might take the population residing within the mapped boundaries of a national state; that would produce a result similar to the first approach, with the main differences due to migration across the boundary in both directions. However, we might also take all native speakers of Russian, all ethnic Kurds, all persons living within 500 kilometers of the Black Sea. Those starting points will produce very different populations, and very different sets of relevant governments. In this approach, the stickiest problem is likely to be how durable the attachment of individuals to the population must be before we include them. Do American tourists in Moscow count? If not, what about American diplomats who spend four or five years in Moscow? Americans whom the Russians put in jail for four or five years? We will solve these problems arbitrarily or—better—as a function of the questions we are asking. The solutions, however, will affect the answers to our questions.

In the primitive, static version of this model, all contenders are attempting to realize their interests by applying pooled resources to each other and to the government. They vary in the success with which they get back resources in return; the biggest division in that regard separates the high-return *members* of the polity from the low-return *challengers*. Among other things, all contenders (members and challengers alike) are struggling for power. In the model, an increase in power shows up as an increasing rate of return on expended resources. All challengers seek, among other things, to enter the polity. All members seek, among other things, to remain in the polity. Changes in the resources controlled by each contender and by the government, changes in the rates at which the contenders and the government give and take resources, and changes in the coalition structure add up to produce entries into the polity, and exits from it. The model conveys a familiar image of interest-group politics.

The second model describes the behavior of a single contender. Let us call it our *mobilization model*. Four important, variable characteristics of contenders are:

Interests: the shared advantages or disadvantages likely to accrue to the population in question as a consequence of various possible interactions with other populations.

Organization: the extent of common identity and unifying structure among the individuals in the population; as a process, an increase in common identity and/or unifying structure (we can call a decline in common identity and/or unifying structure *disorganization*).

Mobilization: the extent of resources under the collective control of the contender; as a process, an increase in the resources or in the degree of collective control (we can call a decline in either one *demobilization*).

Collective action: the extent of a contender's joint action in pursuit of common ends; as a process, the joint action itself.

Interest, organization, mobilization, and collective action are four of the five components we reviewed earlier. The fifth was *opportunity*.

Opportunity describes the relationship between the population's interests and the current state of the world around it. In this first rough statement of the model, it has three elements:

Power: the extent to which the outcomes of the population's interactions with other populations favor its interests over those of the others; acquisition of power is an increase in the favorability of such outcomes, loss of power a decline in their favorability; *political* power refers to the outcomes of interactions with governments.

Repression: the costs of collective action to the contender resulting from interaction with other groups; as a process, any action by another group which raises the contender's cost of collective action; an action which lowers the contender's cost is a form of *facilitation;* let us reserve the terms *political* repression and *political* facilitation for the relationship between contender(s) and government(s).

Opportunity/threat: the extent to which other groups, including governments, are either (a) vulnerable to new claims which would, if successful, enhance the contender's realization of its interests or (b) threatening to make claims which would, if successful, reduce the contender's realization of its interests.

Repression and power refer to closely related transactions. Repression refers to the volume of collective action as a function of the costs of producing it, while power refers to the returns from collective action as a function of its volume. If by some unlikely chance the volume of collective action were to increase while total costs and total returns remained constant, by definition both repression and power would fall. In general, however, a group which is subject to heavy repression—that is, pays a high cost per unit of collective action—also has little power (that is, gets a low return per unit of collective action).

Interests and opportunity/threat are also closely connected. Loosely speaking, interest refers to advantages and disadvantages which would theoretically result from possible interactions with other groups, opportunity/threat to the likelihood that those interactions will really occur.

A SIMPLE ACCOUNT OF COLLECTIVE ACTION

Before moving on to the difficulties hidden behind these elementary concepts, let us consider the simplest version of an argument linking them. Figure 3–2

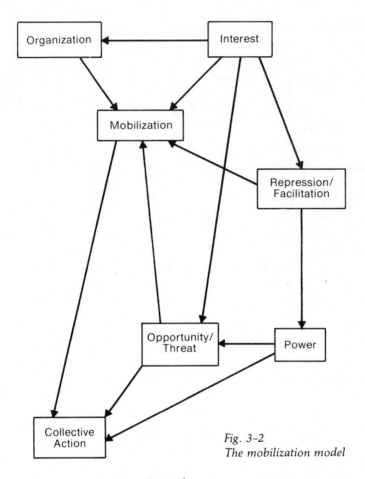

Fig. 3–2
The mobilization model

presents it in schematic form. The diagram declares that the main determinants of a group's mobilization are its organization, its interest in possible interactions with other contenders, the current opportunity/threat of those interactions and the group's subjection to repression. The diagram says that the group's subjection to repression is mainly a function of the sort of interest it represents. It treats the extent of a contender's collective action as a resultant of its power, its mobilization, and the current opportunities and threats confronting its interests. And so on.

It is easy to add hypothetical connections. For instance, it is quite possible that the form of a contender's organization, as such, affects the repression to which other contenders and governments subject it; when voluntary associations become legal vehicles for one kind of interest, they tend to become legal for other kinds of interest. My provisional argument, however, is that such effects are secondary as compared with the particular interest embodied in the contender. Repression depends mainly on that interest, and especially on the degree to which it conflicts with the interests of the government and members of the polity.

Likewise, a number of these connections are reciprocal over the longer run. For example, in the longer run a contender's form, pace, and extent of mobilization surely affect the repression which other groups apply to it. So does power position. A mobilizing group which concentrates on building an arsenal is likely to run afoul of the law, although the more powerful the group is in other respects the more likely it is to get away with it. Over the longer run a group's form of both organization and mobilization affect its interest. Roberto Michels made the classic statement of the dilemma: to act on an interest, a group of people have to organize and mobilize; but complex and effective forms of organization give their managers new interests to advance or defend, and the new interests often conflict with the interests around which the group organized and mobilized in the first place. This, then, is a short-run model; it deals with the determinants of collective action at the moment of action.

Although these short-run connections are plausible, they are not self-evident. Some of them contradict standard arguments concerning political processes. For instance, many "pluralistic" analyses of politics in parliamentary democracies make two assumptions which compete with those of our model: first, that repression is relatively low and spread evenly across the whole range of contenders and potential contenders; second, that the costs of organizing and mobilizing are also fairly low and equal. When he comes to consider the drawbacks of pragmatic two-party politics, Robert Dahl offers some intriguing reflections:

> Consider the lot of the political dissenter . . . If he enters into a third party, he is condemned to political impotence . . . It is natural for him to interpret political conflict among national leaders as sham battles within a unified power elite . . . For the political dissenter, continued political impotence and rejection breed frustration. Frustration may produce apathy and withdrawal from politics, but frustration may also turn to hostility, resentment, vengefulness, and even hatred for national leaders in both parties. The political dissenter, then, is likely to become alienated from the political system—from its prevailing practices, its institutions, its personnel, and their assumptions (Dahl 1966: 65–66).

Dahl does not claim to be building a general account of collective action. The work just quoted deals with the conditions for different patterns of political opposition in democracies. Nevertheless it is legitimate and useful to generalize

Dahl's argument, for it contains the main proposals pluralist theory offers for the analysis of collective action in general.

Dahl's reflections place a remarkable emphasis on individual, as opposed to group, aspirations and grievances. They assume that an individual defines his interest, then searches for a way to forward that interest within the existing political system. They contain an indirect observation that the costs and returns of collective action differ from one potential actor to another as a result of the particular lineaments of the American political system. Neither repression nor mobilizing costs seem to play a significant part in Dahl's explanation of differentials in political participation.

"Political participation" itself, in this view, consists of voting, party work, holding office, and communicating with legislators; people whose problems these procedures won't solve tend to withdraw or to act outside the political system. The extent to which a group's interests are facing new threats or new opportunities becomes, in Dahl's argument and the pluralistic argument in general, the chief determinant of its collective action. Furthermore, the argument draws sharp distinctions among normal politics, abnormal politics, and collective action outside the realm of politics. In all these regards, our collective-action model leads in other directions: assuming groups as the political participants, attributing major importance to repression and to mobilizing costs, minimizing the political/nonpolitical distinction, and arguing that the main difference between "normal" and "abnormal" political action is the power position of the groups involved.

The comparison of our bare-bones mobilization model with the pluralist assumptions also helps display some worrisome gaps in the mobilization argument. For one thing, the model does not directly represent the effects of beliefs, customs, world views, rights, or obligations. Instead, in this elementary version, it assumes that beliefs, customs, world views, rights, and obligations affect collective action indirectly through their influence on interest, organization, mobilization, and repression. This assumption, and others like it, will need attention later on.

For another thing, the model has no time in it. Collective action does. The most obvious defect of the model is that it makes no allowance for the ways a contender's collective action affects its opportunities and its power. The model provides no place for strategic interactions and no place for the conquest or loss of power. Collective action affects a group's power, but that effect takes time. As we move along, we will have to treat time sequences more explicitly and carefully.

Finally, the model is essentially quantitative. It concerns the *amount* of collective action, the *extent* of organization, and so on. Unquestionably, the *type* of organization, of interest, of mobilization affects the *type* of collective action of which a contender is capable; in many circumstances it affects the quantity of collective action as well. In Karl Marx's analysis of 1848, which we looked at in the previous chapter, the social and geographic fragmentation of the peasantry helps explain their inaction in the face of assaults on their interests. We will have much to do with these qualitative relationships later on.

If we were to apply the elementary mobilization model to the changing collective action of different groups of workers in the course of industrialization—which is one of the purposes for which it is intended—we would find ourselves pursuing two somewhat separate bunches of questions: *first*, how the shared interests, general organization, and current mobilization of a trade affected its members' capacity for acting together; *second*, how its current relationship to the government and to powerful contenders affected the costs and returns of each of the available opportunities to act on common grievances and aspirations. Under the first heading come questions about the spatial concentration of the industry, the extensiveness of the internal communications network, the existence of unions, and so on. Under the second are questions concerning the existence of coalitions with power holders, the extent of legislation penalizing labor organizations, the rewards available to victors in elections or in strikes, etc.

Much of the following discussion will propose arguments concerning such specific questions. It will offer concepts to clarify the arguments as well as strategies of measurement and analysis. If, equipped only with our elementary model, we pressed our inquiry into working-class collective action, we would soon need further assumptions about rights, beliefs, and the rules of the political game. The later discussion will often tarry over such problems.

For the moment, nevertheless, we should stick with interests, organization, mobilization, collective action, repression/facilitation, power and opportunity/threat. Let us go around our diagram in that order, refining as we go. Then we can restate the model before applying it to the analysis of different forms of conflict. This chapter will take us through interest, organization, mobilization and collective action. Chapter 4 will then add repression/facilitation, power, and opportunity/threat to the analysis before reconsidering both our models and their implications for real-life conflict.

INTERESTS

Most analyses of mobilization and contention for power take the groups involved, and their interests, for granted. Once we notice who is acting, it rarely seems difficult to explain why they, and not other groups, are acting. Yet many groups fail to mobilize, some mobilized groups fail to act collectively, some collective actors fail to contend for power, and many actors come and go: indignant women now, angry farmers then, temperance advocates some other time. A valid theory of collective action must explain the comings and goings. It must also explain why some groups never show up at all. Part of the explanation lies in the organizational problems we will take up later. But part of it surely resides in the fact that groups have varying interests in collective action.

Theories in the tradition of John Stuart Mill give us little guidance in the identification of a group's interest. Yet they suggest that the nature of the population's central decision-making structures—its market, its system of voting, or something else of the sort—strongly affects which people have an interest in acting together, and will therefore do so.

Durkheimian theories tell us to watch the creation and destruction of groups by the changing division of labor. They tell us to expect greater action (or at least a different kind of action) from the groups being most completely and rapidly transformed. For Durkheim, individual and collective interests generally conflict in the short run. Individual impulses and individual interests are roughly equivalent; the crucial variation from one group or society to another is how much those individual impulses and interests are under social control.

Weberian theories also draw our attention to the division of labor, but lead us to anticipate greater activity from groups which have attached themselves to new systems of belief. Shared belief itself leads to a definition of interest, and stimulates action oriented to that definition.

The Marxian line, finally, is well known: the changing organization of production creates and destroys social classes which are defined by different relationships to the basic means of production; out of the organization of production arise fundamental class differences in interest. A class acts together, in the Marxian account, to the extent that it has extensive internal organization and to the extent that its interests are currently being threatened.

The Millian, Durkheimian, Weberian, and Marxian views produce competing statements about the relationship between interest and organization. A major part of the disagreement concerns the proper way to identify a population's interest in the first place. The basic choices are two. We can

1   infer the interest from the population's own utterances and actions;

2   infer it from a general analysis of the connections between interest and social position.

Millian theorists tend to do some version of the first; they try to ground their analyses on utilities or preferences revealed directly or indirectly by the actors. Marxists often do some version of the second; they determine a group's interest *a priori* from its relationship to the means of production. There are many elaborations and compromises between the two. For example, some analysts infer the interest of workers at one point in time retroactively from an interest they articulate later. Many treatments of social movements take that tack, looking back to the early stages of the movement for traces of awareness of goals which would later become clear and dominant.

The first choice—inferring the interest from the population's own utterances and actions—is open to serious objections. For one thing, many groups appear to be unaware of their own real interests. Either they have not articulated their shared interests or they have articulated them falsely. For another, the appropriate evidence is very hard to identify, assemble and synthesize: people often say conflicting things, or nothing at all. But the second choice—inferring interests from a general analysis of the connections between interests and social position—also has serious drawbacks. It takes confidence, even arrogance, to override a group's own vision of its interests in life. General interest schemes commonly reveal a conflict between short-run and long-run interests. (Much interesting game theory deals with situations in which short-run interest leads to strategies contrary to the long-run interest of the parties.) In that case, which is the "real" interest? Finally, we are trying to explain why people behave as they do; the goals they have fashioned for themselves appear to influence their behavior even when those goals are trivial, vague, unrealistic, or self-defeating. My own response to this dilemma contains two rules: (1) treat the relations of production as predictors of the interests people will pursue on the average and in the long run, but (2) rely, as much as possible, on people's own articulation of their interests as an explanation of their behavior in the short run.

We escape that ferocious dilemma, however, only to rush onto the horns of another: individual interests vs. group interests. Even if we identify both with confidence, they need not coincide, and may well conflict. Much theorizing in the vein of John Stuart Mill has dealt with precisely that dilemma—sometimes by striving to show that individual pursuit of self-interest will serve the common good, sometimes by attempting to identify and explain those situations in which a genuine conflict does emerge, sometimes by looking for decision rules which will cumulate individual interests to the collective advantage. In a famous passage of *The Wealth of Nations* (Chapter 3, Book 4), Adam Smith set the tone of the first alternative:

> Every individual is continually exerting himself to find out the most advantageous employment for whatever capital he can command. It is his own advantage, indeed, and not that of the society, which he has in view. But the study of his own advantage naturally, or rather necessarily, leads him to prefer that employment which is most advantageous to the society.

On the other hand, the argument by Mancur Olson which we reviewed earlier (despite its debt to Adam Smith) indicates that individual interest and group interest usually do conflict. At least they conflict in this sense: each individual actor ordinarily has an incentive to avoid contributing his share to collective actions which will benefit everyone. Adam Smith resolves the dilemma by denying it; by implication, he denies that there is anything special about collective action which the proper study of individual action will not explain. Mancur Olson, however, makes that very link problematic.

We are not defenseless against the dilemma. We should remain clear that collective interests exist, however large a part the pursuit of individual interests may play in the accomplishment of those collective interests. We should deliberately treat the degree of conflict between individual and collective interests as a variable affecting the likelihood and character of collective action. We should treat that degree of conflict, more precisely, as increasing the cost of collective action to the individuals and to the group as a whole. And we should pursue the analysis of the ways that alternative arrangements for making decisions translate individual perferences into collective outcomes. In the analyses that follow, I will occasionally wrestle with these theoretical problems. Usually, however, I will treat them as practical matters: how to determine, in particular times and places, which interests are important and how the people involved aggregate them.

ORGANIZATION

Harrison White has made a powerful distillate of the most insipid wines in the sociological cellar—group taxonomies. There we find only two elements. There are *categories* of people who share some characteristic: they are all female, all Sunni Muslims, all residents of Timbuktu, or something else. A full-fledged category contains people all of whom recognize their common characteristic, and whom everyone else recognizes as having that characteristic. There are also *networks* of people who are linked to each other, directly or indirectly, by a specific kind of interpersonal bond: a chain of people each of whom owes someone else in the set attendance at his or her wedding, let us say, or the set of individuals defined by starting arbitrarily with some person, identifying everyone that person talks with at least once every day, then identifying everyone *they* talk with at least once every day, and so on until no new persons join the list. If the common characteristic of the interpersonal bond is ordinary, the categories and networks defined by them tend to be large. Clearly we can shrink the categories and networks by insisting on criteria (or combinations of criteria) which occur rarely: female Sunni Muslim residents of Timbuktu, perhaps, or daily conversation plus invitability to a wedding.

The more interesting combination is the one White calls a *catnet:* a set of individuals comprising both a category and a network. The catnet catches gracefully the sense of "groupness" which more complicated concepts miss. For that reason, I will substitute the word *group* for the exotic catnet. A set of individuals is a group to the extent that it comprises both a category and a network.

The idea of *organization* follows directly. The more extensive its common identity and internal networks, the more organized the group. CATNESS × NETNESS = ORGANIZATION. Schematically, Fig. 3–3 sums up the relationships among the concepts. "All Brazilians" comprise a set of people only weakly linked by interpersonal networks, but strongly identified by themselves and others as a separate category of being: low on netness, high on catness. The printers' union locals portrayed in Lipset, Trow, and Coleman's

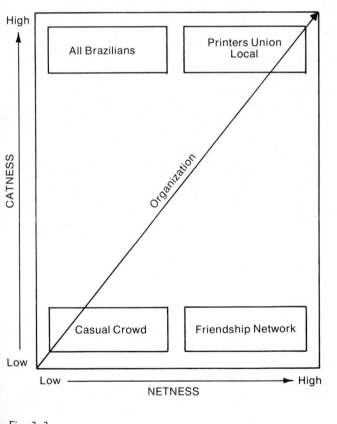

Fig. 3–3
Components of organization

Union Democracy have both distinct, compelling identities and extensive, absorbing interpersonal networks: high on both catness and netness, therefore on organization.

This notion of organization stresses the group's inclusiveness: how close it comes to absorbing the members' whole lives. (For "inclusiveness" we have our choice of three related standards: the amount of time, the amount of energy, or the proportion of all social interaction in which the members and other people are taking into account the fact of group membership.) Other features of a group's structure one might want to consider in judging how "organized" it is are its efficiency and its effectiveness—or the structural features presumably affecting efficiency and effectiveness, such as differentiation, centrality and stratification. I stress inclusiveness on two grounds: (1) the (unproved) hypothesis that it is the main aspect of group structure which affects the ability to mobilize; (2) the intrinsic difficulty of separating effectiveness and efficiency from the mobilization and collective action we are trying to explain. By the standard of inclusiveness, an isolated community will tend to be highly organized, but so will some occupational groups, some religious groups, and some political groups.

We need these definitions in order to think about the groups which could, in principle, mobilize. We also need them to specify what it means to say that organization promotes mobilization. The number of potential mobilizers is enormous. The task of enumerating all of them for a given population would look something like this:

1 Identify every single status distinction employed within the population.

2 Select those distinctions which imply some difference in interest between those in one category and those in another.

3 Produce the (tremendous) list consisting of all combinations of the selected distinctions.

4 Eliminate those which have no real persons within them (e.g., Chinese-Jewish-cowboy-grandmother).

5 Select those with some minimum possibility of identifying and communicating with each other

This fantastic task is probably out of reach for large populations organized in complicated ways, although Edmonson (1958) did analyze apparently exhaustive lists of status terms for North American Indian groups. But one might be able to carry out steps 1 and 2 as sampling operations, if there were an unbiased source of status distinctions; then the list for step 3 could be as small as one desired. If steps 4 and 5 left no categories, one could go back to 1 and 2 over and over.

Gamson's procedure for identifying "challenging groups" in American politics bears a general resemblance to this ideal plan, but starts much further along in the mobilization process. ("Challenging groups" are those which in the period from 1800 to 1945 made a new, contested bid to change the organization or behavior of the national political system; they are a special case of the groups which, not coincidentally, I earlier called "challengers".) Gamson scans numerous historical sources for any mention whatsoever of a group making new claims, and places all group names in a pool from which he then draws groups at random for close study. After some eliminations for duplication, lack of geographic scope, etc., and after a large search for additional information concerning the groups drawn, Gamson has an unbiased, well-documented sample of all challenging groups meeting his criteria over the entire period. Within the sample, he can then study changes in the characteristics of challenging groups over time, differences between successful and unsuccessful challengers, and a number of other important problems. For our purposes, the weakness of Gamson's procedure is that a group must have acted together somehow to be mentioned in historical accounts. It is not, therefore, a reliable way of determining what characteristics set off those groups which mobilize from all those others which, in theory, could have mobilized.

We have an alternative. Instead of attempting to prepare an unbiased list of all potential mobilizers, we can take one or two dimensions of differentiation which are of theoretical interest, search for evidence of group formation, and then of mobilization, at different locations along the dimension, letting the differentials test more general assertions concerning the determinants of organization and mobilization. Voting analysts and students of industrial conflict sometimes do an important part of the necessary work. In voting studies, it is common to take the entire population of potential voters in some territory, divide it up into major demographic categories, then examine differentials among the categories in organization, political activity, and voting propensities. In analyses of strikes, it is common to take an entire labor force, divide it into industries and types of firms, then document variation in the organization of work, type and intensity of unionization, and propensity to strike.

Different ways of dividing up the electorate or the labor force will produce different results. But that can be an advantage: it helps us decide which differentials are durable and general. For example, some years ago Clark Kerr and Abraham Siegel made a plausible and widely accepted analysis of industrial strike propensities. First, they summarized the overall pattern of strike propensities in Australia, Czechoslovakia, Germany, Italy, the Netherlands, New Zealand, Norway, Sweden, Switzerland, the United Kingdom, and the United States during various periods from World War I to the late 1940s. Their description of the general pattern appears in Table 3-1. Having identified the

Table 3-1 *Kerr & Siegel's summary of strike propensities*

Propensity to strike	Industry
High	Mining
	Maritime and longshore
Medium High	Lumber
	Textile
Medium	Chemical
	Printing
	Leather
	General manufacturing
	Construction
	Food & kindred products
Medium Low	Clothing
	Gas, water, electricity
	Hotels, restaurants, & other services
Low	Railroad
	Agriculture
	Trade

Source   Kerr & Siegel 1954: 190

differentials, they tried to explain them. They settled on the presence of an "isolated mass"—a homogeneous workforce, segregated from other workers—as the major condition producing high strike propensity. They also suggested that,

> If the job is physically difficult and unpleasant, unskilled or semiskilled, and casual or seasonal, and fosters an independent spirit (as in the logger in the woods), it will draw tough, inconstant, combative, and virile workers, and they will be inclined to strike. If the job is physically easy and performed in pleasant surroundings, skilled and responsible, steady, and subject to set rules and close supervision, it will attract women or the more submissive type of man who will abhor strikes (Kerr & Siegel 1954: 195).

But this was, fortunately, a secondary hypothesis.

In either version, the argument has two levels: (1) the identification of some standard differentials among industries in strike propensity; (2) the explanation of whatever differentials actually appear. Both facets of the Kerr-Siegel analysis, especially the second, appear to be wrong. For the case of

France, Table 3-2 presents rates of strikes and person days in strikes for major industries from 1890 to 1960. The data show no more than a moderate stability in relative strike propensites from one period to the next. They show a considerable difference in relative strike propensities as measured by frequency of strikes and by total person-days. Although agriculture does stick at the bottom of the list, so do transport and textiles. Food is also consistently low, contrary to the prediction. There is less consistency at the top: quarrying turns out to have many strikes, but relatively short, small ones. Mining turns out to have few strikes, but big, long ones. In any case, the other French industries which rank relatively high in strike propensity—chemicals, construction, building materials, and smelting—are neither high on all indices nor obvious illustrations of the greater strike propensity of isolated, homogeneous and/or "tough" industries.

Table 3-2 *French strike rates by industry, 1890-1960*

Industry	Strikes per 100,000 labor force		Person-days lost per 100 million labor force	
	1890-1914	1915-1935	1915-1932	1950-1960
Quarrying*	30	22	40	111*
Chemicals	24	10	54	62
Construction	24	15	50	31
Building materials ceramics	23	21	91	20
Mining	19	5	151	*
Printing & Paper	16	11	37	15
Smelting	14	17	220	70
Leather & Hides	13	14	77	13
Metalworking	12	10	46	88
Transport	9	8	14	86
Textiles	8	7	72	27
Garments				2
Wood industries	8	9	19	6
Food industries	5	6	10	6
Agriculture, Fish, Forest	0.4	0.3	n.a.	n.a.
Total nonagriculture	7	6	37	39

*Quarrying and Mining combined in 1950-1960.
Source Shorter & Tilly 1974: 201.

In order to get at the "isolated mass" portion of the argument, Edward Shorter and I regrouped the French strike data by small district into three types of areas: mono-industrial, poly-industrial, metropolitan. The Kerr–Siegel analysis predicts a strong tendency for the mono-industrial areas to have higher strike rates, greater militancy, and so on. In fact, it is the other way round: on the whole, metropolitan districts outshadow poly-industrial districts, and the one-industry districts come in last (Shorter & Tilly 1974: 287–295). When Muhammad Fiaz arrayed French industries by their degree of geographic segregation over the country as a whole, he discovered no relationship between isolation and strike propensity; such factors as unionization and plant size, on the other hand, significantly affected the relative propensity to strike (Fiaz 1973). Likewise, the analyses Snyder and Kelly have done for Italy, 1878–1903, indicate that once obvious organizational features such as size and unionization are allowed for, industry as such has no significant effect on the broad quantitative characteristics of strikes (Snyder & Kelly 1976). In these trials, at least, no version of the Kerr–Siegel argument holds up.

These examples offer an important lesson to users of a group-comparison strategy: the less compelling your *a priori* reasons for employing a particular classification as a basis for the study of differentials in organization, mobilization, and collective action, the more important it is to compare the effects of using different classifications. Each application of a new classification to the data is, in its crude way, the trial of a new theory. The corollary applies more generally: the better specified your theory, the more likely you are to find some accessible corner of reality in which to try it out. The better specified your theory, the less you will have to worry about the monumental task of enumerating all groups at risk to organization, mobilization, and collective action. An obvious sermon, but one little heeded.

The Kerr–Siegel analysis provides another lesson as well. Strikes are a form of collective action. To explain group differentials in any kind of collective action, including strikes, we will have to take into account all our components: interests, organization, mobilization, and opportunity. Kerr and Siegel attempt to explain the differentials with interests and organization alone. The reasoning about isolated masses and toughness gives a particular (and inadequate) account of the organizational structure and individual workers' interests characteristic of different industries. But it says nothing about differentials in mobilization or opportunity to strike.

To be more exact, Kerr and Siegel assume implicitly either (1) that mobilization and opportunity are roughly equal across industries or (2) that whatever differences in mobilization and opportunity do exist have no independent effects on strike propensity; they result from the differences in interest and organization. Those assumptions, too, are hypotheses—dubious ones. Before accepting interest and organization alone as full explanations of collective action, we will have to look at the evidence concerning mobilization and opportunity.

MOBILIZATION

The word "mobilization" conveniently identifies the process by which a group goes from being a passive collection of individuals to an active participant in public life. Demobilization is the reverse process. Amitai Etzioni (1968: 388–389) puts it this way:

> We refer to the process by which a unit gains significantly in the control of assets it previously did not control as *mobilization* . . By definition, it entails a decline in the assets controlled by subunits, the supraunit of which the unit is a member, or external units, unless the assets whose control the unit gained are newly produced ones . . . A mere increase in the assets of members, of subunits, or even of the unit itself does not mean that mobilization has occurred, though it increases the mobilization potential. The change in the capacity to control and to use assets is what is significant.

Etzioni offers a rough classification of assets, or resources: *coercive* (e.g., weapons, armed forces, manipulative technologies); *utilitarian* (e.g., goods, information services, money); *normative* (e.g., loyalties, obligations). A group mobilizes if it gains greater collective control over coercive, utilitarian, or normative resources, demobilizes if it loses that sort of control.

In practice, Etzioni's classification of resources is difficult to maintain. It refers to their use rather than their intrinsic character. The service a revolutionary cabal draws from its 272 loyal members is likely to be at once coercive and utilitarian. The resource is labor power of a certain kind. Furthermore, loyalty and obligation are not so much resources as they are conditions affecting the likelihood that resources will be delivered when called for. If we are actually comparing the current mobilization levels of several groups, or trying to gauge a group's change over time, we will ordinarily do better to fall back on the economist's factors of production: land, labor, capital, perhaps technical expertise as well.

To the extent that all of the resources have well-established market values in the population at large, reliance on production factors will help us set rates of return for resources expended in the political arena. We can then represent loyalties, obligations, commitments and so forth as determinants of the probability that each resource nominally under group control will be available:

$$\text{Mobilization level} = \text{sum}\left(\begin{bmatrix}\text{market value} \\ \text{of factor of} \\ \text{production} \\ \text{nominally under} \\ \text{group control}\end{bmatrix} \times \begin{bmatrix}\text{probability} \\ \text{of delivery} \\ \text{when called} \\ \text{for}\end{bmatrix}\right)$$

Political life makes the probabilities hard to estimate *a priori* and unlikely to remain constant from one possible type of action to another: the militants who will vote or picket will not always go to the barricades. This formulation poses the problem explicitly. We can then ask, as a question for research, whether the use of elections as a reference point produces different relative measurements of mobilization for a set of groups at the same point in time (or for the same group at different points in time) than does the use of street demonstrations.

We can also close in on the old problem of differences between a disciplined professional staff and committed volunteers: it should appear not only as a difference in the market value of the labor under group control, but also as a variation in the probability that the available labor will actually do the different things which might be demanded of it: stuff envelopes, picket, lobby, bribe, kidnap, bomb, write legal briefs.

The formulation neatly states an old political dilemma: the choice between loyalty and effectiveness. Effective employees or members often use their effectiveness to serve themselves or to serve others instead of the organization to which they are attached, while loyal employees or members are often ineffective; sometimes the solution of the tax farmer (who uses his power to enrich himself, but at least has enough effectiveness to produce a surplus for his nominal masters) is the best available. Sometimes the disloyalty of the professionals is so great as to make loyal amateurs a more desirable alternative.

Loyalty refers to the breadth of members' commitments to deliver resources. It has three dimensions:

- the amount of resources commited,
- the range of resources involved,
- the range of circumstances in which the resources will be delivered.

A commitment to deliver substantial resources of only one kind in a narrowly specified situation bespeaks relatively little loyalty. A commitment to deliver many resources of different kinds regardless of the situation reveals great loyalty. Real-life organizations lie somewhere between the two extremes.

Albert Hirschman turns this observation inside out; he considers loyalty as one of the major alternative modes of demand for an organization's services. (We looked at Hirschman's analysis briefly while reviewing the Millian approach to collective action.) In the context of response to decline in the performance of organizations, he distinguished three possible reactions of consumers, clients, or members of a given organization: exit, voice, and loyalty. Economics, Hirschman comments, treats exit—a cessation of demand for the commodity or service—as the normal response to declining quality. In the case of schools, governments, and other organizations whose performances fluctuate, he argues, two other responses are common. The relevant public may voice its dissatisfaction, with implicit or explicit threats of exit. Or it may tolerate unsatisfactory performance for a while because the costs of exit or voice are greater than the loss of quality. That tolerance is a measure of subjective returns from the organization, hence of loyalty.

The economic problem is to work out the trade-offs among exit, voice, and loyalty. That specifies the conditions under which one or another occurs. For our purposes, however, the value of Hirschman's analysis is to help us calculate the probability that resources ostensibly on call will actually be delivered. Exit is the analogue of refusal to deliver, while voice and loyalty are alternative ways of continuing to yield. At least in the short run, voice raises the cost of group access to the resources.

In general, a group which puts a large proportion of its membership into remunerated positions within its own organization (for example, a bureaucratized priesthood) raises the cost of exit, and thereby makes voice and loyalty more likely responses to its performance. It does so at the cost of committing an important share of its mobilized resources to the maintenance of the organization itself.

The alternative of placing its members elsewhere—as a victorious political party often disposes of government jobs—reduces the internal drain on the organization. However, it also lowers the cost of exit, unless members continue to hold their posts at the pleasure of the organization. Building an all-embracing moral community also raises the relative costs of exit. Earlier I suggested that the most important element of organization, so far as impact on mobilization was concerned, was the group's inclusiveness of different aspects of social life. The creation of a moral community is therefore an extreme case of organization-building in general. On the whole, the higher the level of organization, the greater the likelihood of voice or loyalty. If a group emphasizes coercion, however, it probably shifts the likelihood away from voice, toward exit or loyalty.

The major variables affecting the probability of delivery are therefore the extent of competing claims on the resources involved, the nature of the action to which the resources are to be committed, and how organized the mobilizing group is. If the resources are free of competing claims, if the action clearly defends the interests of every member, and if the group is an all-embracing moral community, the probability of delivery is close to 100 percent. Loyalty is then at its maximum, the probability of departure or contestation—exit or voice—is at its minimum.

Indeed, a significant part of the work of mobilization goes into changing these three variables: reducing the competing claims on resources controlled by members, developing a program which corresponds to the perceived interests of members, building up a group structure which minimizes exit and voice. In her survey of nineteenth- and twentieth-century American communes, Rosabeth Moss Kanter identifies a series of "commitment mechanisms." "For communes," she tells us:

> the problem of commitment is crucial. Since the community represents an attempt to establish an ideal social order within the larger society, it must vie with the outside for the members' loyalties. It must ensure high member involvement despite external competition without sacrificing its distinctiveness or ideals. It must often contravene the earlier socialization of its members in securing obedience to new demands. It must calm internal dissension in order to present a united front to the world. The problem of securing total and complete commitment is central (Kanter 1972: 65).

She is describing a mobilization program which concentrates on the labor-power and loyalty of the members themselves.

What organizational arrangements promote that sort of mobilization? Kanter compares nine nineteenth-century communal movements (including the Shakers, Harmony, Jerusalem, and Oneida) which lasted thirty-three years or more with twenty-one (including Modern Times, Oberlin, Brook Farm, and the Iowa Pioneer Phalanx) which lasted sixteen years or less. The commitment mechanisms which were substantially more common among the long-lived communes included:

- sexual and material abstinence
- prohibition of nonresident members
- signing over property at admission
- nonreimbursement of defectors for property and labor
- provision of medical services
- insulation mechanisms, such as a special term for the Outside, ignoring of outside newspapers, speaking a foreign language and/or a special jargon
- rules for interaction with visitors
- discouragement of pairing: free love or celibacy required
- physical separation of family members
- communal ownership of clothing and personal effects
- no compensation for labor
- no charge for community services
- communal work efforts
- daily meetings, and most time spent with other group members

- mortification procedures such as confession, mutual surveillance and denunciation, or distinctions among members on moral grounds
- institutionalization of awe for the group and its leaders through the attribution of magical powers, the legitimation of group demands through appeals to ultimate values, and the use of special forms of address (Kanter 1972: chapter 4).

Kanter's list begins to give us a feeling for the real-life manifestations of the process Max Weber called the routinization of charisma. Faith and magic play a part, to be sure. But so do a concrete set of social arrangements which place the available resources at the disposal of the group, and make either voice or exit costly ways to respond to unsatisfactory performance. The social arrangements build loyalty, and enhance mobilization.

Most social groups are unlike communes. They differ in the priorities they assign to exit, voice, and loyalty. The professionals concentrate on accumulating resources free of competing claims, the rationalists on adapting their program to current group interests, the moralists on building an inclusive group which commands assent for its own sake. An exploitative group will concentrate on the first while appearing to concentrate on the second or the third: actually working to free resources while appearing to shape a program to the interests of its members or to build a satisfying group. Religious frauds often take this latter form.

Thus any group's mobilization program breaks down into these components:

1 Accumulating resources.
2 Increasing collective claims on the resources
   a) by reducing competing claims,
   b) by altering the program of collective action,
   c) by changing the satisfaction due to participation in the group as such.

A successful mobilization program does all of them at once.

Groups do their mobilizing in a number of different ways. We can make crude distinctions among *defensive, offensive,* and *preparatory* mobilization. In defensive mobilization, a threat from outside induces the members of a group to pool their resources to fight off the enemy. Eric Wolf (1969) has pointed out how regularly this sort of response to the representatives of capitalism and state power has preceded peasant rebellions. Standard European forms of rural conflict—food riots, tax rebellions, invasions of fields, draft resistance, and so on—typically follow the same sort of defensive mobilization. This large class of actions challenges the common assumption (made by Etzioni, among others) that mobilization is always a top-down phenomenon, organized by leaders and agitators.

Offensive mobilization *is*, however, often top-down. In the offensive case, a group pools resources in response to opportunities to realize its interests. A common form of offensive mobilization consists of the diffusion of a new organizational strategy. In the late 1820s, for example, the success of O'Connell's Catholic Association in forcing the expansion of the political rights of British and Irish Catholics inspired the creation of political associations aimed at expanding the franchise and guaranteeing rights to assemble, organize, and act collectively. A coalition of bourgeois and substantial artisans arose from that strategy, and helped produce the great Reform Bill of 1832. In this instance, the top-down organizational efforts of such leaders as Francis Place and William Cobbett were crucial. Nevertheless, in parish after parish the local dissidents decided on their own that it was time to organize their own association, or (more likely) to convert their existing forms of organization into a political association.

Preparatory mobilization is no doubt the most top-down of all. In this variety, the group pools resources in anticipation of future opportunities and threats. The nineteenth-century trade union is a classic case. The trade union built up a store of money to cushion hardship—hardship in the form of unemployment, the death of a breadwinner, or loss of wages during a strike. It also pooled knowledge and organizational skills. When it escaped the union-busting of employers and governments, the trade union greatly increased the capacity of workers to act together: to strike, to boycott, to make collective demands. This preparatory mobilization often began defensively, in the course of a losing battle with employers or in the face of a threat of firings, wage reductions, or cutbacks in privileges. It normally required risky organizing efforts by local leaders who were willing to get hurt.

The preparatory part of the strategy was always difficult, since it required the members to forego present satisfactions in favor of uncertain future benefits. As we move from defensive to offensive to preparatory mobilization, in fact, we see the increasing force of Mancur Olson's statement of the free-rider problem: a rational actor will ride for nothing if someone else will pay the fuel and let him aboard. But if everyone tries to ride free the vehicle goes nowhere. Preparatory mobilization, especially in the face of high risks, requires strong incentives to overcome the reasonable desire to have someone else absorb the costs.

As we move from defensive to offensive to preparatory mobilization, we also see that the distinction between offensive and preparatory is less clear than the distinction between offensive and defensive. Both offensive and preparatory mobilization require foresight and an active scanning of the world outside the group. Both are unlikely in any but the smallest groups without active leadership and deliberate organizational effort. One frequent pattern is for leaders to employ resources which are already mobilized to assure the commitment of other resources to collective ends. That happens, for example, when priests play on their congregations, already obliged to assemble, for cash contributions. It also happens when landlords send bailiffs to claim part of the crop, or when ward heelers trade jobs for votes. These are concrete examples of the "selective incentives" for participation whose importance Mancur Olson has stressed.

Unlike defensive mobilization, neither offensive nor preparatory mobilization occurs very often as a simple extension of the group's everyday routines for doing its work: gathering at the market, shaping up for hiring at the dock, getting together for a little poaching. Offensive and preparatory mobilization resemble each other; the main difference is whether the opportunities to which the group responds are in the present or the future. So the basic distinction runs between defensive and offensive modes of mobilization.

A population's initial wealth and power significantly affect the probability that its mobilization will be defensive or offensive. Common sense says that the rich mobilize conservatively, in defense of their threatened interests, while the poor mobilize radically, in search of what they lack. Common sense is wrong. It is true that the rich never lash out to smash the status quo, while the poor sometimes do. But the rich are constantly mobilizing to take advantage of new opportunities to maximize their interests. The poor can rarely afford to.

The poor and powerless tend to begin defensively, the rich and powerful offensively. The group whose members are rich can mobilize a surplus without threatening a member's other amusements and obligations. A group with a poor constituency has little choice but to compete with daily necessities. The group whose members are powerful can use the other organizations they control—including governments—to do some of their work, whereas the powerless must do it on their own. The rich and powerful can forestall claims from other groups before they become articulated claims, and can afford to seize opportunities to make new claims on their own. The poor and the powerless often find that the rich, the powerful, and the government oppose and punish their efforts at mobilization. (The main exception, an important one, is the powerless group which forms a coalition with a rich, powerful patron; European Fascists of the 1920s mobilized rapidly in that fashion.) As a result, any mobilization at all is more costly to the poor and powerless; only a threat to the little they have is likely to move them to mobilize. The rich and powerful are well defended against such threats; they rarely have the occasion for defensive mobilization.

If, on the other hand, we hold mobilization constant and consider collective action itself, common sense is vindicated. Relatively poor and powerless groups which have already mobilized are more likely to act collectively by claiming new rights, privileges, and advantages. At the same level of mobilization the rich and powerful are more likely to act collectively in defense of what they already have. Thus the well-documented tendency of strikes to become more frequent and more demanding in times of prosperity, when workers have more slack resources to devote to acting together, and employers have more to lose from the withholding of labor.

Mobilization implies demobilization. Any process by which a group loses collective control over resources demobilizes the group. How could that happen? Anything which destroys resources tends to have that effect: war, neglect, potlatch. But the more common source of demobilization is the transfer of control over certain kinds of resources to another group: a subunit of the group in question, a large unit of which the group itself is a part, a group outside. A lost war, for example, frequently produces all three sorts of demobilization in the losing country. Men and women return from military service to the service of their families; the government, for a time, gives up some of its control over its own operations to a concert of nations of which it is a part; other countries seize some of the loser's territory, population, equipment, or wealth. Whether such processes produce a negative sum, a positive sum, or a zero sum depends entirely on the *relative* rates at which new resources are being created, and old ones destroyed.

Often two groups, one containing the other, mobilize at approximately the same time. A confusion between the two levels has regularly dogged discussions of mobilization, since Karl Deutsch's initial formulation of the ideas (1953). The most notable examples from our own era involve national states and smaller units within them: parties, unions or even organized ethnic groups. (Many Africanists, for instance, have noticed the strengthening of the ostensibly traditional groups which outsiders call "tribes" with the growth of new states.)

Political theorists, both totalitarian and democratic, have often considered the mobilization at one level and at the other to be complementary. The party, in such an account, accumulates loyalties which transfer to the state. There is actually, however, little guarantee that this harmony will prevail. In the usual situation, the smaller and larger units compete for the same resources. They may follow well-defined rules of combat, and one of them may consistently have the upper hand, but they compete nonetheless. Likewise, two or more groups mobilizing simultaneously within some larger group which is also mobilizing commonly struggle over control of the same resources. The Teamsters and the Transport Workers fight for jurisdiction over the same drivers. When union members pay more taxes, they have less money for union dues. When all a person's time goes into a religious sect, he has none left either for union membership or for government service. Military conscription withdraws a man from his obligations to a circle of friends and relatives.

This last example underscores the collective character of the process. We are not simply dealing with the fact that people in some categories give up resources as people in other categories acquire them. When conscription occurs, a group gives up labor power. In the European feudal period, the "group" was characteristically a fief. The vassal's personal obligation to the overlord tied his fief to the overlord's fief, to be sure; but the fief owed the knight service. As states grew stronger, communities typically became the units which owed a certain number of recruits. The usual mechanism of the draft consisted of the assignment of a quota to a commune, with some sort of collective decision (frequently the drawing of lots) determining which of the eligible young men would go. The purchase of substitutes by those who could afford it, as shocking as it appears to egalitarian eyes, expresses precisely this sense of a debt owed by a community, rather than an individual, to the state: Community X owes six conscripts. Under these circumstances, resistance to the draft united a community, not just a group of young people, against the state. The great counterrevolution of the Vendée against the French revolutionary state, in 1793, began with solidary resistance of communities to the demand for conscripts. The community as a whole stood to lose part of its supply of labor, love, loyalty, and procreative power.

The spread of the political theory and practice of "possessive individualism" (as C. B. Macpherson calls it) shifted the military obligation toward the individual, but only incompletely. Within French villages, the *classe* of young men coming up for the draft in the same year remains one of the principal solidary groups, one which symbolizes its loss through rituals, banquets, and ceremonial gifts. In most western countries, religious groups and some of the professions have, in the course of acquiring distinct political identities, worked out special compacts with the state exempting some of their members—at least their priests—from service, and setting conditions for the service of others. In the United States, the American Medical Association has achieved that sort of guarantee for its members, while the American Chiropractic Association has not. The Religious Society of Friends has, the Black Muslims have not. This tying of religious exemptions to specific group memberships caused great confusion in the 1960s as young Americans opposed to the Vietnam war began applying for certification as conscientious objectors on general moral grounds without claiming affiliation with one of the privileged sects.

In the America of the 1960s, something else was going on as well. In different ways, groups of blacks and groups of young people began to claim a collective right to withhold their members from military service. I do not mean they were widely successful either in mobilizing their own populations or in holding off the state. Both groups contain competing mobilizers pursuing competing ends, and have many members who refuse to commit their resources to any of the mobilizers, even though they are willing to yield them to the state. Yet the claim was there, in the form of organized campaigns to resist or evade the draft. The demands for the exclusion of corporate and military recruiters from campuses likewise made claims for collective control of the disposition of manpower. The claim was a sign that some mobilization was occurring; groups, rather than individuals, were struggling over the right to precious resources: the labor power of young people. With the end of the draft and the withdrawal of American troops from the Vietnam war, the groups involved demobilized. I do not think they, or their claims, have disappeared.

Reminder: mobilization refers to the acquisition of collective *control* over resources, rather than the simple accretion of resources. A group that grows in size has more manpower in it. That does not mean the absolute or propor- tionate manpower committed to collective ends increases. An increase of re- sources within a unit normally facilitates its mobilization, simply by permitting subunits to keep receiving resources while the larger unit gains control over more than it had before. But it is that increase in collective control itself which constitutes mobilization. Without some mobilization, a group may prosper, but it cannot contend for power; contending for power means employing mobilized resources to influence other groups.

Ideally, then, we are looking at a set of groups, and trying to estimate for each group and for each resource under the control of any of the groups two different entities (a) the value of the resource nominally under group control and (b) the probability that the resource will be delivered when called for, given some standard assumption about the uses to which the resources will be put. To my knowledge, no one has ever come close to estimating these quanti- ties for any set of groups. We have only rough approximations.

Measuring Mobilization

How to do it? If the mobilization of diverse resources fell into a standard sequence within any particular population, one could produce a scale of mobilization without having direct measures of each of the component resources. We might take as a methodological model the scales for "central- ity" of villages which Frank Young has constructed (see Young 1966). Such a scale would resemble the following set:

1   No one within this category ever identifies it as a group, so far as can be determined from some standard set of sources.

2 Members of this category sometimes identify themselves as a group.

3 The group has a standard name known to members and nonmembers alike.

4 Members of the group sometimes appear in public as a group, identified by name.

5 The group has standard symbols, slogans, songs, styles of dress, and/or other identifying marks.

6 The group contains one or more organizations which some members of the group recognize as having the authority to speak for the group as a whole on some matters.

7 The group contains one or more organizations controlling well-defined buildings and spaces which are at least nominally open to members of the group as a whole.

8 The group has at least one common store of major resources—money, labor, weapons, information, or something else—held in the name of the group as a whole.

9 At least one organization run by group members exercises extensive control over group members' allocation of time and energy in the name of the group as a whole.

10 At least one organization run by group members exercises extensive control over the personal relations of members of the group.

The first four items on the list clearly belong under the heading "organization" rather than "mobilization." The fifth balances uncertainly between the two. Thus the lower end of the scale rests on the assumption of a close association between organization and mobilization. Obviously such a scale could not be used to establish the existence of that relationship.

In my own research group's work on collective action in Europe and America, we have approached the measurement of mobilization in two simple ways. Both fall short of the comprehensive accounts and internally consistent scales we would like to have; the real world is hard.

The first and more obvious way is to take one or two widely available indicators of mobilization, such as union membership, and prepare comparable series of those indicators for the set of groups under study. In this case, we make no *a priori* effort to combine available indicators. On the contrary, we hope to learn something about their relationships from the analysis. In our studies of French strike activity from 1830 to 1968, Edward Shorter and I recurrently use number of union members and/or years of continuous existence of a local general labor organization (a *bourse de travail*) as indicators of a local labor force's mobilization level (Shorter and Tilly 1974). David

Snyder (1974) uses union membership in his time-series analyses of strikes in Italy, France, and the U.S. from various points in the nineteenth century to 1970. Joan Lind, studying strikes and labor-related street demonstrations in Sweden and Great Britain from 1900 to 1950, measures mobilization via union membership and union income. With interesting exceptions to be discussed later on, alternative indicators of mobilization turn out to be strongly correlated with each other, and to have a significant positive effect on the level of strike activity.

The second and riskier way we have indexed mobilization is to build different versions of the sort of ordinal scale I have just sketched from descriptions—statistical or otherwise—of the groups in question. Ronald Aminzade's study of Marseillaise workers illustrates this tack. Aminzade was trying to assess the influence of organizational characteristics, prior experience with collective action, and mobilization level on the involvement of different groups of workers in Marseille from 1830 to 1871. Drawing on evidence from French archives and from published works, he found that he could assemble more or less continuous descriptions for each of twenty-one occupational categories concerning (a) the presence or absence and (b) the general pattern of activity of guilds (more exactly, *compagnonnages*), cooperatives, trade unions, mutual benefit societies, and resistance societies. For 1848, he was also able to ascertain whether the occupational group had its own representation to the Republican Central Committee, its own political club, and any collective privileges formally recognized by government regulations. (Information on membership and on funds controlled was also available, but not regularly enough for the construction of continuous series.)

Aminzade then combined this information into three indicators:

1   Total number of occupational organizations.
2   Total years of prior existence of different organizational forms.
3   Total number of collective actions previously carried out by these organizations.

The third indicator is the most debatable as an index of mobilization. Aminzade essentially ranked each occupational group as high or low on each of the three items (2 = high; 1 = low) and summed them into a six-point scale (6 = three highs; 1 = three lows). Using the scores for the periods just preceding the events in question, he analyzed occupational differentials in arrests during Marseille's insurrection of June 1848 and in the course of Louis Napoleon's 1851 *coup d'état*; for the insurrections of August 1870 and March 1871 in Marseille, he reconstructed a list of 429 participants from police dossiers on persons involved in the revolutionary International, from conviction records for the 1870 insurrection, and from arrest records for the 1871 insurrection. Individual indicators of mobilization correlate with involvement in one or another of these events from 0 to +0.8. The correlations of participation with the combined mobilization index are

1848:	+0.333
1851:	+0.571
1870–71:	+0.473

There is a substantial relationship between mobilization level—as crudely measured by Aminzade—and involvement in Marseille's major revolutionary movements from 1848 to 1871.

General Conditions for Mobilization

According to our mobilization model, the broad factors within a population affecting its degree of mobilization are the extent of its shared interest in interactions with other populations, and the extent to which it forms a distinct category and a dense network: its interest and its organization. Outside the group, its power, its subjection to repression, and the current constellation of opportunities and threats most strongly affect its mobilization level. Power, repression, and opportunity/threat will come in for detailed discussion in the next chapter. Interest and organization have already had their share of attention. Yet it would be good to review their impact on mobilization before rushing on to examine collective action itself.

Anthony Oberschall has provided a neat synthesis of a good deal of recent thinking about these relationships. Oberschall deliberately counters Durkheimian thinking—especially its "mass society" variety—by insisting on the importance of some forms of prior group coherence to the mobilization of conflict groups. Among other things, he points out that newly mobilizing conflict groups usually reduce their organizing costs by building, intentionally or unintentionally, on existing group structure. Instead of starting from a shared interest but no organization, existing groups coalesce and reorganize. Thus the conflict group escapes, to some extent, from the great cost of starting at zero mobilization.

Considering that prior organization, Oberschall calls particular attention to two dimensions: to the character of links within the population (communal organization, associational organization, or little organization of any kind) and to the ties between the population and other groups (integrated with other groups vs. segregated from them). In combination, the two dimensions produce a sixfold classification of populations.

Internal Links

		Communal	Weak	Associational
Ties to Other Groups	Integrated			
	Segregated			

We will use a related classification later on, when we try to distinguish the major varieties of collective action.

Oberschall's analysis directly confronts mass-society theory. The mass-society argument says that populations in the central column, especially those which are segregated from the rest of society, are the great breeders of protest movements. One of the best-known statements of the theory runs:

> Groups which are particularly vulnerable to mass movements manifest major discontinuities in their structure during periods of change. Thus, communism and fascism have gained strength in social systems undergoing sudden and extensive changes in the structure of authority and community. Sharp tears in the social fabric caused by widespread unemployment or by major military defeat are highly favorable to mass politics. Social classes which provide disproportionate support for mass movements are those that possess the fewest social ties among their members. This means above all the lower social classes. However, since there are sections of all social classes which tend to be socially atomized, members of all social classes are to be found among the participants in mass politics: unattached (especially free-lance) intellectuals, marginal (especially small) businessmen and farmers, and isolated workers have engaged in mass politics in times of crisis (Kornhauser 1959: 229).

We have already encountered the same line of argument in our review of Durkheimian analyses of collective action.

Oberschall counters with the argument that populations with weak internal structure rarely act at all. He also argues that each combination of internal structure and external ties produces a different variety of mobilization and collective action. In general, he sees ties to other groups (especially elite groups) as constraints on the formation of conflict groups; in that one regard, he tends to agree with the mass-society theorists. But in his analysis, segmented populations with either extensive communal or extensive associational structure are especially likely to produce—or become—conflict groups. To put it in mass-society terms, they are *more*, not less, "available" for social movements.

Overschall then proposes a useful series of hypotheses about the mobilization of conflict groups:

1   In a segmented context, the greater the number and variety of organizations in a collectivity, and the higher the participation of members in this network, the more rapidly and enduringly does mobilization into conflict groups occur, and the more likely it is that bloc recruitment, rather than individual recruitment, will take place (Oberschall 1973: 125).

2   The more segmented a collectivity is from the rest of the society, and the more viable and extensive the communal ties within it, the more rapid and easier it is to mobilize members of the collectivity into an opposition movement (p. 129).

3   If a collectivity is disorganized or unorganized along traditional communal lines and not yet organized along associational lines, collective protest is possible when members share common sentiments of oppression and targets for hostility. These sentiments are more likely to develop if the collectivity is segmented rather than vertically integrated with other collectivities of the society. Such protest will, however, tend to be more short-lived and more violent than movements based on communal or associational organization (p. 133).

4   Participants in popular disturbances and activitist in opposition organizations will be recruited primarily from previously active and relatively well-integrated individuals within the collectivity, whereas socially isolated, atomized, and uprooted individuals will be underrepresented, at least until the movement has become substantial (p. 135).

Although the third hypothesis provides an escape clause, the main argument strongly emphasizes the influence of prior organization. So does the varied evidence which Oberschall reviews. Perhaps too strongly, or rather too exclusively: the argument I have been building up here gives greater weight to interests, mobilization strategy, repression, and power position. Nevertheless, the two lines of argument agree in denying that unattached individuals and homogenized masses have any special propensity to form or join social movements.

Oberschall's hypotheses focus on just that issue: joining or not joining. For that reason, the communal end of his classification remains more mysterious than the associational end. It is valuable to point out, as Oberschall does, that events such as great peasant revolts do not ordinarily sweep up society's rootless, disorganized, leftover people, but draw in coherent but aggrieved groups of people who remain attached to each other and to their social settings. But to speak of "recruitment" compromises the insight.

The implicit model has modern contours. It applies easily to such membership organizations as labor unions, political parties, and religious

organizations. It does not apply so easily to the eighteenth-century countrymen who tore down poorhouses and then went back to work in their shops
and fields. It distorts the experience of nineteenth-century artisans who built
barricades in the streets near their shops during the revolutions of 1848. The
eighteenth-century people of Nacton and the nineteenth-century people of
Paris mobilized and acted collectively, all right. But they did not form or join a
"social movement" or even a "conflict group" in the sense required by
Oberschall's model.

To cover the whole range from antipoorhouse crowds to revolutionary
artisans to political parties to religious cults, we need a very broad view of
mobilization. It must accomodate a great variety of resources, and not be tied
to any particular organizational form or type of interest. In that spirit, the
three major principles we have laid down so far are broad indeed,
schematically:

1   $$\frac{\text{Quantity of resources}}{\text{collectively controlled}} \times \frac{\text{probability}}{\text{of delivery}} = \text{mobilization}$$

2   Mobilization = f (organization)

3   Organization = catness × netness

The first and third are, obviously, definitions. The second is a proposition, but
one which needs a good deal more specification before it has much value. The
specification will drive us back toward the same problems Oberschall emphasizes: the differences between segmented and integrated populations, the contrasting mobilization patterns of communal and associational groups, the
conditions for organizational effectiveness. In short, we are on the right path,
but not very far along. Let us try to stride on by dealing with collective action
itself.

FROM MOBILIZATION TO COLLECTIVE ACTION

Collective action is joint action in pursuit of common ends. Up to this point, I
have argued that the extent of a group's collective action is a function of (1) the
extent of its shared *interests* (advantages and disadvantages likely to result
from interactions with other groups), (2) the intensity of its *organization* (the
extent of common identity and unifying structure among its members) and
(3) its *mobilization* (the amount of resources under its collective control). Soon
I will add repression, power, and opportunity/threat to those determinants of
a group's collective action. In this general statement, the argument is not very
controversial. It rejects Durkheimian theories which trace routine collective
action back to society's integration and which trace nonroutine collective action back to society's disintegration. Still a great many Weberian, Marxian

and Millian analyses will fit, with a bit of shoving, into the boxes defined by interests, organization, and mobilization.

At this level of argument, the main differences among the Weberian, Marxian, and Millian analyses are in the weights they assign to the various determinants of collective action. On the whole, Weberian arguments—especially as they appear in analyses of social movements and their routinization—assign different weights to interests in routine and nonroutine collective action. In a full-fledged social movement, runs the argument, interests have a less immediate effect because the group's beliefs override or redefine them. The Weberian approach tends to treat the costs and effects of organization as great, but then to consider the group's interests and organization a sufficient explanation of its actions. Implicitly, that is, it treats the costs of mobilization and collective action as slight.

Marxian analyses likewise give high weights to interests and organization, low weights to the costs of mobilization and collective action as such. The difference from the Weberian line, in this regard, is in the strong Marxian emphasis on material interests—more precisely, on interests defined by relationship to the predominant means of production—and in the argument that the organization of production underlies and dominates other forms or organization.

Millians are the only ones of our four clusters who commonly assign major importance to the costs of collective action itself. The standard Millian analysis jumps from defined interests to collective action with scant attention to organization and mobilization. Starting from the challenge laid down by Mancur Olson, Millians have sharpened the analysis of collective action by connecting it to the production of collective goods. The ideal collective good is inclusive and indivisible. If any member of the group receives it, all receive it. There is no way of breaking it up into shares. The draining of a swamp to prevent malaria is a fairly pure example. Real goods vary considerably in how much they approximate that ideal. Police protection, for example, is ideally a pure collective good; ideally, it is inclusive and indivisible. In practice, some people get little or no police protection, and others buy up extra shares for themselves. We therefore have to say that action is collective *to the extent that* it produces inclusive, indivisible goods.

The definition I have proposed is more relaxed in some regards and more restrictive in others. Joint action in pursuit of common ends often fails to produce any goods at all, but so long as it *tends* to produce collective goods I propose to include it. On the other hand, some collective goods (and many collective bads) are produced unintentionally, as by-products of individual efforts. I propose to exclude them from the definition of collective action. That choice has its disadvantages; it requires us to think about what an unsuccessful action might have produced and to be sure that people really did act jointly, instead of simply searching around for the appearance of collective goods. Yet it has the advantage of focusing the analysis more clearly on the explanation of the action itself, instead of aiming at its outcomes.

Let us borrow the basic Millian insight: collective actors are attempting to produce collective goods that have a specific value in relation to their interests, and are expending valuable resources in the effort. If we can imagine assigning relative values to the collective goods produced and the resources expended, we can think of a contender as gaining, losing, or breaking even. Diagrammatically, we have Fig. 3–4. In the shaded area above the diagonal, the value of the collective goods obtained is greater than the value of the resources expended; that is a gain. Below the diagonal we have losses, and the diagonal itself is a break-even line.

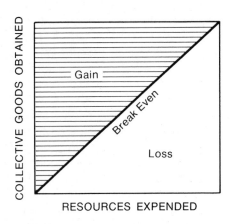

Fig. 3–4
Gains and losses in collective action

In any real collective action, there are real limits on how much of the space in the diagram is available to the actor. We have talked about the two main limits as mobilization and opportunity. To modify the diagram, we create Fig. 3–5.

The group cannot expend more resources than it has currently mobilized; that sets an unbreakable limit in one direction. The opportunities for gain are finite; that sets a limit in the other direction. Later on we will look carefully at limits on opportunity. For the moment it is enough to see that both mobilization and opportunity limit the possible gains from collective action. It follows, clearly, that a change in mobilization or opportunity will produce a change in the set of gains and loses available to a group. Zero mobilization equals zero

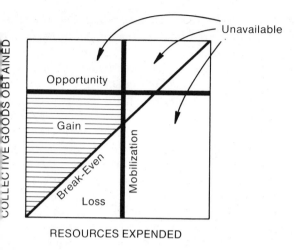

Fig. 3–5
How opportunities and mobilization limit gains and losses

gains or losses. A group can increase the range of gains and losses available by mobilizing or by manipulating opportunities—that is, by increasing its power or reducing its subjection to repression.

If things were this simple, we would expect every group to mobilize to its utmost capacity to manipulate opportunities as much as possible and to maneuver itself into the highest available position above the diagonal. To some extent, that is a reasonable simplification of what goes on in power struggles. But it ignores important realities: mobilization itself is costly. The group's organization itself sets important limits on the collective actions, mobilization strategies, and manipulations of opportunity it can or will undertake. And its interests define which sorts of gains and losses are acceptable or unacceptable.

To put it another way, groups differ considerably in the relative values they assign to collective goods and to the resources which must be expended to acquire them. Many, perhaps most, groups behave like peasants who are seeking to draw a target income from their land; instead of locating themselves at the point of maximum profit, they aim for a certain return. If they can, they expend the minimum resources required for that reason. Thus a group of workers first decide they want an eight-hour day, then calculate what effort they will have to expend in order to win that particular objective.

Some groups value a given collective good so highly that they are willing to incur what other groups regard as net losses in order to achieve their cherished objectives. From the viewpoint of the average group, they are satisfied with a position below the break-even line. We can make a distinction among four group strategies: (1) the *zealots* who, compared to other groups, set an extremely high value on some collective good in terms of the resources required to achieve that good—willing to expend life and limb, for instance, in order to acquire self-government; (2) the *misers,* who value the resources they already hold so highly that hardly any available collective good can draw them into expending their mobilized resources on collective action—we should expect misers to act together defensively when they act at all; (3) the *run-of-the-mill contenders* who aim for a limited set of collective goods, making the minimum expenditure of resources necessary for the acquisition of these goods, and remaining inactive when the current combination of mobilization and opportunity makes a net loss on the exchange likely; (4) the *opportunists* who strive to maximize their net return—the difference in value between resources expended and collective goods obtained—regardless of which collective goods they acquire.

Figure 3-6 presents the four ideal types schematically. In this simplified picture, opportunity and mobilization are the same for all types. The diagrams value the resources expended and the collective goods acquired at averages over all groups instead of showing the relative values usually assigned to mobilized resources and collective goods by each type of group. According to the diagram, zealots find acceptable only a narrow range of collective goods; the goods are not necessarily those that other groups value most highly. They are willing to spend up to the limit of their mobilized resources to acquire those collective goods, even if by the standards of other contenders they are taking losses. Misers will only spend a share of their mobilized resources for a very valuable return in collective goods. They will never spend up to the limit set by their mobilization. Run-of-the-mill contenders resemble zealots, except that they are willing to settle for a wider range of collective goods, and unwilling to settle for a loss. Finally, opportunists will take any collective goods they can get. They will spend up to their limit to get it, just so long as they make a profit.

The diagram invites further theorizing. For example, it is reasonable to suppose that zealots tend to maintain higher levels of mobilization than other kinds of actors. They therefore have more chances to acquire their desired collective goods, but they also run a greater risk of heavy losses. Opportunists, on the other hand, probably work more effectively at moving up the opportunity line by such tactics as forming coalitions with other powerful contenders. Some of these strategic questions will become important in our later discussions of power.

Every political system sorts its contenders among zealots, misers, opportunists, and run-of-the-mill contenders. No doubt every political system

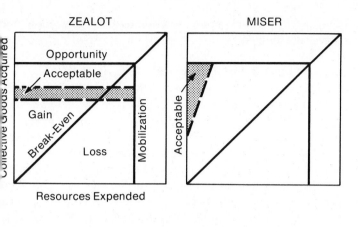

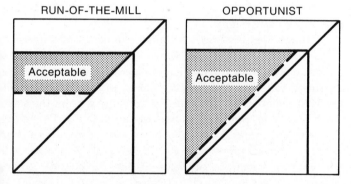

ig. 3–6
our ideal patterns of collective action

ewards the opportunists more than the run-of-the-mill, and the run-of-the-
nill contenders more than the zealots or the misers. That is even true, I fear,
ifter zealots seize power. They, too, reward opportunists and punish zealots.

Oddly enough, the opportunist is the least likely to appear of the four
:xtremes. Regardless of group strategy, the return the group seeks is rarely or
never a simple profit on collective action. Groups care about the character of
he collective goods. Labor unions usually don't want papal dispensations,
:lans usually don't want recognition as bargaining agents. In fact, both the
supply and the demand are "lumpy", clumped, discontinuous. For that reason,
ve cannot simply graft the analysis of collective action on the existing micro-
:conomics of private goods. The existing economics of collective goods comes

closer. But it, too, has yet to solve the problems of interest, organization, and mobilization we have encountered.

THE DETECTION AND MEASUREMENT OF COLLECTIVE ACTION

When trying to study joint action in pursuit of common ends, we face the practical problems of detecting the action, and then determining how joint it is and how common its ends. If we confine our attention to clear-cut examples, such as strikes, elections, petitions, and attacks on poorhouses, we still face the practical problems of gauging their magnitudes—especially if we want to say "how much" collective action one group or another engaged in over some period of time. As with the measurement of mobilization, we commonly have the choice between (a) indicators of collective action which come to us in a more or less quantitative form, but are too narrow or too remote to represent adequately the range of action we have in mind, or (b) indicators derived from qualitative descriptions, which are usually discontinuous, which often vary in coverage from one group or period to another, and which are always hard to convert reliably into meaningful numbers.

David Snyder's time-series analyses of Italian, French, and American strikes provide a case in point. Snyder uses number and proportion of labor union members in the civilian labor force as a mobilization measure. Data for long periods are difficult to locate and hard to make comparable, but when they are available at all they are usually in quantitative form from the start. On the side of collective action, Snyder uses two sets of variables. First come the strike-activity measures: number of strikes, number of participants in strikes, mean duration of strikes, days lost, proportion ending in success or failure, proportion making offensive or defensive demands, and so on. Ultimately, all of these come from official sources, where they appear as summary statistics or as uniform descriptions of all the strikes reported for some period, area, and definition of the relevant labor force. As in the case of union membership, it takes some ingenuity and effort to wrest comparable measures from the sources, but the quantification itself is not very difficult.

That is certainly not true of Snyder's second set of measures. They concern other forms of collective action by workers. Snyder's list (from Snyder 1974: 114) runs:

Economic and directly job-related actions
* employment information and placement
* local control of working conditions, including grievance procedures, local adjustments of national contracts, etc.
* negotiation of extralocal contracts (usually national)
* disbursement of strike funds

Economic, but not job-related actions

    aid to members for accident, sickness, unemployment, burial

•   provision of social/recreational/education facilities

•   financing cooperative efforts (both production and consumption)

Political actions

•   lobbying activities

•   distribution of printed material

    support of candidates for election

•   coalition with political party

Snyder read through a large number of economic, labor, social, and political histories for each of his three countries, abstracting any mention of any of these activities, regrouping the abstracts into organization-year summaries, then coding each of the eleven items in a standard way. For example, the code for support of candidates appears in Fig. 3–7. Snyder summed the scores for each organization into four general scores—one each for his Job-Related, Economic-Not-Job-Related, and Political categories, and a summary Collective Action score. Finally, he weighted each organization for the proportion of

Fig. 3–7
Snyder's Code for labor support of candidates

The coder is evaluating a single-year summary of abstracts from historical sources concerning a particular organization's support of candidates for elective office.

Code	Evaluation	Criteria
0	none at all	no support of candidates
1	small amount	endorsement of candidates in printed material of the organization
2	moderate	speechmaking, etc., by labor leaders/members in support of candidates *and* endorsement in printed material
3	good deal	active campaigning by members for candidates (passing out leaflets, going door to door, etc.) *and* items listed above
4	great deal	financial support of candidates *and* items listed above

Source Snyder 1974: 302

the labor force it contained, and summed each weighted score over all organizations for a country-year total. Snyder's analyses of the unionization collective action and strike variables for France and Italy indicate that the best summary of their relationships runs, schematically:

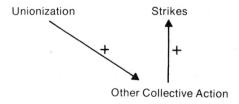

Edward Shorter and I had implicitly adopted a different model:

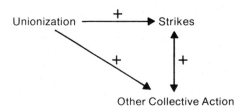

But we neither formulated that model clearly nor (except for some analyses of the relationships between strike activity and collective *violence*) made much of an effort to estimate it. Thus Snyder's work in description and measurement leads us to reconsider the processes we are analyzing.

Aside from strikes, our research group's most extensive forays into the measurement of collective action have dealt with violent events. (For general descriptions and preliminary results, see Tilly, Tilly, and Tilly 1975.) For reasons which will become clearer in the course of my later discussions of violence as such, collective violence serves as a useful "tracer" of collective action in general. Although collective actions which produce damage to persons or objects are by no means a random sample of all collective actions, the presence of violence greatly increases the likelihood that the event will be noticed and recorded. With prudent analysis, the pattern of collective violence will yield valuable information about the pattern of collective action as a whole. My collaborators and I have done detailed enumerations and descriptions of collective violence in Italy, German, France, and England over substantial blocks of time with exactly that purpose in mind.

Let us concentrate on collective violence within a population under the control of a single government. Let us agree to pay attention to war, to full-fledged games, to individual violence, and to highly discontinuous interacions. We are then still free to examine events in which the damage was only ncidental to the aims of most of those involved. In our own investigations, my research group has discovered that we can, without huge uncertainty, single out events occurring within a particular national state in which at least one group above some minimum size (commonly twenty or fifty persons) seizes or damages someone or something from another group. We use newspapers, archival sources, and historical works for the purpose. As the minimum size goes down, collective violence begins to fade into banditry, brawling, vandalism, terrorism, and a wide variety of threatening nonviolent events, so far as our ability to distinguish them on the basis of the historical record is concerned.

We use the community-population-day as an elementary unit. On a particular day, did this segment of the population of this community engage in collective violence, as just defined? If so, we have the elementary unit of a violent event. Did an overlapping set of people carry on the action in an adjacent community? If so, both communities were involved in the same event. Did an overlapping set of people continue the action the following day? If so, the incident lasted at least two days. Introduce a break in time, space, or personnel, and we are dealing with two or more distinct events. The result of this modular reasoning is both to greatly simplify the problem of bounding the "same" incident and to fragment into many separate incidents series of interactions (such as the Spanish Civil War as a whole) which many analysts have been willing to treat as a single unit. More details on definitions and procedures are in the Appendix.

For some purposes, like the comparative study of revolutions, a broader criterion may serve better. Still other investigations will require more stringent standards—more participants, a certain duration, someone killed, a particular minimum of property damage. But the general reasoning of such choices would be the same: identify *all* the events above a certain magnitude, or at least a representative sample of them, before trying to sort them out in terms of legitimacy or in terms of the aims of the participants.

Let us consider some alternative ways of handling the enumeration of events. Reacting to what he regards as the weakness of our concentration on violent events, Heinrich Volkmann has delineated a class of events called "social protests". In general, he thinks of a social protest as "any collective disturbance of public order on behalf of common objectives" (Volkmann 1975: 3). Events qualify when at least twenty persons take part. Looking at Germany (as defined by the frontiers of 1937) during the revolutionary years from 1830 through 1832, he finds 165 events meeting the criteria in the pages of the *Augsburger Allgemeine Zeitung.* Just as in the case of France we use certain key words (multitude, rassemblement, réunion, foule, attroupement, etc.) to establish the presence of at least fifty people when our reports contain no numerical estimate, Volkmann establishes rough numerical equivalents for certain terms. He does so by taking the twenty-two accounts which contain both a numerical estimate and a verbal description of magnitude. The classification runs:

> *20–100 persons:* eine Anzahl, ein Trupp, Schwarm, Haufemeist mit spezifizierenden Zusätzen wie "ein Haufe Arbeiter", "ein Haufe Volks".

> *100–1000 persons:* Rotte, Zusammenrottierung, Haufen, grössere Haufen, zahlreiche oder grössere Menge, einige Hundert.

> *1000–2000 persons:* Menge, grosse Menge, grosser Volksauflauf, Massen, unzählige Menschenmasse (Volkmann 1975: 89).

He is thus able to estimate sizes for another sixty events, leaving almost exactly half without either a numerical statement or a codable verbal description. Presumably Volkmann judged whether at least twenty persons took part from the nature of the action itself.

In a study of "mass disturbances" in Japan from 1952 to mid-1960, done independently of our research group, Yoshio Sugimoto adopted some of our definitions and procedures. He used a number of Japanese newspapers to identify all events, involving at least fifty people, in which the police intervened and there was some detectable violence. He identified 945 such events in his 8.5-year period. Sugimoto's measurement of magnitudes followed the same pattern: number of events, size, duration. But, following Sorokin and Gurr, he added a fourth dimension: intensity. The intensity measurement is unusual. Instead of simply scoring the injuries, property damage, and arrests that occurred in any particular event, Sugimoto attempted to estimate their probability as a function of the various kinds of action that made up the event. Having broken down every event into phases consisting of only one kind of action, he then sorted all action phases from all events in his sample by type of action. Items 31 to 40 on the 70-item list (with numbers of action phases shown in parenthesis) were, for example:

31. protection of individuals from attack (109)
32. picket against cars (105)
33. attempt to break picket line (312)
34. skirmish (1133)
35. attempt to throw someone into the sea (3)
36. forceful removal of objects (10)
37. attempt to trample down fields (1)
38. attempt to dig a well (1)
39. attempt to dam water in a river (5)
40. attempt to hammer pikes into ground (1)

'or each of the seventy types of action distinguished, he summed injuries, property damage, and arrests. The "probability" of injury assigned to each action is the proportion of all actions in the class which produced injuries. Sugimoto then combined the three individual scores for each action phase by means of the weights derived from a factor analysis of the three, computed the magnitude of the action phase by multiplying

intensity × size × duration,

and then computed the magnitude of the event as a whole by summing the magnitudes of all its action phases. The result was probably the most refined measure of magnitude ever computed for a large sample of violent events.

What is more, Sugimoto made good use of his refined measures. He shows that the magnitude of agrarian disturbances was greater in regions where landholding was relatively equal before the land reforms, and where the pace of the reform was more rapid, that the proliferation of labor unions strongly promoted disturbances involving workers, and many other findings of equal interest.

Let us take a last example which is entirely independent of my group's work. Drawing on the *Annual Register* from 1815 to 1848, Charles Taylor (1966) prepared an index of "political articulation" by English workingmen. It singled out efforts to influence the national government, including "meetings to demand a reform of the franchise, riots to protest the introduction of new poor law and demonstrations to support some particular group cause" (Taylor 1966: 15). The context makes it appear that Taylor also scored petitions, group violence, the formation of associations, and the founding of publications, just so long as they bore explicitly on the political system. He weighed each instance from 1 to 5 depending on its duration and the number of participants. He then used the index to demonstrate strong relationships between a county's level of political articulation over the entire period and the county's urban population, density, growth rate, and nonagricultural labor force.

In my own group's effort to index British collective action during the same span of time, we have avoided relying on a political criterion at the start, in hopes of capturing a wide range of action; then we have some chance to determine whether collective action oriented to national politics and collective action in general rise and fall together, or whether the rise of national politics represents a net shift within the body of collective action. (For details, see the Appendix.) That important exception aside, the two approaches to the measurement of collective action have much in common.

In line with the hope of assembling evidence on the pattern of collective action as a whole, we have coded many features of the violent events: characteristics of the setting, types of participants, forms of action, outcomes.

In thinking of the magnitude of collective action involved, we have followed the model of strike analysis. We have attempted to estimate the total person-days absorbed by the action, and to disaggregate that estimate into its components: number of participants, duration. For the total amount of collective action produced by a given population in a certain period of time, we then have a three-dimensional figure which can assume quite different proportions (see Fig. 3–8).

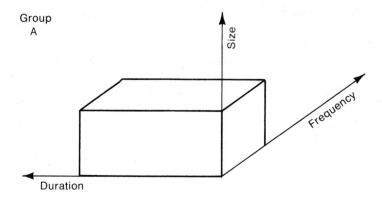

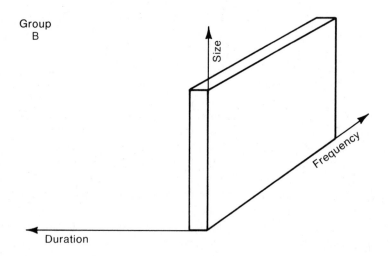

Fig. 3–8
Components of the magnitude of collective action

Group A produces a few long events of medium size, while Group B produces many large, short events; the volume of collective action as measured by person-days, however, is about the same in the two hypothetical cases. This simple sort of representation brings out the fact that in France from the nineteenth to the twentieth century both strikes and collective violence shifted from a pattern of small size and long duration to large size and short duration; the number of strikes and person-days in strikes expanded greatly, while the number of violent events and person-days in violence did not rise significantly faster than the French population.

Some of the reasons for these changes are obvious, and some require reflection and research. The twentieth-century rise of the big demonstration and the one-day protest strike as modes of collective action and as contexts for collective violence played a large part in the net shift toward large, short, violent events. To ask why they rose, however, is to ask about the expanding importance of special-purpose associations, the changing relations between organized labor and the national government, the movement of protests toward large cities and big plants. In short, the alterations in the forms of collective action result from changes in its determinants.

Interest, organization, and mobilization, however, are not the only determinants of the intensity and character of collective action. Opportunity matters, too. We must look at the three major components of opportunity—power, repression/facilitation, and opportunity/threat—before we have a rounded picture of collective action.

4
The Opportunity to Act Together

FROM MOBILIZATION TO OPPORTUNITY

We began the last chapter with two models. The "mobilization model" describes the behavior of a single contender in terms of interest, organization, power, and other variables. That model we have kept much in view. We have, however, looked mainly at one side of it: the side dealing with the contender's internal structure. Schematically, we have concentrated on the following relationships:

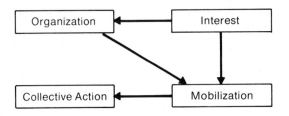

By itself, this portion of the model is inadequate. It deals only with the *capacity* to act, not with the immediate incentive or opportunity to act. Those incentives and opportunities find their places in the other half of the mobilization model, and in the polity model.

The "polity model" relates contenders to a government and to other contenders—both challengers and members of the polity—via coalitions and struggles for power. So long as we were examining the internal structure of a contender, we could take its external relations for granted. As we move into the world of opportunity, we must pay sustained attention to other actors. Their strengths and weaknesses comprise the contender's opportunities to act on its interests.

In Durkheimian thinking, the main word for this set of relations between the collective actor and its environment is *social control*. Social control consists of the efforts of authorities, or of society as a whole, to bring deviants back into line. This idea of social control assigns a passive, uncreative role to collective actors. It fits the reality of collective action too poorly to help us here.

Real contenders are more active than Durkheim's portrait implies. They pursue their interests. They struggle for power. On the way, they maneuver, form and break coalitions, try alternative strategies, win and lose. Our primitive models simplify all this contention by describing it as a series of responses to changing estimates of the costs and benefits likely to result from various possible interactions with governments and with other contenders. The central assumptions run:

1   Collective action *costs* something.

2   All contenders count costs.

3   Collective action brings benefits, in the form of collective goods.

4   Contenders continuously weigh expected costs against expected benefits.

5   Both costs and benefits are uncertain because (a) contenders have imperfect information about the current state of the polity; (b) all parties engage in strategic interaction.

We sum up the relevant costs and benefits under the headings repression/facilitation, power, and opportunity/threat. On the opportunity side, the main relationships in the model run:

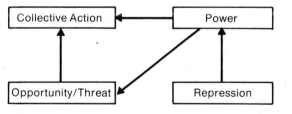

Remember that these relationships refer to the moment of collective action. Over the long run, the extent and form of a contender's collective action affect its power, the repression to which it is subjected, and the further opportunities and threats it faces. This version of the model ignores time. Let us consider each component of the timeless model in turn.

Repression and Facilitation

Contention for power always involves at least two parties. The behavior of the second party runs along a range from repression to facilitation. Let us recall the definitions: *repression* is any action by another group which raises the contender's cost of collective action. An action which lowers the group's cost of collective action is a form of *facilitation*. (We call repression or facilitation *political* if the other party is a government.) A group bent on repressing or facilitating another group's action has the choice of working on the target group's mobilization or directly on its collective action. For example, a government can raise a group's mobilization costs (and thereby raise its costs of collective action) by disrupting its organization, by making communications difficult or inaccessible, by freezing necessary resources such as guns and manpower. Standard repressive measures such as suspending newspapers, drafting strikers, forbidding assemblies, and arresting leaders illustrate the antimobilization avenue. Or a government can operate directly on the costs of collective action by raising the penalties, making the targets of the action inaccessible, or inducing a waste of the mobilized resources; the *agent provocateur*, the barricades around the city hall, the establishment of military tribunals for insurgents fall familiarly into the strategy of moving directly against collective action. Facilitation likewise has two faces, both familiar: promobilization activities such as giving a group publicity, legalizing membership in it, and simply paying it off; activities directly reducing the group's costs of collective action, such as lending information or strategic expertise, keeping the group's enemies out of the action, or simply sending forces to help the action along.

Despite the two faces of repression/facilitation, the elementary mobilization model shows no direct connection between repression/facilitation and collective action. Instead, it portrays repression/facilitation as acting on power, which in turn influences collective action. That is because the elementary model refers to the moment of action alone. At that moment, the prior effects of repression translate into power: into the extent to which the outcomes of the contender's various possible interactions with other contenders favor its interests over those of the others.

Governmental repression is the best-known case. For example, the United States government's outlawing of the Communist Party during the Cold War essentially guaranteed that the party would lose leaders to jail when it acted together in any visible way. That is a high cost to pay for collective action. The law also raised the party's cost of mobilization by penalizing individuals who dared to contribute time, money, or moral support to its work. From a government's point of view, raising the costs of mobilization is a more reliable repressive strategy than raising the costs of collective action alone. The antimobilization strategy neutralizes the actor as well as the action, and makes it less likely that the actor will be able to act rapidly when the government suddenly becomes vulnerable, a new coalition partner arises, or something else quickly shifts the probable costs and benefits of collective action. Raising the costs of collective action alters the pattern of effective demand from mobilized groups, while raising the costs of mobilization reduces demand across the board.

Governmental repression is uniquely important because governments specialize in the control of mobilization and collective action: police for crowd control, troops to back them, spies and informers for infiltration, licensing to keep potential actors visible and tame. Yet groups outside government also repress each other, in the sense of manipulating each other's cost of collective action. That is obvious in the case of quasi-governments such as large firms: simply consider how much the structure and policy of the firm affect the chances for unionization and therefore for strike activity. It is less obvious in the case of routine competition among other groups: the volunteer fire companies which burned each other's premises and held deadly shootouts in the streets of nineteenth-century Philadelphia ended up resetting the relative ability of each fire company to wield political influence (Laurie 1972). The fights between groups of young blacks and Irish for control of local turfs in Boston significantly affect the group's future costs of assembling and acting together. In principle, then, repression sums the effects of the actions of all other groups, including governments, on a particular group's cost of collective action.

If different forms of repression and facilitation sometimes concentrate on mobilization and sometimes on collective action itself, they also select in two other important regards: the target groups and the varieties of collective action encouraged or deterred. Selectivity by group is the more obvious. In recent years, agencies of the U.S. government have worked to impede the collective action of groups as diverse as the Symbionese Liberation Army, the Vietnam Veterans Against the War, and the Democratic Party. Agencies of the government have also worked to facilitate the collective action of the Blackstone Rangers, the American Medical Association and the A.F.L.–C.I.O. Politics as usual involves a great deal of coalition making among and against different contenders for power. Divisions of the government play important parts on both sides.

Selectivity by type of collective action shows up in the very rules of the game, and in their changes; at a given time, it may be legal to petition, associate, vote as a bloc, acquire a patron in the legislature, and assemble as a formally constituted community, but not to demonstrate, strike, boycott, form militias, or invade the legislature. The repression and facilitation reside in the government's action to alter the relative costs of different forms of collective action. Legality matters because laws state the costs and benefits which governments are prepared (or at least empowered) to apply to one form of action or another.

Impressed by that fact, I once thought we should index fluctuations in a government's repressiveness by watching carefully its flow of legislation. A closer look at the way the magistrates of eighteenth- and nineteenth-century Britain did their work of repression and facilitation, however, diminished my confidence. Eighteenth-century legislation multiplied the number of capital offenses. Penalties for offenses against property led the way: plundering shipwrecks, food rioting, many forms of forcible entry and theft became punishable by hanging. Moreover, the bills which extended the death penalty were characteristically special-interest legislation; in fact, the capital offenses often appeared as incidental features of complex bills designed to advance the current interests of shipowners, merchants, landlords or other property holders (Hay 1975).

This much seems quite consistent with the eighteenth-century rise of "possessive individualism." But one fact is inconvenient: the application of the death penalty became less frequent during the eighteenth century (Beattie 1974). What are we to make of that? Perhaps the deterrent worked so well that fewer capital offenses were committed. Perhaps juries tempered the law's severity by refusing to convict. Perhaps, as Douglas Hay suggests, the combination of widespread threats and declining executions resulted from a system of general terror, selective repression, and extensive patronage. In any of these eventualities, the reading of repressiveness from legislation alone is faulty.

E. P. Thompson's analysis of the background of the Black Act of 1723 is a case in point. The Black Act set the death penalty for no fewer than fifty offenses, especially armed and disguised hunting, poaching, rick burning and other attacks on rural property. Thompson shows that it was essentially class legislation; it was engineered by Sir Robert Walpole and his friends to consolidate their exclusive enjoyment of their estates over the resistance of the small farmers nearby. At a superficial reading, one might easily take the Black Act as an illustration of the manner in which legislation makes the rise and fall of repression visible . . . and thus, perhaps, makes it quantifiable.

Thompson, however, points out the difficulty:

> On the one hand, it is true that the law did mediate existent class relations to the advantage of the rulers; not only is this so, but as the century advanced the law became a superb instrument by which these rulers were able to impose new definitions of property to their even greater advantage, as in the extinction by law of indefinite agrarian use-rights and in the furtherance of enclosure. On the other hand, the law mediated these class relations through legal forms, which imposed, again and again, inhibitions upon the actions of the rulers (Thompson 1975: 264).

We have to deal with not one element—legislation alone—but with three: the legislation as such; the interpretation and application of the legislation; the limits set on that legislation's effect by other, existing law.

The first and third elements are both matters of the law as written by judges, legislators, and lawyers. One might hope to get at them by studying current legislation and jurisprudence. But the interpretation and application of existing legislation are subtle, varied and scattered. In Britain, the Justices of the Peace had great discretion. They used it. On the one hand, they never exercised their legal powers to the fullest possible extent; there were groups on which the full rigor of the law did not descend, laws which remained unused, numerous instances in which one person was punished as an example while the other offenders were left to acquire contrition and fear by proxy. In the case of the provincial hunger riots of 1766:

> . . . the magistrates not only refrained from effective measures to crush the initial disorders, they actually abetted other members of the landed and industrial interests in their encouragement of the people to regulate markets and reduce the prices of provisions by force . . . By this means, they diverted the rioters towards middlemen and large farmers, and away from the landed and industrial interests. Unlike other agrarian disorders of the century, the riots of 1766 did not involve direct attacks on landowners or manufacturers. Thus while not actually inciting the riots, the actions of the magistrates certainly gave them direction. Only belatedly, when the scale of disorder frightened them, did the gentry-magistrates close ranks with the aristocracy and other rural leaders to crush what they had come to fear was the start of social revolution (Shelton 1973: 95–96).

When it suited them, on the other hand, the Justices of the Peace often used portmanteau laws concerning public order. They arrested people for vagrancy, trespassing, breach of the peace, unlawful assembly, or hindrance of an officer in the pursuit of his duty. Sometimes they reinterpreted an existing law, such as the law of treason, to cover the form of collective action at hand.

British magistrates of the eighteenth and nineteenth centuries probably had unusual freedom of action, as compared with their counterparts in other western countries. Nevertheless, the Prussian Junker who judged his own tenants as *Landrat* and the humbler French notable who held court over his neighbors as *juge de paix* also chose their weapons from a large legal arsenal.

The exercise of discretion within the system does not mean that the distinction between legal and illegal means of collective action is insignificant. It means we must derive the distinction from legal practice instead of relying naively on the statute books. Criminal statistics thus receive a new lease on life.

Criminal statistics are properly suspect as a comprehensive (or even representative) record of actual violations of the law. Yet they do unquestionably reflect the action of the judicial apparatus, and therefore provide evidence on changes in that action. George Rudé notes the marked decline in the British use of the death penalty against protest after 1800:

> Once arson, riot and attacks on property had virtually ceased to be capital offences, the worse he would have to face—and this was terrifying enough—was a term of transportation. It is not surprising, therefore, that the typical crimes for which protesters were transported in the 1840's—the Chartists and Rebecca's Daughters, for example—were for former capital offenses like demolishing turnpikes, pulling down houses, sedition, "cutting and maiming", "mobbing and rioting" and "attempted murder". And the last batch of transported protesters to be sent to Australia from England were 21 arsonists who arrived there in a half-a-dozen ships in 1852. After this, transportation ceased in Tasmania as it had ten years earlier in Sydney; and when it revived briefly in Western Australia between 1860 and 1868, there was not a single English, Welsh or Scottish protester among the 9,000 convicts that went out. Henceforth, such protesters as remained to be sentenced were confined to jails at home; and, as we noted earlier, indictments for such offenses were, by the 1860's, in fairly steady decline (Rudé 1973: 22–23).

As Rudé points out, this use of the criminal record shifts the analytic shoe to the other foot. Instead of assuming a constant pattern of repression and reading the reported convictions as a history of criminal activity, we want to "hold constant" the criminal activity and force the record to tell us about repression. Not easy, but at least we can analyze the punishment meted out for similar offenses in different times and places, watch the waxing and waning involvement of different types of repressive forces (for example, the increasing role of professional police in the nineteenth and twentieth centuries), studying the changing life histories of typical complaints.

In looking at much the same material as Rudé, E. P. Thompson notes the frequent eighteenth-century use of exemplary punishment—especially the public hanging—instead of widespread prosecution as a deterrent to the rambunctious eighteenth-century English popular classes, and its later decline in favor of a tendency to prosecute all offenders, to incarcerate them instead of subjecting them to banishment or brief agony, to remove punishment from the public view, to dream of reforming the individual. Thompson is therefore properly skeptical that anyone could estimate either the amount of protest or the degree of repression by following such statistics as arrests, imprisonments, and executions. Yet his very objection helps specify what has to be measured. Clearly we have to distinguish between the volume and type of repressive activity, on one hand, and its symbolic significance, on the other hand.

Since groups vary so much in their characteristic use of one sort of collective action or another, the selectivity of repression and facilitation with respect to types of collective action usually entails a selection by kind of actor as well.

No doubt abridging the right of assembly is less selective than outlawing the Communist Party. Even when the assembly laws are equitably enforced, however, they fall with special force on those groups which can only make contact by gathering in public spaces. In the nineteenth century, the workers who customarily got together in pubs or on the street found themselves more greatly hampered by riot acts than did the rich. The rich could escape to their salons and private clubs.

The nineteenth-century case is particularly interesting because of the great professionalization of policing which occurred in most western countries as the century moved on. Some of the apparently huge expansion of police forces in the nineteenth century resulted from the bureaucratization of volunteer and part-time policing. In France, the regular national forces rose from about 5,000 policemen and 16,000 gendarmes (for a combined rate of 57 police per 100,000 population) in 1848 to about 16,000 policemen and 21,000 gendarmes (for a combined rate of 97 per 100,000 population) in 1897. But a significant part of the increase in policemen consisted of the incorporation of irregular local forces into the national police (see Tilly, Levett, Lodhi, and Munger 1975). In the United States, no national police emerged, but parallel changes in policing occurred. There we see the shift from "entrepreneurial" to "bureaucratic" police forces (Levett 1974). In the entrepreneurial stage, three kinds of forces shared the responsibility: (1) citizen forces; they were called such things as posse and deputies when the government did not authorize them; (2) regular troops; (3) constables and similar officers, often short-term or part-time, often given little or no regular remuneration, often drawing most of their police income from fees: fines, a share of recovered property, rewards posted for the apprehension of major criminals, and so on. These forces had little incentive to carry on comprehensive patrols, to deal with routine public order offenses, or to protect the poor. The third group were "entrepreneurial" in that they made their livings by competing for the available fees. With a growing, increasingly segregated and increasingly foreign-born working class gathering in nineteenth-century cities, however, American political officials became increasingly interested in forming regular police forces which would patrol the entire city, deal with victimless offenses such as public drunkenness, and contain major threats of hostile collective action. Thus they organized bureaucratized, salaried, uniformed full-time forces.

The same general change took place in England. Robert Storch points out that as the middle and working classes drew apart, nineteenth-century middle class leaders increasingly felt the need for a force which would contain and civilize the workers:

> The disintegration of a common sphere of enjoyment was of course paralleled by a physical separation of the classes—classically described by Engels—unprece-

dented in western history. The Victorian bourgeoisie which set the moral tone of cities like Manchester and Leeds were not likely to patronize the cockpit as the Preston gentry of the late eighteenth century had done, nor to shower coins on a Guy Fawkes crowd as Wakefield Tories still felt at liberty to do at mid-century. Such gentlemen were much more inclined to either mind their own business and businesses or else to patronize temperance or rational recreation societies or mechanics' institutes. It was also they who supported the moral-reform mission assigned to the police and added to it in the language of numerous local improvement acts. The new demands for civil order in nineteenth-century England produced a novel type of surrogate to replace older and perhaps more personal lines of authority and deference which were now conceived to be moribund. The police, a "bureaucracy of official morality," were produced to try to fill this vacuum and to act as a lever of moral reform on the mysterious terrain of the industrial city's inner core (Storch 1976: 496).

What is more, the poor of English cities resisted the growth of regular police forces. They saw the police, quite rightly, as specialists in intruding on their life space, keeping them under surveillance, interfering in their organization and entertainment. They assaulted police who closed pubs during church services or tried to break up crowds of idlers on the street. The resistance was, to be sure, self-defeating: it only gave the fearful middle classes stronger incentives to expand and regularize the police forces. Thus an ostensibly general protective measure increased the repression directed at urban workers.

Repressive and Tolerant Governments

Let us set these ideas down more systematically. The repressiveness of a government is never a simple matter of more or less. It is always selective, and always consists of some combination of repression, toleration, and facilitation. Governments respond selectively to different sorts of groups, and to different sorts of actions. Sometimes the discriminations are fine indeed: the same government which smiles on church services bringing together a thousand people assembled to pray for salvation shoots without hesitation into a crowd of a thousand workers assembled to pray for justice.

Governments which repress also facilitate. While raising the costs of some kinds of collective action to some kinds of groups, they lower the costs of other kinds of collective action to other kinds of groups. They do so in two different ways: (a) by simply diminishing the difficulty of specific varieties of mobilization and/or collective action, and (b) by providing positive incentives for specific varieties of mobilization and/or collective action. At the extreme, facilitation therefore turns into compulsion: punishing nonperformance instead of simply rewarding performance. For present purposes, however, we can treat facilitation and compulsion as a seamless continuum.

Toleration is the space between repression and facilitation. For some combinations of groups and collective actions, a given government does not react at all: the residents of an urban neighborhood get together to write a letter to the editor about local housing for the elderly, and the government neither impedes them nor helps them; striking students stay away from classes, and the police studiously ignore them.

To the extent that the acceptability of actions and of groups to a given government each fall into a single rank order, we have a simple way of representing both the limits of tolerable behavior and the general level of governmental repressiveness. Figure 4-1 offers a simple description of repression, toleration, and facilitation. In this idealized diagram, any group less acceptable than D gets repressed no matter what it does. Any action less

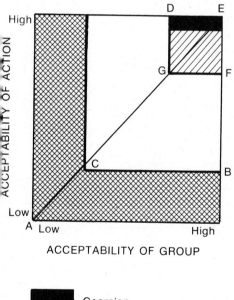

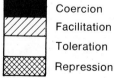

Coercion
Facilitation
Toleration
Repression

Fig. 4-1
Repression, toleration, facilitation, and coercion

acceptable than B gets repressed no matter which group does it. AC therefore represents the amount of repression. Any group more acceptable than E and any action more acceptable than F receive governmental support. EG represents the general extent of governmental facilitation, CG the general extent of governmental tolerance.

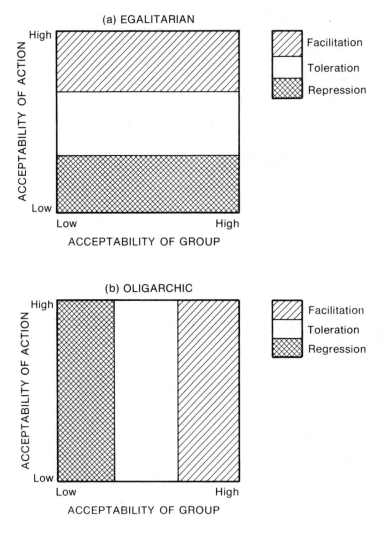

Fig. 4-2
Repression in egalitarian and oligarchic governments

With these tools, we can manufacture the two ideal types of regimes shown in Fig. 4–2: Egalitarian and Oligarchic. In the extreme case of egalitarianism, the acceptability of the group makes no difference to the likelihood that the government will repress or facilitate a given sort of action by that group. In the extreme case of oligarchy, the sort of action undertaken makes no difference to the likelihood that the government will repress the action of a group with a given amount of power.

In that never-never world where evidence is free, clear, and reliable, we can compare real regimes in these regards, and thus be on our way to testing arguments concerning such things as the tempering effects of parliamentary systems on the repression of collective action. Real evidence would also give us the means of judging the utility of the polity model presented earlier: the clearer the distinction between members and challengers, the sharper and more nearly vertical should be the line between repression and toleration. To the extent that governments are truly egalitarian and that the transition from toleration to repression is gradual instead of abrupt, the division of contenders into members and challengers is misleading.

The rectilinear representation we have been using so far is not very realistic. Let us neglect the unreality introduced by having no gray areas, no governmental wavering, and no tactical maneuvering. Even with great certainty as to when the government will and will not repress, tolerate, or facilitate, what Fig. 4–3 shows is more like everyday reality. In both cases shown in the diagrams, even highly unacceptable groups have a few innocuous courses of action open to them. Even highly acceptable groups have some actions barred to them. But the acceptability of the action varies with the acceptability of the group.

In the diagrams, although governments X and Y do about the same amount of facilitating of collective action, Y is substantially more repressive than X. Y is also less tolerant than X. We can represent the difference in repressiveness between the governments as $AC - A'C'$. The same device will serve to portray the change in the repressiveness of a single government over time: the question is how far C moves up and down the diagonal.

The diagram has an interesting by-product: it helps specify some standard intuitions of the repressive patterns in different sorts of regimes. Figure 4–4 lays out the differences among repressive, totalitarian, tolerant, and weak regimes. In this characterization, a *repressive* regime represses many groups and actions, while facilitating few of either. A *totalitarian* regime may repress less, but it facilitates a wide range of actions, even to the point of making them compulsory. As a consequence, the band of merely tolerated actions narrows. The *tolerant* regime widens that middle band: diagram (c) sneaks in the supposition that to do so it must bar some actions to the most powerful groups

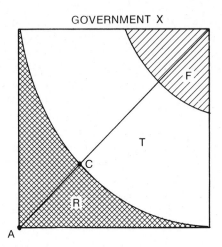

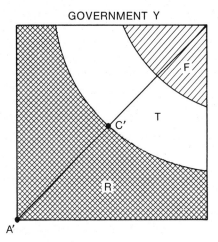

Fig. 4–3
Tolerance versus repression

within it. Finally, the *weak* regime also has a wide band of tolerated behavior, but it facilitates less, and tips its repression toward the weaker groups while doing practically nothing about the collective action of the strong.

So far we have simply been exploring a two-dimensional definition of repressiveness. We can edge a bit further into the world of testable propositions by asking what features of actions make actions acceptable, and what features

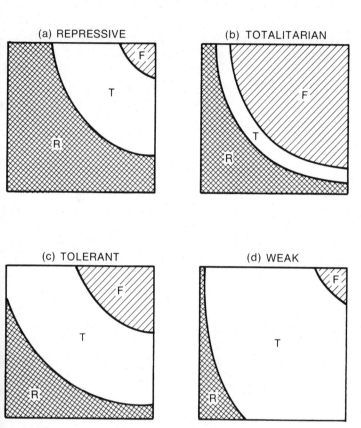

Fig. 4-4
Repressive patterns in different types of regime

of groups make groups acceptable. Those are empirical questions, tough ones. Their detailed answers vary according to the kind of people and the kind of government we are talking about. Regardless of whatever else affects the acceptability of an action, however, its sheer scale certainly does. The larger the scale of a collective action, on the whole, the more repression a government is likely to throw at it. By "scale" we may mean number of participants, duration, geographic range, extent of organization, degree of force mobilized, or some weighted combination of them.

On the side of group acceptability, the group's current power is the most promising single factor. That for two reasons: because might often makes right, and because current power sums up many other kinds of acceptability. The more powerful the group, on the average, the less repression it receives.

Although at first hearing the relationship sounds obvious, it is neither self-evident nor true by definition. Indeed, a government at the edge of a revolutionary situation often concentrates whatever repressive strength it has on its most powerful rivals, and lets the weak run free. Nevertheless, in general an inverse relationship between power and repression probably does hold.

This effect of power on repression and facilitation reverses the main relationship proposed by our elementary mobilization model. There, the contender's current subjection to repression/facilitation affects its power, but not vice versa. Again the difference is due to a shift in perspective. The elementary model deals with the moment of collective action, and aims at the action of the contender. This supplementary model of repression/facilitation, however, deals with a government's decision to repress—either in response to some single collective action, or as a pattern of responses over a longer period.

Our earlier diagrams now translate into Fig. 4–5. In this idealized map, a group weaker than A will be repressed no matter how small the scale of its action. Even the strongest group will be repressed if it undertakes an action

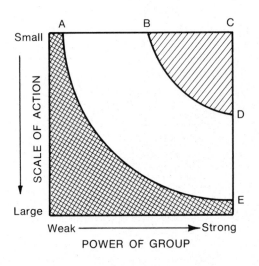

Fig. 4–5
Repression as a function of scale and power

arger than E. Any group stronger than B will receive active support for its
smaller-scale actions, and the strongest groups will receive facilitation from
the government for the full range of actions from C to D. The oddity of some
of these implications makes it clear that a valid map would show more bumps
and depressions. For example, in any particular political system there is no
doubt a threshold below which groups are too weak to bother with; since they
pose no threat, their small-scale collective actions are ignored. Making the
map more realistic is a significant theoretical and empirical problem.

Figure 4-6, the last in this series, offers some speculations about the standard distributions of repression and facilitation in populations with relatively
strong governments. I mean them to apply to major western states over the
last two or three centuries. The repression curve now registers the idea that
groups with a little power pose a greater threat to the government and its main
supporters than do powerless groups. The hypothetical government represses
all but the smallest collective actions of slightly powerful groups, while
allowing more latitude to the genuinely powerless. It also contains the idea
that as the power of a particular group rises—as, for example, it actually becomes identical with the government—the range of collective actions denied to

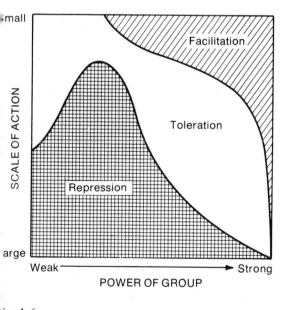

ig. 4-6
Hypothetical distribution of governmental repression
as a function of the scale of collective action and the
power of the actor

it eventually dwindles to nothingness. The facilitation curve tells us that even relatively powerless groups receive incentives to carry out certain highly acceptable collective actions; the result of that circumstance is to squeeze the range of collective action on the part of slightly powerful groups which is simply tolerated: either they can't do it or they must do it. As a result, relatively powerless groups find their world more totalitarian than do the powerful or the completely powerless.

At the other end of the power range, the extremely powerful enjoy governmental support in almost any collective action they carry on. At the extreme, where the government and the most powerful group merge indissolubly, government supports everything the group does. This basic pattern is possible with a smaller or larger area of toleration, smaller or larger zones of repression and facilitation.

If this argument is correct, repression and facilitation should work. It should not be true, for example, that a people long held under a repressive regime will gradually build up so much resentment that it bursts out against the regime. It should be true, on the other hand, that visible changes in a government's repressive policy—cracking down on violators of a certain law or easing up on them—will rapidly encourage or discourage the collective action of many groups besides those most directly affected; the news of the change should quickly affect their estimates of the costs of particular kinds of collective action, and perhaps of collective action in general. To be more exact, shifts in the pattern of repression and facilitation should have two related effects: depressing or raising the overall level of collective action, altering the relative attractiveness of different forms of collective action.

The historical evidence for the impact of repression on the general level of collective action is, I think, quite strong. At the extreme, the Europe of our own time provides the examples of Spain under Primo de Rivera and Franco, Portugal under Salazar, Germany under Hitler, and Soviet Union under Stalin and his successors, Italy under Mussolini, France under Vichy and the Nazis—all times of enormously reduced collective action in those countries except for collective action directly initiated by the state. In general, when a European state temporarily trained its full repressive power on its internal enemies (as when the Italian state attacked the Sicilian Fasci of 1893–94), the enemies subsided.

The alteration of the relative attractiveness of different forms of collective action by repression and facilitation is easy to illustrate and hard to establish as a general rule. The "channeling" of collective action by governments shows up in the nineteenth-century preference for mutual-aid societies over trade unions. Western governments generally discouraged the banding together of workers who sought to control production. They diverted workers into presumably safer organizations oriented to consumption. The tactic worked in the short run; until they became legal, trade unions attracted few members. At first, Friendly Societies and *sociétés de secours mutuels* busied themselves with problems of welfare away from work. In the longer run, however, they became the nuclei of action against employers and against the state. The lower-cost alternative eventually became a very effective one. That repression makes a difference does not mean that it always accomplishes what the repressors had in mind.

POWER

The provisional hypothesis of this last discussion, then, runs as follows: the extent to which a given collective action by a given group is subject to repression, toleration, or facilitation is mainly a function of two factors: (1) the scale of the action, (2) the power of the group. The larger the scale of the action, the more likely its repression; the more powerful the group, the less likely its repression. The later diagrams refined that crude hypothesis by specifying interactions between the scale of the action and the power of the group. But the core of the hypothesis remains.

Scale of action is a fairly clear idea. Power is not. Unfortunately for clarity, the word has many tones and overtones. Enough, I think, to make the search for one essential meaning or one comprehensive definition of power a wild-goose chase. The meaning I have in mind here is simple and common-sense. Suppose we have two or more interacting parties. Suppose each party has an interest in an outcome of the interaction. Suppose at least one such interest of one party to the interaction conflicts with the interest of another party to the interaction. The power of that party is the extent to which its interests prevail over the others with which it is in conflict.

The other actors may range from a single person to the sum of all other persons and groups. The power of a given party is therefore always relative to a specific (1) other party or set of parties; (2) interest or set of interests; (3) interaction or set of interactions. A farmer who tramples the interests of other members of his household sometimes makes no headway in the village council; he has extensive power at home, but not abroad. An industry which gets extensive governmental protection from unionization sometimes fails utterly to arrange protective tariffs; its power is high with respect to labor, low with respect to international trade. A group of revolutionaries who were ineffectual last year sometimes reorganize and start making a revolution this year; in last year's interactions they were powerless, while in this year's they are powerful. When we argue about whether a given group is powerful, we are occasionally disagreeing about the facts. But usually we are contending over which parties, interests, and interactions deserve to be taken into consideration, and how to weigh them.

Now and then someone introduces *potential* power into the discussion. Potential power describes the extent to which the party's interests would prevail if it used all the means at its disposal: if all women used all the wealth, tools, knowledge, etc., they dispose of now to enforce their rights to employment, for example. The trouble with notions of potential power is that by definition they refer to situations we can't observe, that they force us to decide between assuming that the other parties to the interaction continue to behave as before (e. g., that men don't respond by piling up all the wealth, tools, knowledge, etc., *they* control) and theorizing about the whole sequence of interaction likely to follow: war games. Yet we can't simply brush aside potential power as an inconvenient idea, for the implicit threat that a party will use the means it has in reserve often (perhaps always) multiplies the effect of the means actually used.

A related distinction separates power-as-effectiveness from power-as-efficiency. (An exactly parallel distinction appears in discussions of organizational outputs; see, e. g., Yuchtman and Seashore 1967.) A group which accomplishes what it sets out to do is *effective*, regardless of the costs it incurs. To the extent that the group's interests thereby prevail over other interests with which they are in conflict, the group is exercising effective power. On the other hand, a group which gets a large return relative to the means at its disposal is *efficient*, regardless of the specific character of that return. To the degree that the return favors the group's interests and counters the interests of other groups, the group is exercising efficient power.

Both effectiveness and efficiency are relative to the group's defined interests. But an effective group may be rather inefficient; by virtue of their willingness to sacrifice almost anything for their objectives, our "zealots" often fall into that category. Likewise, an efficient group may be relatively ineffective; our "misers" frequently end up there. A very ineffective group tends to demobilize through the process that Albert Hirschman analyzes: a succession from some combination of loyalty + voice to exit. A very inefficient group wastes its mobilized resources and then tends either (a) to become ineffective as a result or (b) to lose its support to other groups pursuing the same interests more efficiently. In order to survive and prosper, real groups must maintain themselves above some minimum of power-efficiency and some minimum of power-effectiveness. The analysis which follows provides a means for dealing with both aspects of power.

Parties

Let us go back to our three points of reference: parties, interests and interactions. Many students of power like to distinguish between "governments" or "authorities," on one hand, and all parties outside the government, on the other. William Gamson, for example, uses *power* to refer to the effect of authorities on other parties, and *influence* to refer to the effects of other parties on authorities (Gamson 1968). To my way of thinking, the distinctions among party, authority, and government are purely relative: an authority is simply a party which controls some concentrated means of coercion; a government is simply the party which controls the most important concentrated means of coercion within some defined population.

Political power, then, is power over governments. Our estimate of a group's political power will depend on which other parties we take into consideration. At one extreme, we can look at the group and the government alone. Then the group's political power is the extent to which its interests prevail over those of the government when the two sets of interests are in conflict. That result is vaguely unsettling, precisely because we usually have some other contenders for the government's favor in mind, and visualize the situation of a perfect coincidence of interests between a given party and the government: surely we wouldn't want to say that such a party had no political power!

An extreme answer to that difficulty is to include all other contenders. The answer is extreme because it entails (a) enumerating all those other contenders, (b) preparing the huge balance sheet of their interests vs. the interests of the group whose power we are trying to assay. The intermediate answer is to limit the set of contenders taken into consideration: one competitor, a limited set of powerful competitors, all those which have made themselves known with respect to some particular issue and/or some particular phase of governmental activity, and so on.

The notion of a "polity" takes a step in that direction by singling out all contenders which have routine access to the government. For this particular notion of polity to be useful, there must be a break in the distribution of power. The break must separate the relatively great power of all contenders ("members of the polity") who have routine access to the government from the relatively small power of all other contenders ("challengers") who lack that routine access. It also implies a break in the life history of a group which moves from challenge to membership or membership to challenge. To the extent that these processes are continuous and gradual, the concept of polity loses its value.

Interests

We face the trilemma which Steven Lukes lays out. Lukes distinguishes among "pluralist," "reformist," and "radical" conceptions of power. The essential distinction rests on the means used to identify the relevant interests of each actor. A "pluralist" view, in Lukes' terminology, takes into account only those interests which groups articulate and press in the political arena. A "reformist" conception of power adds other interests which a group articulates, but has no opportunity to act upon. In a reformist analysis, a truly powerful group not only sees to it that its interests prevail in the event of an open conflict within the political arena, but also manages to keep other group's challenges to its interests off the public agenda. Both the pluralist and the reformist analyses limit the list of relevant interests to those which the groups themselves articulate.

The "radical" analysis, according to Lukes, considers a group's real interests regardless of whether the group has articulated them. We looked at this choice in the previous chapter: (1) infer the interests from the group's own utterances and actions—utterances and actions in the public arena for the pluralists, utterances and actions in any arena for the reformists; (2) derive the interests from a general scheme which relates interest to social position. In the Marxist tradition, the "social position" which counts is the group's relationship to the means of production.

It is easy to accept the reformist conception of power as a substitute for the pluralist conception. The reformist approach simply adds new interests to those already considered relevant by the pluralist. The choice between the radical approach and the other two is more drastic. It leads to the conclusion that some apparent interests which groups articulate and pursue are not really interests. They are chimeras, products of false consciousness, trivialities. The radical approach also leads to the identification of interests which the actors themselves do not—and, sometimes, would not—recognize as their own interests. It second-guesses the actors' own perception of the world.

Substituting one's own assessment of the relevant interests for that of the actors on the scene takes confidence, sometimes even condescension and arrogance. Those interests which groups articulate and pursue, whether an outside analyst rates them as "real" or not, significantly affect real struggles for power. In prudence and humility, then, we should give them priority. Nothing prevents us, however, from posing the following empirical problem:

We may ask, that is, how accurately the interests we impute to a group on general grounds predict to (a) the interests the group articulates and pursues, and/or (b) the power struggles in which the group engages. The Marxist analysis says that both will have predictive power. Over the long run, a group's relationship to the prevailing means of production determines the interests which the group articulates and pursues. The group's relationship to the means of production also affects its contention for power directly, by determining its likely enemies and allies, and by shaping its internal organization. Marxists differ among themselves when it comes to deciding how much importance to attribute to these direct effects of class position on contention for power, and how much to insist on class consciousness as a prerequisite for sustained or effective action. If we can find a reasonable way of gauging class consciousness, this, too, can become an empirical question.

Interactions

Having settled on a particular set of parties and a particular set of interests, we still have to settle on a particular set of interactions. The most obvious limit is time: power today, power this year, power over the last decade, power at some time in the future? Different sets of interactions are relevant. If we want to single out the *effects* of power, we are almost certainly going to attempt the distinction between power today and power tomorrow, on the assumption that today's exercise of power will, directly or indirectly, affect tomorrow's power distribution. In addition to fixing the interactions in time, we have to decide whether to consider all interactions, or only some crucial subset—every communication, direct or indirect, between Standard Oil and the U. S. Government, or just formal requests for rate adjustments?

We sometimes sidestep this difficulty by looking simply at the returns a given group gets from other parties over some period of interaction, without trying to detect the impact of every single interaction. Logically speaking, that is a gross simplification. We also tend to assume that the power which shows up in a visible set of interactions is strongly correlated with the power which would show up in the interactions shielded from our eyes: if J. P. Morgan could do that much in public, then think how much he could do in private! The correlation is nevertheless a matter of fact, a subject of possible dispute, and an assumption we cannot continue to make indefinitely.

THE MEASUREMENT OF POWER

Let us suppose, *mirabile dictu*, that we have settled on a specific set of parties, interests and interactions. We can now use the simplified model of collective action as the pursuit of collective goods to describe a single group's power position. Figure 4-7 refines the earlier collective goods model in two regards. The returns now include the possibility of collective bads: negative returns from collective action. The position −1 might represent the group's complete

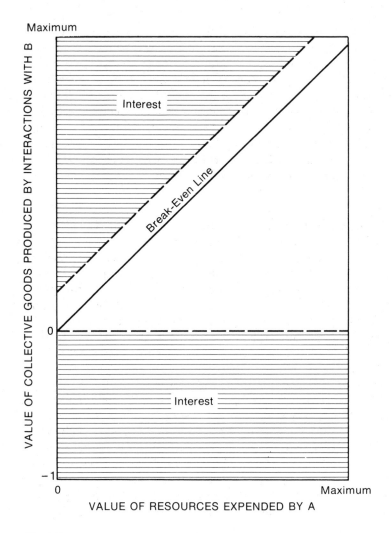

Fig. 4-7
Interests and returns from collective action for an opportunist contender

extinction. The diagram also represents the interests of the sort of contender we earlier called an opportunist: a group which will accept any sort of collective goods, so long as they represent a significant gain over the resources expended to get them. With the additional possibility of collective bads, the diagram also shows that the contender's interest extends to defense against these negative outcomes. Even in the case of the omnivorous opportunist, the collective goods we now take into consideration are those which result from a specified set of interactions with a particular set of parties by reference to which we want to gauge the contender's power.

For simplicity's sake, let us narrow our attention to the interaction of two parties. The narrowing is not quite so drastic as it may seem, since one of the "parties" to the interaction may be a sum of all other parties. We can easily represent the actions of third parties as influences on the outcomes in question. Then, as before, the diagram represents several crucial facts: collective action requires an expenditure of resources; the collective goods obtained are worth something; to the extent that the resources expended and collective goods obtained have comparable values the interaction can result in a gain, a loss or a standoff. Above the diagonal, Party A gets back more than it expends; it thus gains. Below the diagonal, Party A gets back less than it expends; thus it loses. The diagonal is a break-even line.

In any real interaction, a number of things constrain B's response to A's action: the resources under B's control, B's own desire and capacity to resist or cooperate, the interest of third parties in the resources under B's control, and so on. For a number of reasons it is reasonable to suppose the following things.

1 A contender which does not act at all will receive collective bads.

2 A contender which acts on a very small scale will receive even more collective bads, as the other party responds negatively to its efforts.

3 Beyond that point, the contender will receive an increasing return for increasing outputs of collective action, but only up to a limit.

4 The marginal rate of return for collective action eventually becomes negative.

The curve in Fig. 4–8 describes those hypothetical effects. The rate of return eventually declines because B's resources are not inexhaustible, because B will defend itself against threats to its own survival, and because third parties will intervene when A's gains visibly threaten their own interest in the resources under B's control. Under the conditions shown in Fig. 4–8, an unconstrained, coolly calculating Party A—an opportunist—would maximize by expending Z resources, landing at Y on the returns curve and getting back X in collective goods, for a gain of X–Z. The returns curve gives a simple description of A's power over B.

Putting the diagonal back in makes it clearer that some groups might always be in a losing position because their entire returns curve lies below the break-even line. Figure 4–9 states that possibility. There, Party A_2 has little hope; its curve lies too low. Party A_1 is better off; a portion of its curve lies above the break-even line. With respect to this set of parties, interests, and interactions, Party A_1 has more *power* than Party A_2. An opportunist Party

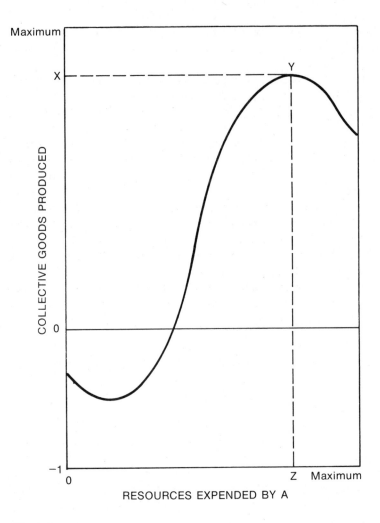

Fig. 4–8
Hypothetical schedule of returns from collective action

A_1 would confine its action to the range producing returns above the diagonal: Z_1 to Z_2. An opportunist Party A_2 would act only enough to forestall collective bads—and work to improve its schedule of returns.

We have forgotten, however, that neither A_1 nor A_2 has unlimited resources to expend. The amount of resources party A currently has under its control (that is, *mobilized resources*) limits how far out on the S-curve of returns A can move. Figure 4–10 identifies that limit. With M_1 in mobilized re-

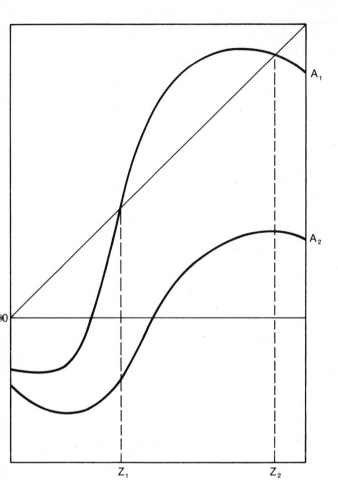

Fig. 4-9
Gaining versus losing schedules of returns

sources, Party A can only lose, despite its theoretically favorable position. If A can arrange to mobilize more resources, then act, that looks like a good strategy. With M_2, expending almost everything on hand will make sense. With M_3, it would still be smart to expend something around M_2, and keep the rest in reserve for another time.

This last diagram permits two refinements to the analysis of power. First, the intersection of the S-curve with the mobilization line is a fairly good ap-

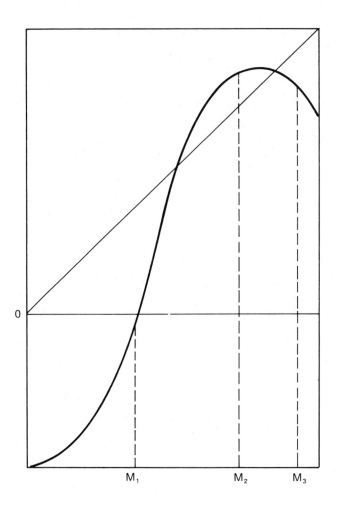

Fig. 4-10
How mobilization limits collective action

proximation of *potential* power. It tells us what effect Party A could have if it expended all the resources under its control. (You may prefer to search for the highest point on the S-curve which falls to the left of the mobilization line, and call *that* A's potential power.) Second, the distinction between power-effectiveness and power-efficiency appears clearly. Power-effectiveness refers to how far up the vertical axis Party A can reach or does reach. Power-efficiency refers to the slope of the return curve at the point Party A can or does reach. In either case, the diagram tells us that the current mobilization level of Party A sets a firm limit on Party A's power.

A prudent description of A's power in the real world disregards the portion of the S-curve to the right of the mobilization barrier. For this state of the world, this set of parties, this set of interests and this set of interactions, the segment of the curve to the left of the mobilization line describes the power of Party A.

POWER AND POLITY MEMBERSHIP

Contention for power links the mobilization model to the polity model. Contention for power consists of the application of resources to influence other groups, and power itself consists of a group's making its interests prevail over others with which they are in conflict. Contention for *political* power involves applying resources to a particular kind of organization: a government. A government is simply the organization, if any, which controls the principal concentrated means of coercion within some population. The contenders for power within a given population include all groups which are collectively applying resources to influence the government. In real life, we usually want to set some threshold for contention, in order to eliminate tiny, evanescent, intermittent applications of resources to the government. In theory, we can generously include all of them.

At any point in time, some (and only some) of the contenders have achieved recognition of their collective rights to wield power over the government, and have developed routine ways of exercising those rights. They are *members of the polity*. All other contenders are *challengers*. They contend without routine or recognition. Membership in the polity gives important advantages to a group. In the most general sense, its power rises: in terms of the diagrams of the previous section, polity membership produces a rise in the curve of returns from collective action. Departure from the polity produces a drop in the curve. Concretely, recognition pays off in collective access to jobs, exemptions from taxation, availability of privileged information, and so on.

Every polity establishes tests of membership. All polities include among such tests the ability to mobilize or coerce significant numbers of people. Furthermore, within the polity members continually test one another; repeated failures of partial tests lead to fuller tests. The fuller tests lead, *in extremis*, to exclusion from the polity. Each new entry or exit redefines the criteria of membership in a direction favorable to the characteristics of the present set of members. In the process, the members tend to become attached to those criteria as a matter of principle.

In theory, a group can mobilize without contending for power; it can apply its collective resources entirely to recreation, the search for enlightenment, or some other nonpolitical end. A commune or religious community retiring from the world moves in that direction. Within the modern world, however, governments are so likely to claim the right to regulate and to extract resources from any mobilizing group that mobilization usually propels a group into contention for power over one government or another—at least into an effort to secure guarantees of its basic rights to exist, assemble, accumulate resources, and carry on its valued activities. Eric Wolf's analysis of the involvement of peasant communities in revolutions, for instance, shows how regularly they mobilize and then contend for power not because they initially want a change in government, but in self-defense.

Wolf's analysis also tells us how crucial to the success of the contention for power are the coalitions peasant communities make with other groups outside. No coalition = lost revolution. In a great many situations, a single contender does not have enough resources—enough committed people, enough guns, enough trained lawyers, enough cash—to influence the government by itself. A coalition with another contender which has overlapping or complementary designs on the government will then increase the joint power of the contenders to accomplish those designs.

Coalitions most commonly occur between members of the polity or between nonmembers of the polity. Nevertheless, coalitions between members and nonmembers often occur when the members are seeking ends for which there are not enough coalition partners within the polity, and for which the resources being mobilized by the nonmembers would be useful. This happens when a party wins an election by buying off the support of a tribe through promises of jobs and influence. It also happens when a dissident but established group of intellectuals forms an alliance with a new worker's movement. These coalitions take on special importance because they often open the way to the new acquisition of membership in the polity, or the way to a revolutionary alliance.

Member–nonmember coalitions also matter because they affect the amount of violence which grows out of contention for power. Under most conditions a coalition with a member reduces the violence with attends a challenger's acquisition of membership. The coalitions of the women's suffrage and temperance movements in England and the United States with other established segments of the middle classes, for example, almost certainly restrained the use of force against them. Where the effect of coalition is to split the polity into factions making exclusive and incompatible claims on the government, however, a high degree of collective violence is likely to follow. That is, in fact, a revolutionary situation.

Detecting Changes in Polity Membership

Political power is a characteristic of the interactions between contenders and governments. In seeking to detect major changes in political power, we have the choice of starting with the contenders or of starting with the government.

What should we look for? A simple, if slightly risky, approach would be to take running accounts of political life as they appear in political histories, yearbooks, memoirs and so on, to determine whether informed observers report changes in the major actors on the scene. Jean Laponce (1969) has invented a refined version of this strategy: he watches the stabilization of party labels in Canadian politics an an indication of the consolidation of various blocs of voters. A successful party such as the Liberals tends, at it succeeds, to drop the qualifiers from its label and to retain a shortened version of its original title. A party still gathering its forces (and perhaps one on the way out, as well) tends to accumulate changes and qualifiers as it makes new, provisional coalitions.

That approach has promise. Another possibility is to examine the expenditure patterns of the government. If a new budget line representing services to linguistic minorities appears, that may be a sign that a linguistically based challenger is breaking into the polity. If an old program disappears (as when special benefits for Spanish–American War veterans melt into the general veterans' program), that probably tells us the bloc itself is dissolving. Major changes in the amounts spent on war, education, or welfare might point in the same direction, although (as Fenno 1966 makes clear) some such changes are mystifications, and others depend mainly on the internal dynamics of the government itself.

Perhaps the actual structure of agencies—a Department of Labor to match the arrival of organized labor, a Department of Veteran's Affairs to match the arrival of veterans—provides evidence of the same kind. But in a parliamentary system, the behavior of the parliament itself probably reflects the *va-et-vient* of contenders more accurately than anything else. Do discussions of issues clearly linked with one contender or another (whether represented in the parliament or not) wax and wane in time with the political fortunes of those contenders? Does the appearance of a reliable split of the vote on such issues signal the arrival of a member? Is there a sort of scale going:

- a discussion of an issue clearly linked with a contender (e. g., putting down unruly workers or racial minorities)
- introduction of bills or resolutions
- bringing such bills or resolutions to a vote
- appearances within the parliament of a bloc, or standard alignment, with respect to issues clearly linked with the contender
- appearance within the parliament of a representative publicly identified with a specific contender
- appearance within the parliament of a party publicly identified with a specific contender?

With the idea that some such process might be going on, Jeff Pearson analyzed roll-call votes in the Ninth Legislature of the French Chamber of Deputies, which met in 1906–1907. Those were turbulent years in France. Socialists had withdrawn their support from the government in the fall of 1905 over the issue of schoolteachers' right to unionize and to strike. The elections of January 1906 renewed the Senate and brought in a new President, Armand Fallières. A strike wave, concentrated in the mines but involving many workers in chemicals and smelting as well, began to roll in March and reached a crest in May. During the legislative elections of May, the Parti Socialiste Unifié conducted a national campaign for the first time; questions of nationalization of railroad lines, retirement plans, and benefits in general figured widely in the campaign debates. The year 1907 featured a massive protest of southern winegrowers resulting from an overproduction crisis. And throughout the period the government was implementing the disestablishment of the Catholic Church which had been decided two years before, and liquidating the Dreyfus Affair which had hung over France for a decade. Judging from the general political histories of the time, one could reasonably assert that two major changes in polity membership were occurring: organized labor was acquiring an established place in the national structure of power and the Catholic Church was losing an important share of power.

Pearson's analysis jibes nicely with the political history of the time. He examined 228 of the 324 roll-call votes which occurred in the parliamentary session. (The issues of the *Journal Officiel* reporting the other 96 roll-calls were unavailable to Pearson at the time.) They fell into three categories: *legislative* roll calls deciding the fate of laws proposed for enactment; *sanctioning* roll calls approving or disapproving an action of the government; *others* which cover a variety of procedural matters, resolutions, and other actions none of which can lead to the passage of a law or the fall of a government. Using the content of the debates and such secondary sources as Bonnefous' *Histoire politique de la Troisième République* as a guide, Pearson coded each vote for the groups outside the Chamber, if any, to which the action was supposed to apply. The results of the coding appear in Table 4–1.

Pearson was able to identify about half the roll calls he examined with some fairly well-defined group. Some of the entries raise doubts: legislative districts, for example, or the Army in general; those doubts involve important questions concerning both the definition of contenders for power in general and the structure of contention within the French political system. In general, however, the list catches exactly the actors one would hope for: winegrowers, postal workers, the Catholic Church, and so on. The issues involved in the roll calls are the issues which rent France as a whole in 1906 and 1907. And the tally of outcomes is suggestive. "Favorable" roll calls are simply those in which the proposal voted on approves or promotes the interests of the group in question. To be the subject of roll calls which actually pass is evidence of power, at least power in the legislature. Although the numbers of roll calls are too small to inspire confidence, Pearson's tabulation suggests that in 1906–07 the power position of miners and railroad workers was superior to that of schoolteachers and postal workers. That remains to be verified with other evidence. But this preliminary investigation makes it seem possible to draw systematic information about contention for power at the national level from the ample proceedings of legislatures.

The use of roll calls and debates has some obvious limitations. It is best suited to the detection of groups whose position is *changing*, rather than calmly enjoying long-established benefits. It assumes that a significant part of public business is actually being done in the legislature. If some contenders (bankers, say, or the military) typically do their work through other branches of government, the procedure will not work so well. One might have to turn to the sort of analysis Tudesq has undertaken for *grands notables* and for *conseillers généraux*, or that many others have undertaken for cabinet members, government officials, or legislators: person-by-person collective biography aggregated into a characterization of the entire category of persons. At the edges of the government, it might be profitable to search for the rise and fall of pressure groups, professional lobbyists and the like. By this point, however, we are beginning to edge back into the study of mobilization and of collective action, away from the acquisition and loss of power as such.

In dealing with relations between major industries and the U.S. government from 1886 to 1906, William Roy has invented some procedures which neatly link the mobilization processes and the power processes, without confounding them. Roy's work focuses on the influence exerted by different industries over interactions between the U.S. government and other countries. He indexes that influence via the frequency and types of explicit mention which the industries in question receive in correspondence between the State Department and ambassadorial officials overseas. The index is imperfect; some important kinds of influence may not appear in the correspondence because they are either too risky or too routine to commit to print. Nevertheless, the basic notion—that to hold power is to be taken account of in your areas of interest—is valid, and the method of implementing it ingenious.

Roy attempts to account for variations in power among industries and over time through three different sets of industrial characteristics: (1) the network position of firms in the industry, as measured especially by interlocking directorates and by relations of industry personnel to government and social organizations; (2) "objective" characteristics of the industry such as size, number of firms, and revenue from foreign trade; (3) mobilization and collec-

Table 4-1 *Groups figuring in 1906–07 roll calls of French Chamber of Deputies*

Group	Issue	Number of roll calls				Percent favorable	Percent favorable and passed
		Legislative	Sanctioning	Other	Total		
Schoolteachers	Right of state employees to strike for wages without government sanctions	0	7	1	8	50	0
Postal workers	Same	6	0	3	9	89	11
Railroad workers	Free from compulsory dependence on employer-run *economats*	2	0	0	2	100	50
Miners	Introduce maximum 8-hour day	1	0	0	1	100	100
Spinners	Emergency funds for unemployed	0	0	1	1	100	0
Winegrowers	Stemming the overproduction crisis of 1907 and safeguards for future	22	0	2	24	83	30
Winegrowers	Punishment for June 1907 demonstrations in South	0	7	2	9	44	0
Wine merchants and middlemen	Safeguards and controls on them to prevent watering wine	1	0	0	1	100	100
Second Army	Discipline regiment which refused to quell demonstrations	2	1	0	3	33	0
Second Army	Provide earlier release of draftees to aid harvest	3	0	0	3	100	33

Army in general	Vindicate Dreyfus and Piquart	4	0	0	4	25	25
Army in general	Increase appropriations	3	0	0	3	67	33
Army in general	Reduce compulsory service by one year	5	2	2	9	33	33
Small grocers	Impose tax on, to regulate sale of sugar to local wine makers	2	0	0	2	50	0
Workers in general	Create Ministry of Labor	1	0	1	2	100	100
Workers in general	Legalize national Sunday holiday for	3	0	0	3	67	33
Workers in general	Abolish private property in behalf of	0	2	0	2	50	0
Left-leaning legislative districts	Institute proportional representation in all elections	0	0	2	2	50	0
Lower classes	Relative tax burden on	1	4	0	5	20	0
Agriculture	Emergency appropriations for	1	0	0	1	100	100
Private railroad company (Chemin de Fer de l'Ouest)	State takeover of	1	0	5	6	67	0
Roman Catholic Church	Right to retain tax-free property	4	5	4	13	23	7
Total classifiable		62	30	21	113	57	19
Unclassifiable					115		
Total roll calls					228		

tive action within the industry, as represented by the intensity of economic cooperation and concentration among firms, the character of trade associations and trade publications, the extent of lobbying, political involvement of executives, and so on.

Roy's research design does not quite bring us to the point of measuring the returns different industries receive for the resources they apply to the government; it therefore falls short of the ideal measure of power proposed earlier. It takes important steps in that direction. Furthermore, it makes possible a valuable partial test of the proposed distinction between challengers and members of the polity. If a "polity" exists in a strong sense of the term, there should be a distinct break in the continuum of influence wielding; the break should correspond to the threshold below which an industry is simply not a polity member to be taken account of.

If, on the other hand, the continuum runs smoothly from zero to infinite power, the notion of a bounded polity is misleading. Likewise the notion requires a break in the *relationship* between level of collective action and amount of influence, corresponding to the significantly higher return polity members should receive for their investments. In any case, if there is no significant relationship between the industry's mobilization and its political influence, the model of the polity laid out here will lose plausibility.

So far, my account makes the process of entry and exit too calm and orderly: stolid Britons waiting in line, ration books in hand. In reality, it is the occasion for some of the greatest struggles in which people engage. If every polity has tests of membership, that does not mean every challenger has equal chances of meeting those tests, or that the leaders of every contender are equally willing to make the effort.

The likelihood that a new contender will accept and employ the means of acquisition of power the members of the polity prescribe (e.g., gathering enough votes to elect a party, sacrificing enough people in war, bringing in enough food from the hunt, buying enough government officials) depends on the congruence of the conceptions of justice which prevail within it to those built into the operation of the polity. Where they diverge widely, the challenger is likely to employ irregular means—which means applying resources to the government and to members of the polity which are rarely used in those relationships. A concrete example: Guatemalan revolutionaries kidnap government officials and American emissaries in order to secure the release of their own members from prison. Another Latin American case: Peruvian trade unions deliberately stage violent demonstrations as a way of pressing their demands on the central government (Payne 1965).

The idea of a polity, then, sums up the major relationships among repression, power, and collective action. Members of the polity have more power and face less repression than challengers do. Challengers become members through collective action, and members defend themselves against loss of power through collective action. This much is a useful simplification. But the polity model lacks an important element: interests. It provides no guide to the opportunities and threats affecting any particular group's interests. Without some idea of the articulation of interest and power position, we can have no clear idea how the extent and character of challengers' and members' collective action differ from one another.

OPPORTUNITY/THREAT

Opportunity has two sides. On the opportunity side, we have the extent to which other groups, including governments, are vulnerable to new claims which would, if successful, enhance the contender's realization of its interests. On the threat side, we have the extent to which other groups are threatening to make claims which would, if successful, reduce the contender's realization of its interests. The analysis of opportunity/threat parallels the analysis of power: in principle, it embraces everything about the surrounding world which is likely to affect the actor's well-being. In practice, we can only deal with it by referring to some specific set of interests, parties and interactions.

One important difference between the analyses of power and of opportunity/threat concerns perceptions and expectations. In the analysis of power we can choose to neglect them: power then refers to the observable transactions among the parties. In the case of opportunity/threat we have no choice but to construct some model of the way that information about the environment comes to the actor's attention. For the moment, let us assume that the contender, who is engaged in frequent interactions with other groups, simply responds to the trend of those interactions. The contender responds individually to the trend of its interactions with each specific group, and collectively to the trend in all interactions. A contender which is encountering increasing attacks on its interests anticipates more attacks; a contender which finds the government increasingly responsive to its overtures anticipates further responsiveness. Later on we will have to consider a contender's observation of interactions among other parties—noting, for example, that when a government shows signs of weakness in dealing with any particular contender, most other contenders read those signs as threats or opportunities with regard to their own interests. We will also have to recognize that strategic interaction usually involves feints and misunderstandings. Let us ignore these interesting complications for the time being.

Figure 4-11 breaks opportunity/threat into two dimensions: (1) the extent of anticipated change in the contender's realization of its interests; it runs from

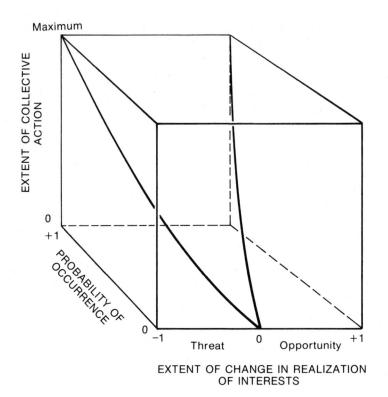

Fig. 4–11
Collective action as a function of threats and opportunities

−1 (complete obliteration of its interests) to 0 (no change) to +1 (complete realization of its interests); (2) the probability that the change will occur (a) if the contender does not act, in the case of threats, (b) if the group acts, in the case of opportunities. The diagram says that the greater the absolute value of the quantity (probability of occurrence × extent of change), the more extensive the contender's collective action. In this simple version, the contender's responses to threat and to opportunity are exactly symmetrical: the more of either, the more collective action. The two curves are gently concave to represent a mild tendency for collective action to accelerate more rapidly with higher levels of threat or opportunity.

An asymmetrical response to threat and opportunity is more plausible than a symmetrical response. Assuming equal probabilities of occurrence, a given amount of threat tends to generate more collective action than the "same" amount of opportunity. On the whole, response to opportunity is likely to require more alteration of the group's organization and mobilization pattern than is response to threat; the group can respond to threat via its established routines. European peasant communities relied on their local communication networks and shared understandings in getting together to chase out the unwanted tax collector. They had much more trouble sending a delegation to the capital to demand an alteration of the tax burden. Furthermore, groups generally inflate the value of those things they already possess, when someone else is seeking to take them away. For equal probabilities, the loss of the existing village common land counts more than the gain of the same amount of common land. Finally, threats generalize more readily than opportunities do. A group is more likely to see a threat to a particular interest as a sign of threats to a wide range of its interests than it is to see an opportunity for enhancement of one of its interests as a sign of opportunity for a wide range of its interests.

These are, of course, not established verities, but hypotheses. Figure 4–12 sums them up: the extent of collective action, it says, mounts more rapidly as a function of threat than as a function of opportunity. On the threat side, it says, collective action rises to the maximum permitted by the group's mobilization level considerably before the point at which the threat means annihilation. The longer the time lag considered, the greater the asymmetry. Over a longer period defensive mobilization in response to threat tends to add its effect more rapidly than offensive or preparatory mobilization in response to opportunity.

The asymmetry, I believe, produces a deep conservatism in every polity. Members of the polity resist changes which would threaten their current realization of their interests even more than they seek changes which would enhance their interests. They fight tenaciously against loss of power, and especially against expulsion from the polity. They work against admission to the polity of groups whose interests conflict significantly with their own.

Existing members tend to be more exacting in their demands of contenders whose very admission would challenge the system in some serious way. Max Heirich points out the stark contrast in the response of University of California officials to two equally obscene events which occurred about the same time in 1965: the campus Ugly Man contest (won by Alpha Epsilon Pi fraternity, whose candidate was Miss Pussy Galore) and the late stages of the Free Speech Movement, now redubbed the Filthy Speech Movement. At that point, the Movement's quintessence was the posting and parading of signs saying, simply, Fuck. Heirich reports a conversation with a faculty member who actively opposed the FSM and was incensed about a recent "obscenity rally" a group of free speech advocates had organized:

When I asked him why he was angry about this but not about the obscene remarks by the fraternity boys, he replied: *That was different.* That was a bunch of fraternity boys blowing off steam. You know that when it's all over they're going to return to their place as respectable members of society. But these people are out to deliberately break every rule they can, to try to tear down society (Heirich 1971: 363).

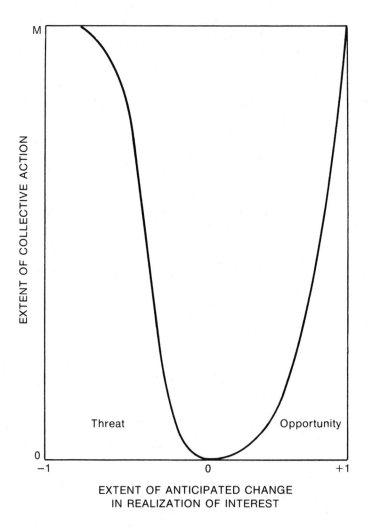

Fig. 4-12
Asymmetrical effect of threat and opportunity on collective action

Throughout 1964 and 1965 the varicolored Movement was, indeed, rapidly mobilizing and demobilizing; it made recurrent, spasmodic bids for power within the structure of the university, ordinarily by testing the Berkeley rules of assembly, speech, or advocacy at their most vulnerable limit, and then claiming some alternative legitimacy for its action. The university's recognition of the claimed right would tend to admit the group making the claim to membership in its polity, and thereby to shift the criteria of membership in general. Something serious is at stake in every such change.

As a consequence, people are exceptionally ready to fight over entries into a polity, and exits from it. As Arthur Stinchcombe (1965) says, leaders of organizations are especially likely to employ, authorize, or tolerate unlimited means of combat when they sense a discrepancy between what their organization is getting and what it is due. That enraging disagreement typically has to do, precisely, with what the organization is due. It is a matter of principle, of rights, of justice. This state of affairs has strong implications for the locus, timing and personnel of major struggles for power.

The recent work of William Gamson (1975) deals effectively with some aspects of the power struggle. Gamson and his associates studied fifty-three "challenging groups" in the U.S. from 1800 to 1945. (The list makes neighbors of the Anarcho-Communists and the National Urban League, of the United Sons of Vulcan, the Tobacco Night Riders and the Steel Workers' Organizing Committee.) The research examines two main sorts of outcomes of the challenges:

- acceptance or nonacceptance of the group by at least one of its antagonists as a legitimate spokesman for the interests it claims to represent

- acquisition or nonacquisition of new advantages for its members.

The acceptance of the group, as defined by Gamson, overlaps to some extent with entrance into a polity, as described earlier. As one might expect, acceptance and the acquisition of new advantages are connected: 80 percent of the groups which gained some acceptance also acquired new advantages, while only 21 percent of those which failed to gain any acceptance acquired any new advantages.

More important, the groups which gained acceptance tended to differ in form and strategy from the others: on the whole, they were groups which did not demand to displace other groups, organized around a single issue, were relatively large, provided selective incentives for participation to their members instead of relying on diffuse appeals to solidarity, and were bureaucratic. Thus far, the results sound like an argument for coolly organized pressure groups. But the successful challengers were also significantly more likely to have used violence and other constraints in their quest for power. The passive recipients of violence had very low rates of success. If it is true that organization pays, it is not so true that patience and moderation pay. Gamson's results are congruent with the general argument which is unfolding here.

Gamson's world is keenly anti–Durkheimian. It opposes the Durkheimian portrayal of collective action in two main ways: (1) its actors approach defined objectives with strategy and tactics—which does not mean they always choose the best strategy or that their objectives are always consistent and attainable; (2) their actions and the outcomes of those actions cannot be explained by looking at the challenging groups alone; they result from an *interaction* between challengers and other groups. In the terms we have been using here, they result from the interplay of interests, organization, and mobilization, on one side, and of repression/facilitation, power, and opportunity/threat, on the other.

THE INTERPLAY OF MOBILIZATION AND OPPORTUNITY

Let us continue to concentrate on the mobilization model. We can crystallize the principal teachings of the last two chapters in a pair of diagrams. Remember the earlier distinctions among four types of contenders: zealots, run-of-the-mill contenders, misers, and opportunists. The run-of-the-mill contenders define their interest in terms of a limited range of collective goods, and are unwilling to act if the action is likely to bring a loss. In Figs. 4–13 and 4–14 we see an idealized run-of-the-mill contender in two contrasting situations. In the first, the preceding arguments say that the contender is likely to produce some collective action. In the second, if the arguments are correct, the contender should not act.

In Fig. 4–13, the run-of-the-mill contender has significant current incentives for collective action. Current opportunity includes the group's narrow area of interest, while current threat includes the possibility of significant loss, although not the -1 of total extinction. If those were the only constraints in operation, we would expect the contender to act both to capitalize on its opportunities and to defend itself against threats of loss.

There is, however, one other constraint: mobilization. In this sketch, the contender's mobilization level is high enough to permit action throughout the range of its current interest and opportunity. Nevertheless, the group's power position would permit it to acquire still more collective goods if it mobilized further; the dotted curve to the right of the mobilization line describes those theoretical possibilities; it also shows the theoretical decline in the group's return if it pushes collective action too far. Beyond a certain point, we expect repression to start diminishing the group's return from collective action.

Repression does not appear in the diagram, but its effect is there. Faithful to the mobilization model, we represent it as one of the factors producing the

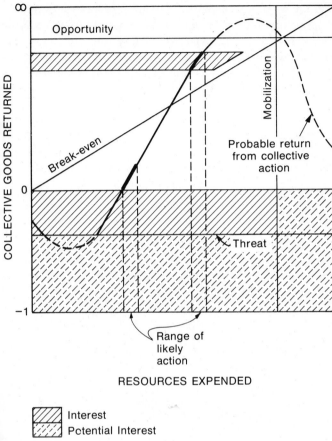

Fig. 4–13
Idealized sketch of conditions for action of a run-of-the-mill contender

current shape and location of the probable-return curve, as well as the current location of the mobilization line. Organization likewise remains hidden from view, as a variable which works through interest and mobilization. Power is present, however. The curve of probable returns gives us a simplified summary of the contender's current power position. Indeed, several different aspects of the contender's power are there: power-efficiency in the rates of return of collective goods for resources expended in the two zones of most likely action; power-effectiveness in the portion of its interest—in this case 100 percent—that the contender can realize; potential power is the high point of the probable-return line.

In our first diagram, then, the current combination of interest, mobilization, power, and opportunity/threat leads us to expect the contender to engage in two kinds and levels of collective action: a low intensity of action to counter threats of loss, a higher intensity of action to take advantage of opportunities for gain in the area of the group's interest. Figure 4-14 shows us the same sort of contender in a very different situation. The situation is a prescription for inaction.

Why? Because all four major variables are now in different positions. Take opportunity/threat: the contender's range of desired collective goods lies above the limit set by current opportunities, and the current threat of loss is very slight. In other words, no other contenders are currently vulnerable to

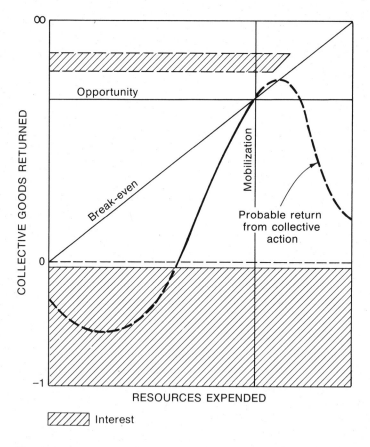

Fig. 4-14
Idealized sketch of conditions for inaction of a run-of-the-mill contender

claims which would enhance this run-of-the-mill contender's realization of its defined interests; hardly any other contender is making plausible threats against its current realization of its interests.

Mobilization likewise inhibits this run-of-the-mill contender's capacity for collective action. The current mobilization level restricts the contender's possible action to the range in which a net loss is almost certain.

The contender's curve of probable returns from collective action is unfavorable as well. It barely crosses the break-even line—and that only in a region which (a) is currently inaccessible because of the mobilization ceiling, (b) does not quite reach to the contender's area of particular interest. Another way of stating these relationships is this: the group's aims are "too high" for its current possibilities of action. A change in any of the four variables could increase the likelihood of collective action. An organizer who wanted to put this hapless run-of-the-mill contender into a better position would attempt to increase its mobilization and try to augment its power by such tactics as forming coalitions. One might also try to foster a redefinition of the contender's interests, in order to bring them within a range of possibility. A powerful coalition partner might try maneuvering to make other contenders or the government more vulnerable to this contender's claims—to raise the limit set by opportunity. Any of these efforts, if successful, would increase the likelihood of the contender's collective action.

In the short run we have been considering, the extent of collective action depends greatly on the degree to which the group involved has previously acquired collective control of resources. Most alternative theories either make mobilization such an immediate function of changing interests that mobilization ceases to act as an independent variable, or maintain that under many circumstances unmobilized groups tend to mobilize so rapidly and effectively as to wipe out any general relationship between prior mobilization and present collective action.

Simple class-voting schemes follow the first line; bloc votes rise and fall as an immediate effect of changing threats to class interests. James Davies's J-curve explanation of rebellions follows the second line; a population which experiences a long period of rising satisfaction of its interests and then experiences a rapid decline in that satisfaction, Davies argues, tends to mobilize and to strike out at once. The argument offered here answers the first line by saying that the effect of changing threats exists, but is not immediate because the speed and intensity of the class' response depends on its prior mobilization. The argument answers the Davies line by saying that the quick response to decline is only characteristic of highly mobilized groups, and that in any case the groups which rebel do not respond to the general fact of deprivation; they respond to the specific fact of another group's making claims which would, if realized, violate their established rights and privileges. The alternative arguments underestimate or eliminate the costs of collective action.

If the mobilization model is an improvement over previous analyses of collective action, it still has some significant weaknesses. It has no time in it. Concentrating on the immediate situation of collective actors greatly simplifies the analysis. But it also makes it difficult to deal with reciprocal influences such as those which link power and collective action: current power position certainly affects the likelihood of collective action, as the model says; current collective action also affects future power position, as the model does not say. The absence of time, furthermore, eliminates the feints and hesitations of strategic interaction. The most the model can do for us in these regards is to help us reduce the blur of the newsreel into many distinct successive frames, each with its own logic.

The mobilization model is essentially quantitative. It deals with *amounts* of collective action, resources and collective goods rather than with their qualities. Unless we can find some way of establishing the quantitative equivalences among different sorts of collective actions, resources, and collective goods, furthermore, the model will only apply to the simplest situations. With the discussion of repression and facilitation, we wandered into the comparison of different kinds of contender and different sorts of collective action. But by and large we noticed qualitative variations without building them into the mobilization model.

We face an important choice. We can continue the step-by-step exploration and elaboration of the mobilization and polity models. Or we can jump headlong into the world of time and qualitative variation. I hope many of my readers will follow the first course: revising the mobilization and polity models to deal effectively with time, quality, and strategic interaction, then scrutinizing the evidence to see if the models work right. I plan to keep at that work myself, but elsewhere. The next three chapters will follow the second course. They will make loose applications of the models to major historical problems in the study of collective action. Chapter 5 treats changes in the prevalent forms of contentious collective action which occurred in western countries as large-scale industry developed, cities grew, powerful national states formed, and capitalism expanded. Chapter 6 deals with the relationship between collective action and collective violence. Chapter 7 discusses rebellion and revolution. Then, at the end, we take one more look at the general logic of collective action.

5
Changing Forms of Collective Action

THE FORMS OF CONTENTION

Real people do not get together and Act Collectively. They meet to petition Parliament, organize telephone campaigns, demonstrate outside of city hall, attack powerlooms, go on strike. The abstract mobilization model we have been using has many virtues, but it tends to obscure two fundamental facts. First, collective action generally involves interaction with specific other groups, including governments. Collective action rarely consists of solitary performances. People do not ordinarily act to influence abstract structures such as polities and markets; they try to get particular other people to do particular things. As a consequence, explanations of collective action which concentrate on the capacities and inclinations of one participant at a time—or the average capacities and inclinations of all participants—will leave us disappointed.

Second, collective action usually takes well-defined forms already familiar to the participants, in the same sense that most of an era's art takes on of a small number of established forms. Because of that, neither the search for universal forms (such as those sometimes proposed for crowds or revolutions) nor the assumption of an infinity of means to group ends will take us very far. Because of that, the study of the concrete forms of collective action immediately draws us into thinking about the cultural settings in which more forms appear. Much of the pleasure and adventure in the historical study of collective action comes from the rich complexity of the material: having to learn how and why the Parisians of 1789 paraded severed heads on pikes, how and why the young people of Berkeley, California occupied a makeshift park in 1969.

Putting the two themes together opens the way to a first rough classification of forms of collective action. The classification stresses the nature of the interaction between other groups and the group whose action we are classifying. More precisely, it depends on the claims the collective actors are asserting in their action: *competitive* claims, *reactive* claims, or *proactive* claims. The classification leaves out pursuit of common ends which involve no claims on other groups: pure recreation, contemplation, escape. In fact, it applies most easily where the claims express a conflict of interest among the parties. I have worked out the categories in studying the evolution of forms of conflict in western Europe, and will illustrate them from European experience.

Competitive actions lay claim to resources also claimed by other groups which the actor defines as rivals, competitors, or at least as participants in the same contest. Take the *charivari*—the American "shivaree"—for an example. Only recently have European historians begun to uncover the large base of competition and control on which this ostensibly frivolous custom rested. John Gillis (1974: 30–31) describes one standard version:

> In a typical rural charivari, a recently remarried widower might find himself awakened by the clamor of the crowd, an effigy of his dead wife thrust up to his window and a likeness of himself, placed backward on an ass, drawn through the streets for his neighbors to see. Paying of a "contribution" to the Lord of Misrule might quiet his youthful tormentors, but by that time the voices of village conscience had made their point. Second marriages invariably drew the greatest wrath and, by contrast, endogamous marriages of young people of roughly the same age were the occasion of the youth group's rejoicing. In that case, the functions of charivari were reversed and the couple were accompanied by a noisy crowd to their wedding bed, the ritual send-off of its former members by the peer group. The marriage feast, and the Abbey's participation in it, symbolized the central purpose of the youth group, which was to provide a prolonged rite of passage from roughly the onset of puberty to the point of marriage.

The English often called their similar custom Rough Music. Most of the time, it was a contained but raucous affair, accompanied by the thumping of pans and blowing of horns. The charivari became a "disorder" to the eyes (and, no doubt, the ears) of the authorities when it persisted more than a night or two, or when dozens of young people joined the fun.

The precise form of the charivari differed considerably from one region of Europe to another. Within Great Britain, E. P. Thompson distinguishes four main variants:

a) *ceffyl pren* (Welsh for "wooden horse"), which is associated with the Rebecca Riots in many parts of Wales;

b) "Riding the stang," commonly practiced in the Scottish Lowlands and the north of England;

c) the Skimmington or Skimmety parade, which still survived in the nineteenth century in the West, as well as in some regions of the South; and finally

d) Rough Music itself, without a parade, but in the course of which people often burned effigies of the victims; a widespread custom, but found especially in the Midlands and the South (Thompson 1972: 287–288).

In addition to the shivaree, variants of these other forms of action remain embedded in American folklore, even if they have come unstuck from daily practice: riding someone out of town on a rail, parading and burning effigies, and so on.

Village age-groups were the typical initiators of charivaris. The organization and functions of age-groups varied considerably from one part of Europe to another. (For regional patterns in France, e.g., see Varagnac 1947.) They often had responsibility for Lenten bonfires and other celebrations. They sometimes controlled the pairing up of young couples for bundling and courting. Village age-groups also fought the youth of neighboring villages, sometimes to the death. They often assembled as a bloc at public ceremonies, sometimes mounting elaborate charades to mock and warn those who had transgressed their rules. All these activities affirmed their priority over the eligible females and over the rituals of courtship within their own villages. Within their limited sphere, the activities were deadly serious.

The charivari, the village fight, and the youth group's mocking ceremony had many kin. There were brawls between student groups, between different detachments of soldiers, between soldiers and civilians, between ethnic and religious groups. There were the more highly routinized struggles of rival groups of artisans to dishonor each other's symbols, impede each other's ceremonies, and challenge each other's priority in processions and other public assemblies. Somehow these forms of action seem trivial and quaint to twentieth-century people. We of this century have seen giant wars and mass murder, and have come to think of "serious" politics as having a national or international scope. The events in question were, indeed, usually small, short-lived, localized. They rarely linked with revolutionary movements or great rebellions. Yet they left their toll of dead and injured. In times of crisis, they blended into major conflicts. They were important forms of collective action.

Some features of collective competition, such as the ritualized mockery, carried over into the second major category: *reactive* collective actions. (We can also call them collective reactions.) They consist of group efforts to reassert established claims when someone else challenges or violates them. Speaking of peasant land invasions in contemporary Peru, E. J. Hobsbawm points out that they take three forms: squatting on land to which no one (or only the government) has a clear title, expropriating land to which the invaders have not previously enjoyed a claim and to which someone else has repossessing land from which the invaders have themselves been expropriated (Hobsbawm 1974: 120–121).

The third variant is the clear reactive case: the dispossessed react. That sort of land reoccupation characterized the first stages of Zapata's rebellion during the Mexican Revolution, recurred through much of southern Italy during the massive nineteenth-century concentration of land in bourgeois and noble hands, and marked the consolidation of bourgeois landownership wherever it developed in the presence of solidary peasant communities. In a standard European scenario, a group of villagers who had long pastured their cattle, gathered firewood, and gleaned in common fields, found a landlord or a local official (or, more likely, the two in collaboration) fencing the fields by newly acquired or newly asserted right of property. The villagers commonly warned against the fencing. If the warning went unheeded, they attacked the fences and the fencers. They acted in the name of rights they still considered valid.

The overlap with collective competition appeared clearly when costumed avengers tore down the fences or occupied the fields, as in the Demoiselles movement of the 1830s in the Pyrenees (see Merriman 1975). In other collective reactions, the overlap was at least as notable, for in both cases the actors commonly assumed, more or less self-consciously, the role of the authorities who were being derelict in their duty, and the groups which reacted were often the same local solidarities: the youth groups, guilds, and so on.

The basic outline of the land occupation applied to the bulk of European food riots, machine breaking, tax rebellions, and local actions against military conscription: all moved directly against someone who had unjustly deprived, or tried to deprive, a local population of a precious resource. Yves-Marie Bercé, expanding on his comprehensive analysis of the seventeenth-century rebellion of the *Croquants* in southwestern France, has proposed that the kernel of European peasant rebellions before the nineteenth century was the resistance of closed, solidary peasant communities to outside attempts to infringe upon their established rights and routines. In the case of seventeenth-century France, he distinguishes four major occasions for rebellions: high food prices, billeting of troops, tax collection, and the imposition of excise taxes by tax farmers. In all these cases, says Bercé, "Revolt is the strategy of the little people, an extraordinary organization for defense against fiscal aggression" (Bercé 1974: II, 680–681).

As community solidarity declined, according to Bercé, the concerted peasant rebellion disappeared. Only much later did farmers and agricultura workers reappear in action; now they were organized around forward-looking special-interest groups. Although (as Bercé himself concedes) the scheme homogenizes unduly the participants and motives in the older forms of conflict, it captures an essential contrast. It is the contrast between reactive and proactive forms of collective actions.

Proactive collective actions assert group claims which have not previously been exercised. (We may also call them instances of collective proaction.) The strike for higher wages or better working conditions provides an everyday illustration. Deliberate work stoppages to gain a point have probably existed since people first worked for one another. Natalie Davis (1975: 1–16) describes well-organized strikes in sixteenth-century Lyons. But the strike only became a common way of doing public business in the nineteenth century. As wage work in organizations larger than households expanded, the number and scale of strikes expanded. In most western countries, fifty to a hundred years went by in which strikes were increasingly frequent but remained illegal—sometimes prosecuted, sometimes broken up by armed force, sometimes tolerated, always disapproved. Under pressure from organized workers and their parliamentary allies, most western governments legalized the strike between 1860 and 1900. Since then, states that have stepped up repression (states of emergency, wartime governments, Fascist regimes) have normally rescinded the right to strike, and all regimes have negotiated continually with workers and employers over who had the right to strike, and how. But in general the strike has been widely available as a means of action since the beginning of the twentieth century.

Government sanction of the strike shows up in strike statistics; they date from the 1880s or 1890s in most western countries. Their appearance reflects the working out of a standard public definition of the word "strike," and the formation of a bureaucracy to monitor and regulate the strike's use. In France, Michelle Perrot (1974) argues that the strike lost much of its expressive function, its festival air, its revolutionary potential, as the bureaucratization of the 1890s set in. By way of compensation, it became a more widely accessible, less risky way of making demands.

Several other forms of collective proaction came into their own during the nineteenth century. The demonstration, the sponsored public meeting and the petition drive began to thrive with the arrival of mass electoral politics. The seizure of premises by an insurrectionary committee also generalized during the nineteenth century, although the ties to electoral politics are more distant. The military *pronunciamento* is of the same vintage. On the other hand, the general strike, the sit-in, and the farmers' dumping of surplus crops in protest are essentially twentieth-century creations. Proactive forms of collective action have proliferated over the last two centuries.

This labeling of forms has two catches. First, although we are dealing with situations in which contenders interact, we are not classifying the interactions themselves. On the whole, if one group is engaging in collective proaction, then at least one of its partners is engaging in collective reaction: a group of dissident colonels attempts a coup, the junta defends itself against the coup. Landlords band together to raise rents, peasants band together to resist the raising of rents. Only the collective competition is usually symmetrical: when one party jockeys for a visible position in a public ceremony, so does another.

Second catch. Strictly speaking, a public meeting or a general strike could fit any of the three types: competitive, reactive, or proactive. Just as the charivari could mock a wrongdoer or celebrate a rightdoer, people can demonstrate for something, against something, or both for one thing and against another thing at the same time. The classification as competitive, reactive, or proactive depends on the claims being asserted, not on the form of the action. The squatting and expropriating land occupations described by Hobsbawm have a far more proactive flavor than the reoccupations of lost land. Workers have often struck in defense of threatened job rights. Those strikes were reactive.

Yet the general correlation persists. In general, the demonstration and the strike have been privileged vehicles for new claims, have risen in periods and places in which ordinary people were articulating new demands, and are peculiarly suitable to the effort to make gains rather than to forestall losses. In general, the tax rebellion, the food riots, and similar events have cascaded when ordinary people were defending their rights against attack, and make little sense as means of stating new claims. On the average, the demonstration and the strike are proactive, the food riot and tax rebellion reactive.

In Europe of the last few hundred years, the three forms of collective action have waxed and waned in sequence. In the fifteenth and sixteenth centuries, competitive actions seem to have predominated. From the seventeenth into the nineteenth century, the reactive forms became much more widespread, while the competitive forms remained steady or perhaps declined. With the nineteenth and twentieth centuries, collective proaction began to predominate, the reactive forms dwindled, while new forms of competition came into existence. If I read the record aright, seventeenth- and eighteenth-century Europeans took collective action in defense of threatened rights much more than their predecessors had, while twentieth-century Europeans became exceptionally prone to act in support of claims they had not previously exercised.

The reasons for the successive changes are, I think, twofold: (1) during the period from 1600 to 1850, more so than before and after, the agents of international markets and of national states were pressing their new (and proactive) claims on resources which had up to then been under the control of innumerable households, communities, brotherhoods, and other small-scale organizations. The small-scale organizations reacted repeatedly, fighting against taxation, conscription, the consolidation of landed property, and numerous other threats to their organizational well-being. Eventually the big structures won, the battle died down, the reactive forms diminished. (2) Increasingly, the pools of resources necessary to group survival came under the control of large organizations, especially governments, which only redistributed them under the pressure of new claims.

There may be a third factor: (3) a general decline in the costs of mobilization and collective action during the nineteenth and twentieth centuries. Such a decline might have resulted from the massing of population in large settlements and big organizations, from the elaboration of communications and from the expansion of elections as a way of doing public business. This is roughly the same set of changes which Karl Deutsch calls Social Mobilization, and which Amitai Etzioni regards as making possible the self-directed Active Society. If the analysis of the previous chapter is correct, however, we could only expect such changes to elevate the level of collective action if the relationship between contenders and their interests altered. For a fixed set of interests and a given level of opportunity/threat, a general decline in the costs of mobilization and collective action could well depress the level of collective action.

Figure 5-1 shows how that could happen. (It illustrates the problem for a zealot—a contender which aims at a narrow range of collective goods and is prepared to take what others would regard as a loss in order to achieve those goods—but applies equally to misers and run-of-the-mill contenders. Opportunists present, as we shall see, another problem.) Under high costs (curve A for expected returns from collective action), our contender would be unable to attain its interest, regardless of its mobilization level or the current constellation of opportunities; all we could reasonably anticipate in that case would be defensive action to forestall threats: collective action of amount A on the resources-expended axis. Under medium costs (curve B), the contender can achieve its entire interest in new collective goods and forestall threats at the same time by placing its action in the range from B_1 to B_2. (Being a zealot, the contender has no interest in the higher returns obtainable by pushing a bit beyond B_2—but not too far—on the resources-expended scale.) But note what happens if costs become very low: curve C applies. In this case, the present levels of opportunity and mobilization permit our contender a very high return indeed. Because the contender's defined interest remains the same, however, it can achieve the same objectives with a smaller amount of collective action than when costs are medium. Now the ideal range of collective action runs from C_1 to C_2. Lowering costs lowers the expected level of collective action.

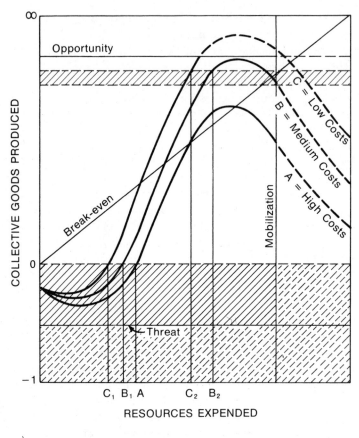

 Interest

Potential Interest

Fig. 5-1
Hypothetical effects of lowered costs of collective action on a zealot

To be sure, the relationship between contenders and their interests may
alter in some regular fashion as costs decline. The most obvious alternative is
the one proposed long ago by Robert Michels. "The revolutionary political
party," said Michels,

> is a state within a state, pursuing the avowed aim of destroying the existing state
> in order to substitute for it a social order of a fundamentally different character.
> To attain this essentially political end, the party avails itself of the socialist orga-
> nization, whose sole justification is found precisely in its patient but systematic
> preparation for the destruction of the organization of the state in its existing form.

The subversive party organizes the *framework* of the social revolution. For this reason it continually endeavors to strengthen its positions, to extend its bureaucratic mechanism, to store up its energies and its funds (Michels 1949: 384-385).

The Iron Law of Oligarchy—that every successful struggle ends with the establishment of a governing elite—thus applies, according to Michels, to democratic revolutionaries as well as to all others.

Translated into the code we have been using, the Iron Law takes two forms. First, the process of mobilization in itself transforms the group's defined interests; those who lead the contender's mobilization acquire the desire and the means to maintain the organization they have built and to identify their special interests with those of the group as a whole. Second, the lowering of costs increases the gap between the group's mobilization level and the resources it must expend to achieve its ends. That produces a surplus. The accretion of a surplus might logically lead to demobilization. But according to Michels it encourages the oligarchs to divert the available resources to ends which they themselves define as desirable. In the extreme case, the new interests which emerge do not even include the interests which originally brought the contender into existence. In the extreme case, a zealot becomes an opportunist, ready to act for a wide variety of collective goods, prepared to strike for the best return available, but unwilling to act in the face of a probable loss. The "social movement organizations" in contemporary America analyzed by McCarthy and Zald (1973) come close to this caricature.

We must also weigh something else against the presumed cost-cutting effects of communications improvements, the installation of free elections, and the like: the increased repressive activity and repressive efficiency of governments and other large organizations. Intrinsic costs are down. But the costs imposed by others are up. I guess that the intrinsic costs have declined more than the imposed costs have risen. In the present state of our knowledge, however, that judgment is both risky and unverifiable.

REPERTOIRES OF COLLECTIVE ACTION

At any point in time, the repertoire of collective actions available to a population is surprisingly limited. Surprisingly, given the innumerable ways in which people could, in principle, deploy their resources in pursuit of common ends. Surprisingly, given the many ways real groups have pursued their own common ends at one time or another.

Most twentieth-century Americans, for example, know how to demonstrate. They know that a group with a claim to make assemblies in a public place, identifies itself and its demands or complaints in a visible way, orients its common action to the persons, properties, or symbols of some other group it is seeking to influence. Within those general rules, most Americans know how to carry on several different forms of demonstration: the massed march, the assembly with speechmaking, the temporary occupation of premises. Moreover, there are some specifiable circumstances in which most Americans would actually apply their knowledge by joining a real demonstration. Americans who have not learned this complicated set of actions through personal participation have nonetheless witnessed demonstrations directly, read about them, watched them on television. Various forms of demonstration belong to the *repertoire* of twentieth-century Americans—not to mention twentieth-century Canadians, Japanese, Greeks, Brazilians, and many others. The repertoire also includes several varieties of strikes, petitioning, the organization of pressure groups, and a few other ways of articulating grievances and demands.

Few Americans, on the other hand, know how to organize the hijacking of an airplane, despite the publicity hijackings have received in recent years; even fewer would seriously consider hijacking as a way of accomplishing their collective objectives. Hijacking belongs to the repertoire of only a few groups anywhere. Machine breaking, once a frequent occurrence, has dropped out of the repertoire. So have the charivari and the serenade. So has the regular intervillage fight; only football remains to remind us of that old form of bloodletting.

Almost no one anywhere is now familiar with a form of action which was once common in Europe: the rebellion in which an existing, functioning group, such as an army or a community assembles, casts off its constituted authorities, commissions that successor (who knows full well that once the action is completed he is likely to be hanged, or worse, for his pains) to present a set of grievances and demands to a higher authority, resists with determination until those demands have been met or until it has been utterly destroyed, then returns to its previous state of submission to the constituted authorities. Remember the recurrent revolts of the victorious but unpaid Spanish armies in the Netherlands toward the end of the sixteenth century: they regularly elected their own chief, the *electo*; they declared they would follow no one else's orders until their demands for back pay and other benefits were satisfied. They sometimes continued to fight, even to fight heroically, but under their own direction. They sometimes pillaged when it appeared their demands would not be met. They always demanded amnesty for all actions committed during the rebellion—and they usually won. Armies mattered to the Spanish king (Parker 1973).

Or recall the Pilgrimage of Grace, the great Yorkshire rising of 1536 against Henry VIII's dispossession of the monasteries and against other measures designed to increase the royal revenues. The "commons" rose by tens of thousands, took gentlemen for their captains and London lawyer Robert Aske as their chief captain. They eventually controlled much of the North. But the Duke of Norfolk's vague, lying promises to take their case to the King dispersed them. By July of 1537 Robert Aske had died on a scaffold at the castle of York, and two hundred other rebels had perished at the executioner's hand (Dodds and Dodds 1915). The word "mutiny" still conveys a sense of that old form of action. But now we use the term almost exclusively in a military context. We fail to recognize that it was once an established, if risky, path out of an intolerable situation.

Hijacking, mutiny, machine breaking, charivaris, village fights, tax rebellions, foot riots, collective self-immolation, lynching, vendetta have all belonged to the standard collective-action repertoire of some group at some time. In one setting or another, people have known routinely how to initiate every one of them. People have at sometime recognized every one of them as a legitimate, feasible way of acting on an unsatisfied grievance or aspiration. Most of these forms of action are technically feasible in contemporary America. Yet they occur rarely, or not at all. More important, no substantial American group with a pressing grievance or aspiration considers any of them to be a genuine alternative to demonstrating, striking, petitioning, or forming a pressure group. They do not belong to the contemporary American repertoire of collective action.

To specify the meaning of repertoire, it helps to ask this question: to what degree does the group prefer the means it has used before over those which are theoretically available for the same purpose? That is a difficult question to answer in the real world. It is hard to know two things: (1) what other forms of action are really "available" to a group, (2) the relative appropriateness and efficiency of the means the group actually uses and the alternative means which are theoretically available. However, two sorts of natural experiments occur often enough to provide information on the subject. First, similar groups in similar settings sometimes use quite different means of collective action. In the 1950s, for example, we find Swedish transport workers taking their grievances to government agencies while their British counterparts go out on strike. Second, the means of collective action alter and spread from one group to another. For instance, in the Italy of 1919 sit-down strikes were rather a novelty. But by August 1920 half a million workers were occupying their factories. Given such events, we can gauge the importance of repertoires by comparing the successive choices of similar groups and by observing innovation and diffusion in the means of action.

Figure 5–2 presents four possible results of such comparisons. In each case, we are dealing with a group which is preparing to act collectively in circumstances similar to other circumstances it has faced before. We identify all the means which are theoretically or practically "available" to the group, and then array them in terms of their similarity to the means the group has previ-

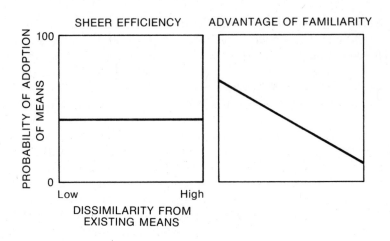

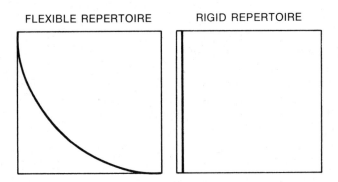

Fig. 5–2
Four models of group readiness to adopt new means of collective action

ously employed. In the sheer-efficiency model, similarity to familiar means makes no difference; the only question is the appropriateness of the means to the end. That model is extreme; it may, in fact, be more efficient to use familiar means because familiarity itself leads to better execution. The advantage-of-familiarity model takes that likelihood into account; it postulates a smooth gradient in the probability of adoption from most familiar to least familiar. The model implies that familiarity is simply one of several factors affecting the choice of a particular means from among all those which are theoretically available. The third model describes a flexible repertoire. In this case, the group has a heavy bias toward means it has previously used, but is not completely closed to innovation. Finally, the rigid-repertoire model describes a group which chooses familiar means unfailingly. To the extent that this model applies, we would expect innovation to be rare, and to occur through breaks and crises.

If the sheer-efficiency or advantage-of-familiarity model applies, it is misleading to speak of repertoires of collective action. Only in the third and fourth cases is the word a useful summary of the reality. Thus we have an empirical test for the utility of the concept: how close the observable behavior of collective actors comes to one or another of the four models. My own hypothesis is that the flexible repertoire is the most general case for organized groups. The less organized the group, the more likely that the advantage-of-familiarity model will describe its behavior. We might reasonably suppose that a contender—especially a member of the polity—which remains in the same power position for a long time tends to move from a flexible to a rigid repertoire. Routinization sets in. It is hard, on the other hand, to imagine any contender maintaining the sheer-efficiency pattern for a significant span of time.

A flexible repertoire permits continuous, gradual change in the group's means. The change may occur through imitation of other groups or through innovation. The imitation of other groups is most likely when the members of one contender observe that another contender is using a new means successfully, or newly using an old means successfully. That is no doubt one of the main reasons "waves" of strikes or demonstrations occur: the fact that a given sort of group gets somewhere with the tactic spreads the expectation that employers or governments will be vulnerable to the same tactic in the hands of other similar groups.

Innovation is rarer, and harder to explain. One of the main processes is surely the stretching of the boundaries of forms of action which already belong to the repertoire. In the early nineteenth century, for instance, we begin to see the French charivari in a new guise. It no longer aimed exclusively at cuckolds, May–September marriages, and couples who failed to treat the local bachelors to the customary nuptial celebration. Many charivaris began to dramatize the opposition of local people to a particular public official or political candidate. Likewise, the complimentary serenade extended to political figures who had enthusiastic popular support. In France, the first half of the nineteenth century was the heyday of the political charivari/serenade. Then the institution gave way to the demonstration, the rally, the public banquet, and the formal meeting.

In a parallel fashion, the American patriots who mobilized from the Stamp Act crisis onward adapted old English customs such as tarring and feathering or riding the stang (riding a reprobate out of town on a rail). Now these shaming actions coupled with mock public trials, and applied to Loyalists and other presumed enemies of the colonists. In the French and American cases, both the form of the action and its object changed. But in both cases the basic action was already part of the popular repertoire.

A population's repertoire of collective action generally includes only a handful of alternatives. It generally changes slowly, seems obvious and natural to the people involved. It resembles an elementary language: familiar as the day to its users, for all its possible quaintness or incomprehensibility to an outsider. How, then, does such a repertoire come into being? How does it change? The answer surely includes at least these elements:

1   the standards of rights and justice prevailing in the population;
2   the daily routines of the population;
3   the population's internal organization;
4   its accumulated experience with prior collective action;
5   the pattern of repression in the world to which the population belongs.

Let us think briefly about each of these elements.

The prevailing standards of rights and justice govern the acceptability of the components of various possible types of collective action. They do not necessarily govern the particular form of action. For example, a group which considers that the set of persons directly producing an object or a service has a prior right to its consumption is likely to condone some kinds of forcible resistance to expropriation of objects and services. That is the implicit rationale of the modern European food riot and tax rebellion. As important rights came to be invested in, and sometimes guaranteed by, the national state, collective action itself nationalized.

The population's daily routines matter because they affect the ease with which one or another of the possible forms of action can actually be carried on. The strike becomes feasible when considerable numbers of people assemble to work in the same location. The notable shift of collective action away from routine assemblies such as markets and festivals toward deliberately called gatherings as in demonstrations and strikes resulted in part from the residential dispersion of occupational groups and of others who shared a common interest. They no longer came together casually and discussed their common grievances or aspirations incidentally. In that process, the participation of European women in collective action declined noticeably; the segregated worlds of politics and labor organization became male preserves.

In European and American cities, that process of segregation passed through three rough stages. In the first, there was little distinction between home and work. For example, craftsmen lived and gathered in their shops and n the nearby streets. The growth of larger firms and workplaces produced a separation of home and work. The typical arrangement, however, was for workers to crowd into dwellings within walking distance of their shops, offices, and hiring sites. Thus distinctive working-class neighborhoods formed. They tended to be small in scale and segregated by craft. Between the workplace and the home grew up gathering places frequented by single groups of workers: pubs, cafes, union halls, social clubs. With the further growth in the size and segregation of workplaces, journeys to work became longer and working-class neighborhoods larger but more heterogeneous with respect to crafts. Gathering with your fellow workers near the workplace became less and less feasible.

These changes in workers' daily routines generally raised the mobilization costs of particular trades. They therefore tended to reduce the level of collective action by trade. At the same time, the changes may have lowered the costs of mobilization for the urban working class as a whole. That possibility deserves further investigation. For the present discussion, however, the important thing to notice is that the *form* of working-class collective action changed in conjunction with the alteration of urban form. To the first of our rough stages (the period of little or no home–work separation) correspond a repertoire of small-scale actions which built directly on the structure of the trade: the petition from the leaders of the craft, the public procession, the staged battle between rival groups of artisans, and so on. In the intermediate stage of larger workplaces and adjacent homogeneous dwelling areas we see the rise of the strike, the blacklist of uncooperative employers, the ostracism or punishment of nonconforming workers, and so forth. At the stage of large firms and extensive home–work separation, the deliberately called meeting, rally, demonstration, and strike took over.

In this set of changes, it is hard to distinguish the effects of alterations in daily routines from the effects of our next factor: changes in the relevant groups' internal organization. Daily routines and internal organization overlap. The three stages correspond approximately to pure craft organization, the organization of proletarianizing trades, and the full-fledged proletarian structure. The religious confraternity is a characteristic expression of solidarity at the first stage, the mutual-benefit society at the second, the bureaucratic trade union at the third. These shifts in organization interact with changing daily routines to make different forms of collective action feasible and advantageous.

Prior experience also counts. The relevant experience includes both the contender's own successes or failures and the contender's observations of other similar groups. We see that blend of previous practice and observation in the rich street theater which grew up in the American colonies from the Stamp Act crisis of 1765 to the Revolution. Mock trials, parading of effigies, ritualized attacks on the homes and offices of royal officials, tarring and feathering of Loyalists accompanied petitions, declarations, and solemn assemblies. Within weeks of Boston's first display of a boot containing a devil as a symbol of Stamp Act promoter Lord Bute, the boot and devil had become standard participants in urban gatherings to oppose the Stamp Act up and down the American coast. The particular form and content of these gatherings were new. But all their principal elements were already well-established ways of dealing with declared enemies of the people. The prior experience of urban sailors, artisans, and merchants shaped the revolutionary repertoire of collective action.

Repression likewise affects the repertoire. Repression makes a large difference in the short run because other powerful groups affect the relative costs and probable returns of different forms of action theoretically available to a particular group. It also matters in the long run because that sort of cost setting tends to eliminate some forms of action as it channels behavior into others. The widespread legalization of the strike in the 1860s and 1870s so increased its attractiveness relative to direct attacks on employers and on industrial property that the latter virtually disappeared from the workers' repertoire. All these changes, however, occur with a lag. The forms of collective action which worked during the last crisis have a special appeal during this one as well. Thus the successes and failures of contention for power produce changes in the repertoire of collective action, but only within the limits set by the actors' own daily routines and conceptions of justice.

The idea of a standard repertoire of collective actions, if correct, simplifies the study of variations in collective action from one place, time, and population to another. It simplifies by breaking the problem into two parts: how the population in question came to have its particular repertoire, how the population selected a particular form of action (or no action at all) from that repertoire. The analysis of innovation in collective action—for example, the invention and diffusion of the sit-in as a way of pressing for equal rights in public accommodations—breaks neatly into the same two parts.

The idea of a standard repertoire also provides insight into "contagion" and "spontaneity" in collective action. It raises the possibility that when a particular form of riot or demonstration spreads rapidly, what diffuses is not the model of the behavior itself, but the information—correct or not—that the costs and benefits associated with the action have suddenly changed. The news that the authorities are (or are not) cracking down on demonstrators in city A filters rapidly to city B, and influences the estimates of potential demonstrators in city B as to the probable consequences of demonstrating. In that regard the grouches who argue that governmental "permissiveness" will encourage more agitation are often right. It is clear, likewise, that an action can be "spontaneous" in the sense of not having been planned in advance by any of the participants, and yet be highly organized, even ritualized. There the grouches are usually wrong; the grouchy inclination is to attribute sustained, concerted action to some sort of conspiracy.

A Case in Point: The Strike

Over the last century or so, the most visible alteration of the working-class repertoire of collective action in western countries has been the rise of the strike. Some form of concerted work stoppage goes far back in time. What is more, the idea must have been invented independently many times; the disparate words for the strike which emerged in various European languages suggest multiple origins: sciopero, turnout, Streik, grève, zabastovka, huelga. Nevertheless, strikes were rare events at the beginning of the nineteenth century. By 1900, they were routine facts of working-class life. They were generally illegal, and frequently prosecuted, in 1800. A century later, they were generally legal, and rarely prosecuted. What is more, in most western countries the intensity of strike activity continued to rise past the middle of the twentieth century (see Hibbs 1976). In the process, strikes routinized: settled down to a few standard formats, acquired their own jurisprudence, became objects of official statistics. By "routinized," I do not mean "calmed down." Despite the complex, standard rules according to which they are played, professional hockey matches are often angry, bone-crunching affairs. The same is true of strikes.

How and why did strikes enter the repertoire? In multiple ways, proletarianization created the strike. By definition, proletarianization created the worker who exercised little or no discretionary control over the means of production and who was dependent for survival on the sale of his or her labor power. That proletarian and the worker threatened with becoming that proletarian have long been the chief participants in strikes. (The word "proletarian" has, alas, recently lost some of the precision Marx gave it in *Das Kapital*. In Marx's analysis the central elements were separation from the means of production + wage labor. Agricultural workers were, in fact, the chief historical case Marx discussed. He certainly did not concentrate on unskilled factory workers.) Of all workers, the proletarian most clearly had interests opposing him directly to his employer. The proletarian had the most to gain through the withholding of labor power, and the least to gain by other means.

Now, the pace of proletarianization increased greatly during the nineteenth century. My own minimum guess is that in Europe as a whole from 1800 to 1900, while the total population rose from about 190 million to 500 million, the proletarian population increased from about 90 million to 300 million. If that is true, the very kinds of workers who were the prime candidates for strike activity were multiplying. Furthermore, many strikes were *about* proletarianization. Whether the immediate issue was wages, hours, or working conditions, the underlying struggle commonly turned about the employer's effort to exercise greater and greater control over the disposition of the means of production, and therefore over the worker's own use of his labor.

In his lucid analysis of "remuneration systems," Bernard Mottez discusses the broad nineteenth-century movement from various forms of task compensation to various forms of time-effort compensation. A clear example of task compensation is the set of contracting systems (*marchandage*) in which a family or work team undertook to produce a certain number of finished objects meeting certain standards at an agreed-upon price. Much mining, woodworking, and textile production once took place under contracting arrangements. Indeed, early quasi-factories often consisted of assemblages of more or less autonomous artisans who brought their own tools and materials into a common workplace. (Michael Hanagan gives the example of the artisanal filemakers of nineteenth-century Le Chambon–Feugerolles, near St. Etienne, who sometimes worked at home and sometimes in small shops, depending on personal inclination and the current level of activity in the trade.)

Time-effort compensation takes many forms, but the two most obvious are the hourly wage and piecework. Piecework differs greatly from taskwork: the employer characteristically owns the materials, tools, and workplace, and controls the basic location, timing, and routines of the work; in addition, the "piece" in question is not normally a finished product, but one small portion of it. Most contemporary forms of production incentives fall into the same category. They assume a proletarian labor force, while taskwork and contracting assume workers who have substantial control over the means and conditions of production.

As Mottez points out, a nineteenth-century entrepreneur who wanted to assemble a group of relatively skilled workers into a good-sized productive unit had no choice but to adopt some form of task compensation. But when capital accumulated, when the scale of production rose, and when innovations in technology and work discipline made it possible to routinize, subdivide, and demystify the basic productive tasks, employers pushed toward greater and greater preplanning and surveillance of the entire process. That included pushing toward time-effort compensation.

In general, workers resisted the entire process when they could. Not that they were simple conservatives; although on the average they did prefer work arrangements they knew and could somehow manage to those they did not know, their resistance sometimes took the form of demands for radical reorganization of work and social life: the word "socialism" itself originally repreented the vision of a *social* order in which producers would control their own ates. The strike grew up as one of the primary means by which artisans threatened with proletarianization and semiproletarians threatened with complete oss of control over the disposition of their labor fought back.

If my analysis is correct, the strike entered the collective-action repertoires of European workers as a reactive means, but later became a primary means of collective proaction. In the process, the strike routinized. One sign is ts legalization. Most western countries legalized some form of strike activity during the latter half of the nineteenth century; Great Britain led the way in 824. Saxony followed in 1861, France in 1864, Belgium in 1866, Prussia in 869, Austria in 1870. Another sign is the advent of regular statistical reporting: the 1880s and 1890s saw the launching of annual strike statistics in many vestern countries, including the United States. A third sign is the growth of professional bureaucracies devoted to monitoring, regulating, reporting and, on occasion, settling strikes. These officials, employers, and organized workers hammered out standard definitions of strikes and lockouts. They worked out rules concerning the proper behavior of the parties to a strike. They developed means of registering and publicizing a strike's end and outcome. They, the courts, police, and other public officials were fixing the precise place of the strike in the day's repertoire of collective action. To be sure, the rules remained uncertain in important regards, the rules changed as the balance of power changed, and most of the rule making occurred as a by-product of bitter struggle. That is the way repertoires of collective action usually change.

Michelle Perrot's collective biography of the roughly 3,000 strikes which occurred in France from 1870 to 1890 catches an important period in the routinization of the strike. The book is a feast: rich with the folklore, rhetoric, and tactics of strike activity, jammed with telling observation on the contexts of the issues about which workers struck. The largest theme of the book, however, is that the 1890s tamed and drilled the strike, which had previously displayed great spontaneity and had expressed the immediate concerns of workers quite directly. The growth of large, centralized labor unions, in Perrot's view, helped smother the strike's creativity, its spontaneity, perhaps its revolutionary potential. On the last point some doubt remains: the 1890s brought a great swelling of strike activity, an outpouring of revolutionary displays on the occasion of May Day and the great strikes, and the heyday of anarcho-syndicalism. Furthermore, smaller-scale workers' organizations had been crucial to the development of local strike activity before 1890. Nevertheless, the main observation stands: through an interplay of unions, workers, government, and employers, the strike was indeed standardizing.

In terms of the checklist of factors in the production of collective-action repertoires which we looked at earlier, the nineteenth-century crystallization of the strike looks something like this:

1 *Prevailing standards of rights and justice:* artisanal view that the contribution of labor gives a right to control the disposition of its product and the conditions of its use, confronting bourgeois view that the ownership of capital bestows a right to its untrammeled disposition.

2 *Daily routines of the population:* increasing concentration of workers in large shops and the equivalent.

3 *Population's internal organization:* combination of residues of craft organization, employer pressure toward proletarianization, increasing residential segregation of workers.

4 *Accumulated experience with collective action:* demonstrated success of artisanal strikes, failure of appeals to officials and patrons.

5 *Pattern of repression:* increasing readiness of governments to tolerate limited forms of strike activity.

None of these explains the *invention* of the strike, which goes back well before the nineteenth century. But they are a convenient inventory of the major factors in the nineteenth-century emergence of the strike as a standard workers' performance in western countries.

The strike continued to change in the twentieth century. Figure 5–3 shows several aspects of that alteration for France from 1890 to 1954. The three-dimensional graphs represent the median duration, the number of strikers per strike, and the strike rate in terms of strikes per year per 100,000 workers in the labor force. The volume of the solid gives an approximation of striker-days per year. The shape of the solid then sums up the combination of length, size, and frequency of strikes. In the 1890s, French strikes were relatively small and infrequent, but they tended to last a long time. In the 1950s, French strikes averaged large and frequent, but short. That general change in shape was very common in western countries (Shorter and Tilly 1974: chapter 12). It reflected among other things, the shift from small shops, artisanal organization, and local unions toward large plants, fully proletarian workers, and large-scale unions.

While these changes were quite general, national patterns of strike activity diverged considerably. The general withering away of the strike which many theorists expected to come with "mature" industrialization failed to materialize; strike frequencies, sizes, and volumes generally rose after World War I and remained high or climbed even higher after World War II. Yet important contrasts opened up.

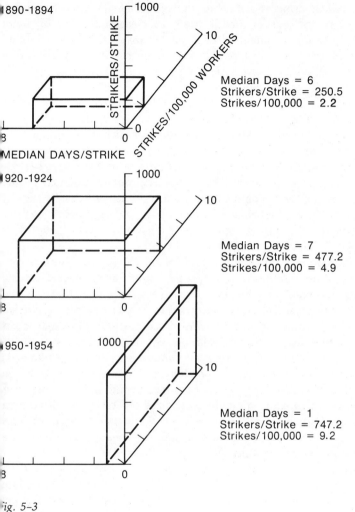

1890-1894

Median Days = 6
Strikers/Strike = 250.5
Strikes/100,000 = 2.2

1920-1924

Median Days = 7
Strikers/Strike = 477.2
Strikes/100,000 = 4.9

1950-1954

Median Days = 1
Strikers/Strike = 747.2
Strikes/100,000 = 9.2

Fig. 5-3
The alteration of French strike shapes, 1890–1954

One of the most dramatic contrasts separated the Scandinavian countries from the rest of the West. While strike levels were reaching new heights elsewhere, they were declining in Scandinavia. Joan Lind's comparison of industrial conflict in twentieth-century Britain and Sweden brings out an important element of that contrast. At first inspection, her findings fall into the pattern we have already discussed at length. Time-series analyses of strike activity in

both countries reveal strong relationships between the level of industrial conflict and the extent of worker mobilization, as measured either by union
membership or by union income. But the finding is less straightforward than i
sounds. In Britain the relationship is positive: the higher the mobilization
level, the more strikes. In Sweden, it is *negative*. Swedish strikes decline
steadily as union membership mounted.

That is not all. In Britain, a monthly time-series analysis indicates that the
repressive measures of World War I had a small depressant effect on the over
all level of strike activity (allowing for the effect of such other variables as
prices and unemployment) and a larger tendency to promote government
aided voluntary negotiations and binding arbitration as an alternative to strike
activity. But a similar analysis of World War II produces no such results
There, strikes rose greatly during the later months of the war, despite the out
lawing of strikes and the establishment of compulsory arbitration in June 1940
They rose despite the rise of prosecutions for strikes and lockouts from fifty in
1941 to 582 in 1942 to 1279 in 1943 (Lind 1973: 156).

The contradictions are troubling. Some of the things going on are clear
enough. In Britain, organized labor, despite the Labor Party, never developed
the continuous, intimate, and reliable tie to the government that the long
incumbency of the Social Democrats afforded to Swedish labor; in Sweden
the stronger labor became the easier it was to settle disputes through means
other than the strike: negotiation, legislation, governmental pressure on the
employers. As labor entered the British polity, multiple trade unions retained a
good deal of autonomy; no central labor organization acquired the power to
negotiate for all its members or to force those members to abide by the term
of their contracts. In Sweden, a highly centralized federation acquired grea
power both as a negotiator and as an enforcer. Under these circumstances
polity membership encouraged strikes in Britain and made routine political
pressure a more attractive alternative to strikes in Sweden.

David Snyder's analyses of industrial conflict in Italy, France, and the
United States likewise point toward a more complex model of power holding
When Snyder tests standard economic models on annual strike series running
from the late nineteenth century to around 1970, he finds they have unsatisfac
tory (although not negligible) predictive power in all three countries before
World War II and in France and Italy since then; for the United States, the pre
dictive power of a pure economic model greatly improves after World War II
A pure political model (in which union membership, Democrats in Congress
party of President, and the presence of national elections figure) provides a
better fit to the observations in all cases but the U.S. after World War II.

As one might expect, a synthesis of the economic and political model
provides the most accurate predictions; even there, the political variable

arry a major part of the explanatory weight except in the recent U.S. experi-nce. Snyder's proposal is essentially that the New Deal and the accommoda-ions of World War II strengthened and stabilized the ties of organized Ameri-an labor to the government. It stabilized those ties so much that previous fforts to influence the government itself by strike activity, or to take advan-age of its momentary favor, subsided in favor of a fundamentally economic ontest between employers and organized workers. The contest was fought ut within limits set and guaranteed by the government. The role of the overnment remained much more contingent, the power of organized labor nuch weaker and more variable, in Italy and France.

Snyder's best-fitting composite models resemble the ones which Edward horter and I found to be most efficient in accounting for year-to-year fluctu-tions in French strike activity between 1885 and 1965 (Shorter and Tilly 1974, sp. chapter 4). Snyder improves on our formulation by clarifying the effect of abor's relation to government. His account of changes in that regard resem-les Lind's comparison of Britain and Sweden.

Douglas Hibbs has brought a similar perspective to bear on twentieth-cen-ury strike trends in Belgium, Canada, Denmark, Finland, France, Italy, apan, Netherlands, Norway, Sweden, United Kingdom, and United States Hibbs 1976). His general conclusions run as follows:

> . . . *strike activity is one manifestation of an ongoing struggle for power between social classes over the distribution of resources, principally although not exclusively national income*. The main thesis of the study is that *long-run changes in the volume of industrial conflict are largely explained by changes in the locus of the distributional struggle*. Strike activity has declined dramatically in nations where Social Democratic or Labor parties assumed power in the 1930s—or just after the second World War—and created the modern "welfare state." In these countries an enormous fraction of the national income now passes through the public sector and is allocated by the *political process*. Political conflict between left- and right-wing parties in the electoral arena . . . has replaced industrial con-flict between labor and capital in the private sector . . . as the ultimate mecha-·nism for the distribution of national income. By comparison, in countries gov-erned more or less continuously by bourgeois parties of the center and right, the private sector continues to dominate the *allocation* as well as the *production* of resources. The economic marketplace remains the primary locus of distributional conflict in these nations, and, consequently, the average level of strike activity has been relatively constant for three-quarters of a century or more (Hibbs 1976: 26–27; italics in original).

ynthesizing the findings of Lind, Snyder, and Hibbs, we arrive at a tripartite livision: (1) countries in which the market is the locus of distributional conflict nd the relationship of labor and management to government relatively stable;

there, market variations strongly affect the level of strike activity; (2) countries in which allocation decisions are basically under political control; there, strike activity is low or nonexistent, and the real distributional conflicts occur in the course of elections and other political contests; (3) countries in which the locus of allocation decisions is itself at issue; there, short-run political fluctuations strongly affect strike activity. The *form* of strike activity—for example, the prevalence of the one-day protest strike—undoubtedly varies in a parallel way.

All these analyses bring out the great importance of mobilization, at least as represented by unionization of the workforce. All of them indicate that the most direct way in which short-run economic fluctuations promote strike activity is not through the imposition of hardships but through the provision of opportunities to act on grievances or aspirations long nurtured. As a result of these and other recent studies, there is little remaining doubt concerning a general tendency of strike activity to rise with economic expansion and fall with contraction (e.g., Knowles 1952, Weintraub 1966, Ashenfelter and Johnson 1969, Vanderkamp 1970, Skeels 1971, Kaelble and Volkmann 1972). None of these analyses attaches much importance to its complement, facilitation, in the sense of government actions lowering the cost of strike activity to workers.

The comparison of different national patterns brings out two interesting difficulties. First, the strike is only one of several means of action open to workers. At different times, political pressure, sabotage, demonstrations, and occupation of the workplace all become attractive alternatives to striking. The workers' repertoire of collective actions always includes more items than the strike. Furthermore, whether a particular struggle actually produces a work stoppage depends on the behavior of the other parties: management first of all, unions and government in many cases. The level of strike activity is therefore at best an imperfect indicator of working-class collective action as a whole. A proper explanation of strike activity must include an account both of the choice among alternative forms of collective action and of the process of negotiation.

The second difficulty is that the *form* of the ties between organized labor and government affects strike activity quite strongly. To the extent that labor organizations become powerful within the government and acquire control over the collective action of workers in general, striking becomes a relatively expensive way of doing labor's business. To the extent that the threat or promise of government intervention in strikes declines, workers become free to tune their strike activity to the rhythms of the economy. The threat or promise of government intervention depends on the structure of power among labor, management, and the government.

ELECTIONS, DEMONSTRATIONS, AND POLITICAL SYSTEMS
The lesson is more general. The simple model of the polity laid out earlier provides a useful starting point, but it misses the importance of political coalitions and of the means of actions built into the existing political organization. The use of elections to do public business is a major case in point. Political scientists have long since noticed that the establishment of binding national elections promotes the growth of political parties—not only because governments tend to legalize elections and parties at the same time but because electoral competition gives such a patent advantage of interests which are organized in parties. I think the effect of electoral systems on the pattern of collective action is even more general. A comparison of the histories of contentious collective action in Italy, Germany, France, and England (Tilly, Tilly and Tilly 1975) suggests a close connection between the institution of national elections and the use of formal associations of all sorts as vehicles for collective action. The great proliferation of clubs, circles, and sodalities in the French, German, and Italian revolutions of 1848 (in which expanding the electorate and increasing the political significance of elections were standard parts of the revolutionary program) illustrates the connection. The experience of those same countries also makes plausible the hypothesis that the growth of elections promotes the crystallization and spread of the demonstration as a form of collective action.

Why? Because of an umbrella effect: the legal umbrella raised to protect the electoral process, and to keep it huddled in the center away from the rain, has a ragged edge. There is shelter for others at its margins. The grant of legality to an electoral association or an electoral assembly provides a claim to legality for associations and assemblies which are not quite electoral, not *only* electoral or not *now* electoral. The grant of legality lowers the group's costs of mobilization and collective action. It also provides a prestigious, accessible model for action in general. In the United States of the 1960s we find a grudging grant of legitimacy to the Black Panther Party, the Mississippi Freedom Democratic Party, the Peace and Freedom Party.

Agents of the government tried to harass all these organizations out of existence at one time or another. But there formed an implicit coalition between the organizations and "white liberals" with a strong interest in a broad definition of acceptable political activity. The coalition made it harder for the government to withhold from the quasi-parties rights to organize, recruit, assemble, solicit, publicize, and demonstrate which established parties exercised as a matter of course. Yet it was not a pure power play. The fact that movements with important activities and objectives besides winning elections had chosen to organize in the guise of political parties itself afforded them a protection unavailable to similar movements which chose to organize as autonomous communities, military units, or conspiratorial networks. Sϵ doing, to be sure, they ran the risk of cooptation, infiltration, and easy surveil lance. There lies the eternal dilemma of the militant group which finds a pro tective cleft in the legal system: solidary resistance with a chance of destruc tion, or adaptation with a chance of absorption or dissolution.

Why should the demonstration prosper as a consequence of the growth o elections? Because its basic form resembles that of the electoral assembly, an because it provides an effective means of displaying the strength of a contes tant, sometimes of influencing the outcome of an election.

The demonstration we know entered the standard repertoire of collectivϵ actions in most western countries during the nineteenth century. In Englan and America, nevertheless, we can see its form crystallizing before 1800. Fo several centuries, Englishmen had gathered in large numbers on certain stan dard holidays, such as Guy Fawkes' Day. During the festivities they ofter expressed their collective opinions of the day's heroes, villains, and fools They paraded effigies, floats, charades, and placards. Hangings, funerals, exit from prison, royal birthdays, announcements of military victories drew crowds and, sometimes, concerted expressions of demands, sympathies, o complaints. In all these cases, the authorities provided the occasion and, tϵ some degree, the sanction for the assemblies in question. Contested election fell easily into the same pattern, and the assemblies of supporters of differen candidates acquired a degree of protection.

In the full-fledged demonstration, the crowd became more autonomous, choosing its own occasion and manner of assembly. After 1750, the presenta tion of a petition to Parliament or to local authorities now and then brough together thousands of people in support of a common position. The famou Gordon riots of 1780 began with a meeting and march organized around th presentation to Parliament of the Protestant Association's petition, signed b some 44,000 people, against the Catholic Emancipation Act of that year. Lor George Gordon led four great columns of demonstrators to the House of Com mons. They were the nucleus of the large crowd that formed and waitec through the session in Parliament Square. Late at night, "one section of the crowd moved off towards the private chapel of the Sardinian ambassador ir Duke Street, Lincoln's Inn Fields, another to the chapel attached to the Bavarian Embassy in Warwick Street, St. James'. The first, known to be fre quented by English Catholic gentry, was burned to the ground; both were plundered and ransacked and their contents burned in the streets" (Rudé 1971 221–222).

The electoral assembly came into its own as the setting of demonstration in the same period. At the finale of the 1769 election campaign of the popular hero John Wilkes:

Wilkes' supporters formed themselves into various cavalcades that paraded peacefully through the streets of London before proceeding to Brentford to cast their votes. One of these set out from the Prince of Orange in Jermyn Street, before whom were carried six or seven flags (Bill of Rights, Magna Carta, etc.), all badges of the different societies of which Mr. Wilkes had been made a member (Rudé 1962: 69).

As it happens, Parliament refused to seat Wilkes after his election by a resounding majority. That fact initiated another great petition drive, this one nationwide in scope; many of the petitions arrived at Parliament or the King's door to the accompaniment of demonstrating crowds. Wilkes's supporters in his repeated struggles with the government employed the mass petition march widely to exhibit their growing strength.

That innovation took a long step toward the creation of the demonstration as a distinctive form of collective action. Two more changes would complete the transformation: the elimination of the petition as a necessary pretext for the show of strength, and the generalization of the form of action beyond King and Parliament. In the struggles between London Radicals and the Crown which blazed in the last decades of the eighteenth century, those further changes began to occur.

By the 1790s, the Radical societies of London and elsewhere organized demonstrations, large ones, with great frequency. In Sheffield, according to E. P. Thompson:

> Demonstrations were held at the end of November to celebrate the success of the French armies at Valmy, and they were reported in the *Sheffield Register* . . . , a weekly newspaper which supported the reformers. A procession of five or six thousand drew a quartered roasted ox through the streets amid the firing of cannon. In the procession were—"a caricature painting representing Britannia—Burke riding on a swine—and a figure, the upper part of which was the likeness of a Scotch Secretary, and the lower part that of an Ass . . . the pole of Liberty lying broken on the ground, inscribed 'Truth is Libel'—the Sun breaking from behind a Cloud, and the Angel of Peace, with one hand dropping the 'Rights of Man', and extending the other to raise up Britannia (Thompson 1963: 104).

The symbols are exotic, reminiscent of William Blake. It is easy to forget, however, that twentieth-century demonstrators often carry symbolic coffins, and dummies, and masks. The basic form of that 1792 demonstration in Sheffield is the one we know today.

During these same years the demonstration was becoming a standard way of doing public business in Britain's North American colonies. Like the contemporaneous battles over Wilkes in England, the American resistance to the Stamp Act of 1765 helped separate the demonstration from the sanctioned assembly, helped establish its importance as a routine instrument for the application of political pressure. On the fourteenth of August two effigies appeared, suspended from a great tree on a strategic street into Boston; one represented the tax-stamp distributor, Andrew Oliver, the other, a large boot containing a devil. The crowd which gathered refused to let the effigies be taken down.

> Towards evening some men cut down the effigy of the stamp-master and placed it on a bier, which was carried through the town accompanied by a cheering and huzzaing multitude: "Liberty and property forever," "No stamps," "No Placemen." In this concourse, "some of the highest Reputation" were walking "in the greatest order," "and in solemn manner." At the head of the procession "Forty or fifty tradesmen, decently dressed, preceded; and some thousands of the mob followed . . ." The concourse, amidst the acclamations of large numbers of people lining the street, went down Main Street, turned into King Street and stopped under the town house where Governor and Council were assembled. The multitude, well knowing this, "gave three huzzas by Way of Defiance, and pass'd on" (Hoerder 1971: 153).

The great elm which held the effigies later became famous as the Liberty Tree. It was the model for thousands of liberty trees consecrated, and struggled over, in America. Later the Liberty Tree became a prime symbol in Revolutionary France. In many histories the resistance to the Stamp Act counts as the beginning of the American Revolution. The demonstration took an important and durable place in the American repertoire of collective actions as that revolutionary movement swelled.

The case of the demonstration teaches a general lesson. The forms, frequencies and personnel of collective action depend intimately on the existing structure of government and politics. When we begin refining the simple model of government, polity and contenders with which we started, we must pay attention to the specific rules of polity membership, the existing pattern of repression and facilitation, the rights claimed by different contenders. Our elementary model does little more than specify in what connections each of these variables should be significant.

On the question of political rights, for instance, the argument unfolded so far favors a view of the right to vote, to petition, to assemble, to publish, and so on as (a) consisting not of a general principle, but of a specific claim of a defined contender on a certain government, (b) coming into being as the result of struggles among mobilized contenders and governments. Thus the common idea that a standard set of political rights gradually extended from a small elite to the general population is misleading. Not wrong, because on the whole the share of the population having enforceable claims on various national governments with respect to voting, petitioning, assembling, and publishing has expanded enormously over the last two centuries, has increased in distinct steps from elites to ordinary people, has not contracted drastically once it has grown. Nevertheless misleading, because the similar claims ordinary people have had on other governments (especially local governments) have generally dwindled in the same process, and because each step of the expansion has usually occurred in response to the demand of some well-defined contender or coalition of contenders.

The fact that the rights consist of enforceable claims on the government by particular groups makes it less puzzling that such elementary rights as assembly and petition should be so easily denied to challengers (prostitutes, millennialists, Fascists, homosexuals) whose personal characteristics, objectives, or activities are unacceptable to most other groups. The denial of rights to a challenger only threatens the rights of existing members of the polity when the challenger's characteristics, organization, objectives, or activities resemble those of some members, or when a coalition between challenger and member has formed.

All our inquiries into the forms and frequencies of collective action eventually lead us back to questions of power. A close look at competitive, reactive and proactive forms of action dissolves the common distinction between "prepolitical" and "political" protest. A careful exploration of the context of strike activity challenges the separation of "economic" and "political" conflicts from each other. A thoughtful reflection on the demonstration, the charivari, and the food riot raises fundamental doubts about any effort to single out a class of spontaneous, expressive, impulsive, evanescent crowd actions—although it confirms the importance of creativity, innovation, drama, and symbolism within the limits set by the existing repertoire of collective action and the existing structure of power.

6

Collective Violence

BRITISH BRAWLS AS COLLECTIVE VIOLENCE

"We all know what a nomination day is like," commented *The Times* in June 1868.

> The presiding functionary bespeaks a fair hearing for both sides, and it is well if he gets to the end of his few sentences without derisive cheers and ironical cries explicable only by a local historian. After that no one gets a hearing. Unceasing clamour prevails; proposers, seconders, and candidates speak in dumb show, or confide their sentiments to the reporters; heads are broken, blood flows from numerous noses, and the judgment of the electors is generally subjected to a severe training as a preliminary to the voting of the following day (Richter 1971: 21).

As Donald Richter says, the jeers and brawls which regularly accompanied nineteenth-century elections belie both the orderly reputation of Victorian Britain and the notion that electoral reform + regular policing = civic calm. Nineteenth-century British elections—and much other public life in Britain as well—ran violent. "Public rowdiness and resistance to authority," concludes Richter, "have been nurtured into the British character through centuries of independence and political intransigeance" (Richter 1971: 28). Richter's idea resembles the sentiment of the nineteenth-century authorities: that they were dealing with naturally unruly people who had to be checked, trained and civilized.

The difficulty with this sort of characterological explanation of violence is that it explains too much, or nothing at all. Too much, in that there is no violent action to which it could not apply in principle, and therefore no way to prove it wrong. Nothing at all, in that it finally reduces to a description of what has to be explained. Available accounts of nineteenth-century British electoral violence, however, give us hope of escaping from tautology and of detecting regular relationships between the pattern of collective violence and the nature of current struggles over rights and power.

As it happens, Richter himself gives us some valuable information on the origins of British electoral rowdiness. "It was not uncommon," he reports:

> for agents of the candidates, not always without the latter's cognizance, to hire gangs of ruffians from nearby collieries to intimidate and bully rival voters. A witness before the Parliamentary Committee investigating the election of 1868 testified that at Bristol Liberal agents from London organized and paid "flying columns," bands of from 200 to 300 men recruited from the Bristol suburbs. Disposed in quasi-military formation and armed with bludgeons, they appeared on election day at various polling booths and drove off Conservative voters" (Richter 1965: 180).

More generally, the supporters of a given candidate—hired or not—often made a holiday of the election, sporting their colors, drinking amply to the health of their champion, jeering his rivals, brawling with the bearers of other colors. This behavior may exemplify "public rowdiness and resistance to authority," but it also identifies a clearer link between violence and organized struggles for power than *The Times* commentator was ready to concede.

Two years before the 1868 election, the Tory government which had newly come to power announced, through Disraeli, that it would not necessarily take up parliamentary reform in the next session. The Reform League called for a mass meeting in Hyde Park on 23 July 1866. The meeting was the occassion for what Francis Sheppard calls the "only significant outbreak of violence" in the great campaign leading up to the Reform Bill of 1867:

> The law officers of the Crown had decided that the Crown had the right to close the gates, and the Home Secretary, Spencer Walpole, now decided to exercise this right. On being informed of this the leaders of the League decided nevertheless to march to Hyde Park, and if prevented from entering, to proceed to Trafalgar Square. Printed leaflets to this effect were distributed in large numbers. When the leaders of the procession reached Marble Arch they found the gates closed and a large body of police assembled. After being refused admission by the police commissioner, Sir Richard Mayne, Beales and the crowd near him left for Trafalgar Square. But other processions were still arriving, control broke down, and soon a densely-packed mass of men were pressing against the railings. The railings and stonework were old and weak, and breach after breach was quickly made along Park Lane and the Bayswater Road. The police resisted these incursions, and scuffling broke out, but many thousands of people were now inside the park, and even a company of the Grenadier Guards, whose arrival was loudly cheered, could not oust the invaders except by the use of firearms. After an hour or two of cheerful speechifying darkness began to fall, and the crowd dispersed voluntarily" (Sheppard 1971: 341).

Except perhaps for the good cheer, the affair was a textbook example of large-scale collective violence: one group undertakes a large action which directly or indirectly states a claim; a second group challenges that claim; they struggle. The group stating the counterclaim is often a specialized repressive force—police, troops, posse, vigilante—acting on behalf of the dominant classes. No doubt some of the demonstrators in 1866 were angry, some were drunk, and some enjoyed the rough-and-tumble. But the breaking down of fences and the scuffling with police was a by-product of the play of claim and counterclaim. That is the standard structure of collective violence.

VIOLENCE: CONCEPT AND REALITY

In order to get that point straight, however, we have to dispose of some serious conceptual problems. "Violence" often serves as a catchall containing all the varieties of protest, militancy, coercion, destruction, or muscle flexing which a given observer happens to fear or condemn. Violence, as Henry Bienen comments, "carries overtones of 'violating', and we often use violence to refer to illegitimate force" (Bienen 1968: 4). Grundy and Weinstein (1974: 113) array competing definitions of violence on a continuum from narrow to broad:

- *narrow:* those uses of physical force which are prohibited by a normative order presumed to be legitimate;
- *intermediate:* any use of physical force;
- *broad:* all deprivations of asserted human rights.

In general, they point out, defenders of constituted authority prefer narrow definitions. Opponents prefer broad ones. In between, they place the "liberal democrats who define violence as any use of physical force, because they would like to justify revolutions against authoritarian regimes which do not have built-in mechanisms for peaceful change" (Grundy and Weinstein 1974: 113).

We have, however, practical as well as political reasons for selecting the middle term. The narrow definition of violence as illegitimate force introduces the debate about the proper scope of the authorities into the very delineation of the phenomenon to be investigated—an unpromising way to begin. The broad definition of violence to include all violations of human rights not only requires agreement on the character of those rights, but also expands the phenomenon to such a large range of social relations as to make systematic study of it almost unthinkable. If we restrict our attention to human actions which damage persons or objects, we have at least a chance to sort out the regularities in the appearance of those actions.

Even that restriction calls immediately for further distinctions. Violence so defined still includes:

- cut thumbs
- murders
- hockey games
- rebellions
- normal wear of automobiles or the roads they travel
- disposal of noxious wastes
- cigarette smoking.

The obvious temptation is to add some qualifications concerning the intentions of the actors: they want to destroy, they are angry, they seek power, or something else. The trouble with letting much depend on intentions is that intentions are mixed and hard to discern. The judgments outsiders make concerning the intentions of participants in conflicts usually include implicit theories of causation and responsibility. Even with full knowledge, intentions often turn out to be mixed and divergent, often change or misfire in the course of the action. We must ask *whose* intentions *when.*

Violence, furthermore, is rarely a solo performance. It usually grows out of an interaction of opponents. Whose intentions should count: the small group of demonstrators who gather on the steps of the capitol, the larger group of spectators who eventually get drawn into the action, the police who first stand guard and then struggle to disperse the crowd? Both in theory and in practice, then, intentions provide shaky criteria for the distinction of violence from nonviolence.

In her brilliant essay on violence, Hannah Arendt urged a fundamental distinction between *power* and *violence.* Power, in her view, is "the human ability not just to act but to act in concert." But the difficulties with which we are wrestling appear in one fact: Arendt never quite defined violence. This was the closest approach:

> *Violence* is distinguished by its instrumental character. Phenomenologically, it is close to strength, since the implements of violence, like all other tools, are designed and used for the purpose of multiplying natural strength until, in the last stage of their development, they can substitute for it (Arendt 1970: 46).

As a distinction in political philosophy—that is, in the principles upon which we can reasonably found a system of government and by which we can justify or condemn public actions—Arendt's treatment of power and violence is illuminating. As a guide to observation of acting people, however, it has the fatal flaw of resting on exactly the features of collective action which observers and participants dispute most passionately. That is precisely because they are the features of the action which will bring on it justification from some and condemnation from others. Justification and condemnation are important business, but they are not our business here.

Nor do any easy alternatives lie close at hand. We may try to define "normal" or "expected" or "legitimate" uses of force in social life, and define deviations from them as violent. That approach not only requires the (difficult) assessment of the normal, expected state of affairs, but also tends to define away violence exerted by professional specialists in coercion: police, soldiers, mafiosi, muggers. If, on the other hand, we turn to the amount of damage sustained by the individuals or objects involved, we face the difficulty of determining how direct and material the damage must be: Does a firm's dumping of garbage which promotes disease count? Does the psychic burden of enslavement count?

I recite these tedious complications in order to emphasize that in the present state of knowledge *any* definition will be arbitrary in some regards and debatable in others. People do not agree on what they will call violent. What is more, their disagreement springs to an important extent from differences in political perspective. My own inclination is toward what Terry Nardin calls a "brute harm" conception of violence: any observable interaction in the course of which persons or objects are seized or physically damaged in spite of resistance. (Direct or indirect resistance, in the form of attacks on persons, erection of barriers, standing in the way, holding on to the persons or objects at issue, and so on, enters the definition in order to exclude self-destruction, potlatches, ceremonial mutilation, urban renewal, and other collective damage in which all parties are more or less agreed to the damage. In short, to certify the presence of competing interests.)

Further distinctions start from there: collective vs. individual, depending on the number of parties to the interaction; games vs. nongames, depending on the extent to which all participants begin with an agreement to work toward a determinate set of alternative outcomes by following some standard rules; continuous vs. discontinuous, depending on how great a time span we observe and how large an interval we permit to elapse before we call the action at an end; and so forth.

Some Lineaments of Violence

Once collective violence is defined in these terms, interesting conclusions begin to emerge from the close examination of the actual record of violent events. Our study of thousands of violent incidents occurring in western Europe since 1800 reveals several strong tendencies which affect our understanding of the roots of violence.

First, most collective violence—in the sense of interactions which produce direct damage to persons and objects—grows out of actions which are not intrinsically violent, and which are basically similar to a much larger number of collective actions occurring without violence in the same periods and settings. The clearest example is the demonstration: some group displays its strength and determination in the presence of the public, of the agents of the state, and perhaps of its enemies as well. The great majority of demonstrations pass without direct damage to persons or property. But a small proportion do turn to violent encounters between police and demonstrators, or attacks on property by the demonstrators. When that happens, we conventionally use a new word for the event—"riot"—and thereby obscure its connection with non-violent events. The demonstration is such a common way of doing political business in modern Europe that even the small proportion of violent outcomes is enough to make the demonstration the most frequent setting for collective violence. The strike, the parliamentary session, the public meeting, the fiesta follow something like the same pattern: the great majority of them going off without violence, the violent ones not differing in any fundamental way from the rest.

A second important feature of collective violence which stands out in the modern European record is the heavy involvement of agents of the state, especially repressive agents like police and soldiers. This is, unsurprisingly, a matter of scale: the fewer the people involved, the less likely that repressive agents will be there. But it does not mean simply that the larger the scale of *violence* the more likely the police are to step in. For in the modern European experience repressive forces are themselves the most consistent initiators and performers of collective violence.

There is a division of labor: repressive forces do the largest part of the killing and wounding, while the groups they are seeking to control do most of the damage to objects. The division of labor follows from the usual advantage repressive forces have with respect to arms and military discipline; from the common tactics of demonstrators, strikers, and other frequent participants in collective violence, which are to violate symbolically charged rules and prohibitions whose enforcement is the affair of agents of government; from the typical sequence of events, in which demonstrators are carrying on an action which is illegal yet nonviolent, and repressive forces receive the order to stop them by whatever means are necessary. The means are often violent.

VIOLENCE IN AMERICA

Since no one has done the necessary detailed studies of contemporary Latin America, North America, Africa, or Asia, it is hard to say how generally these generalizations apply. The fragments of evidence now available indicate that they apply very widely in contemporary countries with strong governments. Jerome Skolnick (1969: 258) says in summary of one part of his analysis of contemporary American protests, "It is misleading to ignore the part played by social control agencies in aggravating and sometimes creating a riot. It is not unusual, as the Kerner Commission observed, for a riot to begin *and* end with police violence."

A chronological review of violence in American labor-management disputes makes it clear both that over the long run police, troops, and plant guards have done the bulk of the killing and wounding, and that the typical starting point has been some sort of illegal but nonviolent collective action by the workers—a walkout, a sitdown, a demonstration, picketing, sending of delegations. In their sketch of the usual circumstances in which the total of at least 700 persons died in American "labor violence" during the nineteenth and twentieth centuries, Taft and Ross report:

> Facing inflexible opposition, union leaders and their members frequently found that nothing, neither peaceful persuasion nor the heads of government, could move the employer towards recognition. Frustration and desperation impelled pickets to react to strikebreakers with anger. Many violent outbreaks followed efforts of strikers to restrain the entry of strikebreakers and raw materials into the struck plant. Such conduct, obviously illegal, opened the opportunity for forceful police measures. In the long run, the employer's side was better equipped for success. The use of force by pickets was illegal on its face, but the action of the police and company guards were in vindication of the employer's rights (Taft and Ross 1969: 289–290).

The same general pattern recurs in the bulk of contemporary American collective violence: a group undertakes an illegal and/or politically unacceptable action, forces of order seek to check the group, a violent encounter ensues, the "rioters"—for that is the label the group acquires at the moment of violent contact with police or troops—sustain most of the casualties.

Reflecting on the long succession of violent encounters between challengers and power holders in America, Richard Rubenstein makes an important observation:

> At the outset, one thing seems clear: those groups which achieved success without participating in sustained rioting, guerrilla terrorism or outright insurrection were not necessarily more talented, hard-working or "American" than those that resorted to higher levels of violence. The resistance of more powerful groups to change is one key struggle; another is the match between out-group characteristics and the needs of a changing political-economic system (Rubenstein 1970: 15–16).

Then he goes on to contrast the fluidity of the economic and political arrangements open to the immigrants of 1880–1920 with the formation, in the 1930s and 1940s, of a new ruling coalition quite resistant to displacement: "Ironically, since these are the groups most wedded to the myth of peaceful progress and the culpability of the violent—it is the existence of this coalition, exercising power through a highly centralized Federal bureaucracy, which helps keep emerging groups powerless and dependent" (p. 17). The consequence, in Rubenstein's view, is that recent bids for power have met determined resistance and brought forth the pious recommendation that the members of the groups involved attempt to enter the system as individuals, on their own merits, rather than destroying the system through collective efforts to wrest benefits from it.

Rubenstein's analysis includes both an idea of how the American system usually works and a notion of the changes it has undergone since the 1930s. The general picture corresponds to William Gamson's portrayal of "stable unrepresentation" in American politics: " . . . the American political system normally operates to prevent incipient competitors from achieving full entry into the political arena" (Gamson 1968: 18). That description applies to all political systems; the real questions are: How great are the obstacles? How do they vary from system to system and time to time?

That brings up the second part. Has the American system closed down since the 1930s? To try that question out seriously, we shall need much more precise information than we now have concerning the fates of successive challengers. Gamson's investigation does not reveal any significantly increased tendency for the recent challengers in his sample to fail. But his investigation deals with small numbers, and stops in 1945. It is not obvious that recent challengers—antiwar students, organized blacks, gay activists, and aircraft manufacturers are likely candidates for the post-1940 list—met more resistance than craft unions, Prohibitionists or Abolitionists had met in the nineteenth century. There is probably variation over time, and there may well be a long-run trend. Both are surely too subtle to show up in a few offhand comparisons.

POLITICAL ACTION AND INVOLVEMENT IN VIOLENCE

In the terms we were using earlier, Rubenstein is saying that members of the polity, acting mainly through agents of the state, have banded together to resist the claims of newly mobilized challengers for membership. His most prominent case is organized blacks. The analysis applies generally to the past and present contention of wheat farmers, women, believers in Temperance, students and organized labor. In these cases and many others, the acceptance of the group's collective claims would significantly reallocate the resources under the control of the polity, redefine the rules of membership for futher challengers, change the likely coalitions inside and outside the polity. In such cases, the main line between violence and contention for power consists of the repeated sequence in which members of the challenging group publicly lay claim to some space, object, privilege, protection, or other resource which they consider due them on general grounds, and the agents of the government (backed by the members of the polity) forcibly resist their claims. Collective proaction on the one side, collective reaction on the other.

A complete picture of the process linking contention and violence, however, requires a distinction between challengers and members on their way out of the polity. Members losing their position are more likely to find themselves trying to maintain exclusive claims to some particular resource—a school, a distinctive costume, a source of income, a tax exemption—and unable to enlist the support of other members or of agents of the government in maintaining those claims. Under those circumstances, they commonly attempt to exert those claims on their own, and to keep others from claiming the same resources.

Then two different sequences are likely to produce collective violence involving declining members of a polity. The first is like the one involving new claimants for membership in the polity, in that agents of the government directly resist the claims of the parting member to keep exerting their former rights to certain resources. The second pits the parting member directly against others seeking to acquire the disputed resources: vigilante movements, private armies, and gangs of thugs are especially likely to enter the action at this point, as the old member seeks to substitute its own force for that of the now unreliable government.

The regional movement of resistance against a centralizing state commonly takes this form (see Hechter 1975). So does the classic European food riot, in which the members of a community collective dispute the right of anyone to store grain in times of hunger or ship grain out of the community when local people still need food, and reinforce their dispute by acting in the traditional role of the authorities: inventorying the grain on hand, accumulating it in a public place, and selling it off at a price locally determined to be just and reasonable (see C. Tilly 1975, L. Tilly 1971). So, finally, do a variety of fascist movements formed in opposition to the threatening claims of a mobilized working class.

The sequences involving new contenders and declining members mean that collective violence tends to cluster around entries into the polity and exits from it. When membership is stable, collective violence is less prevalent. The most important single reason for that clustering is the propensity of the government's repressive forces to act against new contenders and declining members.

Some indications of the links between collective violence and struggles at the edge of the polity appear in Dee Wernette's analysis of the German elections of September 1930 and July 1932—crucial moments in the rise of the Nazis and the disappearance of the communists from German political life. Among other things, Wernette coded "political events" reported in the *Kölnische Zeitung* during the two months preceding each of the elections. The events he enumerated included (1) nonviolent, organized political activities such as electoral rallies; (2) acts of terrorism such as bombings and ambushes touching manifestly political targets; (3) fights and collective violence involving at least one group clearly identified by political affiliation; (4) repressive acts by the state, such as police investigations, arrests, and trials.

As Table 6-1 shows, a significant proportion of all the events included terror or collective violence. More important, the proportions rose as the struggle became more acute: twenty-seven percent of the events involved collective violence, nine percent terror and eight percent attacks on property in 1930, while the figures for 1932 were fifty-seven percent, twenty-five percent and thirteen percent. (The categories are not, of course, mutually exclusive.) The leading participants in violent events, by far, are Nazis, Communists, and police. The chief settings of collective violence were major areas of Communist strength: the regions of Berlin, Cologne, Düsseldorf, and so on—the areas in which the Nazis concentrated their campaign to extirpate the Communists. In fact, the most frequent events were Nazi–Communist clashes and attacks of each on the other's property. The collective violence grew directly from the struggle for places in the German polity.

I do not mean that the sequences I have described are the *only* ones which produce collective violence, just that they are the most regular and reliable.

Table 6-1 *Percent of all political events preceding the German elections of September 1930 and July 1932 involving different types of action*

Type of action	Percent in 1930	Percent in 1932
Election-oriented nonviolent action	33	15
Other nonviolent action	4	17
Acts of terror	8	25
Attacks on property	9	13
Collective violence	27	57
Police investigations	6	10
Arrests	17	22
Reports of trials	19	5
Bans on organizations	2	7
Bans on activities	8	9
Total number of events	316	569

Routine testing among established members of a polity produces a certain amount of violent conflict, but it tends to be limited, and treated as a regret table error. Conventional combats among teams, communities, youth groups or schools sometimes fit the pattern of "testing" violence, but more often escape it; they, too, operate on a small scale, within large restrictions Drunken brawls, private vengeance, festival madness, impulsive vandalism all reach a dangerous magnitude now and then. What is more, the frequency of conventional combats, brawls, vendettas, and so on undoubtedly varies with the basic conceptions of honor, obligation, and solidarity which prevai within a population. Nevertheless, I would say that in populations under the control of states all these forms account for only a small proportion of the collective violence which occurs, and change far too gradually to account for the abrupt surges and recessions of collective violence which appear in such populations. The chief source of variation in collective violence is the operation of the polity.

Nor do I mean that most collective violence goes on in calculating calm Far from it. Both those who are arguing for the acquisition of rights on the basis of general principles and those who are fighting for the defense of privilege on the basis of custom and precedent are usually indignant, and often enraged. Moments of dangerous confrontation (as Louis Girard says of the French Revolutions of 1830 and 1848, and almost everyone says of the French Events of May 1968) frequently bring an air of festival, of exhiliration, of release from ordinary restrictions. Plenty of individual venting of resentments and settling of old scores takes place under the cover of collective action in the name of high principle. The argument up to this point simply denies the common conclusion that the rage, the exhiliration, or the resentment *cause* the collective action.

If these arguments are correct, they produce a paradoxical lesson for researchers: to understand and explain violent actions, you must understand nonviolent actions. Any study which treats violent events alone deals with the product of two different sets of determinants: (1) the determinants of collective action in general, whether it produces violence or not; (2) the determinants of violent outcomes to collective action. We encountered a similar problem in the explanation of strikes: While in some sense a group of workers chooses to strike or not to strike, the strike is simply one of several alternative ways to deal with grievances: slowdowns, political pressure, sabotage, and individual grumbling are also possible. That is why we can't simply infer the level of discontent from the frequency of strike attempts. Furthermore, whether a strike actually occurs is a product of strategic estimates and strategic interaction on the part of at least two contenders; when either party is much stronger and wilier than the other, the grievance is likely to be settled, or squashed, short of a strike.

Snyder and Kelly (1976) find that from 1878 through 1903 Italian strikes were more likely to be violent if they were large, long, and/or oriented to wage demands rather than union organization. Contrary to many arguments which proceed immediately from grievances to strikes, they find no relationship between the frequency of violence in strikes and the rate of industrial growth or wage changes. Contrary to the findings of Shorter and Tilly (1971) for France, they find that on the average violent strikes were less successful than nonviolent strikes. These are important results. They emphasize all the more the necessity of separating the determinants of collective action (in this case, the decision to strike) in general from the determinants of violent outcomes to collective action.

In our first category of determinants, we find such items as the frequency of violations of established rights, the mobilization levels of different contenders for power, the current costs of different forms of action which are in the available repertoire, and so on. In the second, we find the presence or absence of counterdemonstrators, the tactics of repressive forces, the length of time during which opposing parties are in direct contact with each other, and so on. Each of the two sometimes changes while the other remains more or less the same: demonstrations become more frequent, although the percentage of demonstrations which produce street fighting remains the same; the authorities get tougher with strikers, although strike propensities have not altered. Either one changes the frequency of collective violence. A proper explanation of violence levels must decompose into at least these two components.

Out of the entire stream of collective action, only a small part produces violence. The collective action which produces violence attracts disproportionate attention because (1) the immediate costs to the participants tend to be greater, more visible, and more dramatic than in nonviolent collective action; (2) the events in question often involve the intervention of the authorities; the authorities intervene because they find their interests—or those of their allies—threatened by the other actors. Collective violence is not, by and large, the result of a single group's possession by an emotion, sentiment, attitude, or idea. It grows, for the most part, out of strategic *inter*action among groups.

In the modern western experience, the most frequent settings for collective violence are contentious gatherings: assemblies of people who make visible collective claims which conflict with the interests of other groups. Contentious gatherings such as the demonstration, the strike, the so-called food riot, and the tax protest are not, on the whole, intrinsically violent. In fact, most of them occur without violence.

The violent versions of the demonstration, the strike, the food riot, and the tax protest do not form a distinctly separate class of events. They ordinarily occur in the midst of strings of similar events which are quite similar to them except for the fact that they produce no damage or seizure of persons or property. They are, for the most part, the members of the strings in which other parties resist the claims being made. The other parties are more likely to resist if the contender making the claims lacks a large advantage in power or if the claims threaten their survival. But violent and nonviolent events of the same general type cluster together sufficiently for us to employ the visible, violent events as a tracer of the ebb and flow of contentious gatherings in general.

CHANGING CONTEXTS FOR COLLECTIVE VIOLENCE

The competitive/reactive/proactive scheme provides a convenient means of summing up the largest trends in the evolution of the major contexts of collective violence in western countries over the last four or five centuries. Two main processes have dominated all the rest: (1) the rise of national states to preeminent positions in a wide variety of political activities; (2) the increasingly associational character of the principal contenders for power at the local as well as the national level. In 1500, no full-fledged national state with unquestioned priority over the other governments within its territory existed anywhere in the West. England was probably the closest approximation. The England of 1500 was, however, only fifteen years past the slaying of King Richard III by Henry Tudor at Bosworth Field. It was fresh from the widely supported rebellions of Lambert Simnel and Perkin Warbeck. It had yet to effect the union with Scotland. It still harbored a number of great lords who controlled their own bands of armed retainers. Government itself consisted largely of shifting, competing coalitions among great magnates and their retinues, the king being the greatest magnate of the strongest coalition. Become Henry VII, Henry Tudor began the large work of state making which Henry VIII and Elizabeth so vigorously continued.

A century and a half after 1500, a great civil war reopened the question of whether the centralized royal apparatus the Tudors, and then the Stuarts, had begun building would be the dominant political organization in England. In fact, the state which emerged in 1688 had rather different contours from the one the Tudors and Stuarts had been building. The strength and autonomy of Parliament far exceeded anything a cool observer of the England of 1600 or 1620 could reasonably have anticipated.

In 1500 most states faced serious challenges to their hegemony from both inside and outside the territory. Only a small minority of the hundreds of more or less autonomous governments survived the next two centuries of state making. Most power was concentrated in politics of smaller than national scale: communities, city-states, principalities, semiautonomous provinces. Most contenders for power in those polities were essentially communal in structure: craft brotherhoods, families, peasant communities. The predominant forms of collective violence registered those circumstances: wars between rival governments, brawls between groups of artisans, battles among the youth of neighboring communes, attacks by one religious group on another.

The rise of the state threatened the power (and often the very survival) of all these small-scale polities. They resisted. The state makers won their struggle for predominance only over the furious resistance of princes, communes, provinces and peasant communities. For several centuries the principal forms of collective violence therefore grew from reactive movements on the part of different segments of the general population: communally based contenders for power fought against loss of membership in polities, indeed against the very destruction of the polities in which their power was invested. Collective resistance to conscription, to taxation, to billeting, to a whole variety of other exactions of the state exemplify this reactive road to collective violence.

For a century or more in the experience of most West European countries, however, the most frequent form of violence-producing movement aimed at the market more directly than at the state. That was the food riot. The name is misleading: most often the struggle turned about raw grain rather than edibles, and most of the time it did not reach the point of physical violence. The classic European food riot had three main variants: the *retributive action*, in which a crowd attacked the persons, property, or premises of someone believed to be hoarding or profiteering; the *blockage*, in which a group of local people prevented the shipment of food out of their own locality, requiring it to be stored and/or sold locally; the *price riot*, in which people seized stored food or food displayed for sale, sold it publicly at a price they declared to be proper, and handed the money over to the owner or merchant.

In the best-documented cases—England and France of the eighteenth and nineteenth centuries—the blockage occurred more frequently than the price riot, and much more often than the retributive action. In those two countries, the food riot practically disappeared some time during the nineteenth century. Later, questions of food supply motivated dramatic collective actions now and then, but almost always in the form of demonstrations in which producers complained about low prices or consumers complained about high prices.

The timing of the food riot's rise and fall is revealing. In England, France, and some other parts of western Europe, the food riot displaced the tax rebellion as the most frequent violent form of collective action toward the end of the seventeenth century. It declined precipitously in England just after 1820, in Germany and France just after 1850, only to linger on in parts of Spain and Italy into the twentieth century.

The calendar did not conform to the history of hunger; indeed the great killing famines of Medieval and Renaissance Europe were disappearing as the food riot came into its own, and per capita food supply was probably increasing through much of the period. Instead, three conjoint changes account for the timing: (1) the proletarianization of the population, which meant a drastic diminution in the proportion of households which produced enough food for the subsistence of their own members, a great expansion in the number dependent on the market for survival; (2) the commercialization of food production, which included the building of national markets and the promotion of the ideas that the national markets should have priority over local needs and that the market's operation tended to set a just, proper, and efficient price; (3) the dismantling of the extensive previously existing controls over the distribution of food, which gave the local population a prior claim over food produced and sold in a locality, and bound the local authorities to provide for the subsistence of the local poor.

E.P. Thompson has called the entire process a decline in the old Moral Economy, a shift from a *bread nexus* to a *cash nexus*. People resisted the process so long as local solidarity and some collective memory of the locality's prior claims survived. To an important degree, the crowd's actions of blocking, inventorying, storing, declaring a price, and holding a public sale for the benefit of the locals fulfilled what had previously been the obligations of the local authorities in dealing with shortages and high prices. Magistrates or mayors often acknowledged that fact implicitly by acquiescing in the routine; when they took the initiative themselves, the crowd usually stopped its work.

The immediate objects of the crowd's attention were commonly local officials, bakers, rich farmers, and, especially, grain merchants. The struggle pitted the claims of the national market against the claims of the local population. For that reason, the geography of the food riot reflected the geography of the grain market: tending to form a ring around London, Paris, another capital or a major port, concentrating especially along rivers, canals, and major roads. For the acute English crises of 1795–96 and 1800–01, Stevenson remarks: "The map shows the extremely close relationship of disturbances to the communications network in the production areas around London in these two shortages. The most striking pattern overall is that of 1795–96 when at least fifty food disturbances took place at communication centres, either coastal ports, canal or river ports, or towns within easy carting distance of major population centres" (Stevenson 1974: 43). Yet the reflection of the market came through a distorting mirror, for the most thoroughly commercialized areas, adjacent to large old cities, did not typically produce food riots. There, the market had already won out over local rights to the food supply.

Despite the salience of the market, the food riot also resulted in part from the rise of the national state. In general (although with great hesitations, variations, and differences in outcome) European statemakers acted to promote all three of the processes underlying the food riot: proletarianization, commercialization, dismantling of local controls. As their dependent governmental staffs, urban populations, and nonagricultural labor forces swelled, the managers of states intervened increasingly to promote marketing. (There is irony in the fact that they acted thus in the name of freeing the market.) As Stevenson says of the English crisis of 1795:

> The government, however, was determined to keep out of the internal corn trade and attempted to keep up the normal circulation of grain, so that the large urban centres would be supplied. On these grounds the government refused to yield to the pleas of local authorities and interfere with the normal movement of grain. . . It was reported to the Home Office that stopping the movement of grain had become so widespread that country millers were said to be frightened to send grain to the capital except by night. In an attempt to free the circulation of grain from these checks the government passed an act to prevent the stopping of grain by making the whole hundred liable to fine and individuals liable to fine and imprisonment (Stevenson 1974: 41–42).

In that crisis, many local officials sought to restrict the flow of grain away from their own markets. Within three decades, however, the market and the national government had won their battle; few mayors and magistrates chose to counter the national will, and few hungry crowds harbored the hope of making them do so. One of the English forms of collective action had withered away.

Two things eventually put an end to the predominance of the reactive forms, although at times and tempos which varied markedly from one part of the West to another. First, the state won almost everywhere. One may ask how complete the victory of the state was in the remote sections of vast territories such as Canada, Australia, or Brazil, and speculate whether recent surges of sectionalism in Belgium, Great Britain, and even France presage the end of state control. Yet on the whole the two centuries after 1700 produced an enormous concentration of resources and means of coercion under the control of national states, to the virtual exclusion of other levels of government. Second, a whole series of organizational changes closely linked to urbanization, industrialization, and the expansion of capitalism greatly reduced the role of the communal group as a setting for mobilization and as a repository for power; the association of one kind or another came to be the characteristic vehicle for collective action. The rise of the joint-stock company, the political party, the labor union, the club all belong to the same general trend.

Working together, the victory of the state and the rise of the association transformed the collective actions which most commonly produced violence.

In country after country, politics nationalized; the polity which mattered was the one which controlled the national state; the crucial struggles for power went on at a national scale. And the participants in those struggles were most often organized as associations. The strike, the demonstration, the party conspiracy, the organized march on the capital, the parliamentary session, the mass meeting became the usual settings for collective violence. The state became an interested participant in all collective violence—as policemen, as party to the conflict, as *tertius gaudens*.

The discovery that collective violence is a by-product of the same political processes which produce nonviolent collective action does not mean, then, that it is an uninteresting by-product. The occurrence of damage to persons or objects gives us some small assurance that at least one of the parties to the collective action took it seriously. More important, violence makes collective action visible: authorities, participants, and observers tend to set down some record of their actions, reactions, and observations. Collective violence therefore serves as a convenient tracer of major alterations in collective action as a whole. Like all tracers, we must use it with care.

7

Revolution and Rebellion

REVOLUTIONARY SITUATIONS AND REVOLUTIONARY OUTCOMES

We have encountered our share of Big Words on the way from mobilization to revolution. Interest, power, and violence have all turned out to be controversial concepts not only because they refer to complex realities but also because alternative definitions of each of them tend to imply alternative political programs. That is why Stephen Lukes speaks of "pluralist," "reformist," and [truly] "radical" definitions of power. The same is certainly true of our final Big Word: revolution. Revolutionary reality is complex. And whether it includes coups, assassinations, terrorism, or slow, massive changes such as industrialization is controversial not only because the world is complex but also because to call something revolutionary is, within most forms of western political discourse, to identify it as good or bad.

Nevertheless, most western analysts of revolution restrict their definitions by means of two sorts of requirements: (1) by insisting that the actors and the action meet some demanding standards—that they be based on an oppressed class, that they have a comprehensive program of social transformation in view, or some other gauge of seriousness; (2) by dealing only with cases in which power actually changes hands. Peter Calvert, for example, builds the following elements into his conception of revolution:

(a) A process in which the political direction of a state becomes increasingly discredited in the eyes of either the population as a whole or certain key sections of it . . .

(b) A change of government (transition) at a clearly defined point in time by the use of armed force, or the credible threat of its use, namely, an *event*.

(c) A more-or-less coherent programme of change in either the political or the social institutions of a state, or both, induced by the political leadership after a revolutionary event, the transition of power, has occurred.

(d) A political myth that gives to the political leadership resulting from a revolutionary transition short-term status as the legitimate government of the state (Calvert 1970:4).

Thus, he goes on, "in order to investigate fully the concept of revolution, it would be necessary to study in detail process, event, programme, and myth as distinct phenomena" (Calvert 1970:4). He confines his own study to revolutionary events: changes of government accomplished by force. That choice greatly increases the number of cases he has to examine, since most such events do not meet his criteria (a), (b), and (c). Yet the insistence on armed force and on an actual transfer of power eliminates many instances in which competing observers see something revolutionary: the Industrial Revolution, revolutions from above, the legendary General Strike of the syndicalists, and so on. On the other hand, the definition has a hard-nosed quality which many advocates of revolution will find unacceptable; it does not insist that the party which seizes power be dispossessed, progressive, or even angry.

No concept of revolution can escape some such difficulties, because no conceptualizer can avoid making some such choices. Nevertheless, we can clear a good deal of conceptual ground by means of a simple distinction between *revolutionary situations* and *revolutionary outcomes*. Most significant disagreement about the proper definition of revolution falls somewhere along these two dimensions.

Revolutionary Situations

The distinguishing characteristic of a revolutionary situation, as Leon Trotsky said long ago, is the presence of more than one bloc effectively exercising control over a significant part of the state apparatus:

> The historical preparation of a revolution brings about, in the pre-revolutionary period, a situation in which the class which is called to realize the new social system, although not yet master of the country, has actually concentrated in its hands a significant share of the state power, while the official apparatus of the government is still in the hands of the old lords. That is the initial dual power in every revolution.
>
> But that is not its only form. If the new class, placed in power by a revolution which it did not want, is in essence an already old, historically belated, class; if it was already worn out before it was officially crowned; if on coming to power it encounters an antogonist sufficiently mature and reaching out its hand toward the helm of state; then instead of one unstable two-power equilibrium, the political revolution produces another, still less stable. To overcome the "anarchy" of this twofold sovereignty becomes at every new step the task of the revolution—or the counter-revolution (Trotsky 1965: 224).

The shadow of Russia in 1917 falls dark across this passage. From the particular instance, nevertheless, comes an idea of general value. Trotsky's idea of dual sovereignty clarifies a number of features of revolutionary situations. Peter Amann has gone so far as to fashion it into a serviceable definition of revolution itself: for him, a revolution begins when more than one "power bloc" regarded as legitimate and sovereign by some of a country's people emerges, and ends when only one power bloc remains.

Amann's adaptation of Trotsky has the advantage of neatly identifying the common properties of coups, civil wars, and full-scale revolutions without requiring knowledge of what happened next. It still permits their distinction in terms of the identities of the power blocs themselves. At the same time it identifies a weakness in Trotsky's formulation: the insistence that a single class makes a revolutionary situation. Barrington Moore's treatment of the greatest modern revolutions corrects that weakness by tracing out the *coalitions* of classes which tore down the old regimes. Thus for Moore a coalition of workers, bourgeois, and peasants made the French Revolution, even if the workers and peasants lost out fairly soon. What is more, Moore argues that the character of the revolutionary situation shaped the revolutionary outcome. The fact that it was bourgeois + peasants + workers rather than the different coalitions which made the American, English, or Russian revolutions, in Moore's view, pushed France toward the attenuated parliamentary democracy she maintained in the nineteenth and twentieth centuries.

Two of Trotsky's restrictions therefore seem unnecessary: (1) that each of the blocs consist of a single social class; (2) that there be only two such blocs at any point in time. Either of these restrictions would eliminate most of the standard cases of revolution—not least those of France, China, and Mexico.

Trotsky's idea retains its analytic resiliency if expanded to include blocs consisting of coalitions of classes and/or other groups and to allow for the possibility of three or more simultaneous blocs. *Multiple sovereignty* is then the identifying feature of revolutionary situations. A revolutionary situation begins when a government previously under the control of a single, sovereign polity becomes the object of effective, competing, mutually exclusive claims on the part of two or more distinct polities. It ends when a single sovereign polity regains control over the government.

Such a multiplication of polities occurs under four different conditions:

1   The members of one polity attempt to subordinate another previously distinct polity. Where the two polities are clearly sovereign and independent at the outset we are likely to consider this conflict a special variety of war. Circumstances like the annexation of Texas to the United States or the transfers of power to various communist regimes in Eastern Europe at the end of the

Second World War fall, in fact, into an uncertain area between war and revolution.

2   The members of a previously subordinate polity, such as the group of contenders holding power over a regional government, assert sovereignty. Here the words "rebellion" and "revolt" spring readily to mind. Yet in recent years it has become quite usual to call one version of such events a colonial or national revolution—especially if the outcome is independence.

3   Contenders not holding membership in the existing polity mobilize into a bloc successfully exerting control over some portion of the governmental apparatus. Despite the attractiveness of this version to leaders of the dispossessed, it rarely, if ever, occurs in a pure form.

4   The more usual circumstance is the fragmentation of an existing polity into two or more blocs, each exercising control over some part of the government. That fragmentation frequently involves the emergence of coalitions between established members of the polity and mobilizing nonmembers.

How would we recognize the onset of multiple sovereignty? The question is stickier than it seems at first glance. Neither the presence nor the expansion of areas of autonomy or of resistance on the part of the subject population is a reliable sign. All governments excite some sorts of resistance, and all governments exert incomplete control over their subjects. That was the point of the earlier analysis of repression, toleration, and facilitation. Most states face continuing marginal challenges to their sovereignty: from within, bandits, vigilantes, religious communities, national minorities, or uncompromising separatists hold them off. From without, powerful states infiltrate them and encroach on their prerogatives. All of these circumstances have some distant kinship to revolution, but they do not constitute revolutionary situations. Even rival claims to those of the existing polity by the adherents of displaced regimes, military movements, or outside states are quite common. The claims themselves do not amount to a revolutionary situation.

The question is whether some significant part of the subject population honors the claim. The revolutionary moment arrives when previously acquiescent members of that population find themselves confronted with strictly incompatible demands from the government and form an alternative body claiming control over the government, or claiming to *be* the government . . . and those previously acquiescent people obey the alternative body. They pay taxes, provide men to its armies, feed its functionaries, honor its symbols, give time to its service, or yield other resources despite the prohibitions of a still-existing government they formerly obeyed. Multiple sovereignty has begun. When only one polity exerting exclusive control over the government remains,

nd no rivals are successfully pressing their claims—however that happens—
he revolutionary situation has ended.*

evolutionary Outcomes

A revolution," writes Samuel Huntington, "is a rapid, fundamental, and vio-
:nt domestic change in the dominant values and myths of a society, in its
olitical institutions, social structure, leadership, and government activity and
olicies. Revolutions are thus to be distinguished from insurrections, rebel-
ons, revolts, coups, and wars of independence" (Huntington 1968: 264).
luntington's definition stresses *outcomes*, not the political processes which
:ad to those outcomes. Such outcomes are rare. Depending on how generous-
′ one interpreted the words "rapid" and "fundamental", it would be easy to
rgue that no revolution has ever occurred, and hard to argue that the number
f true cases exceeds a half dozen. Peter Calvert's definition of revolution,
/hich we looked at earlier, is somewhat less demanding than Huntington's. It
ierely requires that a government be discredited, that a new group seize the
overnment by force, that the newcomers introduce a program of change, and
iat a myth legitimating the transfer of power come into being. Except for the
iscrediting, these conditions, too, are outcomes; there is no reliable way to
now whether a revolution is occurring until the whole process has ended.

For the moment, I propose an even less demanding standard than Cal-
ert's. A revolutionary outcome is the displacement of one set of power
olders by another. That simple definition leaves many reference points avail-
ble: power over the means of production, power over symbols, power over
overnment. Provisionally, let us take power over government as our refer-
ice point. A revolutionary outcome is the displacement of one set of mem-
ers of the polity by another set. Clearly, a revolutionary situation can occur
ithout a revolutionary outcome; in the simplest case, the existing members of
ie polity beat down their challengers after a period of effective, competing,
iutually exclusive claims. It is at least logically possible for a revolutionary
utcome to occur without a revolutionary situation, through the gradual addi-
on and/or subtraction of members of the polity.

In general, how does the displacement of one set of power holders by
iother happen? The answer depends in part on the time perspective we
lopt. In the short run, the question concerns tactics and the balance of forces.
ı Trotsky's analysis of the October Revolution, for example, the tactical
roblems of winning over the Petrograd garrison and then of capturing the
/inter Palace loom very large; generalized, Trotsky's concerns place the con-

---

regret to say that in an earlier version of this chapter (Tilly 1975), I used the word
evolution" for the circumstances I am here calling a revolutionary situation.

trol or neutralization of the available military force at the center of the short-run conditions for a transfer of power.

In the medium run, we arrive at the considerations which have dominated this book: the presence of mobilized contenders in effective coalitions. The medium run of Trotsky's analysis concerns the peasants who had been mobilized via the army, the organized workers of Petrograd and Moscow, the parties and the processes by which each of them mobilized and formed coalitions. In this medium run, repression and facilitation figure as well—notably in the discrediting and weakening of the Tsarist regime by the war. It is in this medium run that the creation or emergence of a revolutionary situation contributes to—and may be essential to—a revolutionary outcome. Without the appearance of multiple sovereignty a significant transfer of power is either impossible or highly unlikely.

In the long run, interests and organization begin to tell. In this book, we have faced the challenge of long run analysis only intermittently, through quick glimpses at the consequences of proletarianization, the development of capitalism, state making, urbanization, and industrialization. The quick glimpses have, however, been graphic enough to communicate the fundamental importance of threatened class interests. Over the long run, the reorganization of production creates the chief historical actors, the major constellations of interests, the basic threats to those interests, and the principal conditions for transfers of power.

SITUATIONS AND OUTCOMES COMBINED

Our concepts will do better work for us if we turn them into continua. A situation can be more or less revolutionary. The central question is: at the point in time which we are evaluating, how much would it cost to eliminate the split between the alternative polities? How nearly irrevocable is the split? We should try to make that judgment from information available at the point in time we are judging, rather than from eventual outcomes. If we want to judge a completed revolution as a whole, we can fix on the mean split between polities, the maximum split, the initial split, or the time function as a whole. In any case, one extreme is no multiple sovereignty at all, the other an irrevocable split. In between are divisions costing the parties varying amounts to eliminate. The cost definitely includes the cost of repression to the repressor and the repressed. The sum of all payoffs and foregone benefits should also enter in. If so, the estimated cost will obviously depend on the time period considered—and will obviously include some thinking about what might have happened if . . .

An outcome can also be more or less revolutionary. Now the central question is: how close did the existing members of the polity come to being ompletely displaced? We may settle for a simple head count. We may weight he heads by their power prior to the change, but still settle for counting how nany heads rolled. We may try to estimate the power of all previously existing nembers before and after. In any case, one extreme will be the maintenance or estoration of the *status quo ante*, the other extreme the complete elimination f previous members from the polity. In between will be varying degrees of displacement.

The decision whether to call an event a revolution now looks like Fig. 7-1. Politics as usual involves little or no displacement of existing members of the polity, and no more than low-cost splits between alternative polities. Coups nvolve higher-cost splits (although not irrevocable ones), but result in relatively little displacement of existing members. Silent revolutions, if they occur, produce major displacements with little or no development of a revolutionary ituation. Great revolutions are extreme in both regards: extensive splits between alternative polities, large-scale displacement of existing members. In Fig. 7-1, line A represents a generous definition of revolution: everything to he right gets counted. Line B states a restrictive definition; only great revolutions qualify.

Although the diagram is entirely conceptual, it helps pinpoint some mportant theoretical issues. Students of revolution disagree over the ombinations of outcome and revolutionary situation which are actually possible in this world. To simplify a complex set of disagreements, let us look at hree idealized maps of the possible and the impossible: "Syndicalist," "Marxist," and "Brintonian." They appear in Fig. 7-2. The Syndicalist argument, in its simplest form, runs: the more extensive the revolutionary situation, the more sweeping the revolutionary outcome. It is a causal argument. It says the creation of an irrevocable split between alternative polities will, in itself, produce a total displacement of the existing holders of power. It also says: he less extensive the revolutionary situation, the less extensive the transfer of power.

The Marxist argument (especially as articulated by such revolutionary heorists as Gramsci and Lenin) disagrees. It argues that many a revolutionary ituation fails to produce a revolutionary outcome—for lack of a vanguard, or lack of a disciplined revolutionary party, for lack of the right class coalitions, and so on. But it agrees with the Syndicalist argument in one important egard: no revolutionary transfers of power occur without extensive revolutionary situations. Thus a two-part revolutionary strategy: create (or look for) revolutionary situation; organize the political means for a revolutionary outome.

Crane Brinton deliberately took the opposite view. He argued important nternal limits on the creation of any revolutionary situation; reaction was nevitable. He suggested, furthermore, that the relationship between situation

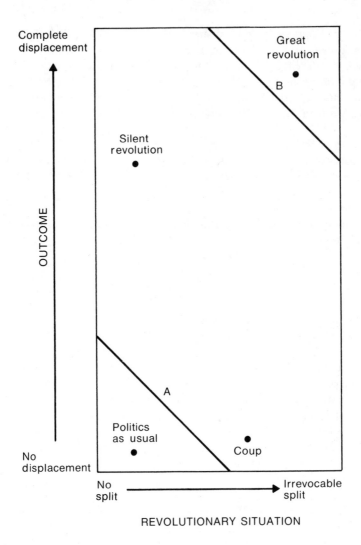

Fig. 7-1
Combinations of revolutionary situations and revolutionary outcomes

and outcome was *negative:* the more revolutionary the situation, the less revolutionary the outcome. A people who went through a major revolution returned, with relief, more or less to the starting point. But the more sensible gradualists, thought Brinton, produced major alterations of the power structure. The arguments among Syndicalists, Marxists, and Brintonians are with us today.

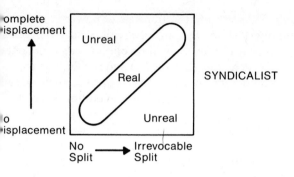

SYNDICALIST

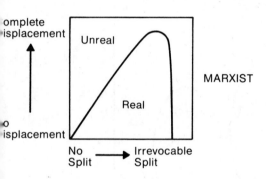

MARXIST

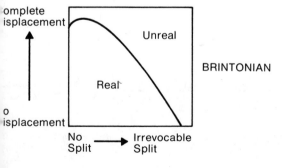

BRINTONIAN

Fig. 7–2

Syndicalist, Marxist, and Brintonian maps of revolutionary reality

Figure 7-3 offers a revised classification of transfers of power in terms of the extent to which revolutionary situations and/or revolutionary outcomes occur. The diagram tells us to take a broad view of revolution, requiring only some minimum combination of revolutionary situation and revolutionary outcome to qualify an event as a revolution. It asserts that the phenomena we call "coups," "insurrections," "civil wars," and "full-scale revolutions" overlap, but not completely. Each has its own characteristic range of outcomes and revolutionary situations. But the basic differences among them regard the

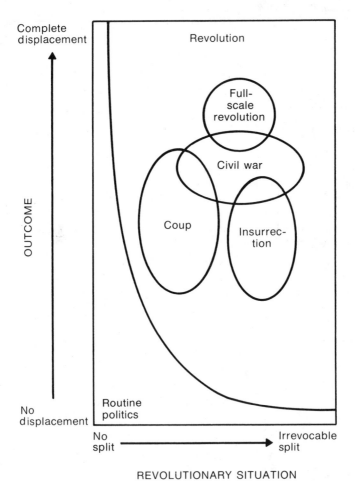

Fig. 7-3
Situations and outcomes in different types of power transfers

dentities of the parties to the transfer of power: in the coup, members of the polity displace each other; in a full-scale revolution much or all of the previously dominant class loses power, and so on.

Although the diagram does not say so explicitly, the oblong for "civil war" brushes the extreme revolutionary situation, irrevocable split, to remind us that one common outcome of civil war is the permanent division of a territory previously controlled by a single government into two or more autonomous territories. The diagram indicates that extensive revolutionary outcomes do not occur without extensive revolutionary situations. But it denies the converse; extremely revolutionary situations do not necessarily produce extremely revolutionary outcomes. The debate over definitions takes us into a debate over the substance of political conflict and the structure of revolution.

Some of our most valuable analyses of revolution and rebellion do not concern the sufficient conditions for one or the other, but the placement of different sorts of groups within some equivalent of the diagram. Some of the analyses concentrate on the mobilizability of different sorts of groups for different kinds of action: for revolutionary activism, for politics as usual, and so on. Eric Wolf's comparison of twentieth-century agrarian rebellions emphasizes the relative ability to mobilize the poor, middle, and rich peasants, although it also says important things about the way expanding capitalism impinges on rural areas and on the interests of different groups of peasants within them.

Some analyses give their primary attention to the correspondence between different forms of political action and different configurations of interests, while saying relatively little about mobilization or about the political processes leading to particular actions and outcomes. They commonly take the form of comparisons of the characteristic forms of action of people in contrasting structural settings. Jeffery Paige's *Agrarian Revolution* is an outstanding case in point. Paige sums up his guiding hypotheses in these terms:

A. A combination of both noncultivators and cultivators dependent on land as their principal source of income leads to an agrarian revolt . . .

B. A combination of noncultivators dependent on income from commercial capital and cultivators dependent on income from land leads to a reform commodity movement . . .

C. A combination of noncultivators dependent on income from capital and cultivators dependent on income from wages leads to a reform labor movement . . .

D. A combination of noncultivators dependent on income from land and cultivators dependent on income from wages leads to revolution (Paige 1975: 70–71).

Paige then conducts two sorts of analysis to verify these hypotheses: a comparison of rural social movements in 135 export sectors of 70 relatively poor countries from 1948 to 1970, and detailed case studies of Peru, Angola, and Vietnam. The evidence looks good for his argument.

Note how the argument works: it cross-tabulates the interests of cultivators and noncultivators, deduces the character and extent of the interest conflict resulting from each combination, and predicts from the conflict of interests to the form of the cultivators' political action. The substance of hypothesis D is that the combination of land and wages

> includes some forms of agricultural organization which combine the inflexible behavior of the cultivators of a landed estate with the strong cultivator organizations of the corporate plantation. When both conditions exist simultaneously, the result is likely to be an agrarian revolution in which a strong peasant-based guerrilla movement organized by a nationalist or Communist party attempts to destroy both the rural upper class and the institutions of the state and establish a new society (Paige 1975: 358–359).

Paige then makes further distinctions concerning the correlates of revolutionary nationalist movements and revolutionary socialist movements. Although in his case studies Paige is sensitive and informative about mobilization, collective action, and strategic interaction, the basic theory predicts action from interests. Here, instead, we are assuming interests and dealing with the political processes which lead from organized and conflicting interests to revolution.

PROXIMATE CAUSES OF REVOLUTIONARY SITUATIONS

Let us look more closely at the implications of the definition of a revolutionary situation as multiple sovereignty. By definition, there are three proximate causes of multiple sovereignty:

1   the appearance of contenders, or coalitions of contenders, advancing exclusive alternative claims to the control over the government which is currently exerted by the members of the polity;

2   commitment to those claims by a significant segment of the subject population (especially when those commitments are not simply acknowledged in principle, but activated in the face of prohibitions or contrary directives from the government);

3   incapacity or unwillingness of the agents of the government to suppress the alternative coalition and/or the commitment to its claims.

The critical signs of a revolutionary situation, in this perspective, are signs of the emergence of an alternative polity. These signs may possibly be related to conditions other analysts have proposed as precipitants of revolution: rising discontent, value conflict, frustration, or relative deprivation. The relationship must, however, be proved and not assumed. Even if it is proved that discontent, value conflict, frustration, and relative deprivation do fluctuate in close correspondence to the emergence and disappearance of alternative policies—a result which would surprise me—the thing to watch for would still be the commitment of a significant part of the population, regardless of their motives, to exclusive alternative claims to the control over the government currently exerted by the members of the polity.

So why didn't the United States break into revolution with the onset of the Depression after 1930? I claim no special wisdom. Assuming the working class as the principal candidate for countermobilization, however, this line of argument singles out factors such as the following: a low initial level of mobilization; lack of alienated coalition partners within the polity; shift of the burden of extraction, at least relatively, to unmobilized groups such as blacks; trading of concessions which were relatively inexpensive to the government (for example, the right of industrial unions to organize) for the granting of loyalty. The fascists of Germany and Italy went another route, by deliberately demobilizing the working class. The other nations of the world paid the cost of the demobilization, in the form of the Second World War.

In an essay which followed his large comparative work, Barrington Moore (1969) proposed four preconditions for major revolutions:

1   the elite's loss of unified control over army, policy, and other instruments of violence;

2   the emergence of acute conflicts of interest within the "dominant classes";

3   the development of widespread challenges to prevailing modes of thought and to the predominant explanations of justifications of human suffering;

4   the mobilization of a revolutionary mass, most probably through some sudden disruption of everyday life coupled with increase of misery.

The first two are essentially the same condition: the fragmentation of the polity into more than one coalition, each a potential claimant to exclusive control of the government, and each a potential coalition partner with challengers that are mobilizing rapidly. Condition (3) may well occur both inside and outside the polity, as those outside express their outrage at being excluded and some of those inside respond to their complaints with sympathy or manipulation.

The mobilization of a revolutionary mass describes the rapid appearance of a new challenger. Nothing in my analysis or in my historical reflection leads me to assume that the mobilization must be sudden or that it must come from immiseration. But lightning mobilization, if it occurs, does reduce the chances for the incremental challenging, testing, and coalition-formation which belong to the routine acquisition of power, and concentrates the attendant collective violence in a short period of time.

We have narrowed the focus of explanation and prediction considerably. It now comes down to specifying and detecting the circumstances under which three related conditions occur: (1) the appearance of contenders making exclusive alternative claims, (2) significant commitments to those claims, (3) repressive incapacity of the government. The short-run conditions of these outcomes may be quite different from the long-run changes which make them possible. Let us concentrate for the moment on the short-run conditions.

Alternatives to the Existing Polity

What I mean by "exclusive alternative claims to control of the government" comes out dramatically in an article written about a year after the October Revolution, as the other parties which had joined the revolutionary coalition were being squeezed out of power:

> Now, however, the course of world events and the bitter lessons derived from the alliance of all the Russian monarchists with Anglo-French and American imperialism are proving *in practice* that a democratic republic is a bourgeois-democratic republic, which is already out of date from the point of view of the problems which imperialism has placed before history. They show that there is no other alternative: *either* Soviet government triumphs in every advanced country in the world, *or* the most reactionary imperialism triumphs, the most savage imperialism, which is throttling the small and weak nations and reinstating reaction all over the world—Anglo-American imperialism, which has perfectly mastered the art of using the form of a democratic republic.
>
> One or the other.
>
> There is no middle course; until quite recently this view was regarded as the blind fanaticism of the Bolsheviks.
>
> *But it turned out to be true* (Lenin 1967a: 35).

These claims came from a party already in power. But they were addressed to revolutionary strategists in other countries who wished to continue a collaborative approach within Russia itself.

When can we expect the appearance of contenders (or coalitions of contenders) advancing exclusive alternative claims to the control of the government currently exerted by the members of the polity? The question is a trifle misleading, for such contenders are almost always with us in the form of millennial cults, radical cells, or rejects from positions of power. The real question is when such contenders proliferate and/or mobilize.

Two paths lead to that proliferation and/or mobilization. The first is the flourishing of groups which from their inception hold to transforming aims which are incompatible with the continued power of the members of the polity. Truly "other-wordly" and retreatist groups seeking total withdrawal from contemporary life do not fully qualify, since in principle they can prosper so long as the rest of the world lets them alone. True radicals, true reactionaries, anarchists, preachers of theocracy, monists of almost every persuasion come closer to the mark.

The second path is the turning of contenders from objectives which are compatible with the survival of the polity to objectives which spell its doom: a claim to all power, a demand for criteria of membership which would exhaust all the available resources, or exclude all its present members.

Why and how the first sort of group—the group committed from the start to fundamental transformation of the structure of power—forms remains one of the mysteries of our time. Max Weber taught that such groups formed around charismatic individuals who offered alternative visions of the world, visions that made sense of the contemporary chaos. Marx suggested that from time to time a few individuals would swing so free of their assigned places in the existing class structure that they could view the structure as a whole and the historical process producing it; they could then teach their view to others who were still caught in the structure. Since Marx and Weber we have had some heroic conceptualizing and cataloging of the varieties of intrinsically revolutionary groups (see Smelser 1963, Lipset and Raab 1970, Gamson 1968). But the rise and fall of diverse movements of protest since World War II has shown us that we still have almost no power to anticipate where and when such committed groups will appear.

The turning of contenders from compatible objectives is rather less of a mystery, because we can witness its occurrence as old members lose their positions in the polity and as challengers are refused access to power. The former is the recurrent history of right-wing activism, the latter the standard condition for left-wing activism. Marx himself gave the classic analysis of the process of radicalization away from some sort of accommodation with the existing system toward an exclusive, revolutionary position. His argument was precisely that through repeated victimization under bourgeois democracy (a victimization, to be sure, dictated by the logic of capitalism) workers would gradually turn away from its illusions toward class-conscious militancy. That he should have overestimated the polarizing effects of industrial capitalism and underestimated the absorptive capacity of the polities it supported does not reduce the accuracy of his perception of the relationships. So far as Marx was concerned a newly forming and growing class was the only candidate for such a transformation. In fact, the general principle appears to apply as well to national minorities, age-sex groups, regional populations, or any other mobilizing group which makes repeated unsuccessful bids for power.

The elaboration of new ideologies, new creeds, new theories of how the world works, is part and parcel of both paths to a revolutionary position: the emergence of brand-new challengers and the turning of existing contenders. Most likely the articulation of ideologies which capture and formulate the problems of such contenders in itself accelerates their mobilization and change of direction; how great an independent weight to attribute to ideological innovation is another recurrent puzzle in the analysis of revolution.

The need for elaboration of ideologies is one of the chief reasons for the exceptional importance of intellectuals in revolutionary movements. The reflections of a leading French Marxist intellectual on current political strategy are revealing:

> The revolutionary party's capacity for hegemony is directly linked to the extent of its influence in the professions and in intellectual circles. It can counter bourgeois ideology to the degree that it inspires their inquiries and draws their vanguard into reflection on an "alternative model," while respecting the independence of these inquiries. The mediation of the intellectual vanguard is indispensable in combatting and destroying the grip of the dominant ideology. It is also necessary in order to give the dominated classes a language and a means of expression which will make them conscious of the reality of their subordination and exploitation (Gorz 1969: 241–242).

This is a congenial doctrine for an intellectual to hold. Yet it corresponds to a vigorous reality: as Barrington Moore suggests, an outpouring of new thought articulating objectives incompatible with the continuation of the existing polity is probably our single most reliable sign that the first condition of a revolutionary situation is being fulfilled.

Acceptance of Alternative Claims

The second condition is commitment to the claims by a significant segment of the subject population. The first and second conditions overlap, since the veering of an already-mobilized contender toward exclusive alternative claims to control of the government simultaneously establishes the claims and produces commitment to them. Yet expansion of commitment can occur without the establishment of any new exclusive claims through (a) the further mobilization of the contenders involved, and (b) the acceptance of those claims by other individuals and groups. It is in accounting for the expansion and contraction of this sort of commitment that attitudinal analyses of the type conducted by Ted Gurr, James Davies, and Neil Smelser should have their greatest power.

Two classes of action by governments have a strong tendency to expand commitment to revolutionary claims. The first is the sudden failure of the government to meet specific obligations which members of the subject populations regard as well established and crucial to their own welfare. I have in mind obligations to provide employment, welfare services, protection, access to justice, and the other major services of government.

Italy, for example, experienced a series of crises of this sort at the end of World War I, despite the fact that she had ended up on the "winning" side. The demobilization of the army threw over two million men on a soft labor market, the fluctuation and relaxation of controls over food supplies and prices aggrieved millions of consumers, and peasants (including demobilized soldiers) began to take into their own hands the redistribution of land they argued the government had promised during the war. The consequent withdrawal of commitment from the government opened the way to fascism. Both Right and Left mobilized in response to the government's inability to deliver on its promises. In the event, the regime chose to tolerate or support the Fascist strong-arm *squadri* in their effort to destroy the most effective working-class organizations. For that reason (rather than any fundamental similarity in their social bases) the initial geographic distribution of Italian Fascism resembled the distribution of socialist strength: the Po Valley, the northern industrial cities, and so forth. The Right: Far Right coalition worked, more or less, in crushing the organized segments of the Left. But it left the Fascists in nearly autonomous control of large parts of Italy: multiple sovereignty.

The case of postwar Italy has a threefold importance, for it illustrates a process which was widespread (although generally less acute) elsewhere in Europe at the same time. It falls into a very general pattern in which the end of war (victorious or not) produces a crisis of governmental incapacity. Finally, it demonstrates the way in which movements of protest themselves not clearly 'right" or "left" in orientation sometimes open the way to a right-wing (or, for that matter, left-wing) seizure of power.

The *second* class of governmental action which commonly expands the commitment of important segments of the population to revolutionary claims is a rapid or unexpected increase in the government's demand for surrender of resources by its subject population. An increase in taxes is the clearest example, but military conscription, the commandeering of land, crops, or farm animals, and the imposition of corvees have all played an historical role in the incitement of opposition. Gabriel Ardant (1965) argues, with widespread evidence, that increased taxation has been the single most important stimulus to popular rebellion throughout western history. Furthermore, he points out that the characteristic circumstances of tax rebellions in Europe since 1500 are not what most historians have thought. Instead of being either the last resort of those who are in such misery that any more taxation will destroy them or the first resort of privileged parties who refuse to let anything slip away from them, the rebellion against new taxes most commonly arises where communities find themselves incapable of marketing enough of their goods to acquire the funds demanded by the government.

Ardant considers "incapable of marketing" to mean either that the local economy is insufficiently commercialized or that the market for the particular products of the community in question has contracted. Eric Wolf's analysis of the relationship between peasants and the market, however, suggests that "incapability" refers more generally to any demands which would make it impossible for people to fulfill the obligations which bind them to the local community, and whose fulfillment makes them honorable men. It follows directly from Wolf's argument that increased taxation in the face of little commercialization or the contraction of demand for the products already being marketed by a peasant community tends to have devastating effects on the structure of the community.

Other types of communities face different versions of the same problems. The consequence is that rapidly increased extraction of resources by the government—which in western countries has most frequently occurred in preparations for war—regularly persuades some segment of the population that the government is no longer legitimate, while those who oppose it are.

Such a shift in position sometimes occurs rapidly, with little advance warning. This appears to be especially likely when a contender or set of contenders mobilizes quickly in response to a general threat to its position—an invasion, an economic crisis, a major attempt by landlords, the state, or someone else to deprive them of crucial resources. We find the villagers of northern England rising in a Pilgrimage of Grace to oppose Henry VIII's dispossession of the monasteries, Mexican peasants banding together to resist the threat of takeover of their common lands, Japanese countrymen recurrently joining bloody uprisings against the imposition of new taxes.

This defensive mobilization is not simply a cumulation of individual dissatisfactions with hardship or a mechanical group response to deprivation. Whether it occurs at all depends very much, as Eric Wolf and others have shown, on the preexisting structure of power and solidarity within the population experiencing the threat. Furthermore, its character is not intrinsically either "revolutionary" or "counter-revolutionary"; that depends mainly on the coalitions the potential rebels make. This defensive mobilization is the most volatile feature of a revolutionary situation, both because it often occurs fast and because new coalitions between a rapidly mobilized group and established contenders for power can suddenly create a significant commitment to an alternative polity.

If that is the case, there may be something to the common notion that revolutions are most likely to occur when a sharp contraction in well-being follows a long period of improvement. James Davies has propounded the idea under the label of "J-curve hypothesis" and Ted Gurr has treated it as one of the chief variants of his general condition for rebellion: a widening of the expectation–achievement gap. All the attempts to test these attitudinal versions of the theory have been dogged by the difficulty of measuring changes in expectations and achievements for large populations over substantial blocks of time and by the tendency of most analysts to work from the fact of revolution back to the search for evidence of short-run deprivation and then further back to the search for evidence of long-run improvement, not necessarily with respect to the same presumed wants, needs, or expectations. The latter procedure has the advantage of almost always producing a fit between the data and the theory, and the disadvantage of not being a reliable test of the theory. The question remains open.

Assuming that sharp contractions following long expansions *do* produce revolutionary situations with exceptional frequency, however, the line of argument pursued here leads to an interesting alternative explanation of the J-curve phenomenon. It is that during a long run of expanding resources, the government tends to take on commitments to redistribute resources to new contenders and the polity tends to admit challengers more easily because the relative cost to existing members is lower when resources are expanding. In the event of quick contraction, the government has greater commitments, new matters of right, to members of the polity, and has acquitted partial commitments to new contenders, perhaps not members of the polity, but very likely forming coalitions with members. The government faces a choice between (1) greatly increasing the coercion applied to the more vulnerable segments of the population in order to bring up the yield of resources for reallocation or (2) breaking commitments where that will incite the least dangerous opposition. Either step is likely to lead to a defensive mobilization, and thence to a threat of revolution. Such a situation does, to be sure, promote the disappointment of rising expectations. But the principal link between the J-curve and the revolutionary situation, in this hypothesis, lies in the changing relations between contenders and government likely to occur in a period of expanding resources.

In a longer historical view, the changes which have most often produced the rapid shifts in commitment away from existing governments and established polities are processes which directly affect the autonomy of smaller units within the span of the government: the rise and fall of centralized states, the expansion and contraction of national markets, the concentration and dispersion of control over property. Prosperity and depression, urbanization and ruralization, industrialization and deindustrialization, sanctification and secularization occur in a dispersed and incremental fashion.

Although state making, the expansion and contraction of markets, and property shifts also develop incrementally most of the time, they are especially susceptible of producing dramatic confrontations of rights, privileges, and principles; this tax collector wants the family cow, this merchant proposes to buy the village commons, this prince fails to protect his subjects from bandits. S. N. Eisenstadt (1963) has brought out the extreme vulnerability of vast bureaucratic empires to overexpansion and to damage at the center; both, in his analysis, tend to produce rebellions in which peripheral agents of the empire seek to establish autonomous control over the lands, men, organizations and wealth first mobilized by the empire. Fernand Braudel (1966) has stressed the frequency with which banditry and related struggles for local power proliferated as the ephemeral states of seventeenth-century Europe contracted. In all these cases, spokesmen for large-scale organization and centripetal processes find themselves locked in struggle with advocates of small-scale autonomy.

In order to produce multiple sovereignty, and thus become revolutionary, commitments to some alternative claimant must be activated in the face of prohibitions or contrary directives from the government. The moment at which some people belonging to members of the alternative coalition seize control over some portion of the government, and other people not previously attached to the coalition honor their directives, marks the beginning of a revolutionary situation. That acceptance of directives may, to be sure, occur as a result of duress or deception as well as of conversion to the cause. A mixture of duress, deception, and conversion will often do the job.

The presence of a coherent revolutionary organization makes a great difference at exactly this point. An organization facilitates the initial seizure of control, spreads the news, activates the commitments already made by specific men. If so, Lenin provides a more reliable guide to revolutionary strategy than Sorel; Lenin's closely directed conspiratorial party contrasts sharply with the spontaneous and purifying rebellion in which Sorel placed his hopes. But the existence of such an organization also makes the start of revolution more closely dependent on the decisions of a small number of men—and thus, paradoxically, subject to chance and idiosyncrasy.

In the last analysis, activation of revolutionary commitments happens through an extension of the same processes which create the commitments. Conspiratorial organization simply happens to be the one which maximizes the opportunity of the committed to calculate the right moment to strike against the government. The government's sudden inability to meet its own responsibilities (as in the German insurrections during the disintegration of the imperial war effort in 1918) or its violation of the established rights of its subject population (as in the 1640 rebellions of Portugal and Catalonia against Castile, which followed Olivares's attempt to squeeze exceptional resources from those reluctant provinces for the conduct of his war with France) can simultaneously spread and activate the commitment to its revolutionary opposition.

In a case like that of the Taiping rebellion, the rapid mobilization of a contender advancing exclusive alternative claims to control over the government itself leads quickly and inevitably to a break and to an armed struggle. The dramatic weakening of a government's repressive capacity through war, defection, or catastrophe can simultaneously create the possibility of revolution and encourage the revolutionaries to make their bid; the quick succession of the French revolution of 1870 to the defeat of the Emperor by Prussia falls into this category.

Governmental Inaction

Condition *three* is the incapacity or unwillingness of the agents of the government to suppress the alternative coalition or the commitment to its claims. Three paths are possible: (a) sheer insufficiency of the available means of coercion; (b) inefficiency in applying the means; (c) inhibitions to their application. The starkest cases of insufficiency occur when the balance of coercive resources between the government and the alternative coalition swings suddenly toward the latter, because the government has suffered a sudden depletion of its resources (as in a lost war), because the alternative coalition has managed a sudden mobilization of resources (as in the pooling of private arms) or because a new contender with abundant coercive resources has joined the coalition (as in the defection of troops or foreign intervention). However, the massing of rebels in locations remote from the centers of coercive strength, the implantation of the alternative coalition in a rough and unknown terrain, and the adoption of tactics unfamiliar to the professional forces of the government all raise the cost of suppression as well.

Ted Gurr (1969: 235–236) develops an interesting argument about the balance of coercive resources between a government and its opponents. In his phrasing, "The likelihood of internal war increases as the ratio of dissident to regime coercive control approaches equality." (For "equality," read "one"; Walter Korpi has expanded a similar argument into a general model of conflict.) Gurr is referring directly to the probable magnitude of collective violence; where the balance strongly favors the government, goes the argument, only dispersed acts of rebellion occur; where the balance strongly favors its opponents, the government tends to be a pawn in their hands. The analysis applies even more plausibly to the likelihood of revolution, for an alternative coalition with large coercive resources is likely to seize control with at most an instant of multiple sovereignty, while an alternative coalition with small coercive resources will never get multiple sovereignty started.

Inefficiency in applying means which are, in principle, sufficient is harder to pin down and explain; the inefficient almost always plead insufficient means. William Langer (1969: esp. 321–322) contends that had the authorities not bungled their repression of various popular movements the European revolutions of 1848 would never have occurred. To have confidence in his conclusion we have to assess the balance of coercive means between popular movements and governments as well as the political inhibitions to repression. In prerevolutionary 1848 the governments clearly had the edge in men, weapons, supplies, and coercive technique. The strong commitment of the new bourgeois, who had been acquiring significant roles in European governments to certain kinds of civil liberties, and various working-class movements, however, both stayed the government's hand. From a strictly instrumental perspective, all such inhibitions are "inefficient." Yet not to distinguish them from the apparent incompetence of the Egyptian regime toppled in 1952 or the Turkish sultanate displaced in 1919 blurs the essential explanation of these events.

Inhibitions to the application of available coercive means are more interesting than shortages or inefficiency, because they are so likely to flow from the political process itself. The great importance of coalitions between established members of the polity and revolutionary challengers exemplifies the point very well. The United States of the 1960s witnessed the constant formation and reformation of coalitions between groups of intellectuals, opposition politicians, Black Liberation movements, students and peace activists, some within the American polity and some outside of it. The total effect of these coalitions fell considerably short of revolution, but while operating they shielded those whose principles offered the greatest challenge to the existing distribution of power from the treatment they received from police, troops, and other repressors when acting on their own.

Despite the implications of this example, however, the most crucial coalitions over the whole range of revolutions surely link challengers directly with military forces. The Egyptian and Turkish revolutions stand near the extreme at which the chief claims to alternative control of the government come from within the military itself; in both cases soldiers dominated a coalition linking dissident politicians and local movements of resistance. In the midst of the range we find events like the Russian revolution, in which the military were far from paramount, but important segments of the military defected, disintegrated, or refused to repress their brethren. The more extensive the prerevolutionary coalitions between challengers and military units, the more likely this is to happen.

In this respect and others, war bears a crucial relationship to revolution. Walter Laqueur (1968: 501) puts it this way:

> War appears to have been the decisive factor in the emergence of revolutionary situations in modern times; most modern revolutions, both successful and abortive, have followed in the wake of war (the Paris Commune of 1871, the Russian revolution of 1905, the various revolutions after the two World Wars, including the Chinese revolutions). These have occurred not only in the countries

that suffered defeat. The general dislocation caused by war, the material losses and human sacrifices, create a climate conducive to radical change. A large section of the population has been armed; human life seems considerably less valuable than in peacetime. In a defeated country authority tends to disintegrate, and acute social dissatisfaction receives additional impetus from a sense of wounded national prestige (the Young Turks in 1908, Naguib and Nasser in 1952). The old leadership is discredited by defeat, and the appeal for radical social change and national reassertion thus falls on fertile ground.

No doubt the statement suffers from a superabundance of explanations. Still it points out the essential relationship between war and the repressive capacity of the government.

Although war temporarily places large coercive resources under the control of a government, it does not guarantee that they will be adequate to the demands placed upon them, that they will be used efficiently, or that they will even remain under the government's firm control. Defeat and/or demobilization provide especially favorable circumstances for revolution because they combine the presence of substantial coercive resources with uncertain control over their use.

War also matters in quite a different way. By and large, wars have always provided the principal occasions on which states have rapidly increased their levies of resources from their subject populations. Conscription is only the self-evident case. Demands for taxes, forced loans, food, nonmilitary labor, manufactured goods, and raw materials follow the same pattern. The increased exactions almost always meet widespread resistance, which the agents of states counter with persuasion and force.

Despite the advantage of having extensive estates to squeeze and a wealthy church to dispossess, the Tudors pressed their England hard to support the military forces they committed to sixteenth-century warfare. They faced serious rebellion in 1489, 1497, 1536, 1547, 1549, 1553 and 1569. The last three—Kett's, Wyatt's and the Northern Rebellion—centered on dynastic issues and consisted largely of risings engineered by regional magnates. The first four, on the other hand, were popular rebellions; every one of them began with the crown's sudden laying hand on resources previously outside its control. The general pattern is the same as I have already described for tax rebellions: the rapid mobilization of an entire population which then challenges the very injustice of the royal demand for men, money, or goods.

PROXIMATE CAUSES OF REVOLUTIONARY OUTCOMES

Let us focus on the short and medium runs, reserving for later another look at long-run conditions for revolutionary outcomes. Three sets of conditions appear to be powerful proximate causes of significant transfers of power: (1) the presence of a revolutionary situation: multiple sovereignty; (2) revolutionary coalitions between challengers and members of the polity; (3) control of substantial force by the revolutionary coalition.

To what extent the development of a revolutionary situation is a symptom, rather than a cause, of a revolutionary outcome is not easy to resolve. In a long view, whether a revolutionary division of the polity occurs depends on the same conditions which determine whether a major transfer of power occurs: the formation of a coalition of mobilized contenders organized around interests which pit them and a substantial segment of the population against the dominant members of the polity. In that long view, whether the transfer of power occurs through a break in the polity, the threat of a break, or a more gradual succession does not matter much. Nonetheless, I would hazard this generalization: the more extensive the revolutionary situation, the greater the likelihood of an extensive transfer of power. That is, indeed, one of the implicit messages of Fig. 7–3, the classification of power transfers.

An extensive revolutionary situation—a costly split between the existing polity and an effective alternative coalition—increases the likelihood of an extensive transfer of power in several ways. The more extensive the revolutionary situation, the harder it is for any organized group or segment of the population to avoid committing itself to one side or the other. That commitment makes it more difficult for any contender to reconstitute its old multiple alliances in the postrevolutionary settlement. The more extensive the revolutionary situation, the more experience the revolutionary coalition will have in forging its own instruments of government independent of the existing holders of power. The party, the army, or the insurrectionary committee becomes the skeleton (or perhaps the blueprint, or both) of the new government. The more extensive the revolutionary situation, the more opportunity and justification the revolutionary coalition will have to attack the persons and resources of the powerholders, and thus to block their chances to regain power later.

These generalizations are not new. They are a standard piece of revolutionary wisdom. Writing in December, 1948, Mao Tse-Tung put it this way:

> The raging tide of China's revolution is forcing all social strata to decide their attitude. A new change is taking place in the balance of class forces in China. Multitudes of people are breaking away from Kuomintang influence and control and coming over to the revolutionary camp; and the Chinese reactionaries have fallen into hopeless straits, isolated and abandoned. As the People's War of Liberation draws closer and closer to final victory, all the revolutionary people and all friends of the people will unite more solidly and, led by the Communist Party of China, resolutely demand the complete destruction of the reactionary forces and the thoroughgoing development of the revolutionary forces until a people's democratic republic on a country-wide scale is founded and a peace based on unity and democracy is achieved (Mao 1961: 305).

The experience of China in the following years confirms the general relationship between the extensiveness of the revolutionary situation and the thoroughness of the transfer of power.

Coalitions between Members and Challengers

The second proximate cause of significant power transfers, however, works against the first to some extent. It is the formation of coalitions between members of the polity and the contenders advancing exclusive alternative claims to control over the government. The relationship is actually curvilinear: If no such coalition exists, that diminishes the chance that the revolutionary coalition will win—that there will be any transfer of power at all. The existence of a coalition increases the likelihood of some transfer of power. But if the coalitions are extensive, the revolutionary settlement will tend to restore the previous *status quo.* The wise revolutionary who wishes to produce a large transfer of power forms the minimum necessary coalition with existing members of the polity, and forces his coalition partners to break irrevocably with other members of the polity.

The nature of such a coalition is for a member of the polity to trade resources with a challenger, for example, an exchange of jobs for electoral support. Such a coalition is always risky, since the challenger will always be on the losing end of the exchange as compared with the value of the resources when traded among members of the polity, and therefore disposed to move its extensive mobilized resources elsewhere. Nevertheless the challenger is likely to accept a coalition where it offers a defense against repression or devaluation of its resources and the member is likely to accept it when the polity is closely divided, or when no coalition partners are available within the polity, or when its own membership is in jeopardy for want of resources.

A classic revolutionary tactic also falls under the heading of challenger–member coalition: the penetration of an organization which already has an established place in the structure of power. As early as 1901, Lenin was enunciating such an approach to trade unions:

> Every Social-Democratic worker should as far as possible assist and actively work in these organizations. But, while this is true, it is certainly not in our interest to demand that only Social-Democrats should be eligible for membership in the "trade" unions, since that would only narrow the scope of our influence upon the masses. Let every worker who understands the need to unite for the struggle against the employers and the governments join the trade unions. The very aim of the trade unions would be impossible of achievement, if they did not unite all who have attained at least this elementary degree of understanding, if they were not very *broad* organizations. The broader these organizations, the broader will be our influence over them—an influence due, not only to the "spontaneous" development of the economic struggle, but to the direct and conscious effort of the socialist trade union members to influence their comrades (Lenin 1967b: 191).

In these cases, the trade unions were normally established members of their respective polities, while the Social Democrats in question were challengers still outside the polity. In this same message, Lenin concludes by recommending the control of the large, open, legal union by the secret, closed, disciplined revolutionary party.

Splinter groups of intellectuals appear to have a special propensity to form coalitions outside the polity. They trade off ideological work, publicity for the demands of the challenger, leadership skills, and access to persons in high places for various forms of support: personnel for demonstrations, electoral strength, defense against other threatening challengers, and so on. Analysts of revolution as diverse as Crane Brinton and Barrington Moore have considered the "desertion of the intellectuals" to be a crucial early omen of a revolutionary situation. The "desertion" may, of course, consist of individual acceptance of exclusive alternative claims to control of the government. It may also take the form of rejecting *all* claims, in good anarchist fashion. But the shifts in commitment by intellectuals which contribute most to hastening a revolutionary situation, in my view, consist of coalitions between revolutionary challengers and groups of intellectuals having membership in the polity. The propensity of French left-wing intellectuals to form such coalitions—without quite relinquishing their own claims to power and privilege—is legendary.

Control of Substantial Force

Control over the major organized means of coercion within the population is pivotal to the success or failure of any effort to seize power. Within all contemporary states, that means control of the military forces. Although defection of the military is by no means a sufficient condition for a takeover by the rebels, no transfer of power at all is likely in a revolutionary situation if the government retains complete control of the military past the opening of that situation (Chorley 1943, Andreski 1968, Russell 1974).

D.E.H. Russell took up the question in the case of fourteen twentieth-century mass rebellions, seven of them successful, seven of them unsuccessful:

Successful	*Unsuccessful*
Afghanistan 1929	Austria 1934
Albania 1924	Burma 1953
Bolivia 1952	Colombia 1948
Brazil 1930	Cuba 1912
China 1949	Honduras 1933
Cuba 1959	Italy 1949
Mexico 1911	Spain 1934

By "rebellion," Russell means "a form of violent power struggle in which the overthrow of the regime is threatened by means that include violence" (Russell 1974: 56). By successful rebellion, which she equates with revolution, Russell means those in which the rebels or their chosen representatives assume the positions of power. Her distinction between rebellion and revolution parallels the distinction between revolutionary situation and revolutionary outcome, except that it excludes the possibility of revolution without rebellion. In the fourteen cases, Russell works out a scale for the disloyalty of the governmental armed forces. The scale appears in Table 7–1. As the table shows, the disloyalty score has three components: the degree of disloyalty (D), the timing of disloyalty (T), and the proportion of the armed forces which were disloyal (P). The basic formula, with adjustments for the number of different armed forces involved and the different phases of their action, is the product of the three components: $D \times T \times P$. Russell found some overlap between the distribu-

Table 7–1 *D.E.H. Russell's armed force disloyalty scale*

---

1. Degree of disloyalty (D)

   0 = willing, enthusiastic fighters

   1 = unwilling fighters, e.g., surrendered readily

   2 = neutral, e.g., stood by without resisting, ran away

   3 = actively helped rebels, e.g., gave arms, informed rebels of troop maneuvers and battle plans

   4 = fought on the side of the rebels

2. Time at which disloyal (T)

   0 = never (in the last 5% of the duration)

   1 = near the end (in the last 6%–25% of the duration)

   2 = about halfway through (from 26%–75% of the duration)

   3 = near the beginning (in the first 6%–25% of the duration)

   4 = from the start (in the first 0%–5% of the duration)

3. Proportion of armed forces disloyal at a particular time (P)

   0 = none (0%–1%)

   0.5 = few (2%–10%)

   1 = some (11%–25%)

   2 = considerable (26%–50%)

   3 = majority (51%–95%)

   4 = all (96%–100%)

Source Russell 1974: 74.

tions of loyalty scores for successful and unsuccessful rebellions. For example, the Burmese rebellion of 1954 failed despite wide support from the armed forces. For another, the defections of Batista's armed forces to Castro's successful Cuban revolution were few and late. On the average, nevertheless, the successful rebellions had much higher disloyalty scores. Furthermore, in no case did success come without some armed force disloyalty significantly before the end of the rebellion. This last is necessarily Russell's most controversial finding; one can easily argue that it merely shows that the armed forces, too, eventually see which way the revolutionary wind is blowing. Since Russell explicitly builds in the timing of disloyalty, however, the general results look solid.

It follows more or less directly that the greater the coercive resources—including private armies, weapons, and segments of the national armed forces—initially controlled by the revolutionary coalition, the more likely a transfer of power. Likewise, the earlier movement of coercive resources to the alternative coalition, the more likely a transfer of power. The mobilization of other resources probably affects the chances of acquiring power significantly as well, but at a lower rate than the mobilization of coercive means. It also follows that the presence of existing members of the polity in the revolutionary coalition will increase the chances for some transfer of power (although it reduces the chances for a *complete* wresting of power from members of the polity) both because of the additional resources it brings to the coalition and because of the greater likelihood that the armed forces will defect, waver, or remain neutral when confronted with established members of the polity.

REVOLUTIONARY SEQUENCES AND COLLECTIVE VIOLENCE

We have explored three proximate causes of revolutionary situations: (1) the appearance of contenders, or coalitions of contenders, advancing exclusive alternative claims to the control over the government which is currently exerted by the members of the polity; (2) commitment to these claims by a significant segment of the subject population; (3) incapacity or unwillingness of the agents of the government to suppress the alternative coalition and/or the commitment to its claims. Another triad summarized proximate causes of revolutionary outcomes: (a) the presence of a revolutionary situation; (b) revolutionary coalitions between challengers and members of the polity; (c) control of substantial force by the revolutionary coalition. Put together, the items are a recipe for revolution.

To sum up the implications of the recipe, we might put together an idealized revolutionary sequence:

1   gradual mobilization of contenders making exclusive claims to governmental control and/or unacceptable to the members of the polity;

2   rapid increase in the number of people accepting those claims and/or rapid expansion of the coalition including the unacceptable or exclusive contenders;

3   unsuccessful efforts by the government (at the behest of members of the polity) to suppress the alternative coalition and/or the acceptance of its claims; this may well include attempts at forced demobilization—seizure, devaluation, or dispersion of the resources at the disposal of contenders;

4   establishment by the alternative coalition of effective control over some portion of the government—a territorial branch, a functional subdivision, a portion of its personnel;

5   struggles of the alternative coalition to maintain or expand that control;

6   reconstruction of a single polity through the victory of the alternative coalition, through its defeat, or through the establishment of a *modus vivendi* between the alternative coalition and some or all of the old members; fragmentation of the revolutionary coalition;

7   reimposition of routine governmental control throughout the subject population.

I lay out the sequence not to propose a new "natural history" of revolution, in the style of Lyford P. Edwards or Crane Brinton, but to identify the logic of the previous discussion.

That logic differs considerably from the common idea of revolution as a sort of tension release. If a tension-release model of revolution were correct, one might reasonably expect the level of collective violence to mount unsteadily to the climax—the revolutionary situation itself—and then decline rapidly. At that point, presumably, the tension is dissipated. The "contention" model I have been following suggests a different sequence. It does not predict clearly to the curve of violence before a revolution, since that depends on the pattern of mobilization and contention leading to the establishment of multiple sovereignty. Yet it does deny the *necessity* of a buildup of violence before a revolution.

On the other hand, the contention model makes it appear likely that once multiple sovereignty begins, collective violence will continue at high levels long after the basic issue is decided, and will taper off gradually. Schematically, the contrast appears in Fig. 7-4. There are several reasons for this general prediction. First, the appearance of multiple sovereignty puts into question the achieved position of every single contender, whether a member of the polity or not, and therefore tends to initiate a general round of mutual testing among contenders. That testing in itself produces collective violence.

Second, the struggle of one polity against its rival amounts to war: a battle fought with unlimited means. Since control of the entire government is

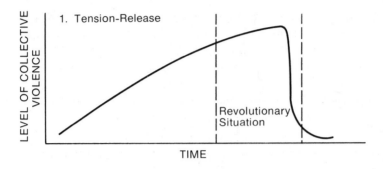

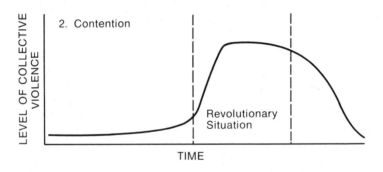

Fig. 7-4
The timing of collective violence in tension-release and contention models of revolution

at stake, high costs and high risks are justified. High costs and high risks include destruction of persons and property.

Third, the revolutionary coalition is likely to fragment once the initial seizure of control over the central governmental apparatus occurs, and that fragmentation itself tends to produce further struggles involving violence. The revolutionary coalition fragments for several reasons: it takes a larger mobilized mass to seize power than to maintain it; the inevitable divergence of some major objectives of the contenders within the coalition will come to the fore once the common objective of seizure of power has been accomplished; those contenders which have mobilized rapidly up to the point of revolution are also likely to demobilize rapidly due to the underdevelopment of their organization for the management of the mobilized resources, and thus will tend to lose position in the next rounds of testing.

Fourth, the victorious polity still faces the problem of reimposing routine governmental control over the subject population even after multiple sovereignty has ended. As the government returns to its work of extracting and redistributing resources, it finds people reluctant to pay taxes, give up their land, send their sons to war, devote their time to local administration. And so a new round of violent imposition and violent resistance begins. Where the initial locus of the revolution is constricted, this is likely to show up as a spread of collective violence to other parts of the population. In a centralized governmental system, the most common sequence is therefore likely to be a large and decisive struggle at the center followed by a more widespread but less critical series of battles through the rest of the territory.

Within this framework, several conditions appear likely to affect the overall level of violence produced by a revolution. In general, the larger the number of contenders involved in the struggle for power (holding constant the number of *people* involved), the higher the level of violence, because the number of mutual tests of position between contenders likely rises exponentially with the number of contenders. The greater the fluctuation in control of various segments of the government by different coalitions of contenders, the higher the level of violence, both because the seizure of control itself brings violent resistance and because each change of control sets off further testing of position.

Finally, the character of the repressive means under government control strongly affects the degree of violence. The connections are obvious yet complicated: the use of lethal weapons for crowd control increases deaths through collective violence, the division of labor between specialists in domestic order (police) and war (armies) probably decreases it, the relationship to overall repressive capacity of the government is probably curvilinear (little damage to persons or property where the government has great repressive capacity, little damage where its repressive capacity is slight), the level of violence probably rises as the armament of the government and of its opponents approaches equality. All of these relationships, and more, are plausible, but no more than slivers of systematic evidence for their actual validity exist.

If these generalizations have something to them, the extent of collective violence produced by a revolution should be only weakly and indirectly related to the extent to which the distribution of power changes. A zero redistribution of power (which most of us would call a failure of the revolution) can occur as an outcome of any of the ideal stages presented before, although it becomes less probable as the stages proceed.

REVOLUTIONARY OUTCOMES AND FURTHER STRUCTURAL CHANGES

Under what conditions does extensive structural change accompany or result from a revolution? To the degree that structural change *means* transfer of power from class to class, party to party, contender to contender, to be sure, we have already examined the question. But if it means further redistribution of resources, changes in the quality of life, urbanization, industrialization, moral reconstruction, everything depends on the time scale one adopts.

Relatively few permanent changes of this sort actually occur in the course of revolutions. Engels, Sorel, and Fanon all held out the hope of a vast moral regeneration within the act of revolution itself; the historical experience is sadly lacking in examples thereof. The other structural rearrangements which occur in the course of revolutions are typically temporary: the mobilization of men, loyalties, organizational talents, and weapons at a national level which recedes as the new structure of power crystallizes; the disruption of daily routines for festivals, deliberations, emergencies; the provisional appearance of commissars, governing committees, task forces. Michael Walzer has brilliantly portrayed a revolutionary outlook for seventeenth-century England, Richard Cobb a revolutionary mentality for eighteenth-century France; nevertheless, for the outlooks and mentalities of most people, revolutions are but passing moments.

A few great revolutions provide exceptions to this absence of short–run transformation; that is perhaps what permits us to call them great revolutions. Although the nobles and the clergy regained some of their position in France with and after Napoleon, the confiscation and sale of aristocratic and ecclesiastical property from 1790 to 1793 permanently shifted the weight away from those two powerful classes. The Soviets survived the Bolshevik Revolution. The Chinese communists began reorganizing village structure almost as soon as they were on the scene. Contrary to the world-weary view of Crane Brinton, who argued that a revolution took a country through tremendous turmoil to a position approximately the same as it would have occupied anyway after an equivalent lapse of time, it may be that the extent of structural alteration occurring while multiple sovereignty persists is our best sign of the depth of the permanent change to be produced by the revolution.

Over the long run, revolutions appear to change the direction of structural transformation to the extent that they produce a transfer of power. Where there is a large transfer of power among classes, the particular coalition which gains profoundly shapes the subsequent political development of the country. Barrington Moore's comparison of India, Japan, China, the United States, France, England, Germany, and Russia makes precisely that point. Military coups almost never produce any significant structural change —despite the declarations of national renovation which ritually accompany them these days—because they involve minor rearrangements among extremely limited sets of contenders. The apparent exceptions to this rule, revolutions from above like those of Japan and Turkey, ordinarily have a reforming segment of the ruling elite effectively cutting off their fellows from further access to power, and forming coalitions with classes previously excluded from power.

However, the organizational means available to those who emerge from the revolution with power affect the degree of structural transformation deliberately promoted by the government in postrevolutionary years. In a discussion of the effect of the "confining conditions" under which a revolutionary coalition seized power on its subsequent capacity to transform social organization, Otto Kirchheimer comes to the conclusion that the emergency powers accruing to states during twentieth-century crises like World War I drastically reduced the confinement of power holders:

> The revolution of the 20th Century obliterates the distinction between emergency and normalcy. Movement plus state can organize the masses because: (a) the technical and intellectual equipment is now at hand to direct them toward major societal programs rather than simply liberating their energies from the bonds of tradition; (b) they have the means at hand to control people's livelihood by means of job assignments and graduated rewards unavailable under the largely agricultural and artisanal structure of the 1790s and still unavailable to the small enterprise and commission-merchant type economy of the 1850s and 1860s; (c) they have fallen heir to endlessly and technically refined propaganda devices substituting for the uncertain leader-mass relations of the previous periods; and (d) they face state organizations shaken up by war dislocation and economic crisis. Under these conditions Soviet Russia could carry through simultaneously the job of an economic and a political, a bourgeois and a post-bourgeois revolution in spite of the exceedingly narrow basis of its political elite. On the other hand, the premature revolutionary combination of 1793–94 not only dissolved quickly, but left its most advanced sector, the *sansculottes,* with only the melancholy choice between desperate rioting—Germinal 1795—or falling back into a preorganized stage of utter helplessness and agony (Kirchheimer 1965: 973).

This analysis can be generalized. Despite the "confining conditions" faced by the French revolutionary coalitions of 1789–94, they seized a state apparatus which was already exceptionally centralized and powerful by comparison with those which had grown up elsewhere in the world. They were able to use that great power, in fact, to destroy the juridical structure of feudalism, effect large transfers of wealth, subjugate the Church, build a mass army. The nineteenth-century revolutionaries who repeatedly seized control of the Spanish state grabbed an apparatus whose extractive and repressive capacities were insufficient to any task of national transformation.

It is true that the mobilization of contenders which occurs before and during a revolution may itself facilitate a further national mobilization, putting resources at the disposal of the state which were simply unavailable before the revolution: property, energy, information, loyalties. That is, indeed, a characteristic strategy of contemporary national revolutions. The Chinese experience indicates that in the course of a long mobilization revolutionaries sometimes build alternative institutions which are potentially stronger than the existing state, and serve as the infrastructure of a strong new state when the revolutionaries come to power. Most revolutionaries, however, seize a state apparatus without that long preparation of an organizational alternative. In those cases, the already-accrued power of the state affects the probability that fundamental structural change will issue from the revolution much more strongly than does the extent of mobilization during the revolution.

These facile generalizations, I confess, do not do justice to a critical question. For on our estimate of the long-run effects of different kinds of revolutions must rest our judgment as to whether any particular revolution, or revolutionary opportunity, is worth its cost. I estimate some revolutions as worth it. But at present no one has enough systematic knowledge about the probable structural consequences of one variety of revolution or another to make such estimates with confidence.

Except, perhaps, in retrospect. Historians continue to debate what the English, French, and Russian revolutions cost and what they accomplished. In those cases (at least in principle) they are dealing with actualities rather than probabilities. That potential certainty, however, has a self-destructive side; when it comes to an event as sweeping as the English Revolution, almost every previous event which left some trace in seventeenth-century England is in some sense a "cause," and almost every subsequent event in the country and its ambit is in some sense an "effect." Making cause-and-effect analysis manageable in this context means reducing the revolution to certain essentials, identifying the sufficient conditions for those essentials, and then specifying subsequent events which would have been unlikely without the revolutionary essentials. So in fact the causal analysis of real, historic revolutions and of revolutions in general converge on statements of probability.

8
Conclusions and New Beginnings

BACK TO THE EIGHTEENTH CENTURY

We began this inquiry together more than two centuries ago, in 1765. At that point we wandered through England, watching people attack poorhouses. We were travelers in time, simply trying to get a sense of the texture and meaning of popular collective action. We went from there to a rather timeless world, a world containing abstract models of collective action. We climbed up the mobilization side from interest to organization to mobilization to collective action. We then climbed down the opportunity side, from repression/facilitation to power to opportunity/threat, only to return to collective action. Next we reentered time, equipped with our models. We made three main circuits: through major changes in repertoires of contentious collective action, through various forms of collective violence, into the turbulence of revolution and rebellion. Here we are now, back near our starting point: general reflection on the texture and meaning of popular collective action.

Suppose we spirited ourselves back to 1765. Armed with the teachings of this book, what would we do? What *could* we do that we couldn't do when first we trod on Nacton Heath?

One of the first things would be to resolve the general "turbulence" of 1765 into specific groups, interests, actions, and relations among groups. We might, for example, start looking hard at such differences as those between the Sussex poorhouse conflicts and the action behind this brief notice for 10 January in the *Annual Register:*

> Some thousands of weavers went in a body to Westminster, and presented petitions to both houses of parliament, in behalf of themselves and their numerous families, most of them now, as they represented, in a starving condition for want of work; and begging, as a relief to their miseries, that they would, in the present session of parliament, grant a general prohibition of foreign wrought silks.

223

We would want to differentiate that from the *Register's* report for 20 April:

> . . . ten journeymen taylors were tried, on an indictment for conspiring together to raise the wages, and lessen the hours of work, settled by an order of sessions, pursuant to an act of parliament for that purpose, when nine of them, who were the principal and committeemen of several of the associations, which raised a fund to support each other in such unlawful meetings, and who had distinguished themselves by the name of Flints, were found guilty, and received sentence according to their several demerits, viz. two to be imprisoned one year in Newgate, five for the space of six months, and two for three months; and were, besides, fined one shilling each and ordered to find security for their behaviour.

At the 30th of June, we would find a brief mention of the fact that "Nine white boys were lately killed, and twenty made prisoners, in a skirmish with a party of dragoons, near Dungannon in Ireland."

The poor on Nacton Heath, the weavers at Westminster, the Flints in London, and the Whiteboys at Dungannon were all acting collectively. That alerts us to an explanatory agenda beginning with the specification of the relevant populations, interests, organization, mobilization, repression/facilitation, power, and opportunity/threat, as well as a close look at the specific forms, intensities, and outcomes of the collective action. It also draws our attention to important differences among the four groups.

For one thing, the poorhouse attacks have a rather reactive tone: an attempt to defend the parish poor against incarceration. The weavers' petition march and the tailors' incipient wage demands lean in the proactive direction: although both groups may well have been responding to threats to their livelihood, the *claims* they made were for advantages they did not currently enjoy. The quick note on the Whiteboys offers no information on the claims at issue. But when we learn that the Whiteboys of Ireland were famous anti-British guerrilla warriors, we receive an indication that their skirmish fell somewhere in the range of collective competition and collective reaction.

For another thing, the contrasting accounts give an inkling of the prevailing schedule of repression: no visible penalties for the petition march, jail sentences for the mobilizing tailors, arrests and shooting for attackers of Sussex poorhouses, nine dead among the Whiteboys. The four incompletely documented cases are a slim basis for any general conclusions, yet they immediately draw attention to the variability of repression with the action and group in question. They also start us thinking about what was changing: sending thousands of weavers to present a petition was a significant innovation, while jailing people for concerting their wage demands would practically disappear over the next century.

Finally, even these fragmentary news stories give us some reason to believe that the repertoire of collective action prevailing in the Britain and

Ireland of 1765 differed significantly from the forms available to ordinary twentieth-century people. Although the petition march would have a significant place in the demonstration's ancestry, the demonstration itself had not yet entered the repertoire. The strike was not then a tool readily available to workers—partly, as we have seen, because of the repression visited upon any workers who attempted to concert their wage demands. The repertoire varied from one part of Britain to another, from one social class to another. But it was distinctly an eighteenth-century repertoire.

If we took a somewhat longer view, we would find the repertoire changing. Indeed, some significant alterations in the whole pattern of collective action were occurring in the Britain of the 1760s and 1770s. The year 1766, for example, brought one of the most widespread series of food riots to appear in modern Britain; in general, food riots became very common in the villages and small towns of Britain during the middle decades of the eighteenth century, and only began their definitive decline after 1830. In London (and, to some extent, in other major cities) we witness a different trend. There we see a Radical movement forming on a middle-class base with important alliances among skilled workers; they brought together, among other things, the demand for domestic political reform and the criticism of the Crown's policy in America. Such skilled workers as the silk weavers who marched on Parliament were building large-scale organizations and applying pressure in the national political arena. The Radicals, the supporters of John Wilkes, the silk weavers, and other organized contenders for power, furthermore, were shaping new means of exercising their strength. They pressed the right to assemble for petitioning and for elections beyond its old limit, and began to create a prototype of the twentieth-century demonstration.

The decade after 1765 was likewise an important time of transition in America. The American transition, to be sure, differed greatly from the British: it went from the great reaction against the Stamp Act to the opening of a truly revolutionary situation—of multiple sovereignty—in all the colonies. To return to the British periodicals of 1765, *The Gentleman's Magazine* stepped up its coverage of American news at the end of the year. For example:

1 October: This day is appointed to be held at *New York* in *North America*, a general congress of all the colonies, in order to draw up a remonstrance to be presented to his majesty against the stamp duties, and other burthens laid upon the colonies, by the late act of the *British* parliament.

5 October: . . . the ships arrived at *Philadelphia*, with the stamps on board, for *Maryland*, *New Jersey*, and *Pennsylvania*, when several thousand citizens assembled in order to consider ways and means for preventing the stamp act taking place in that province, and at last came to a resolution to request the distributor to resign his office; which after some demur he in part did, assuring his countrymen that no act of his, or his deputies, should enforce the execution of the stamp-act in the provinces for which he was commissioned, before the same should be generally put in force in the neighboring colonies. And at the same time the lawyers entered into an agreement not to purchase any of those stamps, giving it as their opinion, that it was impossible the duty imposed by them could be paid for in gold and silver.

4 November [dateline New York]: Some extraordinary preparations in *Fort George,* for the securing the stamped paper in that garrison, having displeased the inhabitants of this city, a vast number of them assembled last *Friday* evening, and proceeded to the fort walls, where they broke open the stable of the *L____t G____r* Cadwallader Colden, Esq; took out his coach and after carrying the same thro' the principal streets of the city, in triumph, marched to the Commons where a gallows was erected; on one end of which was suspended the effigy of the great man, having in his right hand a stamped bill of lading, and on his breast a paper with the following inscription: "The Rebel Drummer in the year 1715." At his back was fixed a drum, at the other end of the gallows hung the figure of the devil. After hanging a considerable time, they carried the effigies, with the gallows intire, being preceded by the coach, in grand procession, to the gate of the fort, from whence it was removed to the bowling green, under the muzzles of the fort guns, where a bonfire was immediately made, and the drummer, devil, coach & c. were consumed amidst the acclamations of some thousand spectators. The whole body next proceeded to Vaux-hall, the house of Major *James,* who, it was reported, was a friend to the Stamp-act, from whence they took every individual article, to a very considerable amount; and having made another bonfire, the whole was consumed in the flames.

The next night, the assembled crowd demanded that the Lieutenant Governor hand over the stamps. After a while, he declared under pressure that he would not distribute the stamps himself, and finally put them into the hands of the municipal corporation, in the New York city hall. *Gentleman's Magazine* of 1765 printed many more reports on American Stamp Act resistance, not to mention multiple essays and commentaries on the political issues.

We already have an idea what happened in the next ten years. In the trading cities of the American coast, anti-British coalitions formed, drawing especially on the merchants, lawyers, tradesmen, and craftsmen, but often aided by such groups as sailors and longshoremen. In a complex interplay between British authorities and American colonists, the Americans moved unsteadily toward a general boycott on political and economic transactions with the British. They moved toward the fashioning of a set of governmental institutions—committees, assemblies, courts, and associations—parallel to British colonial institutions, and independent of them. As significant numbers of Americans began to take their directions from those parallel institutions and to reject the orders of Lieutenant Governors and other British officials, a revolutionary situation was underway. The outcome, too, was at least a limited revolution: thousands of prominent supporters of the British left the colonies, the Americans acquired political independence, and the middle-class members of the revolutionary coalitions wielded exceptional power in the shaping of the new polity.

The struggles of the 1760s in Britain and America clearly belong in the world we have been exploring in this book: the world of contentious collective action. Other people have often portrayed that world as full of "mobs," "disorders," and "mass movements." We have seen many of the events those words refer to, and in the process have noticed repeatedly how misleading the words are. Mob, disorder, and mass movement are top-down words. They are the words of authorities and elites for actions of other people—and, often, for actions which threaten their own interests. The bottom-up approach we have taken identifies the connections between the collective actions of ordinary people and the ways they organize around their workaday interests. That approach also helps clarify how much of the violence which elite observers have been inclined to attribute to the disorganization, desperation, or aggressive impulses of the masses is actually a by-product of interactions between groups which are pursuing their ends in relatively routine ways and rivals or authorities who challenge the claims embodied in those relatively routine actions.

THEORIZING ABOUT COLLECTIVE ACTIONS

We could, if we wanted, now formalize the analysis of the Spitalfields weavers, the Nacton poorhouse wreckers, the Stamp Act crowds in New York. The formalization would consist of mapping the interests of the participants, estimating the current state of opportunity and threat with respect to those interests, checking their mobilization levels, gauging their power positions, then seeing to what extent these variables accounted for the intensity and character of their collective action. One step back from that formalization we would find ourselves examining the prevailing pattern of repression and facilitation, the impact of the various groups' organization on their mobilization and on their interests, the effect of coalitions with other contenders on their current power positions, and so on.

That is the easy part: showing that concepts such as mobilization and repression point to broadly similar processes in different settings, and apply conveniently in those various settings. We would be surprised and disappointed if it came out otherwise; after all, the concepts were *meant* to be quite general. Yet the easy part has its satisfactions. It helps identify some unexpected and potentially fruitful comparisons—between, for instance, the mobilization of British Radicals in the 1760s and the mobilization of American radicals in the 1960s. It brings out the richness and relevance of historical materials for the concerns of contemporary analysts of political processes. These two advantages combine to produce a third advantage: the recognition that historical experiences are an important and accessible domain for the testing and refinement of arguments and explanations of collective action.

There we arrive at the hard part. The hard part is the research agenda: sorting populations into members of the polity, challengers, and nonactors; identifying their interests reliably; measuring the extent and character of repression/facilitation to which they are subject; determining whether it is true, as argued earlier, that rich populations tend to mobilize offensively, poor populations to mobilize defensively; determining whether it is true, as I have asserted repeatedly, that the general effect of sustained repression is not to build up tensions to the point of a great explosion, but to reduce the overall level of collective action.

This is the hard part. It is hard not only because it involves many variables and interactions among the variables. It is hard also because the measurement problems are so large; devising generally comparable and meaningful measures of organization, mobilization, power, repression, and so on lies beyond the present state of the art. That is why this book has so often turned to the problems of measurement. Plenty of work to do there.

The accounts of collective action in Britain and America we have just reviewed also recall a major theoretical problem. In the mobilization model which this book has employed, collective interests are given *a priori.* We impute them from some general historical analysis (my preferred analysis being Marx's relation of different segments of the population to the prevailing means of production) or we determine them empirically (my preferred procedure being to pay attention to what people say are their grievances, aspirations, and rights). The theoretical difficulties multiply. Mobilization, collective action, and acquisition or loss of power frequently alter a group's interests. How should we take that alteration into account? The imputation of interests and the empirical derivation often conflict with each other; Leninists speak of "false consciousness." Does that make sense?

Another problem has been with us from the start, and has refused to go away: the connection between causal and purposive explanations of collective action. We have oscillated between the two without integrating them firmly. The mobilization model serves for short-run analyses. When we take up a series of actions such as the Stamp Act resistance in Philadelphia and New York we sort our observations into interests, organization, mobilization, repression, power, opportunity, and collective action itself. But we ultimately visualize the various groups involved as undertaking their action purposively:

seeking to realize their interests with the means at their disposal within the limits set by their relationship to the world around them. I have already pointed out the limitations of the mobilization model: the lack of allowance for uncertainty and for strategic interaction, the focus on quantity rather than quality, the measurement difficulties inherent in each of its variables. Even if we find ways of overcoming these limitations, however, we are still dealing with a purposive model.

In coping with long-run changes in collective action, we have generally turned from purposive to causal models. The polity model has served us in this way; for example, it provides a crude explanation of the characteristic differences in collective action among groups which are gaining power, groups which are losing power, and groups which are maintaining their power. Challengers gaining political power, runs one part of the explanation, tend to shift toward collective proaction, but at diminished levels; that is because the governmental apparatus protects them from threats and because reduced costs of mobilization and collective action mean they can realize the same interest with less effort. Thus the crucial changes affect constraints, not intentions.

Another kind of causal argument has also figured prominently in the analyses of previous chapters. It concerns the effects of very large social changes, notably state making, proletarianization, and industrialization. There I have argued repeatedly that the change in question simultaneously affected the interests and the organization of various contenders for power, and thereby affected their mobilization and collective action. The case of peasant resistance to the increased taxation accompanying state making is presented in Fig. 8-1.

This is not a complete account, since state making also affects repression/facilitation and power. Nevertheless, this account clearly differs from the standard Durkheimian arguments in which the discrepancy between the pace of structural change and the institutionalization of social control determines the likelihood of conflict and protest. Although the argument has important implications for changes in the purposes of peasant collective action, it is essentially a causal argument.

In principle, it should not be hard to integrate the purposive and causal analyses. In principle, we can integrate them by continuing to think of group decision rules and tactical computations (the purposive part) which operate within severe constraints set by the contender's internal organization, its relationship to other groups, and the current state of opportunities and threats in the world (the causal part). In practice, that is not so easy. We might try to do it by gradually building time into the basic mobilization model: showing, for instance, how a contender's collective action at one point in time changes the conditions which are relevant to the next round of action. In the agenda set by

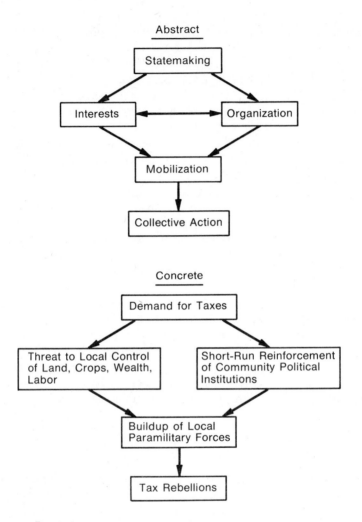

Fig. 8-1
Abstract versus concrete causal accounts of peasant tax rebellions

the model, that means showing how the form, intensity, and outcome of the action affect the contender's interests, organization, and mobilization, its power position, the new opportunities and threats confronting it, and the repression/facilitation to which it is subject. In a very short run, we can ignore some of these relationships because they will remain essentially the same. Over a series of short-run snapshots, however, their effects will begin to accumulate, and to affect the drift of the situation as a whole.

A series of many such short-run portraits should integrate, like a many-framed movie, into a continuous account of the process by which collective action changes and flows. The difficulty, however, is obvious: for the analysis of any particular instant we can afford to treat the actions of other groups (and the contender's relationship to other groups) as features of the environment. As soon as time enters, the actions and reactions of the others become crucial. In the short run, we have strategic interaction. In the longer run, we have changing coalitions, cleavages, and structures of power. The polity model we have used in this book singles out only one aspect—the relationship of contenders to governments—of a complex set of changes. In order to integrate the causal and purposive arguments unfolded in this book, we need more. We need a much fuller analysis of power struggles, coalitions, and other forms of interaction among contenders. For students of collective action, that is the next challenge.

THE IMPORTANCE OF HISTORY

Historical analysis, taken seriously, will help us fashion more adequate models of power struggles. The historical record is rich and relevant. It permits us to follow multiple groups and their relations over substantial blocks of time. Collective action, contention, and struggles for political power are especially likely to leave their traces in the historian's raw materials.

History is more than an abundant source of data. It matters for its own sake; it puts our own experience into perspective and sometimes helps to explain it. The history of collective action is a fascinating inquiry which takes us into different paths from the history of political thought or the history of power holders, although the three sorts of history cross frequently. The different historical trajectories of the demonstration and the strike in western countries, for example, help us understand the different places they occupy in today's political repertoires, help us grasp such peculiar things as the relatively greater frequency with which the demonstrations of our own time produce collective violence; after all, in most western countries strikes were once very common settings for shooting, brawling, and attacks on buildings or equipment.

Historians commonly treat the history of collective action as a subsidiary form of political, social, or economic history: strikes and demonstrations serve as the moral equivalent of the statesman's memoirs, provide evidence of the quality of life among the lower orders, lend themselves to the measurement of the impact of economic fluctuations. Those are all legitimate uses of the evidence on strikes and demonstrations. Taken in its own terms, however, the history of collective action cuts across political history, social history, economic history as we usually imagine them. The categories and periods of collective action's history do not follow simply from those of political, social, or economic history. Collective action follows its own course. Our repeated glimpses of historical experience in this book have given us clear indications of the impact on collective action of changes in power structure and in the organization of production, but they have also shown us how the existing repertoire of collective action and the previous experience of the collective actors constrain the way they act together on interests, aspirations, and grievances. Instead of treating it as a minor elaboration of political or social history—for example, as the subject which George Rudé labeled *The Crowd in History*—we have some warrant to write the history of collective action in its own terms.

Before we stake out a new historical field, however, we should not ask merely whether it is conceivable and interesting. We have to ask whether it is coherent, worthwhile, and accessible. In the case of collective action, the answer to all three seems to be "yes." The subject is coherent in several fundamental regards: any given population tends to have a fairly limited and well-established set of means for action on shared interests, and tends to change those means little by little; the available means of action, the results of action, the intensities and loci of action change in an intelligible manner in the course of such large-scale changes as industrialization and state making; we can reasonably ask the same questions about interest, organization, opportunity, and action in widely different settings, and can even expect similar answers to some questions to come back from very different times and places.

Worthwhile? In the long run, the results of the inquiry will tell us. In advance, we can see at least that the study of collective action gets us to the problems that concerned the ordinary actors of history in a way that almost no other inquiry does. It takes its place with the historical study of work and the family; it is about the logic, framework, and content of everyday life.

The question of accessibility is harder to settle. Too little of the work of making the evidence of collective action available and comprehensible has been done. Interest, opportunity, organization, action—none of them is easy to reconstruct at a distance of a century or two. The action is less difficult than the rest, because the most precise and voluminous records come from legal authorities. The authorities tried to establish what happened in order to punish it this time and prevent it next time. As for interest, opportunity, and organization, we must either infer them from the action itself, guess at them on the basis of general arguments, or piece them together from scattered, brittle materials. When dealing with the actions of ordinary people, most historians content themselves with the first two choices: describe what the people did, then deduce what interests they were pursuing, what opportunities to pursue those interests they faced, and how they were organized from what they said and did during the action, as well as from general arguments concerning the character of crowds, the nature of peasant life, the meaning of resistance to conscription, and similar notions.

In the absence of direct, solid evidence concerning interest, opportunity, and organization, the indirect approach combining general arguments with observations from the action can serve us well. All we need are sound general arguments, well-documented actions, and the wit to correct the general arguments when the actions prove them wrong. In analyzing the actions of the seventeenth-century rural rebels who show up in history books under such quaint names as Bonnets-Rouges, Camisards, and Croquants, Yves-Marie Bercé frames a useful argument. At that time, according to Berce, the local community was the main locus of rural solidarity and the chief repository of rights in which rural people had a strong investment. The expansion of the state under Louis XIII and Louis XIV threatened both the solidarity and the rights.

To each form of local solidarity, Bercé argues, corresponded a form of rebellion: revolts of insecurity based on the institutions of common defense against marauders, food riots based on the communal arrangements for provisioning in hard times, forceful defense of common agricultural rights based on the previous exercise and recognition of those rights, rebellions against direct taxes based on the long participation of the local community in the assessment of those taxes, armed resistance to indirect taxes based on the prior existence of local channels for the trading of the items now subject to inspection, taxation, and seizure. Says Bercé:

> It is roughly from 1660 to 1680 that, irreversibly, communal powers were dismantled, their military, judiciary and fiscal prerogatives choked or revoked, their established rights and privileges crushed. The chronology of great popular rebellions follows the same rhythm. Then these reactions of collective violence died away as the building of the state succeeded (Bercé 1974a: 117).

Bercé's summary underestimates the importance of expanding capitalism. Yet it pinpoints themes which do recur, time and time again, in seventeenth-century revolts: established rights being crushed, long-respected privileges being swept aside. That much appears in the action itself, as when, in 1636, the peasants of Saintonge declared ". . . that they were good Frenchmen and would die, rather than live any longer under the tyranny of Parisians who had reduced them to the despair and extreme poverty in which our province now find themselves because of the great tax assessments and new burdens that they have imposed upon us and invented in this reign . . ." (Bercé 1974b: 736).

The complaint from Saintonge illustrates both the promise and the penalty of working with observations of collective action alone. The promise is that people who act together generally have their own idea of the grievances, hopes, and interests which motivate them, and a notion of their chances of success. If the "tyranny of Parisians" reappears in complaint after complaint, we have some reason to believe that the people of Saintonge had a genuine grievance against demands from outside. The penalty, however, is that the rhetoric of rebellion does not reveal the origin or factual basis of the grievance: how to distinguish, for example, between a long-standing condition recently become intolerable because of changing aspirations or self-definitions, and new privations which violate long-standing rights?

Part of the remedy consists of paying attention to the whole pattern of actions and complaints: in old-regime France, almost everyone who made a public lament complained of "extreme poverty"; if you did otherwise, there was the chance the tax collector would bite harder the next time he passed by. Complaints of "new burdens" and "Parisian tyranny," on the other hand, varied from place to place, time to time, group to group. In that variation over place, time, and group we have a chance to try out our ideas concerning the interests, opportunities, and organization lying behind the collective action. In the case of Bercé's argument, we can determine whether there was, indeed, a tendency for regions just coming under firm royal control to mount major resistance movements, then lapse into docility as the state won out. (There was, although the connections were more complex than Bercé's scheme allows.)

Nevertheless, a broad correlation between the rhythm of state making and the rhythm of rebellion will leave open many alternative interpretations of the interests, opportunities, and organization at work. Eventually we will have to try to observe them directly. Two apparently contradictory strategies apply. The first is the more obvious: dig into the evidence concerning the settings in which collective action occurs. With enough spadework, it is often possible to discover the interests, opportunities, and organization in operation outside the great episodes of action. But eventually we will need comparisons with places, times, and groups in which little or no action occurred: if we find "extreme poverty" in the setting of every seventeenth-century rebellion, does that mean the peasants who did not rebel were less poor? That sort of question leads us to the second strategy: broad comparisons of places, times, and groups which differed in interest, opportunity, and organization. Did their collective action, or lack of it, vary accordingly?

In writing the history of collective action, we have a choice between historical particularism and the attempt to compare and generalize. In one view, all such comparisons are odious, first because they inevitably warp the interpretation of the past to fit the preoccupation of the present, second because they wrench each event from the only context which can give it substance

"The Burgundian of the seventeenth century," Gaston Roupnel tells us, "did not bear the mark of the modern age. At the bottom of his soul there was something so old that it was as if the Gauls were still around him in their new land where history had not yet arrived" (Roupnel 1955: xxx). If so, presumably neither the Burgundian nor the American of our own time can reconstitute or explain the events of seventeenth-century Burgundy without projecting himself across the chasm between the present and an earlier age. Comparisons will only serve to map the depth and contours of the chasm.

The depth and width of the chasm, however, are questions of fact, not of faith. We can, to some degree, determine whether the patterns and explanations which help us order the collective action of the seventeenth century give us any grip on that of the twentieth—provide usable categories for our observations, bring out obscure connections, anticipate features which are not readily visible at first sight. The points at which the seventeenth-century categories fail are clues to change, signals that we have something new to explain. Our attempt to move across the centuries may lead to the conclusion that different centuries require fundamentally different approaches to collective action. Then that conclusion, and the delineation of the essential breaks between one mode of action and another, will be accomplishments in themselves.

THE HISTORY OF COLLECTIVE ACTION IN MODERN FRANCE

How, then, might we set concrete historical experience into the framework this book has built up? The historical work consists of grouping actions within the historical experience into governments, contenders, polities, coalitions, processes of mobilization, and so on. Other fundamental phenomena, such as changes in beliefs, demographic change, or demographic crisis, enter the account only in so far as they affect the pattern of pursuit of interests and contention for power.

In the case of France since 1500, the largest frame for analysis shows us the interplay of a gradually urbanizing, industrializing, and proletarianizing population with a national state which was at first emerging, then establishing priority, then consolidating its hold on the population. The two sets of processes depended on each other to some degree—for example, in the way that expanding taxation drove peasants to market goods they would otherwise have kept at home, on the one hand, and the way that the degree of commercialization of land, labor, and agricultural production set stringent limits on the return from land taxes, income taxes, or excise taxes, on the other. But their timing differed. The epic periods of French state making were the times of Louis XIII and Louis XIV. Those periods had their share of economic turmoil.

Furthermore, they saw both a significant increase in the importance of Paris and a few other major cities for the life of France as a whole and the spread of trade and small-scale manufacturing through the towns and villages of the entire country. Yet in terms of productivity, organization, and sheer numbers of persons involved, the urbanization, industrialization, and proletarianization of the nineteenth and twentieth centuries produced incomparably greater changes. To oversimplify outrageously, the drama consists of two acts: first a fast-growing state acting on a slow-moving population and economy; then a fast-changing population and economy dealing with a consolidating state.

In analyzing this interplay, we need to ask over and over for different places and points in time what contenders for power (potential and actual) the existing social structure made available, and what governments the existing stage of statemaking left them to contend over. The most strenuous current debates over the history of the turbulent French seventeenth century, for example, pivot, first, on the extent to which the national government squeezed out its provincial rivals and acquired firm control over French social life; second, and even more strenuously, on the extent to which the operative divisions of the population were social classes in something like a Marxian sense (see Mousnier 1970, Lebrun 1967, Porchnev 1963, Lublinskaya 1968).

The analytic scheme I have laid out provides no pat answers to those serious questions; if it did, one would have to suspect that its principal assertions were true by definition. It does suggest that the tracing of the actual issues, locations, and personnel of violent encounters in seventeenth-century France will provide crucial evidence on the pace and extent of political centralization, as well as on the nature of the groups which were then engaged in struggles for power. The basic research remains to be done. Yet the recurrent importance of new taxation in seventeenth-century rebellions, the apparent subsidence of those rebellions toward the end of the century, and the frequent involvement of whole peasant communities in resistance to the demands of the crown all point toward a decisive seventeenth-century battle among local and national polities.

Not that all struggle ended then. As Tocqueville declared long ago, the Revolution of 1789 pitted centralizers against guardians of provincial autonomies. The contest between crown and provincial parlements (which led quite directly to the calling for the Estates General, which in turn became the locus of multiple sovereignty in 1789) continued the struggle of the seventeenth century. Throughout the Revolution, in fact, the issue of predominance of Paris and the national government remained open, with tax rebellions, movements against conscription and resistance to the calls of the nation for food recurring when the center weakened and when its demands increased sharply. Most of the events of the so-called peasant revolt of 1789 took the form of food riots and other classic eighteenth-century local conflicts.

Yet they did not represent just "more of the same," because they came in extraordinary clusters, because they occurred in the presence of multiple sovereignty, and because the participants began to form coalitions with other contenders for power. Now, the exact contours of the major contenders and the precise nature of their shifting alliances are the central issues of the big debates about the history of the Revolution (see e.g. Cobban 1964, Mazauric 1970). But it is at least roughly true to say that a loose coalition among peasants, officials, urban commercial classes, and small but crucial groups of urban craftsmen and shopkeepers carried the revolution through its first few years, but began to fall apart irrevocably in 1792 and 1793. Looked at from the point of view of coalition-formation and multiple sovereignty, the Revolution breaks into a whole series of revolutionary situations, from the first declaration of sovereignty by the Third Estate in 1798 to the final defeat of Napoleon in 1815.

Again, in this perspective we begin to grasp the significance of materially trivial events like the taking of the Bastille. For the attack by Parisians on the old fortress finally set a crowd unambiguously against the regime, revealed the uncertain commitment of part of the armed forces to the government, brought the King to his first accessions to the popular movement (his trip to the National Assembly on the 15th of July and his trip to Paris on the 17th), and stimulated a series of minor coups in the provinces:

> Until July 14th the handful of revolutionary institutions set up in the provinces were disparate and isolated. Henceforward most of the towns and many of the villages of France were to imitate Paris with extraordinary swiftness. During the weeks that followed the fall of the Bastille there arose everywhere revolutionary Town Councils of permanent committees, and citizen militias which soon assumed the name of national guards (Godechot 1970: 273).

So if we date the start of multiple sovereignty from the Third Estate's Tennis Court Oath to remain assembled despite the prohibitions of the King, we still have to treat July 15th and its immediate aftermath as a great expansion of the revolutionary coalition.

Obviously the three proximate conditions for a revolutionary situation enumerated earlier—coalitions of contenders advancing exclusive alternative claims, commitment to those claims, failure of the government to suppress them—appeared in the France of 1789. What cannot be obvious from a mere chronicle of the events is how long each of the conditions existed, what caused them, and whether they were sufficient to cause the collapse of the old regime. At least these are researchable questions, as contrasted with attempts to ask directly whether the rise of the bourgeoisie, the increase in relative deprivation, or the decay of the old elite "caused" the Revolution. What is more, they call attention to the probable importance of shifting coalitions among lawyers, officials, provincial magnates, peasants, and workers in the nationwide political maneuvering of 1787 to 1789, as well as to the effect of "defensive" mobilization of peasants and workers in response to the multiple pressures impinging on them in 1789.

The Revolution produced a great transfer of power. It stamped out a new and distinctive political system. Despite the Restoration of 1815, the nobility and the clergy never recovered their prerevolutionary position, some segments of the bourgeoisie greatly enhanced their power over the national government, and the priority of that national government over all others increased permanently. In Barrington Moore's analysis, whose main lines appear correct to me, the predominance of the coalition of officials, bourgeois, and peasant, in the decisive early phases of the Revolution promoted the emergence of the attenuated parliamentary democracy which characterizes post-revolutionary France (Moore 1966, ch. II; for explication and critique see Rokkan 1969, Rothman 1970, Stone 1967). At that scale and in the details of public administration, education, ideology, and life style, the Revolution left a durable heritage.

None of the old conflicts, nevertheless, disappeared completely with the Revolution. The counter-revolutionary Vendée, despite having come close to destruction in 1793, again rose in rebellion in 1794, 1795, 1799, 1815, and 1832. Further revolutions overcame France as a whole in 1830, 1848, and 1870. Most of the characteristic forms of resistance to demands from the center—food riots, tax rebellions, movements against conscription, and so on—continued well into the nineteenth century. Indeed, these reactive forms of collective action reached their climax around the Revolution of 1848, before fading rapidly to insignificance.

From the mid-century crisis we can date the date the definitive reduction of the smaller polities in which Frenchmen had once done most of their political business, the virtual disappearance of communal contenders for power, the shift of all contenders toward associational organization and action at a national level. The massive urbanization and industrialization of France which gained momentum after 1830 transformed the available contenders for power, especially by creating a large, new urban working class based in factories and other large organizations. From that point on, the demonstration, the meeting, the strike were the usual matrices of collective violence as well as the settings in which an enormous proportion of all struggles for power went on. Collective action evolved with the organization of public life.

A Last Case in Point: Rural Collective Action in Burgundy

If this broad sketch of the evolution of collective action holds for France as a whole, it may still lose its verisimilitude when compared to the experience of particular local populations. In Gaston Roupnel's opinion, which I quoted earlier, the old-regime Burgundian was so different from his modern counterpart that a historian has to apply different explanatory principles to his behavior.

Roupnel's challenge to us is to discover whether we can understand and explain the collective action of old-regime Burgundy in terms which are relevant to the time and place, yet still have meaning in other—and especially later—times and places. I think we can. Old-regime Burgundians felt the effects of two momentous processes: the expansion of capitalism and the concentration of power in the French national state. They felt the expansion of capitalism concretely in the growth of an agricultural proletariat, the shift toward cash-crop production, the decline of communal property rights in favor of individual ownership, and a number of other ways. They felt the concentration of state power in the rising importance of royal officials in the region, the declining autonomy of the Parlement and the municipality of Dijon, the increased control, taxation, and sale of local offices by the Crown, and a number of other ways.

The conflicts over state making are most visible in the seventeenth century, especially during the Fronde of the 1640s and 1650s, when Burgundy was the site of major rebellions against the Crown. The conflicts over capitalism are more visible in the eighteenth century, when struggles for control of land, labor, and crops recurred throughout the province. Let us take a brief look at the eighteenth-century struggles, think about their relationship to the expansion of capitalism, and then compare them with the rural collective action of the nineteenth century.

In rural Burgundy, eighteenth-century contention had a strong anticapitalist flavor. It was the golden age of food riots. The crises of 1709, 1758, and 1775 brought their clusters of conflicts, and others appeared between the great crises. That is the meaning of the 1770 edict of the Parlement of Burgundy which forbade, like so many other edicts of the period

> to gather and stop wagons loaded with wheat or other grain, on roads, in cities, towns or villages, on pain of special prosecution . . . (Archives Départementales Côte d'Or [Dijon] C 81).

That blockage of grain expressed the demand of ordinary people that the needs of the community have priority over the requirements of the market. The market, and therefore the merchants as well.

The second common form of anticapitalist action was less routine and more ironic. It was local resistance to the landlord's consolidation of lands and of rights in the land. The irony lies in our normal readiness to place the landlords themselves in the anticapitalist camp. As the great regional historian

Pierre de Saint-Jacob showed, the Burgundian landlords of the period—including both the "old" nobility and the ennobled officials and merchants—played the capitalist game by seizing the forests, usurping common lands, enclosing fields, and insisting on collecting all of the use fees to which their manors gave them claim. Rural people fought back. Suits against landlords multiplied, a fact which de Saint-Jacob interprets as evidence not only of seigniorial aggression but also of an increasing liberation of the peasants from traditional respect.

Where the lawsuit was impossible or ineffective, peasants resisted the seizure of commons by occupying them, resisted enclosures by breaking the hedges or fences. As Pierre de Saint-Jacob describes it:

> The wardens of Athie were attacked by the people of Viserny for trying to forbid entry to a shepherd. On the lands of Bernard de Fontette, Pierre César du Crest, the lord of Saint-Aubin, organized an unusual expedition. He went with 17 men armed with "guns, stakes and staves" to break down the enclosures. They led in 40 cattle under the protection of two guards "with guns and hunting dogs," and kept the tenants of Bernard de Fontette from bringing in their cattle. In Charmois, at the urging of two women, a band of peasants went to break down a fence set up by the overseer of Grenand who could do nothing but watch and receive the jeers of the crowd. In Panthier, a merchant wanted to enclose his meadow; he got authorization from the local court. People assembled in the square and decided to break the hedges, which was done that night. They led in the horses. The merchant wanted to chase them away, but the young people who were guarding them stopped him, "saying that they were on their own property, in a public meadow, that they had broken the enclosures and that they would break them again . . ." (Saint-Jacob 1960: 370–371).

As we can see, the opposition was not directed specifically against the landed nobility, but against the landlords of any class who chewed at the collective rights of the rural community. If in Longecourt in 1764 it was the lord who demanded his own share of the commons, in Darois two years later the Chapter of Sainte-Chapelle, in Dijon, tried to take a share of the communal woods, and in Villy-le-Brûlé in 1769 it was a farmer-notary who enclosed a meadow only to see the ditches filled in by the local people (A.D. Côte d' Or C 509, C 543, C 1553).

What a contrast with rural collective action after the Revolution! Food riots did survive until the middle of the nineteenth century. For example, in April 1829 a crowd in Châtillon forced M. Beaudoin, operator of a flour mill, to sell his wheat at 5 francs and 25 centimes per double bushel, when he had posted the price at 5F30 (A.D. Côte d'Or M 8 II 4). At the next market, several brigades of gendarmes were on hand to prevent such "disorders" (A.D. Côte d'Or 8 M 27). Although the food riot continued to flourish, post revolutionary rural struggles bore hardly a trace of the resistance against the landlords. Instead they concerned the policies, and especially the fiscal policies, of the state.

The active groups of the nineteenth century came especially from the small landholders and the workers of the commercialized, fully capitalist vineyards. Robert Laurent portrays that sort of protest as it took place just after the Revolution of 1830:

> . . . in September, the announcement of the resumption of the inventory of wine on the premises of winegrowers started turbulent demonstrations, near-riots, in Beaune. On the 12th of September at the time of the National Guard review "cries of anger against the Revenue Administration [la Régie] rose from its very ranks." Told that the residents of the suburbs planned to go to the tax offices in order to burn the registers as they had in 1814, the mayor thought it prudent that evening to call the artillery company to arms and convoke part of the National Guard for 5 o'clock the next morning. On the 13th, toward 8 A.M., "a huge crowd of winegrowers and workers," shouting "down with the wolves," "down with excise taxes," occupied the city hall square. To calm the demonstrators the mayor had to send the National Guard home at once. "The crowd then dispersed gradually" (Laurent 1957: I, 484–485).

Despite that peaceful dispersion, the authorities had to delay the inventory of wine. In Meursault it was less peaceful: the winegrowers drove out the tax men.

What is more, the anti-tax movement connected directly to political movements. The winegrowing area stood out for its republicanism; that was especially true of the hinterlands of Dijon and Beaune. All things considered, we observe a significant transformation of the repertoire of collective action in Burgundy. As compared with the means of action prevailing before the Revolution, those of the nineteenth century were less tied to a communal base, more attached to national politics. Associations, clubs, societies played an increasing part. Yet there were important continuities: the survival of the charivari, the food riot, the classic anti-tax rebellion; the persistent orientation to the protection of local interests against the claims of the state and the market rather than to the creation of a better future. The old regime repertoire of collective action survived the Revolution. The forms of action themselves altered, adapted to new conditions; among other things, we notice a sort of politicization of all the forms. New forms of collective action arose; the demonstration and the strike became standard events in Burgundy. That hundred years spanning the Revolution was a period of transformation and of growth of the means of collective action.

What of the Revolution's own place in that transformation and growth of the means of collective action? The Revolution brought an extraordinary level of collective action, a politicization of all interests and thus of almost all the means of action, a centralization of power and thus of struggles for power, a frenzy of association and thus of action on the basis of associations, a promotion of the conditions for the development of capitalism and bourgeois hegemony and thus of a mounting threat to noncapitalist, nonbourgeois interests. If that summary is correct, the Revolution acted as a fundamental stage in the course of a transformation far longer and larger than the Revolution itself. Like the seventeenth-century consolidation of the national state, the changes of the Revolution led to a significant alteration of the prevailing modes of popular collective action.

The evolution of collective action had not ended, however. Although the Dijon winegrowers' demonstrations of the 1830s certainly display many more familiar features than the regional tax rebellions of the 1630s, they also show their age. Nowadays, the successors of those winegrowers typically assemble outside the departmental capital, grouped around placards and banners identifying their organizations and summarizing their demands. The classic charivari and food riot have vanished, along with a number of other forms of action which persisted into the nineteenth century. Today's large-scale actions are even more heavily concentrated in Dijon, Beaune, and other cities than they were in the 1830s. Labor unions and political parties often appear in the action. Although prices and taxes continue to be frequent causes for complaint, such exotic questions as American warmaking in Vietnam and the future of students in sports and physical education exercise many a crowd. As the world has changed, so has its collective action.

Appendixes

Appendix 1

Procedures for the Studies of Strikes and Collective Violence in France

GENERAL

In a nutshell, the strategy of the French study has been to place particular events in time, space, and social setting, not so much to account for any single event as to detect how large-scale social change and alterations of the structure of power affected the pattern of collective action. We deal separately with strikes and with violent events, although violent strikes appear in both halves of the analysis. Strikes represent a frequent, important, well-documented, and usually nonviolent form of collective action. Violent events tend to be better documented than their nonviolent counterparts, and therefore serve as a biased but useful tracer of collective action in general.

The studies' main components are:

1   The enumeration and description of every strike for which we could gather a standard body of information from 1830 to 1968, for a total of approximately 110,000 strikes; the most detailed analysis concentrated on the 36,000 strikes reported in the *Statistique des Grèves* from 1890 through 1935.

2   The enumeration and description of every violent event meeting certain standards (to be discussed in a moment) from 1830 through 1960; our analyses deal with roughly 2000 violent events.

3   Indexing of change in social organization in France as a whole and in its geographic subdivisions—communes, arrondissements and, especially, the 85 to 95 departments—over the period 1830 to 1960.

4   Assembling of (far less complete, far more tentative) information on political structure and activity for France as a whole and for some times and places within it from 1830 to 1960.

5   Use of all three types of evidence in the analysis of variations in the form, intensity, locus, social composition, and precipitating conditions of strikes and

violent events; the analysis stresses the identification of long-run shifts in the pattern of collective action, and the verification or falsification of alternative theories concerning the effects of large-scale social change on collective action.

A comprehensive report of the strike studies appears in *Strikes in France, 1830–1968*, by Edward Shorter and Charles Tilly. The most general summary of the studies of French collective violence is Chapter two of *The Rebellious Century*, by Charles Tilly, Louise Tilly, and Richard Tilly. *The Rebellious Century* also summarizes our studies of Italy and Germany. For more detail on the French, German, and Italian findings, consult the reports listed in the bibliography. Because *Strikes in France* contains an extensive discussion of sources and procedures, while *The Rebellious Century* summarizes them rather quickly, the following discussion will focus on the analysis of collective violence rather than of strikes.

Although in principle our work could be done in other ways, we have relied heavily on high-speed digital computers for tabulation and quantitative analysis. The codebooks mentioned here, for example, are essentially sets of instructions for the preparation of comparable punched cards from the raw descriptions of violent events encountered in archival documents, newspapers, and political histories.

The basic data for the study, indeed, come from (a) documents in French archives, mainly reports on collective conflicts and government responses to them; (b) published series of governmental reports and statistics concerning the administration of justice, population censuses, strikes, special inquiries, labor organization, and so on; (c) long series of political yearbooks, like the *Année politique*; (d) long series of French newspapers, notably the *Moniteur universel*, *Le Constitutionnel*, *La Gazette des Tribunaux*, the *Journal des Débats*, *Le Temps* and *Le Monde*; (e) regular secondary sources, including regional learned and antiquarian journals. We work largely from microfilmed copies of these sources.

There are four overlapping samples of events under consideration. The first includes each strike reported in the *Statistique des Grèves*, the *Statistique annuelle*, the *Revue française de Travail*, the *Associations professionnelles ouvrières*, and several other publications in any year from 1830 to 1960. The second consists of a haphazard collection of conflicts and short periods on which we happen to have exceptionally detailed evidence, evidence permitting careful study of the participants and of the sequence of action: The June Days of 1848, the resistance to Louis Napoleon's 1851 coup d'état, and a number of others. The third—our "general sample"—contains every event meeting certain minimum criteria (to be discussed in a moment) which trained readers encountered in scanning newspapers continuously, day by day, over each year from 1830 through 1860, three randomly chosen months per year from 1861 to

1929, and each year from 1930 through 1960; there were two different news-papers for each day in most years, three newspapers in a few cases of faulty coverage. The fourth—our "intensive sample"—is composed of every event in the general sample estimated to involve at least 1000 person-days (1000 people for one day, or 500 for two days, or 700 on the first plus 300 on the second, and so on), plus every tenth event of all the rest. The general sample has about 2000 incidents in it, the intensive sample about 400.

The actual *description* of the incidents in the two samples comes not only from the newspaper accounts, but also from the archival materials, historical works, and other sources enumerated earlier. The intensive sample receives extensive verification and very detailed coding; the general sample, a less intensive treatment. The systematic, and largely quantitative, analysis of these coded accounts deals with

1 the intensity, form, participants, and geographic incidence of violent events for each major period under study;
2 the relationship between these characteristics of collective violence and the nature of social changes occurring in their settings;
3 covariation of characteristics of individual events, including the identification of common precipitants, standard sequences of events, regular outcomes;
4 connections between the character of industrial conflict and the pattern of collective violence in an area and/or period;
5 changes of these patterns over time.

Obviously, these analyses use standard indexes of various social changes by area and year as well as the coded accounts of violent events.

SOME MATTERS OF DEFINITION*

The study of France also relies for internal consistency on a set of standard definitions. The crucial one identifies the "violent event." Without defending it, I shall have to present that definition and the rules of thumb we have developed for its application. Anyone who has already worked with descriptions of collective conflicts will quickly notice two things about these rules of thumb. First, they form the bridge between an abstract definition and a particular period and place; other periods and different places would no doubt require somewhat different bridges. Second, even in the case of France the rules

---

*I have cribbed most of the following section from the introduction to the intensive sample codebook, which in turn drew heavily from staff memoranda by Lutz Berkner and Charles Tilly.

of thumb leave a good deal of room for judgment and a considerable number of ambiguous cases. I only claim that these criteria in most cases permit a fairly firm determination of whether a particular set of events makes up a "violent event" on the basis of information one has early in the game. Here is the general definition:

A "violent event" is an instance of *mutual and collective coercion within an autonomous political system which seizes or physically damages persons or objects.*

Collective Coercion

One formation of at least fifty persons must be present, representing either the forces of rebellion or the forces of repression. This has been done mainly as a practical measure, since we feel that larger groups are more likely to be reported and relevant information is more readily available on them in the sources.

However, for over half of our incidents, no exact or approximate number of participants is reported. We have decided to adopt a list of words which are often used to describe the incidents, and we are tentatively *assuming* that they mean the involvement of a large group of people, i.e., over fifty.

multitude	troupe	échauffourée
rassemblement	révolte	bagarre
réunion	rébellion	tumulte
foule	insurrection	désordre
attroupement	émeute	trouble

If an incident meets the criteria of damage or violence (below) and no number of participants is given, we include it in the sample if it is described by one of these terms. This does not mean that these are the only terms which could be used (e.g., incident, manifestation, agitation, sédition, rixe, bouleversement, fête), but the ones we have chosen imply the participation of a relatively large group of people. We are *not* using these terms to determine the extent of violence, but only as an indicator of participation.

Adjectives of size used with these words are important. Thus, any adjective suggesting a large size (rassemblements nombreux, foule immense) means it is included. Diminutives (petite foule, etc.) keep the incident out of the sample.

This *excludes* any independent violent activity undertaken by an individual or a small group of individuals. Thus we do not include assassinations, murders, thefts, or other crimes, committed by less than fifty people (or a group defined by other than one of our collective terms). However, we include violence by a group on the periphery of a larger demonstration. This also excludes action by unknown persons such as sabotage, bombs, or fires. We take these into account, but they are not to be included in the basic sample.

Mutual

This means that there must be at least two antagonistic formations involved. However, one may be involved by the proxy of its property or symbols. We include any opposition to the symbols or representatives of authority or another group. Violence must be directed at someone else; thus, workers attacking a newspaper office are included, while farmers destroying their own produce in protest to government farm policies are not.

Seizure or Physical Damage of Persons or Objects

Any dead or wounded make the incident qualify. The major problem cases involve resistance to police when it is not clear whether anyone was hurt, e.g., stones thrown at troops or mounted gendarmes surrounded by a mob. Seizure of persons or objects without physical injury is also a problem. In general, if persons or objects are seized over resistance, that is enough. If the seizing group fights off another group or breaks through a physical barrier of some sort, resistance has occurred.

We include any damage done by one group to someone else's property by attacking or seizing control of it. Besides significant destruction this includes broken windows or symbolic minor damage. It does not include damage to one's own property (farmers destroying own crops, merchants burning their own records in protest) and it must be done by a group—which excludes sabotage, fires, bombings of unknown origins. Seizure of objects includes "taxation populaire"—the forcible seizure of grain or other foodstuffs, followed by their public sale at a proclaimed "just price." It also includes nonviolent occupation of buildings such as sit-down strikes. In order to handle the huge number of sit-downs in 1936, 1937, and 1938, we have grouped them into departmental summaries for each month.

These criteria clearly *exclude* any large political gatherings that do not end in violence or crowds which shout threats of violence but take no action.

Within an Autonomous Political System

This segment of the definition excludes war and border incidents. It also excludes any violence within a closed institution outside the general political sphere such as prisons, asylums and hospitals. If they break out of these institutions, however, they must be included. We include army mutinies since the members of the armed forces are part of the political community.

Boundaries of Violent Events

When one of the actions just discussed has occurred, we must set some limits in time, space, and personnel on the events to be recorded and analyzed. When two or more such actions occur, we must also decide whether they are parts of the "same" event, or related ones. An event begins when at least two of the formations taking part in the violent action begin a continuous interaction and ends when the last two formations end their continuous interaction. It occupies all the space in which a spectator could directly observe the interaction without benefit of mechanical devices. The participants are all persons who perform the crucial action(s), all persons who interact with them directly in the course of that action, plus all persons acting collectively with members of either of the first two categories in the stream of activity including the crucial action(s). Finally, sets of participants fall into separate formations to the extent that they act collectively, communicate internally, oppose other sets of participants, and are given distinct identities by observers. Where we do not have enough information to apply these definitions with any rigor—which is often—we accept the conventional observer's identification of actors, stage, and action.

When two violent actions occur on the same day or consecutive days, in the same commune or adjacent ones (in Paris, Lyon, or Marseille: the same quarter or adjacent ones), and there is a reasonable presumption of an overlap of personnel equal to ten percent or more of the participants in the smaller action, both actions count as part of the same disturbance, and all of the intervening time belongs to the event. Three or more violent actions with such connections may compound into events covering longer periods and larger territories. Two events are distinct but *linked* when they occur in the same or consecutive months, and meet any of these conditions: (a) concerted action of at least one formation in one event with at least one formation in the other; (b) strong evidence of overlap in personnel; (c) strong evidence of the provision of material assistance by the participants in one event to the participants in the other; (d) overt imitation of the action of one event by a formation in another; (e) overt response as indicated by demands, slogans, or ritual acts. Three or more events may be linked in this way.

In summary, the procedure comes to this:

1   Scan the sources for violent actions.
2   Having located a violent action, determine whether the event of which it is a part meets the definition of "violent event."
3   If it does, set its boundaries in space, time, and personnel.
4   Identify the formations taking part in the event.

5 Determine whether it is linked to any other event.

6 Code.

The diagram at the end of this section represents the whole complicated procedure.

SUMMARY

A. *Violence:*
    1. One dead
    2. One wounded
    3. Any damage to objects
    4. Seizure of control of objects

B. *Collective:*
    1. At least fifty persons in one formation (direct evidence through numbers of participants wounded or arrested)
    2. Indirect evidence of a large group through the use of a collective terminology:

multitude	troupe	bagarre
rassemblement	révolte	tumulte
réunion	rébellion	insurrection
foule	émeute	désordre
attroupement	échauffourée	trouble

C. *Mutual:*
    1. Two formations in conflict
    2. A formation versus an individual
    3. A formation versus objects or symbols representing another group

D. *Exclude:*
    1. Sabotage, bombings, fires set by unknown persons
    2. Assassinations, murders, criminal activities by individuals
    3. Large gatherings where no violence breaks out even if they threaten violence
    4. Rebellions within closed institutions: prisons, hospitals, asylums
    5. Symbolic damage to one's own property

E. *Boundaries:*
    1. Begins with continuous interaction of at least two formations.
    2. Ends with termination of continuous interaction of last two formations.
    3. Occupies space within which spectator could observe interaction directly.

    4. Participants: performers of violent acts, others interacting directly with them, plus others acting collectively with either of the first two groups; they are divided into formations.

F. *Multiple violent actions forming single event:*
    1. Same day or consecutive days
    2. Same commune or adjacent communes (in Paris, Lyon, Marseille, same quarter or adjacent quarters)
    3. Overlap in personnel of ten percent or more of the participants in the smaller action

G. *Distinct but linked events:*
    1. Same month or consecutive months
    2. Concerted action of formations
        OR
    3. Overlap in personnel
        OR
    4. Provision of material assistance
        OR
    5. Overt imitation
        OR
    6. Overt response by demands, slogans, ritual acts

This whole system of definitions and procedures works well enough where there are good (and fairly uniform) accounts of many political disturbances, and where there is an identifiable "autonomous political system" with a single central authority tending to monopolize legitimate control over means of collective coercion. In France itself, it weakens during long interregna like the Occupation and the Resistance of World War II. In Italy and Germany, the periods before unification present serious problems. The whole system would probably have to be recast to handle such cases as Zaïre (formerly the Belgian Congo) after 1960, the United States from 1860 to 1865, or western Europe itself before the 17th century. The scheme also has two quite intentional features which suit it well for the kind of analysis we have undertaken, but might unfit it for some other sorts of inquiry: (1) it ignores the political *effects* of the event, giving no special weight, for example, to the rebellion which topples a regime; (2) although the criterion of "violence" is a fairly generous one, the scheme bypasses instances of nonviolent coercion unless they are coupled with violence. Neither a palace revolution nor an unfulfilled threat of mass rioting is likely to qualify as a violent event under its restrictions. These are costs we have accepted because of the advantages of economy and precision they bring; for other investigators and other purposes, they may be costs too great to bear.

Sample Selection Procedure

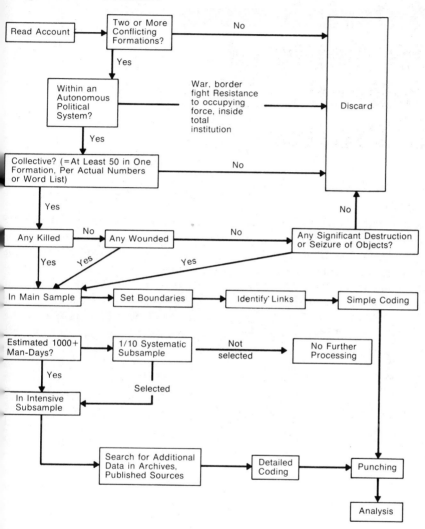

Appendix 2

Materials from the Study of Collective Violence in France

GENERAL

The material follows a single relatively well-documented event from narrative account through coding and transcription in machine-readable form to its integration into a quantitative analysis. Forest invasions of this sort (although not this scale) were frequent events in the Pyrenees from the late 1820s through the Revolution of 1848. The Forest Code enacted by the French government in 1828 curtailed common rights to glean, graze, and gather firewood, in favor of the consolidation of bourgeois property in woodlands. Poor people of the mountains challenged the Code for twenty-five years, especially at moments when the government weakened, as in the revolutions of 1830 and 1848. The conflict of la Barousse took place just one month after the February Revolution of 1848.

When I developed the procedures for sampling and coding violent events in the mid-1960s, I used the word "political disturbance" to describe the events under study. As I worked with the material, I realized the phrase contained an unjustified presumption and a misleading metaphor. Since we enumerate events on the basis of size and the presence of violence regardless of political context or content, the word "political" presumes what is to be proven: that the bulk of collective violence does, indeed, grow out of political processes. The word "disturbance" implies malfunction, abnormality, a break with ordinary life which our analyses of the evidence generally contradict. I now prefer the colorless "violent event," "violent incident", or even "collective action producing violence." However, the older vocabulary pervades our material; it would be dishonest to expunge it.

The violent events studied in France included every one meeting our criteria (some damage or seizure of persons or objects, at least one formation of fifty persons or more, at least one formation nonmilitary) we encountered in

254

reading two daily national newspapers for each day from 1830 through 1860 and 1930 through 1960, plus three randomly selected months per year from 1861 through 1929. The General Sample includes all those events. The Intensive Sample, for the periods 1830–60 and 1930–60 only, includes all events we estimated to involve at least 1000 person-days plus a systematic ten percent of the remaining events. The information coded comes from the newspaper accounts, from historical works, from political yearbooks, and from French archival documents.

The items in this set include:

1 Excerpts from reports of a conflict between troops and "invaders of forests" in la Barousse, March 1848.

2 Reports on Political Disturbance used for abstracting from newspapers, archival documents and secondary sources and as a cover sheet for photocopies of excerpts from those sources.

3 Excerpt from the Intensive Sample Codebook used in coding the event in la Barousse.

4 Excerpts from the coded version of the event, including the complete set of coder's comments.

5 Segments of computer printout including a partial listing of the card-image version of the Intensive Sample coding.

6 Segment of computer printout including a complete listing of the OSIRIS version of the Intensive Sample coding.

7 Machine version of Table 15 from Charles Tilly, "How Protest Modernized in France" in William Aydelotte, Allan Bogue, and Robert Fogel, eds., *The Dimensions of Quantitative Research in History* (Princeton: Princeton University Press, 1972).

8 Table 4 from Charles Tilly, "The Chaos of the Living City" in Charles Tilly, ed., *An Urban World* (Boston: Little, Brown, 1974).

9 Graph representing a five-year moving average of our estimates of total participants in French collective violence, 1830–1960.

EXCERPTS FROM REPORTS ON EVENT 848 02 29 01

"Letters from Saint-Gaudens written the 4th of March announce that order has been restored . . . The band of looters consisted of almost 2,000 people; at the approach of the line troops and the National Guard they retreated toward the mountains of la Barousse; but having arrived in the defiles, they resumed the offensive. The front ranks, armed with guns, fired; the troops replied and rushed toward their enemy with bravery. The evildoers then escaped in every direction across the rough mountain terrain, and it was impossible to follow them. It appears that many of them were shot as they tried to enter caves in the mountainsides . . ." (*Le Siècle*, 11 March 1848).

"The troubles which broke out in the valley of la Barousse were started by illegal users of the forest. A large number of inhabitants of that valley went to the Guard General of the Forests, who was assigned to execute the warrants issued against them and burned all his papers while he was gone. Thence they went to the office of the Collectors for National Lands, where they likewise destroyed all the registers and forced the officers to pay a certain sum of money as reparation for the latest fines the officers had collected. Finally the same people did some damage to the chateau of Lussan, belonging to M. Goulard, the ex-deputy of Bagnères, who has been disputing the ownership of certain forests with the communes in the valley. We learn that a fairly large number of troublemakers have been arrested and have arrived at Bagnères." (*Le Moniteur*, 10 March 1848)

"A band of about 1,000, most of them armed, organized in the Hautes-Pyrénées . . . During the night of 2–3 March, that horde invaded the cantons of Saint-Bertrand and Saint-Béat in the arrondissment of Saint-Gaudens (Haute-Garonne), pillaged the chateau of M. Goulard, the former deputy, at Lassan, and that of the Duke of Rovigo at Barbazon, and finally collected a kind of tribute from a few well-to-do landowners in the same area. The National Guard of various communes joined with line troops sent from Toulouse and Tarbes to restore order. The detachments sent after the miscreants found them. We are told that 25 were taken prisoner, 3 killed and 6 or 7 wounded." (Archives Nationales BB 18 1461, report of procureur général, Cour d'Appel, Toulouse, 4 March 1848)

"The change of regime occasioned fairly serious disorders in the arrondissement of Saint-Gaudens. A band of peasants from the mountains of la Barousse (Hautes-Pyrénées) spread through the lowlands in hopes that the fall of the monarchy might cause an economic overturn which could hardly fail to be profitable to them. On the 2d of March, the coach from Bagnères-de-Luchon was robbed between Bertran and Bagiry, and the news soon spread that 1,500 or 1,800 peasants armed with clubs, pitchforks, picks and hunting rifles were pillaging the houses and castles of the area, and holding their inhabitants for ransom . . ." (Antonin Cayré, "Des journées de février aux journées du juin," in Jacques Godechot, ed., *La Révolution de 1848 à Toulouse et dans la Haute-Garonne* (Toulouse, 1948). (The fullest account, however, appears in Louis Clarenc, "Les troubles de la Barousse en 1848," *Annales du Midi* 65 (1951), 329–348.)

REPORT ON POLITICAL DISTURBANCE (4-65)

1. Title _____ 2. No. _____ 3. Recorder _____

4. Date _____ 5. Source _____

6. Location	7. Antecedents/Presumed Origins

8. Precipitating Events _____

_____

9. Description _____

_____

_____

_____

_____

_____

_____

10. Objectives: none ☐   observer's inference ☐   explicit ☐

11. Casualties _____

12. Property Damage _____ 13. Duration _____

14. Participants _____

_____

15. Repressive Forces _____

_____

16. Linkage with Other Disturbances	17. Consequences

18. References _____

☐ Notes on back   ☐ Additional Sheets Dealing with this Disturbance

                       ☐ Further Information on Continuation Sheet

A NOTE ON FORMATIONS

Some violent action (killing or wounding of persons, damage or seizure of property) brought the events under consideration into the sample of disturbances. The participants in the disturbance include all persons who performed the violent action, all persons who interacted with them directly in the course of that action, and all persons acting collectively with members of either of the first two categories in the continuous stream of activity which contains the violent action.

We divide the participants into formations. Sets of participants belong to distinct formations to the extent that they act collectively, communicate internally, oppose other sets of participants, and/or are given specific identities meaningful outside the disturbance itself (e.g., "socialistes," "paysans," "gendarmes") by the observers. Many formations, however, compound several different kinds of people—for example, maîtres and compagnons; we do not assign them to separate formations unless they are reported to act independently or in significantly different ways.

Most disturbances involve two or three easily distinguishable formations. In an extreme case, a formation can have only one member—for example, the victim of a lynching. At another extreme, a disturbance can involve only one formation—for example, the unanimous destroyers of a chateau. In very complicated disturbances, where these principles would permit the distinction of ten or more different formations, we combine the participants into nine or fewer formations representing the most important divisions in collective action. For example, if the bijoutiers, the ébénistes, and the orfévriers each have their own barricade, they would appear as separate formations in the coding of a small disturbance, but in a very large one could be combined into a single formation. In this case, choose the code in cols. 37–38 with great care, and COMMENT.

Even in small disturbances, groups specialized in the maintenance and restoration of public order (which this codebook will call Repressive for short) can always be combined into a single formation to the extent that their actions are indistinguishable. Thus when National Guards and troops of the line under a single command disperse a group of demonstrators, treat them as a single formation unless they begin to act in significantly different ways. Be sure to COMMENT if the code leaves any doubt how and what you have combined.

In any case, identify the formations before starting to code. When a formation has a public identity more specific than words like foule, attroupement, people, and so on, indicate (for example, "Protestants," "CRS," "les habitants de _____," "Anarchistes"), spell out the identity in columns 12–36.

Cards 31–39: Formation Background

cols. 1–2   *CARD NUMBER*

NUMBER FORMATIONS ARBITRARILY AND NOTE
IN FILE

31	Formation 1	to 39	Formation 9
32	Formation 2		

cols. 3–11   *IDENTIFYING DATA*

DO NOT CODE—WILL BE DUPLICATED AUTOMATI-
CALLY FROM FIRST CARD

cols. 12–36   *PUBLIC IDENTITY OF FORMATION: ALPHABETIC*

If the formation has no definite public identity, leave
blank. If it has a name, put it here.

cols. 37–38   *TYPE OF FORMATION*

01   Crowd (further identifying information unavailable)
10   Crowd of common ideology
         11   Crowd of common political attachment
         12   Crowd of common religion
20   Activist group
         21   Political cadres, hacks
         22   Terrorists
         23   Criminal group (brigands)
         24   Guerrilla insurgents
         25   Private (party) army
         26   Secret society
30   Military or paramilitary group
         31   National guard
         32   Civil guard
         33   Regular army
         34   Garde mobile
         35   Milice bourgeoise
         36   Palace guard
         37   Bons citoyens (volunteers)
         39   Any military group plus public officials:
                 MANDATORY COMMENT

40   Police
    41   Gendarmes
    42   CRS
    43   Military police
    48   Police and military group: comment encouraged
    49   Police plus public officials: MANDATORY COMMENT
50   Occupational group
    51   Workers of same industry
    52   Workers of same factory
    53   Workers of same locality
    54   Union
    55   Students
60   Outsiders (group representing a locality)
    61   Group coming directly from a foreign country
    62   Group coming from an outside locality
    63   Group of migrants from outside France
    64   Group of migrants from another area of France
70   Consumer group
    71   Users of the same market
    72   Users of the same water supply
80   Public officials
90   Combinations: MANDATORY COMMENT
    91   Deliberate combination for purposes of brevity in coding: MANDATORY COMMENT
99   Others: MANDATORY COMMENT

FORMATION BACKGROUND

Content of Code	ITEM NO	CARD 31	CARD 32	CARD 33	CARD 34	CARD 35	CARD 36	CARD 37	CARD 38	CARD 39	Comments
Card Number	1	3	3	3	3	3	3	3	3	3	
Code 31-39	2	1	2	3	4	5	6	7	8	9	
IDENTIFICATION	3	x	x	x	x	x	x	x	x	x	
DO NOT CODE	4	x	x	x	x	x	x	x	x	x	
	5	x	x	x	x	x	x	x	x	x	
	6	x	x	x	x	x	x	x	x	x	
	7	x	x	x	x	x	x	x	x	x	
	8	x	x	x	x	x	x	x	x	x	
	9	x	x	x	x	x	x	x	x	x	
	10	x	x	x	x	x	x	x	x	x	
	11	x	x	x	x	x	x	x	x	x	
PUBLIC IDENTITY	12	B	V	R							
of FORMATION	13	R	I	E							
Spell	14	I	C	P							
Name of	15	G	T	R							
Formation	16	A	I	E							
	17	N	M	S							
	18	D	E	S							
	19	S	S	I							
	20		V								
	21		D	E							
	22		E								
	23			F							
	24	B	O								
	25	R	R								
	26	I	C								
	27	G	E								
	28	A	S								
	29	N									
	30	D									
	31	A									
	32	G									
	33	E									
	34										
	35										
	36										
Type of formation	37	5	9	9							
	38	3	1	0							
Age-Sex	39	1	1	1							
	40	2	2	2							

6) Brigands
8) Victimes de Brigandage
33) Repressive Forces

(37/32) Numerous incidents of brigandage + destruction occurred in the various communes. For the sake of brevity, I have grouped all victims together. These victims include public officials (conducteur de diligence, p.m. Receveur de l'Enregistrement etc), propriétaires, et usuriers. (8/33) garde nationaux, militaires, gendarmes, and some priests

FORMATION BACKGROUND (2)

Content of Code		METHOD	CARD 31	CARD 32	CARD 33	CARD 34	CARD 35	CARD 36	CARD 37	CARD 38	CARD 39	Comments
Birthplace of members	41	0	0	0								
Present residence	42	1	2	1								
Occupational	43	0	0	o								(43-2) Administrateur, Employés
composition	44	1	2	2								des contributions etc, propri-
Political	45	0	0	0								etaires, et usuriers.
attachments	46	0	0	1								(45-32) Police, militaires, national
Immediate	47	0	0	0								guarde, and priests
background	48	1	1	3								
Code in units	49	0	0	0								
of 2	50	0	0	0								
Legality of 1st Act	51	7	1	1								
Precipitating	52	3	2	4								(52-3) News of change in regime
factor	53	3	6	4								gives brigands a pretext for
	54	0	0	0								revolt + an unsettled situation
Type of violence	55	3	2	7								making violence easier to
Response to violence	56	1	1	7								commit without immediate
other forms of	57	4	1	1								reprisals
participation	58	2	0	0								(56-3) For the first 3 days, the
Concerted Action	59	1	1	1								rebels responded to no violence.
Mutual Aid	60	1	1	1								However, on March 3rd, they
Overt Imitation	61	1	1	1								met the repressive formation
Objectives	62	3	8	8								in a battle, both sides using
Code in	63	2	1	3								firearms. This, however, was
units of	64	4	8	7								not the predominant form of
two	65	0	3	4								violence used or responded
	66	2	8	0								to by the rebels.
	67	0	5	0								(62-3) Code forestier
Explicitness of	68	2	1	0								(64-3) Conditions of usury + enclosure
objectives	69	1	0	1								(66-3) Destruction of private
Unity of objectives	70	4	5	3								property in revenge against
	71	1	0	1								proprietaires + usurers
Homogeneity of	72	2	2	2								
objectives	73	0	0	0								
Autonomy of objectives	74	2	2	6								
Fluctuation in focus	75	3	1	1								
Territory controlled	76	5	0	0								(76-3) "Controlled" is a poor word.
	77	4	1	2								The brigands pillaged at will,
Fluctuation in	78	6	1	3								without major opposition, but
territory controlled	79	1	0	0								they did not occupy the terri-
	80	.										tory in the normal sense that
												'control' would imply.

848 02 29 01   La Brousse

21/12. Twelve communes. The three not listed are Bertren (H-P), Troubat (H-P), and
Bagiry (H-G). The communal information for them is the same as for those communes
listed on the cards.

21 to 29/27. No political tendency or apathy noted. Clarenc states that this disturbance had nothing to do with politics.

21 to 29/39. Change in regime created uncertainty as to whether former officials were
still legally in office. Insurgents claimed that they were not and treated them as such.
This uncertainty may also explain why repressive action was not taken until 3 March.

31 to 29/39. Resentment against Code Forestier and enforcement of it. Resentment against
state and certain proprietaires who were felt to be usurpateurs de droits legitimes.

21 to 29/42. Resentment against usurers.

21 to 29/45. Actions by national government which delivered into hands of certain proprietaires land which was felt to be common.

21 to 29/48. Numerous proces-verbaux etc. against violators of Code Forestier.

32/37. Numerous incidents of brigandage and destruction occurred in various communes.
I have grouped all victims together. These include public officials (conducteur du
Diligence, maires, Receveur de l'Enregistrement etc.) proprietaires and usurers.

33/37. Garde nationaux, militaires, gendarmes, and some priests.

32/43. Administration, employes des contribution, proprietaires etc.

33/43. Police, militaires, national guard, and priests.

31/52. News of change in regime gives brigands a pretext for revolt and an unsettled
situation to take advantage of.

31/56. For the first three days, the rebels responded to no violence. On 3 March,
they met the repressive formation in battle, both sides using firearms.

31/62. Code Forestier.

31/64. Conditions of usury.

31/66. Destruction of private property in revenge.

41/43. Estimates are 15-1800, and 2000.

42/43. Different individuals throughout area, a rough estimate.

43/43. About 50 soldiers and gendarmes (Clarenc). The rest was national guard of five
towns of over 11,000 inhabitants total . . National guard strength inferred from nature
of action and sizes of towns.

41/55. Formation generally expanding. Man-days = 1 x 200 + 1 x 800 + 2 x 1800 = 4600.

42/55. Each participant in this formation was involved during only one day.

42/67. Clarenc mentions no wounded and states that none were killed. Newspapers vary
from one to seven wounded and one to three killed.

41/72. Some estimates are lower (97 and 81), but 98 is often repeated, and used by
Clarenc. Ten were prosecuted and found guilty.

51-52/13. The sequence presented between the two XX codes is not a true sequence but
a recreation of a typical incident. Ten to twelve incidents of a similar nature took
place between 29 February and 3 March, and there is no room to code them sequentially.
After the second XX, the battle of 3 March is coded as usual.

51/17. Invasion of mairie, bureau de l'enregistrement or bureau of the forestier.
Subsequent burning of records and mistreating of officials.

52/31. A different victim: a chateau owner.

51-53/43. 3 March, noon, at Antichan. Rounding up of prisoners continues until 5:00 p.m.

848 02 29 01   La Barousse (cont., p. 2)

65/14. Change in regime.

65/44. Formation 53 is law enforcement force. However, division between 51 and 52 combines differences of occupation and property.

66/51. A great number of public records burned in almost every town, mostly pertaining to Code Forestier, lists of offenses, fines and proces-verbaux. Records of debts also buried. Minor property damage to public buildings. A huissier's house was pillaged and horse stolen in Mauleen-Barousse. A pig, some pork, and some wine was taken in Sost, arms and insignia of administrateur forestier stolen. Pillage in Loures-Barousse, house invaded and pillaged in Antichan, six men ransommed in Trobat and Bertren, money and provisions stolen in Anla. Flag torn in Izaourt. Largest damage at a proprietaire's chateau in Luscan where trees were cut, grilles broken, doors broken in, furniture broken or stolen and linen and books destroyed or taken.

66/55. This is a low estimate. 30,000 francs damage alone at chateau de Luscan.

66/73. Although completely stifled, this disturbance stimulated later incidents, notably a plot to assassinate Receveur de l'enregistrement, the 17 April disturbance at Signac, and the incident at Bize-Nistos at the end of April.

70/18. MC 1848-03-10 (582-583)
        LS 1848-03-11

71-78. Comments
     Very difficult to code because of the great number of small incidents. See the model sequence code devised to handle this and note that there are twelve communes involved.

79. Bibliography
79...01 Clarenc, Troubles de Barousse, Annales du Midi, 1951, 329-348.
79...02 Cayne, in Godechot, La Revolution de 1848 à Toulouse, 153-154.

```
LL          IIIIIIIII   SSSSSSSSSS   TTTTTTTTTTT
LL          IIIIIIIII   SSSSSSSSSSSS TTTTTTTTTTT
LL             II       SS        SS     TT
LL             II       SS               TT
LL             II       SSS              TT
LL             II       SSSSSSSSS        TT
LL             II        SSSSSSSSS       TT
LL             II              SSS       TT
LL             II               SS       TT
LL             II       SS       SS      TT
LLLLLLLLLLLL  IIIIIIIII  SSSSSSSSSSSS    TT
LLLLLLLLLLLL  IIIIIIIII   SSSSSSSSS      TT
```

```
2184802290165115221        0012240008105101006207100015OST
2284802290165080428        0012240008105101006207100015MAULEON BAROUSSE
2384802290165010638        00122400081051010062071000014NTICHAN
2484802290165010418        0012240008105101006207100001ANLA
2584802290131076213        0012240008105101006207100001LUSCAN
2684802290165111028        00122400081051010062071000015ARP
2784802290131016037        0012240008105101006207100001BARBAZON
2884802290165066209        00122400081051010062071000017ZNAOURT
2984802290165075413        0012240008105101006207100001LOURES BAROUSSE
3184802290BRIGANDS          5312010100010073303142111324020214120235461
3284802290VICTIMES DE BRIGANDAGE   9112020200010012602110111818385105020210110
3384802290REPRESSIVE FORCES        901201020103001440771011118374000131206102 30
4184802290111431212 0BANDE CONSIDERABLE   0180020477430460005200000005300981118
4284802290100000000010NO KEY WORDS         00030901724300030014000000005600000011
4384802290144611312 0DEUX COLONNES        0080090405110080004100000000000000011
5184802290 ..1183358281403564838582 8164..264545535199
5284802290 ..0251355157515157515 1530202..020202020202
5384802290 020202020202020202020202020202020225453 8334040
5084802290 00030505060605051105050505051103040507 1213
6584802290131330121023.1025103              ..21535JACQUERIE GRAVES DESORDRES
6684802290100026303057743000543006200000001030098190..343112542015012347171111 0
7084802290140100313001399660719660817755028      VERY DIFFICULT TO CODE
7184802290BECAUSE OF GREAT NUMBER OF SMALL INCIDENTS.  SEE THE MODEL
7284802290SEQUENCE CODE DEVISED TO HANDLE THIS AND NOTE THAT THERE ARE 12
7384802290COMMUNES INVOLVED
7984802290101CLARENC. TROUBLES DE BAROUSSE, ANNALES DU MIDI, 1951 329-348
7984802290102CAYNE, IN GODECHOT, LA REVOLUTION DE 1848 A TOULOUSE, 153-154
8084802290101211212 COMMUNES.  THE THREE NOT LISTED ARE BERTREN %H-P<.
8084802290102211224AND BAIGRY %H-G<, THE COMMUNAL INFORMATION FOR THEM IS THE
8084802290103211235AME AS FOR THOSE COMMUNES LISTED ON THE CARDS
8084802290104211271NO POLITICAL TENDENCY OR APATHY NOTED.  CLARENC STATES THAT
8084802290105211272THIS DISTURBANCE HAD NOTHING TO DO WITH POLITICS.
8084802290106221271NO POLITICAL TENDENCY OR APATHY NOTED.  CLARENC STATES THAT
8084802290107221272THIS DISTURBANCE HAD NOTHING TO DO WITH POLITICS.
8084802290108231271NO POLITICAL TENDENCY OR APATHY NOTED.  CLARENC STATES THAT
8084802290109231272THIS DISTURBANCE HAD NOTHING TO DO WITH POLITICS.
8084802290110241271NO POLITICAL TENDENCY OR APATHY NOTED.  CLARENC STATES THAT
8084802290111241272THIS DISTURBANCE HAD NOTHING TO DO WITH POLITICS.
8084802290112251271NO POLITICAL TENDENCY OR APATHY NOTED.  CLARENC STATES THAT
8084802290113251272THIS DISTURBANCE HAD NOTHING TO DO WITH POLITICS.
8084802290114261271NO POLITICAL TENDENCY OR APATHY NOTED.  CLARENC STATES THAT
8084802290115261272THIS DISTURBANCE HAD NOTHING TO DO WITH POLITICS.
8084802290116271271NO POLITICAL TENDENCY OR APATHY NOTED.  CLARENC STATES THAT
8084802290117271272THIS DISTURBANCE HAD NOTHING TO DO WITH POLITICS.
8084802290118281271NO POLITICAL TENDENCY OP APATHY NOTED.  CLARENC STATES THAT
8084802290119281272THIS DISTURBANCE HAD NOTHING TO DO WITH POLITICS.
8084802290120292271NO POLITICAL TENDENCY OR APATHY NOTED.  CLARENC STATES THAT
8084802290121292272THIS DISTURBANCE HAD NOTHING TO DO WITH POLITICS.
8084802290122221391CHANGE IN REGIME CREATED UNCERTAINTY AS TO WHETHER FORMER
8084802290123213920FFICIALS WERE STILL LEGALLY IN OFFICE.  INSURGENTS CLAIMED
```

```
8084802290124213933THAT THEY WERE NOT AND TREATED THEM AS SUCH.  THIS
8084802290125213944UNCERTAINTY MAY ALSO EXPLAIN WHY REPRESSIVE ACTION WAS NOT
8084802290126213955TAKEN UNTIL MARCH 3
8084802290127223911CHANGE IN REGIME CREATED UNCERTAINTY AS TO WHETHER FORMER
8084802290128223920OFFICIALS WERE STILL LEGALLY IN OFFICE.  INSURGENTS CLAIMED
8084802290129223933THAT THEY WERE NOT AND TREATED THEM AS SUCH.  THIS
8084802290130223944UNCERTAINTY MAY ALSO EXPLAIN WHY REPRESSIVE ACTION WAS NOT
8084802290131223955TAKEN UNTIL MARCH 3
8084802290132233911CHANGE IN REGIME CREATED UNCERTAINTY AS TO WHETHER FORMER
8084802290133233920OFFICIALS WERE STILL LEGALLY IN OFFICE.  INSURGENTS CLAIMED
8084802290134233933THAT THEY WERE NOT AND TREATED THEM AS SUCH.  THIS
8084802290135233944UNCERTAINTY MAY ALSO EXPLAIN WHY REPRESSIVE ACTION WAS NOT
8084802290136233955TAKEN UNTIL MARCH 3
8084802290137243911CHANGE IN REGIME CREATED UNCERTAINTY AS TO WHETHER FORMER
8084802290138243920OFFICIALS WERE STILL LEGALLY IN OFFICE.  INSURGENTS CLAIMED
8084802290139243933THAT THEY WERE NOT AND TREATED THEM AS SUCH.  THIS
8084802290140243944UNCERTAINTY MAY ALSO EXPLAIN WHY REPRESSIVE ACTION WAS NOT
8084802290141243955TAKEN UNTIL MARCH 3
8084802290142253911CHANGE IN REGIME CREATED UNCERTAINTY AS TO WHETHER FORMER
8084802290143253920OFFICIALS WERE STILL LEGALLY IN OFFICE.  INSURGENTS CLAIMED
8084802290144253933THAT THEY WERE NOT AND TREATED THEM AS SUCH.  THIS
8084802290145253944UNCERTAINTY MAY ALSO EXPLAIN WHY REPRESSIVE ACTION WAS NOT
8084802290146253955TAKEN UNTIL MARCH 3
8084802290147263911CHANGE IN REGIME CREATED UNCERTAINTY AS TO WHETHER FORMER
8084802290148263920OFFICIALS WERE STILL LEGALLY IN OFFICE.  INSURGENTS CLAIME4
8084802290149263933THAT THEY WERE NOT AND TREATED THEM AS SUCH.  THIS
8084802290150263944UNCERTAINTY MAY ALSO EXPLAIN WHY REPRESSIVE ACTION WAS NOT
8084802290151263955TAKEN UNTIL MARCH 3
8084802290152273911CHANGE IN REGIME CREATED UNCERTAINTY AS TO WHETHER FORMER
8084802290153273920OFFICIALS WERE STILL LEGALLY IN OFFICE.  INSURGENTS CLAIMED
8084802290154273933THAT THEY WERE NOT AND TREATED THEM AS SUCH.  THIS
8084802290155273944UNCERTAINTY MAY ALSO EXPLAIN WHY REPRESSIVE ACTION WAS NOT
8084802290156273955TAKEN UNTIL MARCH 3
8084802290157283911CHANGE IN REGIME CREATED UNCERTAINTY AS TO WHETHER FORMER
8084802290158283920OFFICIALS WERE STILL LEGALLY IN OFFICE.  INSURGENTS CLAIMED
8084802290159283933THAT THEY WERE NOT AND TREATED THEM AS SUCH.  THIS
8084802290160283944UNCERTAINTY MAY ALSO EXPLAIN WHY REPRESSIVE ACTION WAS NOT
8084802290161283955TAKEN UNTIL MARCH 3
8084802290162293911CHANGE IN REGIME CREATED UNCERTAINTY AS TO WHETHER FORMER
8084802290163293920OFFICIALS WERE STILL LEGALLY IN OFFICE.  INSURGENTS CLAIMED
8084802290164293933THAT THEY WERE NOT AND TREATED THEM AS SUCH.  THIS
8084802290165293944UNCERTAINTY MAY ALSO EXPLAIN WHY REPRESSIVE ACTION WAS NOT
8084802290166293955TAKEN UNTIL MARCH 3
8084802290167213911RESENTMENT AGAINST CODE FORESTIER AND ENFORCEMENT OF IT.
8084802290168213922RESENTMENT AGAINST STATE AND CERTAIN PROPRIETAIRES WHO WERE
8084802290169213933FELT TO BE USURPATEURS DE DROITS LEGITIMES
8084802290170223911RESENTMENT AGAINST CODE FORESTIER AND ENFORCEMENT OF IT.
8084802290171223922RESENTMENT AGAINST STATE AND CERTAIN PROPRIETAIRES WHO WERE
8084802290172223933FELT TO BE USURPATEURS DE DROITS LEGITIMES
8084802290173233911RESENTMENT AGAINST CODE FORESTIER AND ENFORCEMENT OF IT#
8084802290174233922RESENTMENT AGAINST STATE AND CERTAIN PROPRIETAIRES WHO W5R5
8084802290175233933FELT TO BE USURPATEURS DE DROITS LEGITIMES
8084802290176243911RESENTMENT AGAINST CODE FORESTIER AND ENFORCEMENT OF IT.
8084802290177243922RESENTMENT AGAINST STATE AND CERTAIN PROPRIETAIRES WHO WERE
8084802290178243933FELT TO BE USURPATEURS DE DROITS LEGITIMES
8084802290179253911RESENTMENT AGAINST CODE FORESTIER AND ENFORCEMENT OF IT.
8084802290180253922RESENTMENT AGAINST STATE AND CERTAIN PROPRIETAIRES WHO WERE
8084802290181253933FELT TO BE USURPATEURS DE DROITS LEGITIMES
8084802290182263911RESENTMENT AGAINST CODE FORESTIER AND ENFORCEMENT OF IT.
8084802290183263922RESENTMENT AGAINST STATE AND CERTAIN PROPRIETAIRES WHO WERE
8084802290184263933FELT TO BE USURPATEURS DE DROITS LEGITIMES
8084802290185273911RESENTMENT AGAINST CODE FORESTIER AND ENFORCEMENT OF IT.
8084802290186273922RESENTMENT AGAINST STATE AND CERTAIN PROPRIETAIRES WHO WERE
8084802290187273933FELT TO BE USURPATEURS DE DROITS LEGITIMES
8084802290188283911RESENTMENT AGAINST CODE FORESTIER AND ENFORCEMENT OF IT.
8084802290189283922RESENTMENT AGAINST STATE AND CERTAIN PROPRIETAIRES WHO WERE
8084802290190283933FELT TO BE USURPATEURS DE DROITS LEGITIMES
```

```
B08480229019129391RESENTMENT AGAINST CODE FORESTIER AND ENFORCEMENT OF IT.
B08480229019229392RESENTMENT AGAINST STATE AND CERTAIN PROPRIETAIRES WHO WERE
B08480229019329393FELT TO BE USURPATEURS DE DROITS LEGITIMES
B08480229019421421RESENTMENT AGAINST USURPERS
B08480229019522421RESENTMENT AGAINST USUR 'ERS
B08480229019623421RESENTMENT AGAINST USURPERS
B08480229019724421RESENTMENT AGAINST USURPERS
B08480229019825421RESENTMENT AGAINST USURPERS
B08480229019926421RESENTMENT AGAINST USURPERS
B08480229019927421RESENTMENT AGAINST USURPERS
B08480229019928421RESENTMENT AGAINST USURPERS
B08480229019929421RESENTMENT AGAINST USUR'ERS
B08480229019921451ACTIONS BY NATIONAL GOVT WHICH DELIVERED INTO HANDS OF
B08480229019921452PROPRIETAIRES LAND WHICH WAS FELT TO BE COMMON
B08480229019922451ACTIONS BY NATIONAL GOVT WHICH DELIVERED INTO HANDS OF
B08480229019922452PROPRIETAIRES LAND WHICH WAS FELT TO BE COMMON
B08480229019923451ACTIONS BY NATIONAL GOVT WHICH DELIVERED INTO HANDS OF
B08480229019923452PROPRIETAIRES LAND WHICH WAS FELT TO BE COMMON
B08480229019924451ACTIONS BY NATIONAL GOVT WHICH DELIVERED INTO HANDS OF
B08480229019924452PROPRIETAIRES LAND WHICH WAS FELT TO BE COMMON
B08480229019925451ACTIONS BY NATIONAL GOVT WHICH DELIVERED INTO HANDS OF
B08480229019925452PROPRIETAIRES LAND WHICH WAS FELT TO BE COMMON
B08480229019926451ACTIONS BY NATIONAL GOVT WHICH DELIVERED INTO HANDS OF
B08480229019926452PROPRIETAIRES LAND WHICH WAS FELT TO BE COMMON
B08480229019927451ACTIONS BY NATIONAL GOVT WHICH DELIVERED INTO HANDS OF
B08480229019927452PROPRIETAIRES LAND WHICH WAS FELT TO BE COMMON
B08480229019928451ACTIONS BY NATIONAL GOVT WHICH DELIVERED INTO HANDS OF
B08480229019928452PROPRIETAIRES LAND WHICH WAS FELT TO BE COMMON
B08480229019929451ACTIONS BY NATIONAL GOVT WHICH DELIVERED INTO HANDS OF
B08480229019929452PROPRIETAIRES LAND WHICH WAS FELT TO BE COMMON
B08480229019921481NUMEROUS PROCES-VERBAUX ETC AGAINST VIOLATORS OF CODE
B08480229019921482FORESTIER
B08480229019922481NUMEROUS PROCES-VERBAUX ETC AGAINST VIOLATORS OF CODE
B08480229019922482FORESTIER
B08480229019923481NUMEROUS PROCES-VERBAUX ETC AGAINST VIOLATORS OF CODE
B08480229019923482FORESTIER
B08480229019924481NUMEROUS PROCES-VERBAUX ETC AGAINST VIOLATORS OF CODE
B08480229019924482FORESTIER
B08480229019925481NUMEROUS PROCES-VERBAUX ETC AGAINST VIOLATORS OF CODE
B08480229019925482FORESTIER
B08480229019926481NUMEROUS PROCES-VERBAUX ETC AGAINST VIOLATORS OF CODE
B08480229019926482FORESTIER
B08480229019927481NUMEROUS PROCES-VERBAUX ETC AGAINST VIOLATORS OF CODE
B08480229019927482FORESTIER
B08480229019928481NUMEROUS PROCES-VERBAUX ETC AGAINST VIOLATORS OF CODE
B08480229019928482FORESTIER
B08480229019929481NUMEROUS PROCES-VERBAUX ETC AGAINST VIOLATORS OF CODE
B08480229019929482FORESTIER
B08480229019932371NUMEROUS INCIDENTS OF BRIGANDAGE AND DESTRUCTION OCCURRED IN
B08480229019932372VARIOUS COMMUNES.  I HAVE GROUPED ALL VICTIMS TOGETHER.
B08480229019932373THESE INCLUDE PUBLIC OFFICIALS *CONDUCTEUR DU DILIGENCE.
B08480229019932374MAIRIES, RECEVEUR DE L*ENREGISTREMENT ETC< PROPRIETAIRES
B08480229019932375AND USURERS
B08480229019933371GARDE NATIONAUX, MILITAIRES, GENDARMES, AND SOME PRIESTS
B08480229019932431ADMINISTRATION, EMPLOYES DES CONTRIBUTION, PROPRITAIRES ETC
B08480229019933431POLICE, MILITAIRES, NATIONAL GUARD, AND PRIESTS
B08480229019931521NEWS OF CHANGE IN REGIME GIVES BRIGANDS A PRETEXT FOR REVOLT
B08480229019931522AND AN UNSETTLED SITUATION TO TAKE ADVANTAGE OF
B08480229019931561FOR THE FIRST 3 DAYS, THE REBELS RESPONDED TO NO VIOLENCE.
B08480229019931562ON MARCH 3 THEY MET THE REPRESSIVE FORMATION IN BATTLE, BOTH
B08480229019931563SIDES USING FIREARMS
B08480229019931621CODE FORESTIER
B08480229019931641CONDITIONS OF USURY
B08480229019931661DESTRUCTION OF PRIVATE PROPERTY IN REVENGE
B08480229019941431ESTIMATES ARE 1500-1800, AND 2000
B08480229019942431DIFFERENT INDIVIDUALS THROUGHOUT AREA, A ROUGH ESTIMATE
B08480229019943431ABOUT 50 SOLDIERS AND GENDARMES *CLARENC<.  THE REST WAS
```

```
808480229019943432NATIONAL GUARD OF 5 TOWNS OF OVER 11000 INHABITANTS TOTAL.
80848022901994343NATIONAL GUARD STRENGTH INFERRED FROM NATURE OF ACTION AND
80848022901994343SIZES OF TOWNS
80848022901994155FORMATION GENERALLY EXPANDING.  MANDAYS # 1X200 & 1X800 &
80848022901994155222X1800 # 4600
80848022901994255EACH PARTICIPANT IN THIS FORMATION WAS INVOLVED DURING ONLY
80848022901994255ONE DAY
80848022901994267THERE WERE SOME OFFICIALS MALTRAITES OR STONED.  THIS FIGURE
80848022901994267IS A GUESS
80848022901994167CLARENC MENTIONS NO WOUNDED AND STATES THAT NONE WERE KILLED.
80848022901994167NEWSPAPERS VARY FROM 1 TO 7 WOUNDED AND 1 TO 3 KILLED
80848022901994172SOME ESTIMATES ARE LOWER 397 AND 81< BUT 98 IS OFTEN REPEATED
80848022901994172AND USED BY CLARENC.  10 WERE PROSCECUTED AND FOUND GUILTY
80848022901995113THE SEQUENCE PRESENTED BETWEEN THE TWO XX CODES IS NOT A TRUE
80848022901995113SEQUENCE BUT A RECREATION OF A TYPICAL INCIDENT.  10-12
80848022901995113INCIDENTS OF SIMILAR NATURE TOOK PLACE BETWEEN FEB 29 AND
80848022901995113MAR 3. AND THERE IS NO ROOM TO CODE THEM SEQUENTIALLY.  AFTER
80848022901995113THE SECOND XX, THE BATTLE OF MAR 3 IS CODED AS USUAL
80848022901995213THE SEQUENCE PRESENTED BETWEEN THE TWO XX CODES IS NOT A TRUE
80848022901995213SEQUENCE BUT A RECREATION OF A TYPICAL INCIDENT.  10-12
80848022901995213INCIDENTS OF SIMILAR NATURE TOOK PLACE BETWEEN FEB 29 AND
80848022901995213MAR 3. AND THERE IS NO ROOM TO CODE THEM SEQUENTIALLY.  AFTER
80848022901995213THE SECOND XX, THE BATTLE OF MAR 3 IS CODED AS USUAL
80848022901995117INVASION OF MAIRIE, BUREUA DE L'ENREGISTREMENT OR BUREAU OF
80848022901995117THE FORESTIER.  SUBSEQUENT BURNING OF RECORDS AND MISTREATING
80848022901995117OFFICIALS
80848022901995231A DIFFERENT VICTIM - A CHATEAU OWNER
80848022901995143MARCH 3, NOON, AT ANTICHAN.  ROUNDING UP OF PRISONERS
80848022901995143CONTINUES UNITL 5 P M
80848022901995343MARCH 3 NOON AT ANTICHAN.  ROUNDING UP OF PRISONERS CONTINUES
80848022901995343UNTIL 5 P M
80848022901996514CHANGE IN REGIME
80848022901996544FORMATION 53 IS LAW ENFORCEMENT FORCE.  HOWEVER DIVISION
80848022901996544BETWEEN 51 AND 52 COMBINES DIFFERENCES OF OCCUPATION AND
80848022901996544PROPERTY
80848022901996651A GREAT NUMBER OF PUBLIC RECORDS BURNED IN ALMOST EVERY TOWN.
80848022901996651MOSTLY PERTAINING TO CODE FORESTIERS. LISTS OF OFFENCES. FINE
80848022901996651AND PROCES-VERBAUX. RECORDS OF DEBTS ALSO BURIED.  MINOR
80848022901996651PROPERTY DAMAGE TO PUBLIC BUILDINGS.  A HUISSIER'S HOUSE WAS
80848022901996651PILLAGED AND HORSE STOLEN IN MAULEEN-BAROUSSE.  A PIG, SOME
80848022901996651PORK AND SOME WINE WAS TAKEN IN SOST, ARMS AND INSIGNE OF
80848022901996651OF ADMINISTRATEUR FORESTIER STOLEN.  PILLAGE IN LOURES-
80848022901996651BAROUSSE, HOUSE INVADED AND PILLAGED IN ANTICHAN. 6 MEN
80848022901996651RANSOMED IN TROBAT AND BERTREN. MONEY AND PROVISIONS STOLEN
80848022901996651IN ANLA. FLAG TORN IN IZAOURT.  LARGEST DAMAGE AT A
80848022901996651PROPIETAIRE'S CHATEAU IN LUSCAN WHERE TREES WERE CUT.
80848022901996651GRILLES BROKEN, DOORS BROKEN IN, FURNITURE BROKEN OR STOLEN.
80848022901996651AND LINEN AND BOOKS DESTROYED OR TAKEN
80848022901996655THIS IS A LOW ESTIMATE.  30,000 FRANCS DAMAGE ALONE AT CHATEA
80848022901996655DE LUSCAN
80848022901996673ALTHOUGH COMPLETELY STIFLED, THIS DISTURBANCE STIMULATED
80848022901996673LATER INCIDENTS, NOTABLY A PLOT TO ASSASSINATE RECEVEUR DE
80848022901996673L'ENREGISTREMENT, THE APRIL 17 DISTURBANCE AT SIGNAC. AND
80848022901996673THE INCIDENT AT BIZE-NISTOS AT THE END OF APRIL
80848022901997018MO 1848-03-10%582-583<.LS 1848-03-11
```

8480229012198651152210000000001220400000081051010062071 0001SOST   122986508042800
000000012204000000810510100620710001MAULEON PAROUSSE   1239865010638000000000012204 00000081051
0100620710001ANTICHAN   1249855010418000000000012204000000081051010062071 0001ANLA
            12598310762130000000000122040000000810510100620710001LUSCAN   1269865
111028000000000012204000000810510100620710001SARP   127983101603700000000012204000
00810510100620710001BARBAZON   128986506620900000000001220400000008105101006207100011Z
N-OURT   12998650754130000000000012204000000081051010062071 0001LOURES BAROUSSE
   31BRIGANDS   5312000101000100073300301420101013204202141 20020354060132VICTIMES DE BR
1GANDAGE   9112000202000100012600201100101018183851050200201 01010033REPRESSIVE FORCES   9012000
10201030001440070710010101837400013120060102030034   9898989898989898989898 98
9898989898989898989398989898989835   98989898989898989898989898989898 9898989898989898
98989898989836   98989898989898989898989898989898989898989898 9898989898989898989837
         989898989898989898989898989898989898989898989898989898 9898989898989838
    98989898989898989898989898989898989898989898989898989898989898989839   989898989898989
89898989898989898989898989898989898989898410101040301020120BANDE CONSIDERABLE   0180002040774304 6000
50200000000503009801110842000000000000000010NO KEY WORDS   00030090107243000300104000000000050600
0000010143040406010103012 0DEUX COLONNES   008000904005110080004010000000000000000010144989898
9898989888   98989898989898989898989898989898989898989898459898989898989888
          989898989899898989898989898989898989898989898989898469898989898989888
98989898989898989898989898989898989898989898984798989898989898 9888   9898998989989898
98998989898989898989898989898498989898989898 9888   9898998989989898989898989898989898
989898989849989898989898 9888   98989898989898989898989898989898989898989898985100
0118335828140356483858281640026454553519900000000000000 00000000000000152000025135515751575151530202 00
0202020202020200000000000000000000000153002020202020202020202020202020202254538334040000000000 0000000000
000000001540000000000000000000000000000000000000000000000000000000000000000000000055000000000000000000
000000000000000000000000000000000000000000000000000005600000000000000000000000000000000000000000000000
0000000000000000000000000005700000000000000000000000000000000000000000000000000005800000
000000000000000000000000000000000000000000000000000000000005900000000000000000000
00000000000000000000000000000000006000030505060605051105050505051103040507121398989898989898989898 9
898016503013300 1021023 102&103   9802015305JACQUERIE GRAVES DESORDRES   166000263003050774
300054300602000000001003009801909834310125402015001020304071701010110704010031300010399660719660817 7
55028989898

8480300012101540740270000000001310000000037200100100100100 1001LIXHEIM   122989998989800
000098989898989898989899899899899899898998   23989998989800000009898989898989899899
8998998998998   249899998989800000009898989898989899899899899899898998
        25989999898980000009898989898989899899899899898998998   269899
98989800000000989898989898989899899899899898998   27989998989800000009898989898989
989899989998998998998   289899998989800000009898989898989899899899899898998998
      2989999989898000000098989898989898998998998998998998
   31MEN LIVING NEAR LIXHEIM   62100003000040000000000100250000017000021102002001006003 2CURE
     9910000274000000003400102000101018000000010200400010 10033   9898989
898989898989898989898989898989898989898989898989834   9898989898989898989899898
989898989849989898989898989898989835   98989898989898989898999898989898989899 898
98989898989836   9898989898989898989898999898989898989898989899898989898989837
       9898989898989898989898989898989898989898989898989898989898989838
    98989898989898989898989898989898989898989898989898989839   989898989898989
89899989898989898989898989898989898989898989841000000000000000121NO KEY WORDS   0020001029981000 2000
203000000000009898000000429803989898980101NO KEY WORDS   00001010099810000010001000000000000 0
00000000 89898989898989888   9898998989989898989898989898989898989898989844989 8
9898989888   98989898989899898989898989898989898989898989898984598989898989888
       9898998989989898989898989898989898989898989898989846989898989898989888

989899898998989898998989998989898989898989898984798989898989888   9898998989989898
989899898998989898998989898989848989898989898888   9898998989989898989898998989898989898
98989898989849989898989898989888   9898998989989898989898998989898989898989898985102
5952583850000000000000000000000000000000000000000000000000000000000000001520171700020200000000000000000000
0000000000000000000000000000000000000000153000000000000000000000000000000000000000000000000000000000000000
0000000000540000000000000000000000000000000000000000000000000000000000000000000000000005500000000000000000
0000000000000000000000000000000000000000000000000000005600000000000000000000000000000000000000000005800000
0000000000000000000000005700000000000000000000000000000000000000000000000000000000000000000000000000000000
0000000000000000000000000000000000000005900000000000000000000000000000000000000000000000000000000000000000
000000000000000000000000000000000000060011103101098989898989898989898989898989898989898989898989898989989
898016502030000198   9800022403DESORDRES GRAVES   166000020101029981
00000201020300000000000000009898009090800210012902404301000404000000002070326803200000003266071966081601

848031401210159073430075430000111010509021101204133722614521LILLE   122989998989800
0000989898989898989899899899899899899899898998   2398999898980000000989898989898999899
8998998998998   2498999898980000000989898989898989899899899899899899899899899899899
                          2598999898980000000989898989898989899899899899899899   269899
98989800000098989898989898989899899899899899899   27989998989800000009898989898989
89899899899899899899899   2898999898980000000989898989898989899899899899899899899899
                          2998999898980000000989898989898989899899899899899899899
310UVRIERS   537100023000304201000000035010006374411605120020100000232NATIONAL GUARD
311000038401454501260000010010001708000013120060102000033   9898989
8989898989898998989898989898989898989898989898989834   98989898989898998998989898
98989898989898989898989898989898989835   9898989898989898998989898989898989898989898
98989898989836   98989898989898989898998989898989898989898989898989898989898989337
                          989898989898989898998989898989898989898989898989898989898989898989898838
                          98989898989898989899898989898989898989898989898989898989839   9898989898989989
8989998989898989898989898989898989898984100040000020001410OUVRIERS, EMEUTIERS 01000070401210010000
40000000001505001701100042040406010203012ONO KEY WORDS   00200040401210002000401000000015040C
0000010043989898989898888   98989989898989898989989898989898989898989984459898989898989888
9898989888   98989989899899898989898989898989898989898989898984698989898989888
                          989899898998989898989898989898989898989898984798989898989898888   9898998989989898
989899898998989898998989898989848989898989898888   9898998989989898989898998989898989898
98989898989849989898989898989888   9898998989989898989898998989898989898989898985103
842235200000000000000000000000000000000000000000000000000000000000000000000152033333333000000000000000000C
0000000000000000000000000000000000000000153000000000000000000000000000000000000000000000000000000000000000C
0000000000540000000000000000000000000000000000000000000000000000000000000000000000000005500000000000000000C
0000000000000000000000000000000000000000000000000000005600000000000000000000000000000000000000000005800000C
0000000000000000000000005700000000000000000000000000000000000000000000000000005900000000000000000000000000C
00000000000000000000000000000000000006005050513989898989898989898989898989898989898989898989898989898989C
89801652002601021102 102&102&102   800202401TROUBLES, SCENES TO MULTEUSES16600012007050121
00001200050000000000300500170100980000099851020143010001070615000005107032680371000003706607206608172
85098989898

848032201210143103249000000000112010000000001001001999000000000PUY   12298999898980C
0000989898989898989899899899899899899899898998   2398999898980000000989898989898989899899
8998998998998   2498999898980000000989898989898989899899899899899998998

```
RUN VII--FORMATION TYPE X-TABS CORRECTION
QUALIFYING DATA ONLY
GENERAL SAMPLE 1830-1960
                                    COUNT OF
                                    FORMATION TYPES
                                    BY YEAR, 1845-51
```

ROWS = FORMATION TYPE.   COLUMNS = YEAR OF ANALYSIS.

Formation Type	1845	1846	1847	1848	1849	1850	1851	SUM	KEY
SIMPLE	2	7	29	40	4	5	16	103	RAW
CROWD	2	8	29	42	4	5	18	108	WTD
	1	1.14	1	1.05	1	1	1.12	1.04	MEN
IDEO-		3		32	16	5	26	82	RAW
LOGICAL		5		39	18	5	27	94	WTD
CROWD		1.66		1.21	1.12	1	1.03	1.14	MEN
GUERRIL				1			25	26	RAW
BANDITS				1			26	27	WTD
PVTARMY				1			1.04	1.03	MEN
OTHER				3			26	29	RAW
ACTIV-				3			26	29	WTD
ISTS				1			1	1	MEN
PUBLIC		2	1	24	4	2	8	41	RAW
OFFCIAL		2	1	25	4	2	8	42	WTD
		1	1	1.04	1	1	1	1.02	MEN
OFFCIAL	2	4	4	16	4	5	26	61	RAW
TROOPS	2	4	4	16	4	5	28	63	WTD
POLICE	1	1	1	1	1	1	1.07	1.03	MEN
REGULAR		1		8	6	1	12	28	RAW
TROOPS		1		10	6	1	12	30	WTD
		1		1.25	1	1	1	1.07	MEN
OTHER		6	2	44	6	2	5	65	RAW
MILITRY		6	2	46	9	3	6	72	MTD
		1	1	1.04	1.5	1.5	1.2	1.1	MEN
POLICE		9	3	9	3	2	12	38	RAW
AND		9	3	9	3	2	12	38	WTD
MILITRY		1	1	1	1	1	1	1	MEN
POLICE	2	2	13	12	8	3	19	59	RAW
	2	2	13	12	8	3	20	60	WTD
	1	1	1	1	1	1	1.05	1.01	MEN

RUN VII--FORMATION TYPE X-TABS CORRECTION
QUALIFYING DATA ONLY
GENERAL SAMPLE 1830-1960

COUNT OF
FORMATION TYPES
BY YEAR, 1845-51

ROWS = FORMATION TYPE.   COLUMNS = YEAR OF ANALYSIS.

	1845	1846	1847	1848	1849	1850	1851	SUM	KEY
CCUPA	1	4	1	13				19	RAW
W/SAME	1	4	1	15				21	WTD
LOCALE	1	1	1	1.15				1.1	MEN
OCCUPA	1	3	2	18	3	4	2	33	RAW
W/SAME	1	1	2	22	5	5	2	41	WTD
INDSTRY	1	1.33	1	1.22	1.66	1.25	1	1.24	MEN
OTHER	1	3	15	16	5	1	1	42	RAW
OCCUPA	2	3	16	16	5	1	1	44	WTD
GROUP	2	1	1.06	1	1	1	1	1.04	MEN
GROUP				12			1	13	RAW
OUTSIDE				12			1	13	WTD
ORIGIN				1			1	1	MEN
USERS		11	1	2		1	1	16	RAW
SAME		12	1	2		1	1	17	WTD
RESOURC		1.09	1	1		1	1	1.06	MEN
OTHERS	1	6	12	18	4	3	14	58	RAW
	1	6	19	20	4	3	15	68	WTD
	1	1	1.58	1.11	1	1	1.07	1.17	MEN
SUMS	10	61	83	268	63	34	194	713	RAW
	11	66	91	290	70	36	203	767	WTD
	1.1	1.08	1.09	1.08	1.11	1.05	1.04	1.07	MEN

*****TABLE TOTALS...   RAW=   713   WTD=   767

Table 4 *Participants in collective violence per 100,000 population by urbanity of department, 1830–1859, corrected to annual rates*

Percent of population in cities of 10,000 or more	1830–34	1835–39	1840–44	1845–49	1850–54	1855–59
0.0	17	4	40	25	152	0
0.1–5.0	23	22	16	70	70	0
5.1–10.0	53	22	48	68	43	9
10.1–15.0	104	19	10	81	15	2
15.1+	731	57	64	689	86	0
Total	147	22	37	210	56	3
Total participants (thousands)	240	41	64	371	101	5

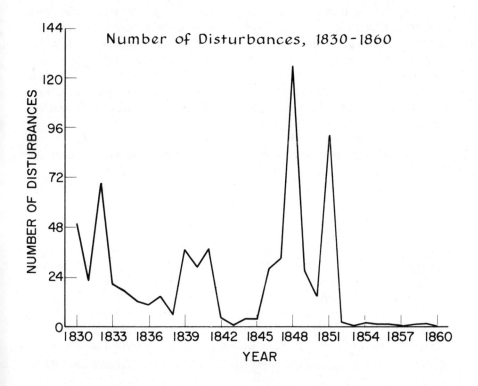

Number of Disturbances, 1830-1860

Appendix 3
Procedures for the Study of Contentious Gatherings in Great Britain

GENERAL

Our newest large effort is a study of conflicts in Great Britain from 1828 through 1834. We have several different incentives for undertaking the new analysis. First, our analyses of violent events in Italy, Germany, and France appeared to confirm our supposition that the violence was on the whole the by-product of the intervention of further interested parties in actions which were not intrinsically violent and which occurred frequently without significant violence. In particular, we were interested in the frequency with which the violence began with the intervention of troops, police, and other specialized repressive forces. Since the only nonviolent events of which we had made large, systematic enumerations for some of the same periods and places were strikes, however, we did not have the evidence to look closely at that relationship between nonviolent and violent collective actions.

Second, it seemed worth making a sustained comparison between patterns of conflict in nineteenth-century Britain and those we had found on the Continent. Students of modern Europe often think of nineteenth-century Britain's experience as a kind of success story—at least in "avoiding" the revolutions which occurred in France, Germany, Italy, and elsewhere. A close study of conflicts in Britain should give us the means to rethink that question. More important, it should provide firmer ground for choosing among obvious alternative explanations of the differences between Britain and the continent: that Britain had fewer of the kinds of people who made nineteenth-century revolutions and rebellions, that the most likely rebels had fewer grievances, that repression was more effective in Britain, and so on.

Our original hope was to examine the changing patterns of conflict in Britain throughout the nineteenth century. With a wide range of nonviolent events to consider, however, that action would have required an enormous effort—many times the already formidable effort per year in our studies of

France and Germany. After some preliminary enumerations in scattered years from the end of the eighteenth century to the end of the nineteenth, we narrowed our attention to 1828–1834. That period recommends itself for several reasons. First, it was a time of major movements, conflicts and collective actions: Catholic Emancipation, Reform agitation, industrial conflict, the attack on select vestries, and the great agrarian rebellions of 1830. Second, there exist excellent historical studies of some of the period's conflicts—for example, *Captain Swing*, by E. J. Hobsbawm and George Rudé—with which we can compare our own results. Third, we have some reason to believe that the period acted as an historical pivot in something like the same way that the revolutions of 1848 did in France and Germany: marking, and perhaps producing, a shift from reactive to proactive, from "backward-looking" to "forward-looking" collective action on the part of ordinary people.

In that period, we are attempting to enumerate, describe, and analyze a large share of all the "contentious gatherings" which occurred in England, Scotland, and Wales. Roughly speaking, a contentious gathering is an occasion in which ten or more persons outside the government gather in the same place and make a visible claim which, if realized, would affect the interests of some specific person(s) or group(s) outside their own number. In principle, these gatherings include just about all the events covered in our earlier enumerations of strikes and collective violence. They also include a great many other events: demonstrations, petition meetings, delegations, group poaching, and plenty of others. Drawing the boundaries both generously and consistently is a delicate and laborious task.

We are still adjusting the procedures for that task. After doing a trial enumeration and summary coding of some events from 1830, we did a preliminary scanning of thirty randomly selected ten-day blocks from the entire six-year period, then proceeded to enumerate systematically from the beginning of 1828. We have completed the preliminary enumeration of 1828. We find the events via a complete issue-by-issue reading of the *Morning Chronicle, The Times, Gentlemen's Magazine, Hansard's Parliamentary Debates, The Mirror of Parliament*, and the *Annual Register*. Once the events are enumerated, we plan to look for more information about them in the papers of the Home Office (of which we have already built up substantial selections via photocopy and microfilm), in other periodicals, and in secondary historical works. We are still making plans for coding of the information in machine-readable form. The file for the six-year period will probably describe on the order of 25,000 events.

We are also slowly making plans for the collection of data on the populations and areas "at risk" to contentious gatherings. The units of observation will certainly include all counties of England, Scotland, and Wales. They will probably include complete sets of hundreds of parishes within selected counties. If possible, they will also include particular populations of potential actors—for example, the handloom weavers of Lancashire and the agricultural laborers of Leicestershire. Ultimately the choice of units and of kinds of data concerning those units will result from a compromise between the arguments we are seeking to test and the costs of getting the relevant evidence.

Events to be Enumerated

The events are "contentious gatherings" (CGs), occasions in which ten or more persons outside the government gather in the same place and make a visible claim which, if realized, would affect the interests of some specific person(s) or group(s) outside their own numbers. Most CGs in our period fall into one or more of the following categories: (1) collective violence, (2) meetings, (3) demonstrations, (4) parades, (5) assemblies, (6) rallies, (7) celebrations, (8) delegations, (9) strikes, (10) union activities. More precisely, the events included are all occasions:

1   reported in the *London Times, Morning Chronicle, Hansard's Parliamentary Debates, Annual Register, Gentlemen's Magazine* and/or *The Mirror of Parliament;*

2   occurring in England, Scotland, or Wales;

3   beginning on any date from 1 January 1828 through 31 December 1834;

4   in which ten or more persons outside the government:
     a)   gather in the same place,
     b)   make a visible claim which, if realized, would affect the interests of some specific person(s) or group(s) outside their own number.

Terms which therefore require working definitions

reported	outside the government
occurring	gather same place
in England, Scotland, or Wales	visible claim affecting interests
beginning	specific person(s) or group(s)
persons	

DEFINITIONS AND RULES OF THUMB

Reported

Any mention in any context. If, for example, an M.P. lays on the table a petition "from a numerous meeting in Oldham" which conforms to all our other criteria, that meeting enters the sample. In parliamentary debates, mentions of meetings do not need numerical information to be included. For example, if *Mirror of Parliament* reports a meeting of parishioners at Preston to petition Parliament, but makes no mention of how many people attended the meeting, we will assume provisionally that at least ten people took part.

Occurring in England, Scotland or Wales

Ten or more people must have gathered within the political boundaries (including territorial waters) of England, Scotland, or Wales. If any part of the action occurs within those boundaries, the entire event falls into the sample.

Sometimes it is difficult to determine how many people are involved in an event or action. In vague cases take the following terms to mean at least ten people:

AFFRAY	GENERAL BODY/BODY
ASSEMBLY	MOB
BRAWL	MULTITUDE
CONCOURSE	NUMEROUS
CROWD	RALLY
DEMONSTRATION	RIOT
DISTURBANCE	RIOTOUS ASSEMBLAGE
GANG	THRONG
GATHERING	TUMULTUOUS ASSEMBLY

Beginning on any date from 1 January 1828 through 31 December 1834

The event begins at the first point at which at least ten of the people who eventually make the visible claim are gathered without further dispersal before they make the claim. The day begins at midnight.

Persons

Any human being who can reasonably be presumed to have intentionally participated in the making of the claim.

Outside the government

When officers are acting in the capacity given them by their offices and no group of ten or more nonofficers is acting with them, we *exclude* the action. If ten or more officers act together but on their own responsibility, we *include* their action. Among the sets of people commonly named in discussions of English governments in the nineteenth century, we are actually distinguishing three categories, (a) officers, (b) public committees, and (c) citizenry. As *officers*, we are considering

Alderman	Horse Guards	Paymasters
Bailiffs	Judges	Police
Beadles	Justices	Police Constables
Boroughreeves	Justices of the Peace	Privy Councilers
Burgesses	Lord Lieutenants	Schoolboards
Churchwardens	Magistrates	Sheriffs
Common Councilers	Mayors	Scotch Guards
Constables	Members of Parliament	Special Constables
Coroners	Military*	Surveyors
Directors of the Poor	Militia	Town Councilers
Grand Juries	Ministers	Yeomanry
Guardians of the Poor	Overseers of the Poor	

and others of essentially similar position.

As *public committees* we are considering Town Meetings, Vestries, Select Vestries, Liveries, Improvement Commissions, Police Commissions, and essentially similar organizations.

As segments of the *citizenry* we are considering Freeholders, Householders, Inhabitants, Landowners, Leypayers, Occupiers, Parishioners, Ratepayers, Tithepayers, and essentially similar collections of people. One day we may well want to analyze the actions of public committees, of segments of the citizenry, and of other groups (such as members of particular crafts, associations, age-sex groups or families) separately. For the present, the crucial distinction separates officers from all the rest. Officers often appear as parties in collective actions involving public committees, segments of the citizenry, and/or other groups. But the only circumstances under which their concerted action qualifies by itself is when they take part in a group of ten or more persons who on their own responsibility assemble to make a publicly visible claim, demand, or complaint.

As *citizens* we are considering everyone else.

Gather same place

Ten or more persons, meeting, assembling, or any of the key words listed earlier to define a get-together. Place is defined as:

a) specific location, church, inn, field;

b) secondary location, town, parish, city;

c) area location, county, hundred, etc.;
   or any combination of (a), (b), and (c).

---

*Cavalry, Infantry, Dragoons, Hussars, Marines, Blues, Grays

Visible claims affecting interests of some specific persons or groups

We are trying to prepare a comprehensive list of occasions where people outside the government assemble to make a publicly visible claim, demand, or complaint. At one time or another, we use all the following words to describe what we're after: claims, demands, complaints, grievances, aspirations, interests, dissatisfactions. Some of these words, such as "demands," clearly have an object outside the group. Others, like "dissatisfactions," do not necessarily have outside objects; one can easily be dissatisfied with oneself. We want to concentrate on actions which *do* have a target outside the acting group. Let's talk about *claims* and *objects of claims*. We are trying to build a sample of gatherings in which—or by which—people articulate claims on actors outside their own group.

What sorts of claims? Basically, any expectation which would, if realized, require the other actor to expend valued resources: money, labor-power, information, and so on. What sorts of actors? Basically, any other set of real people. That excludes a group's claims on itself. It excludes a group's claims on supernatural or imaginary beings. It does not however, exclude claims on an imaginary "power structure," if the group identifies some real people with that structure. Nor does it exclude claims on real people in their capacities as self-declared agents of supernatural beings or imaginary groups: priests, soothsayers, charlatans, members of invented conspiracies. It does not exclude claims on real people present at the same gathering, just so long as there is a we/they separation between actors and objects which is not simply an internal division of the acting group and which is more durable than the gathering itself. In fact, "any other set of real people" does not exclude any individual anywhere, just so long as there is a gathering in which enough people articulate claims on that individual.

When describing the possible content of such claims, we enumerate:

a) petitioning or addressing or memorializing local or national government, either for or against government;

b) opposition to government policy, form of government, or particular agents of it;

c) support for government;

d) support for an enemy of government;

e) control of local government or institution;

f) other grievances and dissatisfactions, including religious, social or economic issues, discussion of complaints about wages, hours, or conditions of work;

Here are some rules of thumb for the identification of qualifying and non-qualifying claims:

1 In the absence of contradictory information, collective violence constitutes *prima facie* evidence of a claim. If ten or more persons act together to attack, damage, or forcibly seize a person or object, that is provisional evidence of a claim.

2 Even if the ultimate aim of the activity is the making of some sort of claim, purely organizational efforts do not qualify in themselves. For example, the creation of a local Reform Association does not in itself constitute a claim. If, on the other hand, ten or more persons who are organizing an association state a qualifying claim as they do so, that claim counts.

3 Benefit suppers, balls, expositions, and the like do not qualify in themselves, regardless of the cause for which they are conducted. If, however, we acquire further evidence of the making of a claim (e.g., a claim-making proclamation by the organizers of the benefit, or a widely-cheered claim-making speech in the course of the event), a benefit qualifies in the same way any other gathering qualifies.

4 A speech by a single person which states a claim, articulates a grievance, or makes a demand constitutes evidence of a collective claim under any of these conditions: (a) the group formally adopts the speaker's views by petition, resolution, or memorial; (b) the reporter explicitly imputes approval of the claim to the participants in the gathering; (c) the group manifestly voices an opinion by cheering, jeering, or other vocal display.

5 If a gathering includes two or more factions, at least one of which has ten or more participants, claims made by one of the factions on another qualify if the issues and divisions in question extend beyond the particular gathering and the particular set of participants. For example, when Henry Hunt and his supporters show up at a parish vestry meeting and challenge the powers of the local elite to control the election of new vestry officers, the division extends beyond that meeting, and the claim qualifies.

6 Explicit support for government, or denial of support to government, qualifies. It can take the form of support for institutions (Parliament, the present government, the constitution) or of support for specific officers of government: the aldermen, bailiffs, beadles, boroughreeves, and so on, listed earlier. It can take the form of deliberate denial of support for these institutions or officers. The institutions and officers must be currently in office; for example, a celebrating banquet for a member-elect of Parliament does not in itself qualify. Evidence of such support or denial includes (a) participation in events, including celebrations and festivities, whose commonly understood

purpose is the display of support, e.g., Lord Mayor's Day parade; (b) the reporter's imputation of support or rejection; (c) articulation of a sentiment through cheering, jeering, and so on. However, a simple toast (e.g., "To the King") does not quality in itself, even if participants cheer.

7 Gatherings explicitly conducted to support or condemn an action of government state qualifying claims if the participants themselves articulate sentiments by passing resolutions, cheering speeches, and so on.

8 Simple expressions of support or rejection do *not* qualify if the objects are (a) nongovernmental institutions or officers in Britain or elsewhere, (b) governmental institutions or officers outside of Britain. If a gathering makes further claims on either of these categories of objects, however, the claims qualify. For example, a banquet in honor of the deposed king of Spain would not qualify unless the participants directly stated the demand that he be reinstated.

BOUNDARIES OF CONTENTIOUS GATHERINGS

Most CGs will occur on one day at one location; however, many will last longer and/or will take place at several sites, so we must delineate boundaries in time and space. Activities will be considered to be part of the same CG if:

1 they occur on the same day, or on consecutive days *and*

2 there is strong evidence of overlapping personnel within the citizen formation(s), such as continuous interaction between two or more of the formations identified in the initial activity *and*

3 the activities involve the same issue, or some directly related issue (e.g., the escalation of demands).

Activities that meet the above criteria will be defined as one CG even though they occur in different locations (e.g., different towns).

If an event qualifies on the grounds of the kind of action and kind of group involved, but we lack sufficient information to assign it a time and place in Britain from 1828 through 1834, we exclude the event pending further information. If only one of these elements—time or place—is uncertain, we *include* the event pending further information.

GENERAL AGENDA FOR CODING

This is a provisional set of plans for the preparation of a machine-readable description of each CG. The record for a single event will contain the following sections:

1   EVENT as a whole, including identification and summary description of all major features.
2   PLACE: one unit per place in which the event occurred.
3   FORMATION: one unit per formation participating in the event.
4   ACTION-PHASE: one unit per action by any formation.
5   SOURCE: one unit per source from which information concerning this event was drawn.
6   COMMENTS: one unit per comment—all keyed to specific locations in sections 1–5.

1. Event Section

Identification number: starting date plus sequence number on that date
Accuracy of starting date
Day of week on which event began
Date on which event ended
Accuracy of ending date
Duration: days
Duration: hours
Low estimate of total participants
High estimate of total participants
Best estimate of total participants
Best estimate of person-days + margin of error
Best estimate of person-hours + margin of error
Best estimate of arrests during event + margin of error
Best estimate of arrests after event + margin of error
Best estimate of wounded during event + margin of error
Best estimate of killed during event + margin of error
Number of formations
Summary of formation type(s)
Summary of participation by authorities
Summary of repression exercised during event
Summary of repression exercised after event
Summary of major target(s) of action
Broad event type
Summary of background
Summary of outcome

2. Place Section

One unit per place in which the action occurred. A "place" is any named location, plus any unnamed location in which we have strong reason to believe that some portion of the action occurred. We produce a unit for "someplace" in two circumstances: (1) we cannot locate the action in at least one specific parish; (2) we have strong reason to believe that some portion of the action occurred outside the places for which the account contains specific names. A "name" can be very general: by the river, on the road, at the market, and so on.

a) *For initial coding*

Principal name of place, alphabetic. Parish takes priority. If it is impossible, name county; if county is impossible, country. Place inferred locations in parentheses. Thus OXFORD means the account specifically mentions Oxford, (OXFORD) that we have inferred the location from the account or its context.

Detailed name of place, alphabetic. Blank if we have a parish name and no other place information. SOMEPLACE if the principal place is a county or a country (England, Scotland, Wales) and we have no further information on location within the county or country; a more specific designation such as "near Norwich" (in parentheses if inferred) takes precedence over SOME-PLACE. SOMEPLACE ELSE for additional places not specifically named.

b) *For coding after alphabetic sort of place sections*

Sequence number for grid square location: 0 if some portion definitely took place in this grid square location; 1 to 9 if one of a cluster of 1 to 9 possible continuous grid square locations, used to describe irregular shapes, e. g., a street, town, riverbank, road. *Note*: this means that a single place record may contain 1 to 9 subrecords for grid square location.

Grid square location per Gazetteer: two letters plus five digits

Vertical location within grid square: 0 if not known, 1 to 9 if known

Horizontal location within grid square; 0 if not known, 1 to 9 if known

Margin of error for grid square location

Location in British census of 1831: nine digits

NOTE on the Place Section. This is not the only information on places that we will eventually have available for analysis. We plan to construct a separate Place File including at least all parishes in which events occurred and all counties, whether or not events occurred in them. The addition of further places, if any, will depend on cost, convenience, and analytic urgency. The likely items of information in such a file are name of the administrative unit (parish, etc.)

proper name of the place

position within administrative hierarchy: parish, hundred, county, etc.

grid square location per Gazetteer

location in 1831 census

population in 1831

other characteristics of that place: presence or absence of market, extent of manufacturing, etc.

characteristics of specific location within that place: inn, church, public square, shop, etc.

enumeration of all events occurring in that place

3. Formation Section

One unit per formation known to be present. Every participant must be assigned to at least one formation. So must every action: if we know some action occurred, but can't assign it to a specific formation, we create a formation named SOMEONE. There may be more than one SOMEONE. In that case, we name them SOMEONE 1, SOMEONE 2, ...

A formation is a set of people who act together and/or interact with another formation in the course of the event. The first formation named must have 10+ members. We divide the remainder into as few formations as possible: generally one formation for each set of people who act distinguishably in the course of the event.

Formation numbers: two digits

Overlap with other formations: list of other formation's numbers

Relation of this formation to event: participant, spectator, etc.

Name(s) of formation: alphabetic, including SOMEONE (in parentheses if the name is inferred rather than given explicitly)

Social composition of formation: alphabetic, including DK (don't know)

Other words describing formation: alphabetic, including NONE [in parentheses if inferred from account, e.g., (LED BY TAILOR)]

Place of origin or normal residence: alphabetic, including DK

Words used to describe magnitude of formation: alphabetic, including NONE [in parentheses if inferred from account, e.g., (GROUP FILLED SQUARE)]

Number of participants: low estimate (50+ = at least 50, 101+ = more than 100, etc.)

Number of participants: high estimate

Number of participants: best estimate

Source of best estimate: code (when the available accounts contain more than one estimate, write COMMENT)

Number of person-days: best estimate (00 = unknown, 01 = participation lasted less than one day)

Number of person hours: best estimate. 00 = unknown, 01 = less than 1 hour. Person-days and person-hours are *additive.* For example, 025, 075 means 25 person-days + 75 person-hours, a reasonable estimate for a formation of 25 people in continuous action for 1 day plus three more hours. 01, 75 means 0 person-days + 75 person-hours. Note alternative estimates as COMMENTS.

Source of best estimate: code

Best estimate of number arrested. Note alternative estimates as COMMENTS.

Source of best estimate: code

Best estimate of number wounded. Note alternative estimates as COMMENTS.

Source of best estimate: code

Best estimate of number killed. Note alternative estimates as COMMENTS.

Source of best estimate: code

Note: best estimates of person-days, person-hours, arrests, wounded, killed must each sum to totals given in EVENT SECTION.

4. Action-Phase Section

An event begins at the first point at which at least ten of the people who eventually make a claim which would qualify the event for inclusion in our sample are gathered without dispersing before they make the claim. The event ends when the last set of people which has made such a claim in the course of the event disperses. If new claims by 10+ people which would independently qualify the event for inclusion arise in the course of the event, they keep the event going.

A new action-phase begins when *any* formation begins a new action. At least one phase must describe action before the event begins; when possible, there should be one such unit for each formation present at the beginning of the event. At least one phase must describe action after the event ends; when possible, there should be one such unit from each formation which survived to the end of the event.

If more than one formation changes action at the same time, we make a phase unit for each formation and assign each unit the same time.

The minimum record contains at least one phase each: (1) before the event begins; (2) at the beginning of the event; (3) in the course of the event; (4) at the end of the event; (5) after the event.

Every formation named must appear in at least one action-phase.

Sequence number: first new phase at this time. Two digits; 00 = SOMETIME

Order number for multiple phases which start simultaneously: one digit

Date: year, month, day

Clock time: 2400 = midnight; 0000 = unknown

Relation to event: 1 = before event begins; 2 = action initiating event; 3 = in course of event; 4 = action ending event; 5 = after event ends

Formation number: 00 = someone (if used, we must enumerate a SOMEONE formation; 99 = all formations)

Action: alphabetic, including DK (definitely permits phrases such as ATTEMPT TO . . . . ; in parentheses if our summary or inference, without parentheses if direct transcription of words in account)

Object of action: alphabetic, including DK, NONE, FORMATION 23, etc.

Immediate consequences for object: alphabetic, including DK, NONE (consequences occurring during same action-phase only; use after-event phases for later consequences)

5. Source Section

One unit per source. In principle, there should be one source unit per cover sheet and one cover sheet per source unit.

Name of source: alphabetic. Standard abbreviations for major sources

Location within source: information will vary with type of source. For newspapers, for example, location will typically be date, page, location on page

Further identifying information: includes NONE. May cite headline, indicate location in footnote, and so on.

Comments on source: alphabetic. Includes NONE. May mention quality, contradiction of other sources, use made in coding.

6. Comment Section

One unit per comment. May be keyed to any location within EVENT, PLACE, FORMATION, ACTION-PHASE, or SOURCE sections. In some cases, the codebook will require the coder who uses a certain code to make a COMMENT.

Location in record: numerical code

Comment: alphabetic

Appendix 4

Materials from the Study of Contentious Gatherings in Great Britain

Provisional List of Contentious Gatherings in February 1828:

Type of CG	Place	Date	Issue
meeting	Weymouth	02–02	parliamentary election
meeting	London	02–03	protection of victualler trade
meeting	Poultry	02–04	test corporation acts
meeting	Edinburgh	02–04	petition king about political favors
gathering	Liverpool	02–05	election to parliament
gathering	Durham	02–05	local election
gathering	Dover	02–06	election to parliament
violence	London	02–06	crowd attacks informer
parade*	Weymouth	02–07	election
meeting	Sheffield	02–07	vestry, church rates
violence	Newbury	02–07	crowd attacks informer
demonstration	Weymouth	02–09	election
meeting	Windsor	02–10	tax on carts
gathering-crowd	Weymouth	02–11	election
gathering-mob	London	02–13	threatens informer
gathering-crowd	Durham	02–13	county elections
meeting*	London	02–15	licensed vs. nonlicensed sellers
violence	Atherstone	02–16	poaching affray
meeting	Leicester	02–18	coin laws
gathering	Weymouth	02–18	election victory celebration

Reports for this event follow.

meeting	Mary-la-bonne	02–20	parish rates
violence	Scarborough	02–28	smuggling affray
meeting	Sheffield	February (approx.)	test and corporation acts
meeting	Islington	February (approx.)	test and corporation acts
meeting	London	February (approx.)	test and corporation acts
meeting	Honiton	February (approx.)	test and corporation acts
meeting	Dorchester	February (approx.)	test and corporation acts
meeting	Manchester	February (approx.)	stamp duties

GREAT BRITAIN STUDY COVERSHEET

Today's date 0/ - 06-1977

( ) Schweitzer
(✓) Lord   ( ) Guest
( ) Kelly   ( ) Sanchez
( ) Gray   ( ) Stewart
( ) Zizka   ( ) Bloomingdale
( ) Shore   ( ) Teixeira
( ) Burke   ( ) Peterson

( ) LONDON TIMES   page __3__   column __2__   Top

(✓) MORNING CHRONICLE   date _02-//-1828_   day _M_   Middle   Bottom

First Line: _ _ _ _ _weymooth —_ _ _ _ _ _ _ _ _ _ _ _ _ _ _ _ _ _ _ _

GENERAL DESCRIPTION: CHECK AS MANY AS APPLY (see memo #6)

(1) VIOLENCE ( )
    property damage ( ),   seizure of property, spaces or persons ( ),
    personal injury ( ),   threat of any of the above ( ).

(2) MEETINGS ( )
    ( ) Election   ( ) support for enemy of government
    ( ) Vestry   ( ) control of local government/institution
    ( ) Livery   ( ) other grievances and dissatisfactions
    ( ) Dinner   ( ) opposition to other peoples or groups
    ( ) Political club/party   ( ) objectives unclear
    ( ) with petition, address, etc. ( ) notices, requests (for future meetings)
    ( ) opposition to government   ( ) other (list)_____
    ( ) support for government

(3-8) GATHERINGS
    demonstrations (✓),   parade ( ),   (assemblies,) crowds, mobs (circle one) (✓),
    gatherings ( ),   rallies ( ),   special celebrations ( ),
    other (list)_____

(9) DELEGATIONS, DEPUTATIONS ( )

(10) LABOR ACTIVITIES ( )
    strike, turnout ( ),   lockout ( ),   combination or union mention ( ),
    threats to stop work ( ),   work stoppages ( ),   return to work ( ),
    deputations of workers ( ).

(11) LEGAL ACTIONS ( )
    arrests ( ),   examinations ( ),   pretrial info. ( ),   trials/court actions ( ),
    sentences, executions, etc. ( ).   Be sure to check the appropriate areas above
    that pertain to the action that brought about the arrest or trial.

Objective of action___ELECTION   TO   PARL.___

Participants___FRIends   or   MR.   Sugden___

Number_"LARGE   CONCOURSE"___   Leaders_MR.   SUGDEN___

Date_Feb. 07, 1828 Thurs.___   Duration (if known)_____
    Yesterday, last week, a few days ago   (one day or less,) a few days, more

Location_"AT the GATE"___,   weymooth___,   _____
    Specific place, inn, field, etc.   village or town/city   parish

COMMENTS ON BACK? ( )   4-76, Rev. 4-77 Bobbi/CML

NA
county

WEYMOUTH, Friday, Feb. 8.

Mr. Sugden made his public entry into this town yesterday afternoon. About five o'clock, a large concourse of his friends and adherents assembled at the triumphant gate (less than a quarter of a mile hence), where they awaited his arrival amid the clang of military music. When the carriage drove up, the horses were taken from it; and " See the conquering Hero comes" was struck up by the band & chorussed by the multitude. Just as the array was setting forward, some purple lights illuminated the scene, which, by throwing their broad glare on the congregated masses around, and casting fitful gleams on the bosom of the bay on the right, produced a coup d'œil equally pleasing and romantic. The carriage was dragged through the town amid the shouts and acclamations of the purple party; although these were partially interrupted by the unwelcome bray of the " Blues," who were not a little assisted on the occasion by the shrill treble of the females, and the tiny voices of the children, who are all devoted Blues. The assemblage stopped at Luce's Hotel, where Mr. Sugden alighted, and mounted the coach box to address the people. " I promised to be here," said the Learned Gentleman, "and here I am [loud applause]. I will give up to no Blue in devotion to the inhabitants of this town, for whose welfare I feel the strongest attachment. If, indeed, a love for the people, and a regard for their rights, are the characteristics of a True Blue man, I at once avow myself to be one [bursts of applause—' Go it, little fellow!']. I trust, by your exertions, that I shall be completely successful in the approaching contest; but, whatever may be the result of it, you may rely on my sacred promise, that I shall not quit the field until the last freeholder has been polled [continued applause; ' Huzza for the game little chap']. Accept of my warmest thanks for the cordial welcome you have given me this evening [The shouts which followed the conclusion of this brief address were quite deafening.] Mr. Sugden afterwards, amidst a profusion of well wishes, with difficulty effected an entrance into the hotel.

In reference to a paragraph from the Insolvent Debtors' Court in *The Morning Chronicle* of Friday, we are informed that there is no person of the name of Ogston holding the situation of Writer to the East India Company.

On Saturday an Inquisition was held at the Nag's Head, Bethnal Green, on the body of a well-dressed man, name unknown, apparently about twenty-three years of age. It appeared

```
┌─┬─┬─┬─┬─┬─┐
│ │ │ │ │ │ │
└─┴─┴─┴─┴─┴─┘
```

Today's date 7 - 9 197,

GREAT BRITAIN STUDY COVERSHEET

( )LONDON TIMES   page___/___ column___/___ Top

(✓)MORNING CHRONICLE   date O2·18·1828 day M

First Line:__ A T   A   VERY __ NUMEROUS ···

(✓)Schweitzer
( )Lord ( )Guest
( )Kelly ( )Sanchez
( )Gray ( )Stewart
( )Zizka ( )Bloomingdale
( )Shore ( )Teixeira
( )Burke ( )Peterson

Middle
Bottom

GENERAL DESCRIPTION: CHECK AS MANY AS APPLY (see memo #6)

(1) VIOLENCE ( )
    property damage ( ),   seizure of property, spaces or persons ( ),
    personal injury ( ),   threat of any of the above ( ).

(2) MEETINGS (✓)
    ( ) Election   ( ) support for enemy of government
    ( ) Vestry   ( ) control of local government/institution
    ( ) Livery   (✓) other grievances and dissatisfactions
    ( ) Dinner   (✓) opposition to other peoples or groups
    ( ) Political club/party   ( ) objectives unclear
    ( ) with petition, address, etc. (✓) notices, requests (for future meetings)
    ( ) opposition to government   ( ) other (list)_____
    ( ) support for government

(3-8) GATHERINGS
    demonstrations ( ),   parade ( ),   assemblies, crowds, mobs (circle one) ( ),
    gatherings ( ),   rallies ( ),   special celebrations ( ),
    other (list)_____

(9) DELEGATIONS, DEPUTATIONS ( )

(10) LABOR ACTIVITIES ( )
    strike, turnout ( ),   lockout ( ),   combination or union mention ( ),
    threats to stop work ( ),   work stoppages ( ),   return to work ( ),
    deputations of workers ( ).

(11) LEGAL ACTIONS ( )
    arrests ( ),   examinations ( ),   pretrial info. ( ),   trials/court actions ( ),
    sentences, executions, etc. ( ).   Be sure to check the appropriate areas above
    that pertain to the action that brought about the arrest or trial.

Objective of action___ AGAINST   NON-LICENSED   Sellers

Participants___ LICENSED   VICTUALLERS

Number___ "NUMEROUS"___ Leaders___ CHAS. BLEADEN

Date FRI.   O2·15·1828_____ Duration (if known)_____
    Yesterday, last week, a few days ago   one day or less, a few days, more

Location___ LONDON TAVERN___ ,___ LONDON___ ,_____
    Specific place, inn, field, etc.   village or town/city   parish

                                        MIDDLESEX
COMMENTS ON BACK? ( )   4-76, Rev. 4-77 Bobbi/CML   county

Freemasons' Tavern, on Friday, the 19th day of February instant, to
consider the expediency of making an alteration in the first Regulation
of the Institution, by confirming the Resolution of the last General
Meeting, respecting the terms upon which Parochial Paupers and Domestic Servants of Persons not Governors of the Institution, shall in
future be received into the Hospital.

The Chair to be taken at Three o'clock precisely.

CHARLES MURRAY, Sec.

AT a very numerous MEETING of LICENSED
VICTUALLERS, held at the London Tavern, on Friday, the
16th day of February, 1828,

CHARLES BLEADEN, Esq. having been called to the Chair.

It was Resolved unanimously, That it is the opinion of this Meeting
that the privileges and business of the Licensed Victuallers have for a
long time past been grievously interfered with and injured by various
persons opening and conducting houses of entertainment without a Magistrate's License.

That it is the opinion of this Meeting that the Legislature, in enacting
and wording the Foreign Wine License, has expressly prohibited unlicensed persons from allowing any exciseable articles to be consumed
upon their premises.

That it is the opinion of this Meeting that no individual can open or
conduct any house of entertainment without a License from the Magistrate so to do.

That it is the opinion of this Meeting, that under the sanction which
the Magistrate's License gives to the house of a Licensed Victualler, the
greater part of this Meeting give large premiums and pay high rents
for the houses they occupy, and which will cease to be of any more value
than other premises of a similar magnitude, if persons can conduct
houses of entertainment without the License of the Magistrates.

That this Meeting, viewing with satisfaction the proceedings that have
already taken place under the superintendance of the Committee, resolve
to support the proceedings of the Committee in such way as may be
deemed most expedient; and that the Committee have the power to
add to their number, and that they be requested to form four District
Committees as soon as they find it advisable so to do.

That the Thanks of this Meeting be given to the Treasurer and Committee for their past services, and that they be requested to continue to
act in those offices.   CHARLES BLEADEN, Chairman.

Also, that the Thanks of this Meeting be given to Charles Bleaden,
Esq. for his especial and valuable attention to the business of the Association, and for his excellent conduct as Chairman on this occasion.

HOPE LIFE ASSURANCE COMPANY, No. 6,
New Bridge-street, London; No. 5, St. Andrew's-square, Edin-
burgh; and No. 18, Westmorland-street, Dublin.

8	2	8	0	2	0	7	0	1

Today's date **2 - 22** 197/

( )Schweitzer
( )Lord (✓)Guest
( )Kelly ( )Sanchez
( )Gray ( )Stewart
( )Zizka ( )Bloomingdale
( )Shore ( )Teixeira
( )Burke ( )Peterson

GREAT BRITAIN STUDY COVERSHEET

(✓)LONDON TIMES   page __3__   column __3__   Top
                                          (Middle)
( )MORNING CHRONICLE   date __02·11·1828__ day __M__   Bottom

First Line: __Weymouth, FRIDAY, FebRuARY 8__

GENERAL DESCRIPTION: CHECK AS MANY AS APPLY (see memo #6)

(1) VIOLENCE ( )
     property damage ( ),   seizure of property, spaces or persons ( ),
     personal injury ( ),   threat of any of the above ( ).

(2) MEETINGS ( )
     ( ) Election   ( ) support for enemy of government
     ( ) Vestry   ( ) control of local government/institution
     ( ) Livery   ( ) other grievances and dissatisfactions
     ( ) Dinner   ( ) opposition to other peoples or groups
     ( ) Political club/party   ( ) objectives unclear
     ( ) with petition, address, etc.   ( ) notices, requests (for future meetings)
     ( ) opposition to government   ( ) other (list)_____
     ( ) support for government

(3-8) GATHERINGS
     demonstrations (✓),   parade ( ),   assemblies, (crowds), mobs (circle one) (✓),
     gatherings ( ),   rallies ( ),   special celebrations ( ),
     other (list)_____

(9) DELEGATIONS, DEPUTATIONS ( )

(10) LABOR ACTIVITIES ( )
     strike, turnout ( ),   lockout ( ),   combination or union mention ( ),
     threats to stop work ( ),   work stoppages ( ),   return to work ( ),
     deputations of workers ( ).

(11) LEGAL ACTIONS ( )
     arrests ( ),   examinations ( ),   pretrial info. ( ),   trials/court actions ( ),
     sentences, executions, etc. ( ). Be sure to check the appropriate areas above
     that pertain to the action that brought about the arrest or trial.

Objective of action __ADDRESSING OF FreehoLDERS AT eLECTION__

Participants __FRIeNDS OF MR. SugdeN__

Number __NA__   Leaders _____

Date __02·07·1828__   Duration (if known)_____
     Yesterday, last week, a few days ago   one day or less, a few days, more

Location __NA__ , __Weymouth__ , _____
     Specific place, inn, field, etc.   village or town/city   parish

COMMENTS ON BACK? ( )   4-76, Rev. 4-77 Bobbi/CML   county

Feb. 8.

WEYMOUTH, FRIDAY, FEB. 8.

Mr. Sugden made his public entry into this town yesterday afternoon. About five o'clock a large concourse of his friends and adherents assembled at the triumphant gate (less than a quarter of a mile hence), where they awaited his arrival amid the clang of military music. When the carriage drove up, the horses were taken from it; and " See the conquering hero comes" was struck up by the band, and chorussed by the multitude. Just as the array was setting forward, some purple lights illuminated the scene, which, by throwing their broad glare on the congregated masses around, and casting fitful gleams on the bosom of the bay on the right, produced a *coup d'œil* equally pleasing and romantic. The carriage was dragged through the town amid the shouts and acclamations of the purple party; although these were partially interrupted by the unwelcome bray of the " Blues," who were not a little assisted on the occasion by the shrill treble of the females, and the tiny voices of the children, who are all devoted Blues. The assemblage stopped at Luce's hotel, where Mr. Sugden alighted, and mounted the coach-box to address the people. " I promised to be here," said the learned gentleman, " and here I am. (Loud applause.) I will give up to no Blue in devotion to the inhabitants of this town, for whose welfare I feel the strongest attachment. If, indeed, a love for the people, and a regard for their rights, are the characteristics of a True Blue man, I at once vow myself to be one. (Bursts of applause—' Go it, little fellow.') I trust, by your exertions, that I shall be completely successful in the approaching contest ; but, whatever may be the result of it, you may rely on my sacred promise, that I shall not quit the field until the last freehol er has been polled. (Continued applause ; ' Hurra for the game little chap.') Accept of my warmest thanks for the cordial welcome you have given me this evening." The shouts which followed the conclusion of this brief address were quite deafening. Mr. Sugden afterwards, amidst a profusion of good wishes, with difficulty effected an entrance into the hotel.

In the evening the learned gentleman again addressed his friends ; and, after thanking them for their zeal and services, and expressing the highest hopes of success, admonished them to be peaceable and orderly, and not to injure the cause which they supported by riot or disorder. The same sentiment was also fervently echoed by Major Weyland on the same evening; but, much as we wish to see their exhortations attended to, I still dread the repetition of the scenes of violence and outrage which stained the annals of the last election.

8	2	8	0	2	0	7	0	1

Today's date 4 - 16 197/

( )Schweitzer
( )Lord ( )Guest
( )Kelly ( )Sanchez

GREAT BRITAIN STUDY COVERSHEET

(✓)LONDON TIMES   page ___3___ column ___3___ Top   (✓)Gray ( )Stewart
                                               (Middle)   ( )Zizka ( )Bloomingdale
( )MORNING CHRONICLE date _02·11·1828_ day __M__ Bottom   ( )Shore ( )Teixeira
                                                          ( )Burke ( )Peterson

First Line: _ _ _ _ _weymouth_ , _Friday_ , _Feb._ 8 _ _ _ _ _ _ _ _ _ _

GENERAL DESCRIPTION: CHECK AS MANY AS APPLY (see memo #6)

(1) VIOLENCE ( )
    property damage ( ),   seizure of property, spaces or persons ( ),
    personal injury ( ),   threat of any of the above ( ).

(2) MEETINGS ( )
    ( ) Election   ( ) support for enemy of government
    ( ) Vestry   ( ) control of local government/institution
    ( ) Livery   ( ) other grievances and dissatisfactions
    ( ) Dinner   ( ) opposition to other peoples or groups
    ( ) Political club/party   ( ) objectives unclear
    ( ) with petition, address, etc. ( ) notices, requests (for future meetings)
    ( ) opposition to government ( ) other (list)_____
    ( ) support for government   _____

(3-8) GATHERINGS
    demonstrations ( ),   parade ( ),   assemblies, crowds, mobs (circle one) (✓),
    gatherings (✓),   rallies ( ),   special celebrations ( ),
    other (list)_____

(9) DELEGATIONS, DEPUTATIONS ( )

(10) LABOR ACTIVITIES ( )
    strike, turnout ( ),   lockout ( ),   combination or union mention ( ),
    threats to stop work ( ),   work stoppages ( ),   return to work ( ),
    deputations of workers ( ).

(11) LEGAL ACTIONS ( )
    arrests ( ),   examinations ( ),   pretrial info. ( ),   trials/court actions ( ),
    sentences, executions, etc. ( ).   Be sure to check the appropriate areas above
    that pertain to the action that brought about the arrest or trial.

Objective of action__WELCOMING   MR.   Sugden_____

Participants_____FRIENDS & ADHERENTS_____

Number__LARGE CONCOURSE__ Leaders _NA_

Date__FRiday 02·08_____ Duration (if known)_____
    Yesterday, last week, a few days ago   one day or less, a few days, more

Location_____, _weymouth_ , _____
    Specific place, inn, field, etc.   village or town/city   parish

COMMENTS ON BACK? (✓)   4-76, Rev. 4-77 Bobbi/CML   county

Feb. 8.

WEYMOUTH, FRIDAY, FEB. 8.

Mr. Sugden made his public entry into this town yesterday afternoon. About five o'clock a large concourse of his friends and adherents assembled at the triumphant gate (less than a quarter of a mile hence), where they awaited his arrival amid the clang of military music. When the carriage drove up, the horses were taken from it; and " See the conquering hero comes" was struck up by the band, and chorussed by the multitude. Just as the array was setting forward, some purple lights illuminated the scene, which, by throwing their broad glare on the congregated masses around, and casting fitful gleams on the bosom of the bay on the right, produced a *coup d'œil* equally pleasing and romantic. The carriage was dragged through the town amid the shouts and acclamations of the purple party; although these were partially interrupted by the unwelcome bray of the " Blues," who were not a little assisted on the occasion by the shrill treble of the females, and the tiny voices of the children, who are all devoted Blues. The assemblage stopped at Luce's hotel, where Mr. Sugden alighted, and mounted the coach-box to address the people. "I promised to be here," said the learned gentleman, " and here I am. (Loud applause.) I will give up to no Blue in devotion to the inhabitants of this town, for whose welfare I feel the strongest attachment. If, indeed, a love for the people, and a regard for their rights, are the characteristics of a True Blue man, I at once vow myself to be one. (Bursts of applause—' Go it, little fellow.') I trust, by your exertions, that I shall be completely successful in the approaching contest; but, whatever may be the result of it, you may rely on my sacred promise, that I shall not quit the field until the last freehol er has been polled. (Continued applause; ' Hurra for the game little chap.') Accept of my warmest thanks for the cordial welcome you have given me this evening." The shouts which followed the conclusion of this brief address were quite deafening. Mr. Sugden afterwards, amidst a profusion of good wishes, with difficulty effected an entrance into the hotel.

In the evening the learned gentleman again addressed his friends; and, after thanking them for their zeal and services, and expressing the highest hopes of success, admonished them to be peaceable and orderly, and not to injure the cause which they supported by riot or disorder. The same sentiment was also fervently echoed by Major Weyland on the same evening; but, much as we wish to see their exhortations attended to, I still dread the repetition of the scenes of violence and outrage which stained the annals of the last election.

GREAT BRITAIN STUDY COVERSHEET

Today's date 6 -29- 197,

```
( ) ( ) ( ) ( ) ( ) ( )
```

(✓)Schweitzer
( )Lord   ( )Guest
( )Kelly ( )Sanchez
( )Gray   ( )Stewart
( )Zizka ( )Bloomingdale
( )Shore ( )Teixeira
( )Burke ( )Peterson

(✓)LONDON TIMES   page____/____ column __2__ Top____
( )MORNING CHRONICLE date _02·18·1828_ day __M__   Middle / Bottom

First Line: _AT_ _A_ _VERY_ _NUMEROUS_ _ _ _meeTING_ _ _ _ _ _ _

GENERAL DESCRIPTION: CHECK AS MANY AS APPLY (see memo #6)

(1) VIOLENCE ( )
    property damage ( ),   seizure of property, spaces or persons ( ),
    personal injury ( ),   threat of any of the above ( ).

(2) MEETINGS (✓)
    ( ) Election   ( ) support for enemy of government
    ( ) Vestry   ( ) control of local government/institution
    ( ) Livery   (✓) other grievances and dissatisfactions
    ( ) Dinner   (✓) opposition to other peoples or groups
    ( ) Political club/party   ( ) objectives unclear
    ( ) with petition, address, etc. ( ) notices, requests (for future meetings)
    ( ) opposition to government   ( ) other (list)_____
    ( ) support for government   _____

(3-8) GATHERINGS
    demonstrations ( ),   parade ( ),   assemblies, crowds, mobs (circle one) ( ),
    gatherings ( ),   rallies ( ),   special celebrations ( ),
    other (list)_____

(9) DELEGATIONS, DEPUTATIONS ( )

(10) LABOR ACTIVITIES ( )
    strike, turnout ( ),   lockout ( ),   combination or union mention ( ),
    threats to stop work ( ),   work stoppages ( ),   return to work ( ),
    deputations of workers ( ).

(11) LEGAL ACTIONS ( )
    arrests ( ),   examinations ( ),   pretrial info. ( ),   trials/court actions ( ),
    sentences, executions, etc. ( ). Be sure to check the appropriate areas above
    that pertain to the action that brought about the arrest or trial.

Objective of action _STOP_ _INTERFERENCE_ _IN_ _THEIR_ _TRADE_

Participants _LICENSED_ _VICTUALLERS_

Number _"NUMEROUS"_   Leaders _Charles_ _BLEADEN_

Date _FRI_ _02·15·1829_   Duration (if known)_____
    Yesterday, last week, a few days ago   one day or less, a few days, more

Location _LONDON_ _TAVERN_ , _LONDON_ ,_____
    Specific place, inn, field, etc.   village or town/city   parish

COMMENTS ON BACK? ( )   4-76, Rev. 4-77 Bobbi/CML

Middlesex
county

commence on Tuesday Evening, Feb. 21, at half-past 8 o'clock precisely. For a syllabus and terms apply to Mr. H. Butterworth, law bookseller, 7, Fleet-street; or Mr. Petersdorff's clerk, New-court, Temple.

AT a very numerous MEETING of LICENSED VICTUALLERS, held at the London Tavern, on Friday, the 15th day of February, 1828;

CHARLES BLEADEN, Esq., having been called to the chair:

It was resolved unanimously, That it is the opinion of this Meeting that the privileges and business of the Licensed Victuallers have for a long time past been grievously interfered with, and injured by various persons, opening and conducting houses of entertainment without a magistrate's license.

That it is the opinion of this Meeting, that the Legislature, in enacting and wording the Foreign Wine License, has expressly prohibited unlicensed persons from allowing any exciseable articles to be consumed on their premises.

That it is the opinion of this Meeting, that no individual can open or conduct any house of entertainment without a license from the magistrates so to do.

That it is the opinion of this Meeting, that under the sanction which the magistrate's license gives to the house of a Licensed Victualler, the greater part of this Meeting give large premiums and pay high rents for the houses they occupy, and which will cease to be of any more value than other premises of a similar magnitude, if persons can conduct houses of entertainment without the license of the magistrates.

That this Meeting, viewing with satisfaction the proceedings that have already taken place, under the superintendence and direction of the Committee, resolve to support the proceedings of the Committee in such way as may be deemed most expedient, and that the Committee have the power to add to their number, and that they be requested to form four District Committees as soon as they find it advisable so to do.

That the thanks of this Meeting be given to the Treasurer and Committee for their past services, and that they be requested to continue to act in their offices.   CHARLES BLEADEN, Chairman.

Also that the thanks of this Meeting be given to Charles Bleaden, Esq., for his especial and valuable attention to the business of the Association, and for his excellent conduct as chairman on this occasion.

PRESENT DISTRESS.—The present inclement aspect of the weather induces the Committee of the WIDOWS' FRIEND and BENEVOLENT SOCIETY to press their appeal to

GREAT BRITAIN STUDY
Event Section
Bobbi 5-77 Form 76-3

CODER [_ _ _ _]

CA ID# (9 digits) [_ _ _ , _ _ , _ _ , _ _]

Day of Event
[| | | | | | |]
S M T W T F S NA

Accuracy of starting date: [ ] Exact.   App. w/in [   ]

Date event ends: [ ] Same as start.   App. w/in [   ]

Duration: Days [   ]   NA [ ]   Answers a guess [ ]   Hours [   ]   NA [ ]   Guess [ ]

Type of event: [ ] Violence   [ ] Meeting   [ ] Gathering   [ ] Delegation   [ ] Other

Major issue, or claim: [   ]

Location:

	Location code #'s
[ ]	/
[ ]	/
[ ]	/
[ ]	/
[ ]	/
[ ]	/
[ ]	/

Sources: [ ] MC [ ] LT [ ] GM [ ] AR [ ] HPD [ ] MOP [ ] Other [   ]

Total participants: Low [   ]   High [   ]

Best guess [   ]   Impossible to judge [ ]

How determined: [ ] Guess   [ ] #s in report   [ ] Other (list) [   ]

# of person-days: Estimate [   ]   Margin of error + [   ]

# of person-hours: Estimate [   ]   Margin of error + [   ]

Arrests during event: [   ]   Margin of error + [   ]

Arrests after event: [   ]   Margin of error + [   ]

Wounded during event: [   ]   Margin of error + [   ]

Killed during event: [   ]   Margin of error + [   ]

Assembler [   ]   Date [/ /]   Coder [   ]   Date [/ /]

Check coder, [   ]   Date [/ /]   Punched [   ]   Date [/ /]

Section coded [ ] A [ ] B [ ] C [ ] D [ ] E [ ] F [ ] G

Total number of formations enumerated [   ]   # of formations participating directly in the event [   ]

For coder use only [   ]

Formation Section: Fill out one sheet per formation.   Coder # [___ ___ ___ ___]

Year	Month	Day	No.		Total # of formations

Event [___ ___ ___   ___ ___   ___ ___   ___ ___]

Number of this formation [_____]

Summary name for this formation [_____]

Does this formation overlap with any other formation(s) in the same event?

[ ] No   [ ] Yes: Which ones? Give formations #s [___] [___]

[___] [___]

What is the relationship between this formation and the Contentious Gathering?

[ ] Participants, making a claim

[ ] Participants, object of a claim

[ ] Participants, both making and receiving claims

[ ] Spectator, bystander

[ ] Involved in action before or after CG only:

How? [_____]

[ ] Other: [_____]

Name(s) given to this formation in account(s):   [ ] None

1 [_____]   4 [_____]

2 [_____]   5 [_____]

3 [_____]   6 [_____]

If the account(s) list any individual names of formation members, list them:

1 [_____]   6 [_____]

2 [_____]   7 [_____]

3 [_____]   8 [_____]

4 [_____]   9 [_____]

5 [_____]   10 [_____]

[ ] None

Individual names mentioned in account(s):   (continued)

11. ☐   16. ☐

12. ☐   17. ☐

13. ☐   18. ☐

14. ☐   19. ☐

15. ☐   20. ☐

If more than 20 names, use another page.

The normal residence of this formation is:

☐ No information given, can't guess residence.

☐   ☐

Specific place   Town

☐   ☐

Parish   County

☐ Other   ☐   Use parentheses if making a guess.

Words in account(s) describing and/or geographic extent of this formation:

None ☐

1. ☐   3. ☐

2. ☐   4. ☐

Do the accounts report a specific number (approximate or exact) for this formation?

☐ No

☐ Yes   ☐

☐ Yes, multiple reports   ☐

☐

Your estimates of the number of people in this formation:

Low [   ]

High [   ]

Best guess [   ]

Impossible to judge [   ]   Source(s) of your best guess:

[   ] Couldn't guess   [   ] Number in text

[   ] Word(s) in text [   ]

[   ]

[   ] Inferred   How? [   ]

Your estimate of the number of person-days in this formation:

[   ] ←

00 = Impossible to judge
01 = CG less than 1 day

Your estimate of the number of person-hours in this formation:

[   ] ←

00 = Impossible to judge
01 = CG less than 1 hr.

Source of your estimate:

[   ] Impossible to judge (must be 00,00 above)

[   ] Number in text

[   ] Word(s) in text [   ]

[   ] Inferred   How? [   ]

[   ] Dates in text make it clear less than one day, NA exact amount of hours:
must be 01-00 above.

How many members of this formation were:

	#	Can't tell	None	Basis of estimate: In text	Inferred	From
Arrested?	[ ]	[ ]	[ ]	[ ]	[ ]	[ ]
Wounded?	[ ]	[ ]	[ ]	[ ]	[ ]	[ ]
Killed?	[ ]	[ ]	[ ]	[ ]	[ ]	[ ]

Any other word(s) in account(s) describing this formation?   None [   ]

[   ]   [   ]

[   ]   [   ]

[   ]   [   ]

[   ]   [   ]

SOURCE SECTION

1. Name of Source [   ]

   Locations: Date [| |]   [   ] [   ]
                     Month   Day   Year   Page   Column

                     [| |]   [   ]
                     Top Middle Bottom   Volume Number
                                                  (if needed)

   Type of Report:

   [ ] Editorial/letter in newspaper   [ ] Trial (legal activity) report

   [ ] Advertisement or notice   [ ] Parliamentary report

   [ ] Eyewitness report   [ ] Regular article

   [ ] Another newspaper's account   [ ] Other

             List name [   ]   List [   ]

2. Name of Source [   ]

   Locations: Date [| |]   [   ] [   ]
                     Month   Day   Year   Page   Column

                     [| |]   [   ]
                     Top Middle Bottom   Volume Number
                                                  (if needed)

   Type of Report

   [ ] Editorial/letter in newspaper   [ ] Trial (legal activity) report

   [ ] Advertisement or notice   [ ] Parliamentary report

   [ ] Eyewitness report   [ ] Regular article

   [ ] Another newspaper account   [ ] Other

             List name [   ]   List [   ]

Additional materials that pertain to this event, specifically or in general.

   [ ] Dissertation   [ ] None

   [ ] Background paper: list title [   ]

   [ ] Book: list title [   ]

   [ ] Other: list [   ]

   Comments [   ]
   [ ] None

PLACE NAME SECTION: Fill out one section for each place an action occurs.

1. Principal place

   List parish first,
   then county.

   Detailed place

   A)

   B)

2. Principal place

   List parish first,
   then county.

   Detailed place

   A)

   B)

3. Principal place

   List parish first,
   then county.

   Detailed place

   A)

   B)

4. Principal place

   List parish first,
   then county.

   Detailed place

   A)

   B)

5. Principal place

   List parish first,
   then county.

   Detailed place

   A)

   B)

6. Principal place

   List parish first,
   then county.

   Detailed place

   A)

   B)

GBS / CGC

F.   COMMENT SECTION   (use one square per/comment only)

1)   Location, section letter _____   item #_____

2)   Location, section letter _____   item #_____

3)   Location, section letter _____   item#_____

GBS / CGC

G.   CODING INFO.

1)   Name of coder; _____   2)   Coder number; _____

3)   Date coded; _____

┌───┐
│ 4)   General notes on coding of this event;   │
│   │
│   │
│   │
│   │
│   │
│   │
│   │
│   │
└───┘

5)   Check coder name; _____   6)   Check coder number; _____

┌───┐
│ 7)   General notes on check coding;   │
│   │
│   │
│   │
│   │
│   │
│   │
│   │
│   │
└───┘

Bibliography

The bibliography falls into eight sections, corresponding to the book's eight chapters. In each section you will find the references cited in the chapter, some background material and a few examples of further work along the same lines.

1 Introduction

CARDEN, MAREN LOCKWOOD (1974). *The New Feminist Movement*. New York: Russell Sage Foundation.

CLARK, SAMUEL D.; J. PAUL GRAYSON; and LINDA M. GRAYSON, eds. (1975). *Prophecy and Protest: Social Movements in Twentieth-Century Canada*. Toronto: Gage.

COLEMAN, JAMES S. (1973). *The Mathematics of Collective Action*. Chicago: Aldine.

FEUER, LEWIS S. (1969). *The Conflict of Generations: The Character and Significance of Student Movements*. New York: Basic Books.

HUME, DAVID (1875). *Essays. Moral, Political and Literary*. 2 vols. London: Longmans, Green. Originally published in 1740.

KLAPP, ORRIN E. (1969). *Collective Search for Identity*. New York: Holt, Rinehart & Winston.

KRIESBERG, LOUIS (1973). *The Sociology of Social Conflict*. Englewood Cliffs, New Jersey: Prentice-Hall.

KUCZYNSKI, JÜRGEN (1967). *The Rise of the Working Class*. New York: McGraw-Hill.

LANDSBERGER, HENRY A., ed. (1974). *Rural Protest: Peasant Movements and Social Change*. London: Macmillan.

LIPSET, SEYMOUR MARTIN (1970). *Revolution and Counter-Revolution: Change and Persistence in Social Structures*. Rev. ed. Garden City, New York: Doubleday Anchor.

MACPHERSON, C. B. (1962). *The Political Theory of Possessive Individualism.* Oxford: Clarendon Press.

MANN, MICHAEL (1973). *Consciousness and Action among the Western Working Class.* London: Macmillan.

MÜHLMANN, WILHELM E. (1961). *Chiliasmus und Nativismus.* Berlin: Dietrich Reimer.

NORDLINGER, ERIC A. (1972). *Conflict Regulation in Divided Societies.* Cambridge, Massachusetts: Harvard University Center for International Affairs. *Occasional Papers in International Affairs 29.*

OHNGREN, BÖ (1974). *Folk i rörelse. Samhällsutveckling, flyttningsmönster och folkrörelser i Eskilstuna 1870–1900.* Uppsala, Sweden: Almqvist & Wiksell. *Studia Historica Upsaliensia 55.*

PEREIRA DE QUEIROZ, MARIA ISAURA (1968). *Réforme et révolution dans les sociétés traditionnelles. Historie et ethnologie des mouvements messianiques.* Paris: Anthropos.

PICKVANCE, C. G. (1975). "On the Study of Urban Social Movements." *Sociological Review* 23: 29–49.

RANULF, SVEND (1964). *Moral Indignation and Middle Class Psychology.* New York: Schocken. First published in 1938.

NATIONAL ADVISORY COMMISSION ON CIVIL DISORDERS (1968). Report. Washington: U. S. Government Printing Office. Known informally as "The Kerner Report."

RICHARDSON, LEWIS F. (1960). *Statistics of Deadly Quarrels.* Pittsburgh: Boxwood Press.

RIDKER, RONALD (1962). "Discontent and Economic Growth." *Economic Development and Cultural Change* 10: 1–15.

ROSENAU, JAMES N., ed. (1964). *International Aspects of Civil Strife.* Princeton: Princeton University Press.

SCHWARTZ, MICHAEL (1976). *Radical Protest and Social Structure.* New York: Academic Press.

SHARP, GENE (1973). *The Politics of Nonviolent Action.* Boston: Porter Sargent.

SMITH, ADAM (1910). *The Wealth of Nations.* 2 vols. London: J. M. Dent. First published in 1776; many editions.

SPIELBERG, JOSEPH, and SCOTT WHITEFORD, eds. (1976). *Forging Nations: A Comparative View of Rural Ferment and Revolt.* East Lansing: Michigan State University Press.

THOMPSON, E. P. (1971). "The Moral Economy of the English Crowd in the Eighteenth Century." *Past and Present* 50: 76–136.

TILLY, CHARLES (1974). "Do Communities Act?" *Sociological Inquiry* 43: 209–240.

TILLY, RICHARD (1970). "Popular Disorders in Nineteenth Century Germany: A Preliminary Survey." *Journal of Social History* 4: 1–40.

WALLACE, ANTHONY F. C. (1956). "Revitalization Movements." *American Anthropologist* 58: 264–281.

WEBB, SIDNEY, and BEATRICE WEBB (1963). *English Poor Law Library. Part I: The Old Poor Law.* Hamden, Connecticut: Archon Books. Volume I of English Local Government. First Published in 1927.

2 Theories and Descriptions of Collective Action

ALBERONI, FRANCESCO (1968). *Statu nascenti. Studi sui processi colletivi.* Bologna: Il Mulino.

ALLAN, GRAHAM (1974). "A Theory of Millennialism: The Irvingite Movement as an Illustration." *The British Journal of Sociology* 25: 296–311.

ANDERSON, BÖ (1968). "Revitalization Movements: An Essay on Structure and Ideology in a Class of Exclusive Underdog Systems." *Acta Universitatis Upsaliensis* 17: 347–375.

ARROW, KENNETH J. (1963). *Social Choice and Individual Values.* 2d. ed. New York: Wiley.

ASH, ROBERTA (1972). *Social Movements in America.* Chicago: Markham.

ASHENFELTER, ORLEY, and GEORGE E. JOHNSON (1969). "Bargaining Theory, Trade Unions and Industrial Strike Activity." *American Economic Review* 59: 35–49.

BANKS, J. A. (1970). *Marxist Sociology in Action. A Sociological Critique of the Marxist Approach to Industrial Relations.* London: Faber & Faber.

BERK, RICHARD A. (1974). "A Gaming Approach to Crowd Behavior." *American Sociological Review* 39: 355–373.

BOULDING, KENNETH E. (1962). *Conflict and Defense. A General Theory.* New York: Harper & Row.

BRETON, A., and R. BRETON (1969). "An Economic Theory of Social Movements." *American Economic Review, Papers and Proceedings* 59: 198–205.

BUCHANAN, JAMES M., and GORDON TULLOCK (1962). *The Calculus of Consent. Logical Foundations of Constitutional Democracy.* Ann Arbor: University of Michigan Press.

CHEVALIER, LOUIS (1958). *Classes laborieuses et classes dangéreuses à Paris pendant la premiére moitiè du XIXe siécle.* Paris: Plon.

COBB, RICHARD (1961–63). *Les armées révolutionnaires, instrument de la Terreur dans les départements.* 2 vols. Paris: Mouton.

_____ (1964). *Terreur et subsistances, 1793–1795.* Paris: Clavreuil.

_____ (1970). *The Police and the People. French Popular Protest, 1789–1820.* Oxford: Clarendon Press.

COLEMAN, JAMES S. (1973). *The Mathematics of Collective Action.* Chicago: Aldine.

_____ (1974). *Power and the Structure of Society.* New York: W. W. Norton.

COOPER, MARK N. (1974). "A Reinterpretation of the Causes of Turmoil: The Effects of Culture and Modernity." *Comparative Political Studies* 7: 267–291.

DAUMARD, ADELINE (1963). *La bourgeoisie parisienne de 1815 à 1848.* Paris: SEVPEN.

DUNCAN, GRAEME (1973). *Marx and Mill. Two Views of Social Conflict and Social Harmony.* Cambridge: Cambridge University Press.

DURHAM, WILLIAM H. (1976). "Resource Competition and Human Aggression, Part I: A Review of Primitive War." *Quarterly Review of Biology* 51: 385–415.

DURKHEIM, EMILE (1933). *The Division of Labor in Society.* New York: Macmillan.

_____ (1951). *Suicide. A Study in Sociology.* Glencoe, Illinois: Free Press.

_____ (1961). *The Elementary Forms of the Religious Life.* New York: Collier Books

FELDMAN, ALLAN, and ALAN KIRMAN (1974). "Fairness and Envy." *American Economic Review* 59: 995–1005.

FIREMAN, BRUCE, and WILLIAM A. GAMSON (1977). "Utilitarian Logic in the Resource Mobilization Perspective." Working Paper 153, Center for Research on Social Organization, University of Michigan.

FISHBURN, PETER (1973). *Mathematics of Decision Theory.* The Hague: Mouton.

FOSTER, JOHN (1974). *Class Struggle and the Industrial Revolution. Early Industrial Capitalism in Three Towns.* London: Weidenfeld & Nicolson.

FROLICH, NORMAN; JOE A. OPPENHEIMER; and ORAN R. YOUNG (1971). *Political Leadership and Collective Goods.* Princeton: Princeton University Press.

FROLICH, NORMAN et al. (1975). "Individual Contributions for Collective Goods." *Journal of Conflict Resolution* 19: 310–329.

FURET, FRANÇOIS (1963). "Pour une définition des classes inférieures à l'époque moderne." *Annales; Economies, Sociétés, Civilisations* 18: 459–474.

FURET, FRANÇOIS; CLAUDE MAZAURIC; and LOUIS BERGERON (1963). "Les sans-culottes et la Révolution française." *Annales; Economies, Sociétés, Civilisations* 18: 1098–1127.

GOSSEZ, RÉMI (1967). *Les Ouvriers de Paris. I. L'Organisation, 1848–1851.* La Roche-sur-Yon: Imprimerie Centrale de l'Ouest.

GURR, TED ROBERT (1968). "A Causal Model of Civil Strife: A Comparative Analysis Using New Indices." *American Political Science Review* 62:1104–1124.

_____ (1969). *Why Men Rebel.* Princeton: Princeton University Press.

GURR, TED ROBERT, and RAYMOND DUVALL (1973). "Civil Conflict in the 1960s: A Reciprocal System with Parameter Estimates." *Comparative Political Studies* 6: 135–169.

GUSFIELD, JOSEPH R. (1966). *Symbolic Crusade. Status Politics and the American Temperance Movement.* Urbana: University of Illinois Press.

HAUSER, PHILIP (1963). "The Social, Economic and Technological Problems of Rapid Urbanization," in Bert Hoselitz and Wilbert Moore, eds., *Industrialization and Society.* The Hague: Mouton for UNESCO.

HIBBS, DOUGLAS A., JR. (1973). *Mass Political Violence. A Cross-National Causal Analysis.* New York: Wiley.

HIRSCHMAN, ALBERT O. (1970). *Exit, Voice and Loyalty: Responses to Decline in Firms, Organizations, and States.* Cambridge: Harvard University Press.

HOBSBAWM, E. J., and GEORGE RUDÉ (1969). *Captain Swing.* London: Lawrence & Wishart.

HOLSTI, K. J. (1975). "Underdevelopment and the 'Gap' Theories of International Conflict." *American Political Science Review* 69: 827–839.

HUNTINGTON, SAMUEL P. (1968). *Political Order in Changing Societies.* New Haven: Yale University Press.

JOHNSON, CHALMERS (1966). *Revolutionary Change.* Boston: Little, Brown.

KRAMER, GERALD H., and JOSEPH E. HERTZBERG (1975). "Formal Theory," in vol. 7 of Fred I. Greenstein and Nelson Polsby, eds., *Handbook of Political Science.* Reading, Massachusetts: Addison-Wesley.

LEFEBVRE, GEORGES (1924). *Les paysans du Nord pendant la Révolution française.* Lille: Robbe.

———— (1962–63). *Etudes orléanaises.* 2 vols. Paris: Commission d'Histoire Economique et Sociale de la Révolution.

LOWY, MICHEL (1970). *La théorie de la révolution chez le jeune Marx.* Paris: Maspéro.

MARX, GARY T., and JAMES L. WOOD (1975). "Strands of Theory and Research in Collective Behavior." *Annual Review of Sociology, I.* Beverly Hills, California: Sage.

MARX, KARL (1935). *The Civil Wars in France.* New York: International Publishers.

———— (1958). "The Class Struggles in France, 1848–1850" and "The Eighteenth Brumaire of Louis Bonaparte" in Karl Marx and Frederick Engels, *Selected Works.* Moscow: Foreign Languages Publishing House.

McCARTHY, JOHN D., and MAYER N. ZALD (1973). *The Trend of Social Movements in America: Professionalization and Resource Mobilization.* Morristown, New Jersey: General Learning Corporation.

McPHAIL, CLARK (1971). "Civil Disorder Participation: A Critical Examination of Recent Research." *American Sociological Review* 36: 1058–1073.

MILL, JOHN STUART (1950). *Utilitarianism, Liberty, and Repressive Government.* London: J. M. Dent.

MOORE, BARRINGTON, JR. (1966). *Social Origins of Dictatorship and Democracy.* Boston: Beacon.

NAMIER, LEWIS (1961). *The Structure of Politics at the Accession of George III.* 2d. ed. London: Macmillan.

NELSON, JOAN (1970). "The Urban Poor: Disruption or Political Integration in Third World Cities?" *World Politics* 22: 393–414.

OBERSCHALL, ANTHONY (1973). *Social Conflict and Social Movements.* Englewood Cliffs, New Jersey: Prentice-Hall.

O'BRIEN, DAVID J. (1974). "The Public Goods Dilemma and the 'Apathy' of the Poor Toward Neighborhood Organization." *Social Service Review* 48: 229–244.

OLSON, MANCUR, JR. (1965). *The Logic of Collective Action.* Cambridge: Harvard University Press.

PARSONS, TALCOTT (1960). "Durkheim's Contribution to the Theory of Integration of Social Systems," in Kurt H. Wolff, ed., *Essays on Sociology and Philosophy.* New York: Harper & Row.

PLAMENATZ, JOHN (1949). *Mill's Utilitarianism, reprinted with a study of the English Utilitarians.* Oxford: Basil Blackwell.

PRICE, ROGER (1972). *The French Second Republic. A Social History.* London: B. T. Batsford.

PRZEWORSKI, ADAM (1975). "Institutionalization of Voting Patterns, or Is Mobilization the Source of Decay?" *American Political Science Review* 69: 49–67.

RIKER, WILLIAM H., and PETER C. ORDESHOOK (1968). "A Theory of the Calculus of Voting." *American Political Science Review* 62: 25–42.

RUDÉ, GEORGE (1959). *The Crowd in the French Revolution.* Oxford: Oxford University Press.

———— (1964). *The Crowd in History. A Study of Popular Disturbances in France and England, 1730–1848.* New York: Wiley.

RUMMEL, RUDOLPH J. (1966). "Dimensions of Conflict Behavior Within Nations." *Journal of Conflict Resolution* 10: 65–74.

SCOTT, MARVIN B., and STANFORD M. LYMAN (1970). *The Revolt of the Students.* Columbus, Ohio: Charles E. Merrill.

SHILS, EDWARD (1962). *Political Development in the New States.* The Hague: Mouton.

SOBOUL, ALBERT (1958). *Les sans-culottes parisiens en l'an II.* La Roche-sur-Yon: Potier.

TAYLOR, MICHAEL (1975). "The Theory of Collective Choice," in vol. 3 of Fred I. Greenstein and Nelson Polsby, eds., *Handbook of Political Science.* Reading, Massachusetts: Addison-Wesley.

THOMPSON, E. P. (1963). *The Making of the English Working Class.* London: Gollancz.

TØNNESSON, KÅRE (1959). *La défaite des sans-culottes.* Paris: Clavreuil.

TURNER, RALPH H. (1967). "Types of Solidarity in the Reconstituting of Groups," *Pacific Sociological Review* 10: 60-68.

USEEM, MICHAEL (1973). *Conscription, Protest, and Social Conflict. The Life and Death of a Draft Resistance Movement.* New York: Wiley.

_____ (1975). *Protest Movements in America.* Indianapolis: Bobbs-Merrill.

VON NEUMANN, JOHN, AND OSKAR MORGENSTERN (1947). *Theory of Games and Economic Behavior.* 2d. ed. Princeton: Princeton University Press.

WEBER, MAX (1972). *Wirtschaft und Gesellschaft.* 5th ed. Tübingen, Germany: J. C. B. Mohr. (English translation: Guenther Roth and Claus Wittich, eds., *Economy and Society.* 3 vols. New York: Bedminster Press, 1968.)

WELLER, JACK M., and E.L. QUARANTELLI (1973). "Neglected Characteristics of Collective Behavior." *American Journal of Sociology* 79: 665-685.

WHITE, LOUISE (1976). "Rational Theories of Participation." *Journal of Conflict Resolution* 20: 255-278.

WILKINSON, PAUL (1971). *Social Movement.* London: Pall Mall.

WILSON, KENNETH L., and ANTHONY ORUM (1976). "Mobilizing People for Collective Political Action." *Journal of Political and Military Sociology* 4: 187-202.

WOLF, ERIC (1969). *Peasant Wars of the Twentieth Century.* New York: Harper & Row.

3 Interests, Organization and Mobilization

AGULHON, MAURICE (1966). *La sociabilité méridionale.* 2 vols. Aix-en-Provence: La Pensée Universitaire.

ALAPURO, RISTO (1976). "On the Political Mobilization of the Agrarian Population in Finland: Problems and Hypotheses." *Scandinavian Political Studies* 11: 51-76.

AMINZADE, RONALD (1973). "Revolution and Collective Political Violence: The Case of the Working Class of Marseille, France, 1830-1871." Working Paper 86, Center for Research on Social Organization, University of Michigan.

CAMERON, DAVID R. (1974). "Toward a Theory of Political Mobilization." *Journal of Politics* 36: 138-171.

COHN, NORMAN (1957). *The Pursuit of the Millennium.* Fairlawn, New Jersey: Essential Books.

DAHL, ROBERT A. (1966). "The American Oppositions: Affirmation and Denial," in Robert A. Dahl, ed., *Political Oppositions in Western Democracies.* New Haven: Yale University Press. Cited from paperback edition.

DEUTSCH, KARL (1953). *Nationalism and Social Communication.* Cambridge: MIT Press.

DOWE, DIETER (1970). *Aktion und Organisation. Arbeiterbewegung, sozialistische*

und kommunistische Bewegung in der preussischen Rheinprovinz 1820–1852.
Hannover: Verlag für Literatur und Zeitgeschehen.

EDMONSON, MUNRO S. (1958). *Status Terminology and the Social Structure of North American Indians.* Seattle: University of Washington Press.

ETZIONI, AMITAI (1968). *The Active Society.* New York: Free Press.

FIAZ, MUHAMMAD (1973). Interindustry Propensity to Strike in France, 1891 to 1930. Unpublished Ph.D. dissertation in sociology, University of Toronto.

FIREMAN, BRUCE et al. (1976). "Catalyzing Rebellion: An Introduction to the Mobilization in Miniature Project." Working Paper 138, Center for Research on Social Organization, University of Michigan.

GAMSON, WILLIAM A. (1968a). *Power and Discontent.* Homewood, Illinois: Dorsey.

—— (1968b). "Stable Unrepresentation in American Society." *American Behavioral Scientist* 12: 15–21.

—— (1975). *The Strategy of Social Protest.* Homewood, Illinois: Dorsey.

GESCHWENDER, BARBARA A., and JAMES A. GESCHWENDER (1973). "Relative Deprivation and Participation in the Civil Rights Movement." *Social Science Quarterly* 54: 403–411.

GURR, TED ROBERT (1969). *Why Men Rebel.* Princeton: Princeton University Press.

HANAGAN, MICHAEL (1976). "The Logic of Solidarity: Social Structure in a French Town," *Journal of Urban History,* forthcoming.

HIRSCHMAN, ALBERT O. (1970). *Exit, Voice, and Loyalty: Responses to Decline in Firms, Organizations, and States.* Cambridge: Harvard University Press.

JACOBSON, ALVIN (1973). "Some Theoretical and Methodological Considerations for Measuring Intrasocietal Conflict." *Sociological Methods and Research* 1: 439–461.

KANTER, ROSABETH MOSS (1972). *Commitment and Community. Communes and Utopias in Sociological Perspective.* Cambridge: Harvard University Press.

KERR, CLARK, and ABRAHAM SIEGEL (1954). "The Inter-Industry Propensity to Strike," in Arthur Kornhauser et al., *Industrial Conflict.* New York: Wiley.

KORNHAUSER, WILLIAM (1959). *The Politics of Mass Society.* Glencoe, Illinois: Free Press.

KRIEGEL, ANNIE (1966). *La Croissance de la C. G. T., 1918–1921: Essai Statistique.* Paris: Mouton.

KUHNLE, STEIN (1973). *Social Mobilization and Political Participation: The Nordic Countries, c. 1850–1870.* Bergen: Institute of Sociology.

LAUMANN, EDWARD O., and FRANZ U. PAPPI (1976). *Networks of Collective Action. A Perspective on Community Influence Systems.* New York: Academic.

LEGGETT, JOHN C. (1968). *Class, Race, and Labor: Working-Class Consciousness in Detroit.* New York: Oxford University Press.

LIND, JOAN (1973). Foreign and Domestic Conflict: The British and Swedish Labor Movements, 1900–1950. Unpublished Ph.D. dissertation in sociology, University of Michigan.

———— (1974). "Political Power and Collective Action: British and Swedish Labor Movements, 1900–1950." Working Paper 100, Center for Research on Social Organization University of Michigan.

LIPSET, S. M.; MARTIN TROW; and JAMES S. COLEMAN (1956). *Union Democracy.* Glencoe, Illinois: Free Press.

MACPHERSON, C. B. (1962). *The Political Theory of Possessive Individualism.* Oxford: Clarendon Press.

MARX, KARL (1973). *Surveys from Exile. Political Writings,* Vol. 2. London: Allen Lane.

McPHAIL, CLARK, and DAVID L. MILLER (1973). "The Assembling Process. A Theoretical and Empirical Examination." *American Sociological Review* 38: 721–735.

MICHELS, ROBERT (1949). *Political Parties.* Glencoe, Illinois: Free Press. First published in 1915.

MORGAN, WILLIAM R., and TERRY NICHOLS CLARK (1973). "The Causes of Racial Disorders: A Grievance-Level Explanation." *American Sociological Review* 38: 611–624.

NETTL, J. P. (1967). *Political Mobilization. A Sociological Analysis of Methods and Concepts.* London: Faber & Faber.

OBERSCHALL, ANTHONY (1973). *Social Conflict and Social Movements.* Englewood Cliffs, New Jersey: Prentice-Hall.

OLSON, MANCUR, JR. (1965). *The Logic of Collective Action.* Cambridge: Harvard University Press.

PROST, ANTOINE (1964). *La C. G. T. à l'époque du Front Populaire, 1934–1939: Essai de description numérique.* Paris: Colin.

ROY, WILLIAM (1977). Inter-industry Vesting of Interests in a National Polity Over Time: The United States, 1886–1905. Unpublished doctoral dissertation in Sociology, University of Michigan.

SEWELL, WILLIAM (1971). "La classe ouvrière de Marseille sous la Seconde République. Structure sociale et comportement politique." *Le Mouvement Social* 76: 27–66.

SHORTER, EDWARD, and CHARLES TILLY (1974). *Strikes in France, 1830–1968.* Cambridge: Cambridge University Press.

SMITH, ADAM (1910). *The Wealth of Nations.* 2 vols. London: J. M. Dent.

SNYDER, DAVID (1974). Determinants of Industrial Conflict: Historical Models of Strikes in France, Italy and the United States. Unpublished Ph.D. dissertation in sociology, University of Michigan.

SNYDER, DAVID, and WILLIAM R. KELLY (1976). "Industrial Violence in Italy 1878–1903." *American Journal of Sociology* 82: 131–162.

SOROKIN, PITIRIM A. (1962). *Social and Cultural Dynamics. III. Fluctuation of Social Relationships, War and Revolution*. New York: Bedminster.

SUGIMOTO, YOSHIO (1973). Equalization and Turbulence: The Case of the American Occupation of Japan. Unpublished Ph.D. dissertation in sociology, University of Pittsburgh.

TAYLOR, CHARLES LEWIS (1966). Toward an Explanation of the Rise of Political Activity among English Working Men, 1790–1850. Unpublished paper presented to the annual meeting of the American Political Science Association.

TILLY, CHARLES; LOUISE TILLY; and RICHARD TILLY (1975). *The Rebellious Century, 1830–1930*. Cambridge: Harvard University Press.

UHEN, LEO (1964). *Gruppenbewusstsein und informelle Gruppenbildungen bei deutschen Arbeitern im Jahrhundert der Industrialisierung*. Berlin: Duncker & Humblot.

VERDERY, KATHERINE (1976). "Ethnicity and Local Systems: The Religious Organizations of Welshness," in Carol A. Smith, ed., *Regional Analysis. Volume II: Social Systems*. New York: Academic.

VOLKMANN, HEINRICH (1975). Die Krise von 1830: Form, Ursache and Funktion des soziales Protests im deutschen Vormärz. Unpublished Habilitationsthesis, Free University of Berlin.

WHITE, HARRISON (n.d.). Notes on the Constituents of Social Structure. Unpublished paper, Harvard University.

WOLF, ERIC (1969). *Peasant Wars of the Twentieth Century*. New York: Harper & Row.

YOUNG, FRANK W. (1966). "A Proposal for Cooperative Cross-Cultural Research on Intervillage Systems." *Human Organization* 25: 46–50.

ZWAHR, HARTMUT (1976). "Zur Strukturanalyse der sich konstituierenden deutschen Arbeiterklasse." *Beiträge zur Geschichte der Arbeiterbewegung* 4: 605–628.

4   The Opportunity to Act Together

BAÎLEY, F. G. (1969). *Stratagems and Spoils*. Oxford: Blackwell.

BALBUS, ISAAC D. (1971). "The Concept of Interest in Pluralist and Marxist Analysis." *Politics and Society* 1: 151–177.

BEATTIE, J. M. (1974). "The Pattern of Crime in England, 1660–1800." *Past and Present* 62: 47–95.

BOISSEVAIN, JEREMY (1976). Of Men and Marbles: Factionalism Reconsidered. Unpublished paper, European-Mediterranean Study Group, University of Amsterdam.

BONNEFOUS, GEORGES (1956). *Histoire politique de la Troisième République*. Vol. I. Paris: Presses Universitaires de France.

BRILL, HARRY (1971). *Why Organizers Fail. The Story of a Rent Strike.* Berkeley: University of California Press.

CHAPMAN, BRIAN (1970). *Police State.* London: Pall Mall.

CHAZEL, FRANÇOIS (1974). "Pouvoir, cause et force." *Revue française de sociologie* 15: 441–457.

CONNOLLY, WILLIAM E. (1972). "On 'Interests' in Politics." *Politics and Society* 2: 459–477.

DAVIES, JAMES C. (1962). "Toward a Theory of Revolution." *American Sociological Review* 27: 5–19.

_____ (1969). "The J-Curve of Rising and Declining Satisfactions as a Cause of Some Great Revolutions and a Contained Rebellion," in Hugh Davis Graham and Ted Robert Gurr, eds., *Violence in America.* Washington: U.S. Government Printing Office.

FENNO, RICHARD F., JR. (1966). *The Power of the Purse.* Boston: Little, Brown.

GAMSON, WILLIAM A. (1968). *Power and Discontent.* Homewood, Illinois: Dorsey.

_____ (1975). *The Strategy of Social Protest.* Homewood, Illinois: Dorsey.

GROH, DIETER (1973). *Negative Integration und revolutionärer Attentismus. Die deutsche Sozialdemokratie am Vorabend des erstes Weltkrieges.* Frankfurt a/M: Ullstein.

GOULD, JOHN P. (1973). "The Economics of Legal Conflicts." *Journal of Legal Studies* 2: 279–300.

HAY, DOUGLAS (1975). "Property, Authority and the Criminal Law," in Douglas Hay et al., *Albion's Fatal Tree. Crime and Society in Eighteenth-Century England.* New York: Pantheon.

HEIRICH, MAX (1971). *The Spiral of Conflict: Berkeley, 1964.* New York: Columbia University Press.

HIRSCHMAN, ALBERT O. (1970). *Exit, Voice and Loyalty: Responses to Decline in Firms, Organizations, and States.* Cambridge: Harvard University Press.

JENKINS, CRAIG, and CHARLES PERROW (1974). *Protest and Power: Farm Worker Insurgency (1945–1972).* Unpublished paper, Department of Sociology, State University of New York, Stony Brook.

LAPONCE, JEAN (1969). "Canadian Party Labels: An Essay in Semantics and Anthropology." *Canadian Journal of Political Science* 2: 141–157.

LAURIE, BRUCE G. (1973). "Fire Companies and Gangs in Southwark: The 1840s," in Allen F. Davis and Mark H. Haller, eds., *The Peoples of Philadelphia. A History of Ethnic Groups and Lower-Class Life, 1790–1940.* Philadelphia: Temple University Press.

LEITES, NATHAN, and CHARLES WOLF, JR. (1970). *Rebellion and Authority. An Analytic Essay on Insurgent Conflicts.* Chicago: Markham.

LEVETT, ALLAN (1974). Centralization of City Police in the Nineteenth Century

United States. Unpublished Ph.D. dissertation in sociology, University of Michi gan.

LIPSKY, MICHAEL (1970). *Protest in City Politics: Rent Strikes, Housing and the Power of the Poor.* Chicago: Rand McNally.

LOWI, THEODORE (1971). *The Politics of Disorder.* New York: Basic.

LUKES, STEVEN (1974). *Power: A Radical View.* London: Macmillan.

MAYHEW, ANNE (1972). "A Reappraisal of the Causes of Farm Protest in the United States, 1870–1900." *Journal of Economic History* 32: 464–475.

MILIBAND, RALPH (1969). *The State in Capitalist Society.* London: Weidenfeld & Nicolson.

NAGEL, JACK H. (1975). *The Descriptive Analysis of Power.* New Haven: Yale University Press.

O'DONNEL, GUILLERMO A. (1972). *Modernización y autoritarismo.* Buenos Aires Paidós.

PAYNE, JAMES L. (1965). *Labor and Politics in Peru.* New Haven: Yale University Press.

PEARSON, JEFF (1970). On Watching the State and Contenders in a Parliamentary Context. Unpublished paper, Center for Research on Social Organization University of Michigan.

PENNINGS, JOHANNES M. (1975). "The Relevance of the Structural-Contingency Model for Organizational Effectiveness." *Administrative Science Quarterly* 20 393–410.

PENROSE, L. S. (1952). *The Objective Study of Crowd Behavior.* London: Lewis.

PERROW, CHARLES (1967). "A Framework for the Comparative Analysis of Orga nizations." *American Sociological Review* 32: 194–208.

RADZINOWICZ, LEON (1968). *A History of English Criminal Law and its Administra tion from 1750. IV: Grappling for Control.* London: Stevens.

ROY, WILLIAM G. (1975). "Integration of a National Business Elite: The U.S 1890–1905." Working Paper 120, Center for Research on Social Organization University of Michigan.

RUDÉ, GEORGE (1973). "Protest and Punishment in Nineteenth-Century Britain." *Albion* 5: 1–23.

RUSSETT, BRUCE M. (1964). "Inequality and Instability: The Relation of Land Tenure to Politics." *World Politics* 16:442–454.

SAMAHA, JOEL (1974). *Law and Order in Historical Perspective.* New York Academic.

SHELTON, WALTER J. (1973). *English Hunger and Industrial Disorders. A Study of Social Conflict during the First Decade of George III's Reign.* London: Macmillan.

SIMON, HERBERT (1957). "Notes on the Observation and Measurement of Political Power," in *Models of Man, Social and Rational.* New York: Wiley.

SPIELMAN, JOHN V. (1939). "Labor Disputes on Rights and Interests." *American Economic Review* 29: 299–312.

STINCHCOMBE, ARTHUR (1965). "Social Structure and Organizations," in James March, ed., *Handbook of Organizations.* Chicago: Rand McNally.

_____ (1974). *Creating Efficient Industrial Administrations.* New York: Academic.

_____ (1975). "Social Structure and Politics," in vol. 3 of Fred I. Greenstein and Nelson Polsby, eds., *Handbook of Political Science.* Reading, Massachusetts: Addison-Wesley.

STORCH, ROBERT D. (1976). "The Policeman as Domestic Missionary: Urban Discipline and Popular Culture in Northern England, 1850–1880." *Journal of Social History* 9: 481–509.

THOMPSON, E. P. (1975). *Whigs and Hunters. The Origin of the Black Act.* New York: Pantheon.

TILLY, CHARLES; ALLAN LEVETT; A. Q. LODHI; and FRANK MUNGER (1975). "How Policing Affected the Visibility of Crime in Nineteenth-Century Europe and America." Working Paper 115, Center for Research on Social Organization, University of Michigan.

TUDESQ, ANDRÉ-JEAN (1964). *Les Grands Notables en France.* Paris: Presses Universitaires de France.

WICKBERG, EDGAR (1975). "The Taiwan Peasant Movement, 1923–1932: Chinese Rural Radicalism under Japanese Development Programs." *Pacific Affairs* 48: 558–582.

WILSON, JAMES Q. (1973). *Political Organizations.* New York: Basic.

WOLF, ERIC (1969). *Peasant Wars of the Twentieth Century.* New York: Harper & Row.

YUCHTMAN, EPHRAIM, and STANLEY E. SEASHORE (1967). "A System Resource Approach to Organizational Effectiveness." *American Sociological Review* 32: 891–903.

5 Changing Forms of Collective Action

ACCATI, L. (1972). "Vive le roi sans taille et sans gabelle: una discussione sulle rivolte contadine." *Quaderni Storici* 7: 1071–1104.

AGUET, JEAN-PIERRE (1954). *Contribution à l'histoire du mouvement ouvrier français: les grèves sous la Monarchie de Juillet (1830–1847).* Geneva: Droz.

AGULHON, MAURICE (1970). *La République au village.* Paris: Plon.

ALAPURO, RISTO (1974). "Peasants, States and the Capitalist World System: A Review." Working Paper 103, Center for Research on Social Organization, University of Michigan.

AMINZADE, RONALD (1976). "Breaking the Chains of Dependency: From Patronage to Class Politics." *Journal of Urban History*, forthcoming.

AMSDEN, JON, and STEPHEN BRIER (1977). "Coal Miners on Strike: The Transformations of Strike Demands and the Formation of a National Union." *Journal of Interdisciplinary History* 7: 583–616.

ASHENFELTER, ORLEY, and GEORGE E. JOHNSON (1969). "Bargaining Theory, Trade Unions and Industrial Strike Activity." *American Economic Review* 59:35–49.

BENDIX, REINHARD (1964). *Nation-Building and Citizenship.* New York: Wiley.

BERCÉ, YVES-MARIE (1974). *Histoire des Croquants.* 2 vols. Paris: Droz.

BLACK, EUGENE C. (1963). *The Association. British Extraparliamentary Political Organization, 1769–1793.* Cambridge: Harvard University Press.

BLOK, ANTON (1974). *The Mafia of a Sicilian Village.* New York: Harper & Row.

BRITT, DAVID, and OMER GALLE (1972). "Industrial Conflict and Unionization." *American Sociological Review* 37: 46–57.

———— (1974). "Structural Antecedents of the Shape of Strikes: A Comparative Analysis." *American Sociological Review* 39: 642–651.

CARTER, APRIL (1973). *Direct Action and Liberal Democracy.* London: Routledge & Kegan Paul.

CAVALLI, ALESSANDRO, and ALBERTO MARTINELLI (1971). *Il campus diviso.* Padua: Marsilio.

CANNON, JOHN (1973). *Parliamentary Reform, 1640–1832.* Cambridge: Cambridge University Press.

CEDERQVIST, JANE (1975). Collective Behavior in Stockholm 1850–1910. Unpublished paper, University of Stockholm.

CHIROT, DANIEL (1976). *Social Change in a Peripheral Society. The Creation of a Balkan Colony.* New York: Academic.

DAHL, ROBERT A. (1975). "Governments and Political Oppositions," in vol. 3 of Fred I. Greenstein and Nelson Polsby, eds., *Handbook of Political Science.* Reading, Massachusetts: Addison-Wesley.

DAVIS, C. S. L. (1968). "The Pilgrimage of Grace Reconsidered." *Past and Present* 41: 54–76.

———— (1969). "Révoltes populaires en Angleterre (1500–1700)." *Annales; Economies, Sociétés, Civilisations* 24: 24–60.

DAVIS, NATALIE ZEMON (1975). *Society and Culture in Early Modern France.* Berkeley: University of California Press.

DEUTSCH, KARL (1953). *Nationalism and Social Communication.* Cambridge: MIT Press.

DODDS, MADELEINE HOPE, and RUTH DODDS (1915). *The Pilgrimage of Grace. 1536–1537, and the Exeter Conspiracy, 1538.* Cambridge: Cambridge University Press.

DUNBABIN, J. P. D. (1974). *Rural Discontent in Nineteenth-Century Britain.* New York: Holmes & Meier.

DUNLOP, JOHN T. (1958). *Industrial Relations Systems.* New York: Holt.

DURAND, CLAUDE, and PAUL DUBOIS (1975). *La grève. Enquête sociologique.* Paris: Colin.

DUVERGER, MAURICE (1963). *Political Parties.* New York: Wiley.

EISENSTADT, S. N. (1966). *Modernization: Protest and Change.* Englewood Cliffs, New Jersey: Prentice-Hall.

EISINGER, PETER K. (1973). "The Conditions of Protest Behavior in American Cities." *American Political Science Review* 67: 11–68.

ELDRIDGE, J. E. T. (1968). *Industrial Disputes: Essays in the Sociology of Industrial Relations.* London: Routledge & Kegan Paul.

ETZIONI, AMITAI (1968). *The Active Society.* New York: Free Press.

FRASER, DEREK (1970). "The Agitation for Parliamentary Reform," in J. T. Ward, ed., *Popular Movements, c. 1830–1850.* London: Macmillan.

GAIGNEBET, CLAUDE (1972). "Le combat de Carnaval et de Carême de P. Bruegel (1559)." *Annales; Economies, Sociétés, Civilisations* 27: 313–345.

GILLIS, JOHN (1974). *Youth and History. Tradition and Change in European Age Relations, 1770–present.* New York: Academic.

GROH, DIETER (1974). "La Grève de masse, arme politique de la social-démocratie allemande en 1905/1906: mais à quoi sert une épée, si elle n'a pas de poignée?" *Revue belge d'histoire contemporaine* 5: 339–359.

GURR, TED ROBERT (1976). *Rogues, Rebels, and Reformers. A Political History of Urban Crime and Conflict.* Beverly Hills, California: Sage.

HANAGAN, MICHAEL (1976). Artisans and Industrial Workers: Work Structure, Technological Change, and Worker Militancy in Three French Towns: 1870–1914. Unpublished Ph.D. dissertation in history, University of Michigan.

HEERS, JACQUES (1971). *Fêtes, jeux et joutes dan les sociétés d'Occident à la fin du Moyen Age.* Paris: Vrin.

HIBBS, DOUGLAS, A., JR. (1976a). "Industrial Conflict in Advanced Industrial Societies." *American Political Science Review* 70: 1033–1058.

―――― (1976b). "Long-Run Trends in Strike Activity in Comparative Perspective." Paper C/76-18, Center for International Studies, Massachusetts Institute of Technology.

HOBSBAWM, E. J. (1959). *Primitive Rebels.* Manchester: Manchester University Press.

―――― (1974). "Peasant Land Occupations." *Past and Present* 62: 120–152.

HOERDER, DIRK (1971). *People and Mobs: Crowd Action in Massachusetts during the American Revolution. 1765–1780.* Berlin: privately published.

INGHAM, GEOFFREY K. (1974). *Strikes and Industrial Conflict. Britain and Scandinavia.* London: Macmillan.

KAELBLE, HARTMUT, and HEINRICH VOLKMANN (1972). "Konjonktur und Streik in

Deutschland während des Übergangs zum organisierten Kapitalismus." *Zeitschrift fur Wirtschafts-und Sozialwissenschaften* 92: 513–544.

KARLBOM, ROLF (1967). *Hungerupplopp och strejker, 1793–1867.* Lund: Gleerup.

KAY, MARVIN L. MICHAEL (1976). "The North Carolina Regulation, 1766–1776: A Class Conflict," in Alfred F. Young, ed., *The American Revolution.* DeKalb: Northern Illinois University Press.

KNOWLES, K. G. J. C. (1952). *Strikes: A Study in Industrial Conflict with Special Reference to British Experience.* 2d. ed. Oxford: Basil Blackwell.

KORNHAUSER, ARTHUR et al., eds., (1954). *Industrial Conflict.* New York: McGraw-Hill.

LAFFERTY, WILLIAM (1971). *Economic Development and the Response of Labor in Scandinavia.* Oslo: Universitets forlaget.

LAMMERS, CORNELIUS (1969). "Strikes and Mutinies: A Comparative Study of Organizational Conflicts Between Rulers and Ruled." *Administrative Science Quarterly* 14: 448–472.

LAUBIER, PATRICK DE (1968). "Esquisse d'une théorie du syndicalisme." *Sociologie du Travail* 10: 362–392.

LIND, JOAN (1973). Foreign and Domestic Conflict: The British and Swedish Labor Movements 1900–1950. Unpublished Ph.D. dissertation in sociology, University of Michigan.

LORWIN, VAL (1958). "Working-Class Politics and Economic Development in Western Europe." *American Historical Review* 63: 338–351.

LUNDKVIST, SVEN (1977). *Folkrörelserna i det svenska samhallet, 1850–1920.* Stockholm: Almqvist & Wiksell.

MARAVALL, JOSÉ ANTONIO (1972). *Estado moderno y mentalidad social. Siglos XV a XVII.* 2 vols. Madrid: Ediciones de la Revista de Occidente.

MARX, GARY T. (1971). "Civil Disorder and the Agents of Social Control," in Gary T. Marx, ed., *Racial Conflict.* Boston: Little, Brown.

———— (1974). "Thoughts on a Neglected Category of Social Movement Participant: The Agent Provocateur and the Informant." *American Journal of Sociology* 80: 402–442.

MARX, KARL (1970–72). *Capital.* 3 vols. London: Lawrence & Wishart.

MCCARTHY, JOHN D., and MAYER N. ZALD (1973). *The Trend of Social Movements in America: Professionalization and Resource Mobilization.* Morristown, New Jersey: General Learning Corporation.

MERRIMAN, JOHN (1975). "Radicalisation and Repression: A Study of the Demobilization of the 'Democ-Socs' during the Second French Republic," in Roger Price, ed., *Revolution and Reaction. 1848 and the Second French Republic.* London: Croom Helm.

MICHELS, ROBERT (1949). *Political Parties.* Glencoe, Illinois: Free Press. First published in 1915.

MOORE, SALLY FALK, and BARBARA G. MYERHOFF (1975). *Symbol and Politics in Communal Ideology.* Ithaca: Cornell University Press.

MOTTEZ, ROBERT (1966). *Systèmes de salaire et politiques patronales. Essai sur l'évolution des pratiques et des idéologies patronales.* Paris: Editions du Centre Nationale de la Récherche Scientifique.

NIPPERDEY, THOMAS (1972). "Verein als soziale Struktur in Deutschland im späten 18. und frühen 19. Jahrhundert," in Hartmut Boockman et al., *Geschichtswissenschaft and Vereinswesen im 19. Jahrhundert.* Göttingen, Germany: Vandenhoeck & Ruprecht.

OZOUF, MONA (1975). "Space and Time in the Festivals of the French Revolution." *Comparative Studies in Society and History* 17: 372–384.

PARKER, GEOFFREY (1973). "Mutiny and Discontent in the Spanish Army of Flanders 1572–1607." *Past and Present* 58: 38–52.

PENCAVEL, JOHN H. (1970). "An Investigation into Industrial Strike Activity in Britain." *Economica* 37: 239–256.

PERROT, MICHELLE (1974). *Les ouvriers en grève.* 2 vols. Paris: Mouton.

REES, ALBERT (1952). "Industrial Conflict and Business Fluctuations." *Journal of Political Economy* 60: 371–382.

RIMLINGER, GASTON V. (1960). "The Legitimation of Protest: A Comparative Study in Labor History." *Comparative Studies in Society and History* 2: 329–343.

ROKKAN, STEIN (1970). *Citizens, Elections, Parties. Approaches to the Comparative Study of the Processes of Development.* Oslo: Universitets forlaget.

ROSS, ARTHUR M., and GEORGE W. HARTMAN (1960). *Changing Patterns of Industrial Conflict.* New York: Wiley.

RUDÉ, GEORGE (1962). *Wilkes and Liberty.* London: Oxford University Press.

_____ (1971). *Hanoverian London.* London: Secker & Warburg.

SHORTER, EDWARD, and CHARLES TILLY (1973). "Les vagues de grèves en France, 1890–1968." *Annales; Economies, Sociétés, Civilisations* 28: 857–887.

_____ (1974). *Strikes in France, 1830–1968.* Cambridge: Cambridge University Press.

SKEELS, JACK W. (1971). "Measures of U.S. Strike Activity." *Labor and Industrial Relations Review* 24: 515–525.

SMITH, A. W. (1966). "Some Folklore Elements in Movements of Protest." *Folklore* 77: 241–252.

SNYDER, DAVID (1974). Determinants of Industrial Conflict: Historical Models of Strikes in France, Italy and the United States. Unpublished Ph.D. dissertation in sociology, University of Michigan.

_____ (1975). "Institutional Setting and Industrial Conflict: Comparative Analyses of France, Italy and the United States." *American Sociological Review* 40: 259–278.

THOMPSON, E. B. (1963). *The Making of the English Working Class.* London: Gollancz.

_____ (1972). " 'Rough Music': Le Charivari anglais." *Annales; Economies, Sociétés, Civilisations* 27: 285–312.

TILLY, CHARLES; LOUISE TILLY; and RICHARD TILLY (1975). *The Rebellious Century, 1830–1930.* Cambridge: Harvard University Press.

TILLY, RICHARD, and CHARLES TILLY (1971). "An Agenda for European Economic History in the 1970s." *Journal of Economic History* 31: 184–197.

VANDERKAMP, JOHN (1970). "Economic Activity and Strikes in Canada." *Industrial Relations* 9: 215–230.

VARAGNAC, ANDRÉ (1947). *Civilisation traditionnelle et genres de vie.* Paris: Albin Michel.

WEINTRAUB, ANDREW (1966). "Prosperity versus Strikes: An Empirical Approach." *Industrial and Labor Relations Review* 19: 231–238.

6   Collective Violence

ADAMS, GRAHAM, JR. (1966). *The Age of Industrial Violence.* New York: Columbia University Press.

AFRICA, THOMAS W. (1971). "Urban Violence in Imperial Rome." *Journal of Interdisciplinary History* 2: 3–22.

AMIOT, MICHEL et al. (1968). *La violence dans le monde actuel.* Paris: Desclée de Brouwer for Centre d'Etudes de la Civilisation Contemporaine.

ARENDT, HANNAH (1970). *On Violence.* New York: Harcourt, Brace and World.

BERGESEN, ALBERT J. (1976). White or Black Riots? A Reconsideration of the Sources of Violence during the Detroit and Newark Race Riots of 1967. Unpublished paper presented to the annual meeting of the American Sociological Association.

BERNOUX, PHILIPPE et al. (1969). *Violences et société.* Paris: Editions Economie et Humanisme/Editions Ouvrières.

BIENEN, HENRY (1968). *Violence and Social Change: A Review of Current Literature.* Chicago: University of Chicago Press.

BLUMENTHAL, MONICA et al. (1972). *Justifying Violence: Attitudes of American Men.* Ann Arbor: Institute for Social Research, University of Michigan.

BOHSTEDT, JOHN (1972). Riots in England, 1790–1810, with Special Reference to Devonshire. Unpublished Ph.D. Dissertation in history, Harvard University.

BROWN, RICHARD MAXWELL (1975). *Strain of Violence. Historical Studies of American Violence and Vigilantism.* New York: Oxford University Press.

CALHOUN, DANIEL (1970). "Studying American Violence." *Journal of Interdisciplinary History* 1: 163–185.

CONANT, RALPH W., and MOLLY APPLE LEVIN, eds. (1969). *Problems in Research on Community Violence.* New York: Praeger.

CONNERY, DONALD, ed. (1968). "Urban Riots: Violence and Social Change." *Proceedings of the Academy of Political Science* 29: entire issue.

CONOT, ROBERT (1968). *Rivers of Blood, Years of Darkness.* New York: Bantam.

COUNTRYMAN, EDWARD (1976). " 'Out of the Bounds of the Law': Northern Land Rioters in the Eighteenth Century," in Alfred F. Young, ed., *The American Revolution.* DeKalb: Northern Illinois University Press.

CRITCHLEY, T. A. (1970). *The Conquest of Violence: Order and Liberty in Britain.* London: Constable.

DÍAZ DEL MORAL, JUAN (1967). *Historia de las agitaciones campesinas andaluzas—Córdoba.* 2d. ed. Madrid: El Libro del Bolsillo.

ELLUL, JACQUES (1970). *Violence.* London: S. C. M. Books.

FARRÉ MOREGO, J. M. (1922). *Los atentados sociales en España.* Madrid: Artes Gráficas.

FEAGIN, JOE R. and HARLAN HAHN (1973). *Ghetto Revolts.* New York: Macmillan.

FEIERABEND, IVO K., and ROSALIND L. FEIERABEND (1966). "Aggressive Behaviors within Polities, 1948–1962: A Cross-National Study." *Journal of Conflict Resolution* 10: 249–271.

FISCHER, WOLFRAM (1966). "Social Tensions at Early Stages of Industrialization." *Comparative Studies in Society and History* 9: 64–83.

FOGELSON, ROBERT M. (1971). *Violence as Protest: A Study of Riots and Ghettos.* Garden City, New York: Doubleday.

GAMSON, WILLIAM A. (1968). "Stable Unrepresentation in American Society." *American Behavioral Scientist* 12: 15–21.

—————— (1975). *The Strategy of Social Protest.* Homewood, Illinois: Dorsey.

GEERTZ, CLIFFORD (1968). "Is America by Nature a Violent Society?" *New York Times Magazine*, April 28.

GIRARD, LOUIS (1961). *Etude comparée des mouvements révolutionnaires en France en 1830, 1848, et 1870–71.* 3 parts. Paris: Centre de Documentation Universitaire.

GRAHAM, HUGH DAVIS, and TED ROBERT GURR, eds. (1969). *Violence in America: Historical and Comparative Perspectives.* Washington, D.C.: U.S. Government Printing Office.

GRIMSHAW, ALLEN D. (1969). *Racial Violence in the United States.* Chicago: Aldine.

GROFMAN, BERNARD N., and EDWARD N. MULLER (1973). "The Strange Case of Relative Gratification and Potential for Political Violence: the V-Curve Hypothesis." *American Political Science Review* 67: 514–539.

GRUNDY, KENNETH W., and MICHAEL WEINSTEIN (1974). *The Ideologies of Violence.* Columbus, Ohio: Charles E. Merrill.

GURR, TED ROBERT; PETER N. GRABOSKY; and RICHARD C. HULA (1977). *The Politics of Crime and Conflict. A Comparative History of Four Cities.* Beverly Hills, California: Sage.

GUZMÁN, GERMÁN et al. (1962). *La violencia en Colombia.* 2 vols. Bogota: Universidad Nacional.

HECHTER, MICHAEL (1975). *Internal Colonialism. The Celtic Fringe in British National Development, 1536–1966.* Berkeley: University of California Press.

HIRSCH, HERBERT and DAVID PERRY, eds. (1973). *Violence as Politics.* New York: Harper & Row.

HOBSBAWM, E. J. (1969). *Bandits.* New York: Delacorte.

HOFSTADTER, RICHARD (1970). "Reflections on Violence in the United States," in Richard Hofstadter and Michael Wallace, eds., *American Violence: A Documentary History.* New York: Knopf.

HOLMBERG, JAMES C. (1971). "The Rush to Violence in Social Analysis: A Review Essay." *Historical Methods Newsletter* 4: 88–99.

HUDSON, MICHAEL C. (1970). *Conditions of Political Violence and Instability.* Beverly Hills, California: Sage. Sage Professional Papers, 01–005.

JIOBU, ROBERT M. (1974). "City Characteristics and Racial Violence." *Social Science Quarterly* 55: 52–64.

KIRKHAM, JAMES F.; SHELDON G. LEVY; and WILLIAM J. CROTTY (1970). *Assassination and Political Violence.* Washington, D.C.: U.S. Government Printing Office.

LODHI, A. Q., and CHARLES TILLY (1973). "Urbanization, Criminality and Collective Violence in Nineteenth Century France." *American Journal of Sociology* 79: 296–318.

LUPSHA, PETER (1969). "On Theories of Urban Violence." *Urban Affairs Quarterly* 4: 273–296.

———— (1971). "Explanation of Political Violence: Some Psychological Theories versus Indignation." *Politics and Society* 2: 89–104.

McHALE, VINCENT E., and ERIC A. JOHNSON (1976). "Urbanization, Industrialization and Crime in Imperial Germany, Part I." *Social Science History* 1: 45–78.

MEHDEN, FRED VON DER (1973). *Comparative Political Violence.* Englewood Cliffs, New Jersey: Prentice-Hall.

NARDIN, TERRY (1971a). "Theories of Conflict Management." *Peace Research Reviews* 4: 1–93.

———— (1971b). *Violence and the State: A Critique of Empirical Political Theory.* Beverly Hills, California: Sage Publications. Sage Professional Papers, Comparative Politics Series, series 01–020, vol. 2.

———— (1972). "Conflicting Conceptions of Political Violence," in Cornelius P. Cotter, ed., *Political Science Annual*, vol. 4. Indianapolis: Bobbs-Merrill.

NESVOLD, BETTY A. (1969). "Scalogram Analysis of Political Violence." *Comparative Political Studies* 2: 172–194.

OBERSCHALL, ANTHONY (1977). "The Decline of the 1960's Social Movements," in Louis Kriesberg, ed., *Research in Social Movements, Conflict, and Change.* Greenwich, Conn.: JAI Press, forthcoming.

PARET, PETER, and JOHN W. SHY (1964). *Guerrillas in the 1960s.* New York: Praeger.

PORTER, RANDALL C., and JACK H. NAGEL (1976). "Declining Inequality and Rising Expectations: Relative Deprivation and the Black Urban Riots." Philadelphia: School of Public and Urban Policy, University of Pennsylvania. Fels Discussion Paper 96.

PRICE, RICHARD N. (1975). "The Other Face of Respectability: Violence in the Manchester Brickmaking Trade, 1859–1870." *Past and Present* 66: 110–132.

RICHTER, DONALD (1965). Public Order and Popular Disturbances in Great Britain, 1865–1914. Unpublished Ph.D. dissertation in modern history, University of Maryland.

———— (1971). "The Role of Mob Riot in Victorian Elections, 1865–1885." *Victorian Studies* 14–15: 19–28.

RUBENSTEIN, RICHARD E. (1970). *Rebels in Eden: Mass Political Violence in the United States.* Boston: Little, Brown.

RUMPF, E. (1959). *Nationalismus und Sozialismus in Irland.* Meisenheim: Hain.

SHEPPARD, FRANCIS (1971). *London 1808–1870: The Infernal Wen.* London: Secker & Warburg.

SHORTER, EDWARD, and CHARLES TILLY (1971). "Le déclin de la grève violente en France de 1890 à 1935." *Le mouvement social* 79: 95–118.

SKOLNICK, JEROME (1969). *The Politics of Protest: Violent Aspects of Protest and Confrontation.* Washington: U.S. Government Printing Office.

SNYDER, DAVID, and WILLIAM R. KELLY (1976). "Industrial Violence in Italy, 1878–1903." *American Journal of Sociology* 82: 131–162.

———— (1977). "Conflict Intensity, Media Sensitivity and the Validity of Newspaper Data." *American Sociological Review* 42: 105–123.

SNYDER, DAVID, and CHARLES TILLY (1972). "Hardship and Collective Violence in France, 1830 to 1960." *American Sociological Review* 37: 520–532.

SPILERMAN, SEYMOUR (1976). "Structural Characteristics of Cities and the Severity of Racial Disorders." *American Sociological Review* 41: 771–792.

STEVENSON, JOHN (1974). "Food Riots in England, 1792–1818," in John Stevenson and Roland Quinault, eds., *Popular Protest and Public Order. Six Studies in British History, 1790–1920.* London: George Allen & Unwin.

STOHL, MICHAEL (1976). *War and Domestic Political Violence. The American Capacity for Repression and Reaction.* Beverly Hills, California: Sage.

TAFT, PHILIP, and PHILIP ROSS (1969). "American Labor Violence: Its Causes, Character and Outcome," in Hugh Davis Graham and Ted Robert Gurr, eds., *Violence in America.* Washington, D.C.: U.S. Government Printing Office.

THOMPSON, E. P. (1971). "The Moral Economy of the English Crowd in the Eighteenth Century." *Past and Present* 50: 76–136.

TILLY, CHARLES (1970). "The Changing Place of Collective Violence," in Melvin Richter, ed., *Essays in Social and Political History.* Cambridge: Harvard University Press.

_____ (1975). "Food Supply and Public Order in Modern Europe," in Charles Tilly, ed., *The Formation of National States in Western Europe.* Princeton: Princeton University Press.

TILLY, LOUISE A. (1971). "The Food Riot as a Form of Political Conflict in France." *Journal of Interdisciplinary History* 2: 23–57.

TILLY, RICHARD (1975). Protest and Collective Violence in Germany During Modernization (1800–1914). Unpublished manuscript, Institut für Wirtschafts- und Sozialgeschichte, Westfälische Wilhelms-Universität.

TOCH, HANS (1969). *Violent Men: An Inquiry into the Psychology of Violence.* Chicago: Aldine.

WALTER, E. V. (1969). *Terror and Resistance: A Study of Political Violence.* New York: Oxford University Press.

WERNETTE, DEE RICHARD (1974). Political Violence and German Elections: 1930 and July, 1932. Unpublished Ph.D. dissertation in sociology, University of Michigan.

WOLFGANG, MARVIN E., and FRANCO FERRACUTI (1967). *The Subculture of Violence.* London: Tavistock.

7 Revolution and Rebellion

AMANN, PETER (1962). "Revolution: A Redefinition." *Political Science Quarterly* 77: 36–53.

ANDRESKI, STANISLAV (1968). *Military Organization and Society.* Berkeley: University of California Press.

ARDANT, GABRIEL (1965). *Théorie sociologique de l'impôt.* 2 vols. Paris: SEVPEN.

ARENDT, HANNAH (1963). *On Revolution.* London: Faber & Faber.

_____ (1971). "Thoughts on Politics and Revolution." *New York Review of Books* 16: 8–20.

AYA, RODERICK (1975). "The Missed Revolution. The Fate of Rural Rebels in Sicily and Southern Spain, 1840–1950." Papers on European and Mediterranean Societies, Antropologisch-Sociologisch Centrum, University of Amsterdam, no. 3.

BAECHLER, JEAN (1970). *Les phénomènes révolutionnaires.* Paris: Presses Universitaires de France.

BELL, DAVID V. J. (1973). *Resistance and Revolution.* Boston: Houghton Mifflin.

BEZUCHA, ROBERT (1974). *The Lyon Uprising of 1834. Social and Political Conflict in the Early July Monarchy.* Cambridge: Harvard University Press.

BRAUDEL, FERNAND (1966). *La Méditerranée et le monde méditerranéen à l'époque de Philippe II.* 2d. ed. Paris: Colin.

BRENAN, GERALD (1943). *The Spanish Labyrinth: An Account of the Social and Political Background of the Civil War.* Cambridge: Cambridge University Press.

BRINTON, CRANE (1965). *The Anatomy of Revolution.* Rev. ed. New York: Knopf.

CALVERT, PETER (1970). *A Study of Revolution*. Oxford: Clarendon Press.

CANTOR, NORMAN ·F. (1970). *The Age of Protest. Dissent and Rebellion in the Twentieth Century*. London: George Allen & Unwin.

CHIROT, DANIEL, and CHARLES RAGIN (1975). "The Market, Tradition and Peasant Rebellion: The Case of Romania in 1907." *American Sociological Review* 40: 428–444.

CHORLEY, KATHERINE (1943). *Armies and the Art of Revolution*. London: Faber & Faber.

CLARK, MARTIN (1973). "The Failure of Revolution in Italy, 1919–1920." Centre for the Advanced Study of Italian Society, University of Reading, Occasional Papers No. 5.

COBB, RICHARD (1957). "The Revolutionary Mentality in France, 1793–1794." *History* 42: 81–96.

DALY, WILLIAM T. (1972). "The Revolutionary: A Review and Synthesis." Beverly Hills, California: Sage. Sage Professional Papers, Comparative Politics Series, 01–025.

DAVIES, JAMES C. (1962). "Toward a Theory of Revolution." *American Sociological Review* 27: 5–19.

DEBRAY, REGIS (1967). *Revolution in the Revolution? Armed Struggle and Political Struggle in Latin America*. New York: Grove.

DEL CARRIA, RENZO (1966). *Proletari senza rivoluzione: Storia delle classe subalterne italiane dal 1860 al 1954*. 2 vols. Milan: Oriente.

DUNN, JOHN (1972). *Modern Revolutions*. Cambridge: Cambridge University Press.

DUVEAU, GEORGES (1965). *1848*. Paris: Gallimard.

ECKSTEIN, HARRY (1965). "On the Etiology of Internal Wars." *History and Theory* 4: 133–163.

ECKSTEIN, SUSAN (1976). "The Impact of Revolution: A Comparative Analysis of Mexico and Bolivia." Beverly Hills, California: Sage. Sage Professional Papers, Contemporary Political Sociology Series, 06–016.

EDWARDS, LYFORD P. (1927). *The Natural History of Revolution*. Chicago: University of Chicago Press.

EISENSTADT, S. N. (1963). *The Political Systems of Empires*. New York: Free Press.

ELLUL, JACQUES (1969). *Autopsie de la révolution*. Paris: Calmann-Levy.

ENGELS, FRIEDRICH (1886). *Herrn Eugen Dührings Umwälzung der Wissenschaft*. Zurich: Volksbuchhandlung.

FANON, FRANTZ (1964). *The Wretched of the Earth*. New York: Grove.

FLETCHER, ANTONY (1968). *Tudor Rebellions*. London: Longmans.

FRIEDRICH, CARL J., ed. (1966). *Revolution*. New York: Atherton.

GAMSON, WILLIAM A. (1968). *Power and Discontent*. Homewood, Illinois: Dorsey.

GILLIS, JOHN (1970). "Political Decay and the European Revolutions, 1789–1848." *World Politics* 22: 344–370.

GLUCKMAN, MAX (1963). *Order and Rebellion in Tribal Africa.* New York: Free Press.

GORZ, ANDRÉ (1969). *Réforme et révolution.* Paris: Seuil.

GREENE, THOMAS H. (1974). *Comparative Revolutionary Movements.* Englewood Cliffs, New Jersey: Prentice-Hall.

GURR, TED ROBERT (1969). *Why Men Rebel.* Princeton: Princeton University Press.

_____ (1973). "The Revolution–Social Change Nexus. Some Old Theories and New Hypotheses." *Comparative Politics* 5: 359–392.

HERMASSI, ELBAKI (1976). "Toward a Comparative Study of Revolutions." *Comparative Studies in Society and History* 16: 211–235.

HILTON, RODNEY (1973). *Bond Men Made Free. Medieval Peasant Movements and the English Rising of 1381.* London: Temple Smith.

HOBSBAWM, E. J. (1962). *The Age of Revolution. Europe, 1789–1848.* London: Weidenfeld & Nicolson.

_____ (1973). *Revolutionaries.* London: Weidenfeld & Nicolson.

HUIZER, GERRIT (1973). *Peasant Rebellion in Latin America.* Harmondsworth, England: Penguin.

HUNTINGTON, SAMUEL (1968). *Political Order in Changing Societies.* New Haven: Yale University Press.

JANOS, ANDREW (1966). *Revolutionary Change.* Boston: Little, Brown.

JESSOP, BOB (1972). *Social Order, Reform and Revolution. A Power, Exchange and Institutionalization Perspective.* London: Macmillan.

KAUTSKY, JOHN H. (1975). *Patterns of Modernizing Revolution: Mexico and the Soviet Union.* Beverly Hills, California: Sage. Sage Professional Papers, Comparative Politics Series, 01-056.

KIM KYUNG-WON (1970). *Revolution and International System.* New York: New York University Press.

KIRCHHEIMER, OTTO (1965). "Confining Conditions and Revolutionary Breakthroughs." *American Political Science Review* 59: 964–974.

KORPI, WALTER (1974a). "Conflict and the Balance of Power." *Acta Sociologica* 17: 99–114.

_____ (1974b). "Conflict, Power and Relative Deprivation." *American Political Science Review* 68: 1569–1578.

KORT, FRED (1952). "The Quantification of Aristotle's Theory of Revolution." *American Political Science Review* 46: 486–493.

LANGER, WILLIAM L. (1969). *Political and Social Upheaval, 1832–1852.* New York: Harper & Row.

LAQUEUR, WALTER (1968). "Revolution." *International Encyclopedia of the Social Sciences* 13: 501–507.

LARSON, REIDAR (1970). *Theories of Revolution, from Marx to the First Russian Revolution*. Stockholm: Almqvist & Wiksell.

LEGGETT, JOHN (1973). *Taking State Power*. New York: Harper & Row.

LENIN, V. I. (1967a). "The Valuable Admissions of Pitirim Sorokin," in *Selected Works*. New York: International Publishers.

_____ (1967b). "What Is to Be Done? Burning Questions of Our Movement," in *Selected Works*. New York: International Publishers.

LEWIS, JOHN WILSON, ed. (1974). *Peasant Rebellion and Communist Revolution in Asia*. Stanford: Stanford University Press.

LIDA, CLARA E. (1972). *Anarquismo y revolución en la España del XIX*. Madrid: Siglo.

LIPSET, S. M., and EARL RAAB (1970). *The Politics of Unreason: Right-Wing Extremism in America, 1790–1970*. New York: Harper & Row.

LUKES, STEVEN (1974). *Power: A Radical View*. London: Macmillan.

MAO TSE-TUNG (1961). "Carry the Revolution Through to the End," in vol. 4 of *Selected Works*. Peking: Foreign Languages Press.

_____ (1965a). "The Chinese Revolution and the Chinese Communist Party," in vol. 2 of *Selected Works*. Peking: Foreign Languages Publishing House.

_____ (1965b). "On Protracted War," in vol. 2 of *Selected Works*. Peking: Foreign Languages Publishing House.

MELOTTI, UMBERTO (1965). *Rivoluzione et societá*. Milan: La Culturale.

MITCHELL, HARVEY (1968). "The Vendée and Counterrevolution: A Review Essay." *French Historical Studies* 5: 405–429.

MOLLAT, MICHEL, and PHILIPPE WOLFF (1973). *The Popular Revolutions of the Late Middle Ages*. London: George Allen & Unwin.

MONNEROT, JULES (1969). *Sociologie de la révolution*. Paris: Artheme Fayard.

MOORE, BARRINGTON, JR. (1966). *Social Origins of Dictatorship and Democracy*. Boston: Beacon.

_____ (1969). "Revolution in America?" *New York Review of Books*, January 30: 6–12.

NOYES, P. H. (1966). *Organization and Revolution. Working Class Associations in the German Revolutions of 1848–49*. Princeton: Princeton University Press.

PAIGE, JEFFERY (1975). *Agrarian Revolution. Social Movements and Export Agriculture in the Underdeveloped World*. New York: Free Press.

PINKNEY, DAVID (1964). "The Crowd in the French Revolution of 1830." *American Historical Review* 70: 1–17.

ROMANO, SALVATORE FRANCESCO (1959). *Storia dei Fasci Siciliani*. Bari: Laterza.

RULE, JAMES, and CHARLES TILLY (1972). "1830 and the Unnatural History of Revolution." *Journal of Social Issues* 28: 49–76.

RUSSELL, D. E. H. (1974). *Rebellion, Revolution, and Armed Force*. New York: Academic.

SABEAN, DAVID (1972). *Landbesitz und Gesellschaft am Vorabend des Bauernkriegs*. Stuttgart: Gustav Fischer.

SALERT, BARBARA (1976). *Revolutions and Revolutionaries. Four Theories*. New York: Elsevier.

SCHEINER, IRWIN (1973). "The Mindful Peasant: Sketches for a Study of Rebellion." *Journal of Asian Studies* 32: 579–591.

SKOCPOL, THEDA (1976). "France, Russia, China: A Structural Analysis of Social Revolution." *Comparative Studies in Society and History* 16: 175–210.

SMELSER, NEIL J. (1963). *Theory of Collective Behavior*. New York: Free Press.

SOLDANI, SIMONETTA (1973). "Contadini, operai e 'popolo' nella rivoluzione del 1848–49 in Italia." *Studi Storici* 14: 557–613.

SOREL, GEORGES (1961). *Reflections on Violence*. New York: Macmillan.

STARBUCK, WILLIAM H. (1973). "Tadpoles into Armageddon and Chrysler into Butterflies." *Social Science Research* 1–2: 81–109.

STONE, LAWRENCE (1972). *The Causes of the English Revolution, 1529–1642*. London: Routledge & Kegan Paul.

TANTER, RAYMOND, and MANUS MIDLARSKY (1967). "A Theory of Revolution." *Journal of Conflict Resolution* 11: 264–280.

TILLY, CHARLES (1964). "Reflections on the Revolutions of Paris: An Essay on Recent Historical Writing." *Social Problems* 12: 99–121.

———— (1973). "Does Modernization Breed Revolution?" *Comparative Politics* 5: 425–447.

———— (1975). "Revolutions and Collective Violence," in vol. 3 of Fred I. Greenstein and Nelson Polsby, eds., *Handbook of Political Science*. Reading, Massachusetts: Addison-Wesley.

TILLY, CHARLES, and LYNN LEES (1974). "Le peuple de juin 1848." *Annales; Economies, Sociétés, Civilisations* 29: 1061–1091.

TILLY, LOUISE A. (1972). "I Fatti di Maggio: The Working Class of Milan and the Rebellion of 1898," in Robert J. Bezucha, ed., *Modern European Social History*. Lexington, Massachusetts: D.C. Heath.

TROTSKY, LEON (1965). *History of the Russian Revolution*. 2 vols. London: Gollancz.

WAKEMAN, FREDERIC, JR. (1966). *Strangers at the Gate: Social Disorders in South China, 1839–1861*. Berkeley: University of California Press.

WALDMAN, ERIC (1958). *The Spartacist Uprising of 1919*. Milwaukee: Marquette University Press.

WALZER, MICHAEL (1970). "The Revolutionary Uses of Repression," in Melvin Richter, ed., *Essays in Theory and History: An Approach to the Social Sciences.* Cambridge: Harvard University Press.

WILKIE, JAMES W. (1970). *The Mexican Revolution. Federal Expenditure and Social Change since 1910.* Berkeley and Los Angeles: University of California Press.

WOLF, ERIC (1969). *Peasant Wars of the Twentieth Century.* New York: Harper & Row.

WOMACK, JOHN, JR. (1969). *Zapata and the Mexican Revolution.* Cambridge: Harvard University Press.

ZAGORIN, PEREZ (1976). "Prologomena to the Comparative History of Revolution in Early Modern Europe." *Comparative Studies in Society and History* 18: 151–174.

8 Conclusions and New Beginnings

BERCÉ, YVES-MARIE (1974a). *Croquants et Nu-Pieds. Les soulevèments paysans en France du XVIe au XIXe siècle.* Paris: Gallimard/Juilliard.

_____ (1974b). *Histoire des Croquants.* 2 vols. Paris: Droz.

BROWN, RICHARD MAXWELL, and DON E. FEHRENBACHER, eds. (1977). *Tradition, Conflict, and Modernization: Perspectives on the American Revolution.* New York: Academic, forthcoming.

COBBAN, ALFRED (1964). *The Social Interpretation of the French Revolution.* Cambridge: Cambridge University Press.

DARVALL, F. O. (1934). *Popular Disturbances and Public Order in Regency England.* Oxford: Oxford University Press.

GODECHOT, JACQUES (1970). *The Taking of the Bastille.* New York: Scribner.

GRATTON, PHILIPPE (1971). *Les luttes de classes dans les campagnes.* Paris: Anthropos.

HAMBURGER, JOSEPH (1963). *James Mill and the Art of Revolution.* New Haven: Yale University Press.

HAY, DOUGLAS et al. (1975). *Albion's Fatal Tree. Crime and Society in Eighteenth-Century England.* New York: Pantheon.

HINDUS, MICHAEL S. (1971). "A City of Mobocrats and Tyrants: Mob Violence in Boston, 1747–1863." *Issues in Criminology* 6: 55–83.

HOERDER, DIRK (1977). *Crowd Action in a Revolutionary Society. Massachusetts 1765–1780.* New York: Academic.

HOFFMAN, RONALD (1976). "The 'Disaffected' in the Revolutionary South," in Alfred F. Young, ed., *The American Revolution.* DeKalb: Northern Illinois University Press.

JONES, DAVID J. V. (1973). *Before Rebecca. Popular Protests in Wales, 1793–1835.* London: Allen Lane.

LAURENT, ROBERT (1957). *Les Vignerons de la 'Côte d'Or' au dix-neuvième siècle.* 2 vols. Paris: Les Belles Lettres.

KNOLLENBERG, BERNHARD (1965). *Origins of the American Revolution: 1759-1766.* Rev. ed. New York: Free Press.

LEBRUN, FRANCOIS (1967). *Le XVIIe siècle.* Paris: Colin. Collection "U."

LE GOFF, T. J. A., and D. M. G. SUTHERLAND (1974). "The Revolution and the Rural Community in Eighteenth-Century Brittany." *Past and Present* 62: 96-119.

LEMISCH, JESSE (1968). "The American Revolution Seen from the Bottom Up," in Barton J. Bernstein, ed., *Towards a New Past.* New York: Vintage.

LEMISCH, JESSE, and JOHN K. ALEXANDER (1972). "The White Oaks, Jack Tar, and the Concept of the 'Inarticulate'." *William and Mary Quarterly* 29: 109-142.

LOCKRIDGE, KENNETH P. (1976). "The American Revolution, Modernization, and Man." Working Paper 139, Center for Research on Social Organization, University of Michigan.

LUBLINSKAYA, A. D. (1968). *French Absolutism: The Crucial Phase, 1620-1629.* Cambridge: Cambridge University Press.

LUCAS, COLIN (1973). *The Structure of the Terror. The Example of Javogues and the Loire.* London: Oxford University Press.

MAIER, PAULINE (1972). *From Resistance to Revolution. Colonial Radicals and the Development of American Opposition to Britain, 1765-1776.* New York: Random House.

MATHER, F. C. (1959). *Public Order in the Age of the Chartists.* Manchester: Manchester University Press.

MAZAURIC, CLAUDE (1970). *Sur la révolution française.* Paris: Editions Sociales.

MERRIMAN, JOHN (1974). "Social Conflict in France and the Limoges Revolution of April 27, 1848." *Societas* 4: 21-38.

_____ (1975). "The Demoiselles of Ariège," in John Merriman, ed., *1830 in France.* New York: Franklin Watts.

MOORE, BARRINGTON, JR. (1966). *Social Origins of Dictatorship and Democracy.* Boston: Beacon.

MOUSNIER, ROLAND (1970). *La plume, la faucille et le marteau.* Paris: Presses Universitaires de France.

MUNBY, LIONEL M., ed. (1971). *The Luddites and Other Essays.* London: Katanka.

MUNGER, FRANK W., JR. (1974). "A Comparison of the Dissatisfactions and Collective Action Models of Protest: The Case of the Working Classes of Lancashire, England, 1793-1830." Working Paper 105, Center for Research on Social Organization, University of Michigan.

_____ (1977). Popular Protest and its Suppression in Early Nineteenth Century Lancashire, England: A Study of Historical Models of Protest and Repression. Unpublished manuscript, University of Michigan.

NASH, GARY B. (1976). "Social Change and the Growth of Prerevolutionary Urban Radicalism," in Alfred F. Young, ed., *The American Revolution*. DeKalb: Northern Illinois University Press.

PALMER, R.R. (1977). "The Fading Dream: How European Revolutionaries Have Seen the American Revolution," in Bede Lackner and Kenneth R. Philp, eds., *The Walter Prescott Webb Memorial Lectures. Essays on Modern European Revolutionary History*. Austin: University of Texas Press.

PEACOCK, A. J. (1965). *Bread or Blood: The Agrarian Riots in East Anglia: 1816*. London: Gollancz.

PILLORGET, RÉNÉ (1975). *Les mouvements insurrectionnels de Provence entre 1596 et 1715*. Paris: Pedone.

PORCHNEV, BORIS (1963). *Les soulèvements populaires en France de 1623 à 1648*. Paris: Mouton.

POWELL, G. BINGHAM (1973). "Incremental Democratization: The British Reform Act of 1832," in Gabriel A. Almond, Scott C. Flanagan and Robert J. Mundt, eds., *Crisis, Choice and Change. Historical Studies of Political Development*. Boston: Little, Brown.

ROGERS, ALAN (1974). *Empire and Liberty. American Resistance to British Authority, 1755-1763*. Berkeley: University of California Press.

ROKKAN, STEIN (1969). "Models and Methods in the Comparative Study of Nation Building." *Acta Sociologica* 12: 52-73.

ROTHMAN, STANLEY (1970). "Barrington Moore and the Dialectics of Revolution: An Essay Review." *American Political Science Review* 64: 61-82.

ROUPNEL, GASTON (1955). *La Ville et la campagne au XVIIe siècle. Etude sur les populations du pays dijonnais*. Paris: Colin.

RUDÉ, GEORGE (1964). *The Crowd in History. A Study of Popular Disturbances in France and England, 1730-1848*. New York: Wiley.

———— (1967). "English Rural and Urban Disturbances on the Eve of the First Reform Bill, 1830-1831." *Past and Present* 37: 87-102.

———— (1970). *Paris and London in the 18th Century*. London: Collins.

RYERSON, R. A. (1974). "Political Mobilization and the American Revolution: The Resistance Movement in Philadelphia, 1765 to 1776." *William and Mary Quarterly* 31: 565-588.

SAINT-JACOB, PIERRE DE (1960). *Les Paysans du Bourgogne du Nord*. Paris: Les Belles Lettres.

SMITH, W. A. (1965). Anglo-Colonial Society and the Mob, 1740-1775. Unpublished Ph.D. dissertation in history, Claremont Graduate School and University Center.

STONE, LAWRENCE (1967). "News from Everywhere." *New York Review of Books*, August 24, 31-35. [Review of Barrington Moore, Jr., *Social Origins of Dictatorship and Democracy*.]

TOCQUEVILLE, ALEXIS DE (1955). *The Old Regime and the French Revolution.* New York: Doubleday Anchor.

VESTER, MICHAEL (1970). *Die Entstehung des Proletariats als Lernprozess. Die Entstehung antikapitalistischer Theorie und Praxis in England 1792-1848.* Frankfurt a/Main: Europäische Verlaganstalt.

WILLIAMS, GWYN W. (1968). *Artisans and Sans-Culottes. Popular Movements in France and Britain during the French Revolution.* London: Arnold.

WOOD, GORDON S. (1966). "A Note on Mobs in the American Revolution." *William and Mary Quarterly* (3d series) 23: 635-642.

YOUNG, ALFRED F. (1973). "Pope's Day, Tar and Feathers and 'Cornet Joyce, Jun.' From Ritual to Rebellion in Boston, 1745-1775." Unpublished paper presented to the Anglo-American Labor Historians' Conference, Rutgers University.

Index

A.F.L.-C.I.O., 101
Abolition, 42, 179
Advantage-of-familiarity model, 154–55
Africa, 76
Aged, 107
Age-groups, 145
Age-sex groups, 203
Agriculture, 221, 235, 239; disturbances, 95, 199–200, 233, 239–40; workers, 146–47, 159. *See also* Farmers; Land; Peasantry
Aircraft industry, 179
Alberoni, Francesco, 38, 42
Algeria, 45
Amann, Peter, 191
American Chiropractic Association, 77
American Medical Association, 77, 101
Aminzade, Ronald, 80
Amnesty, 152
Anarchists, 214
Anarcho-Communists, 137
Anarcho-syndicalism, 161
Angola, 200
Anomic collective action, 17, 18, 19, 23, 29
Arbitration and negotiation, 164, 166
Ardant, Gabriel, 205–6
Arendt, Hannah, 175
Aristocracy, 103, 146, 185, 220, 238, 239. *See also* Landlords

Army, 101, 128, 130–31, 145, 152, 176, 177, 178, 189, 194, 201, 205, 210, 211, 214–16, 219, 221; billeting of, 146, 185; private, 180, 184, 216
Artisans, 74, 84, 145, 156, 157, 160, 161, 162, 170, 185, 221, 237
Ash, Roberta, 41, 42
Ashenfelter, Orley, 33–35
Aske, Robert, 153
Assassination, 189
Assembly, assemblies, 74, 101, 103, 137, 168, 170, 171, 183, 225
Association, associations, 81, 83, 101, 132, 167, 187, 188, 241, 242
Australia, 65, 104, 187
Austria, 161
Authority, authorities, 37, 38, 117, 174, 180, 183, 186. *See also* Government; Public officials

Bastille, fall of, 237
Belgium, 161, 165, 187
Beliefs, belief systems, 8–10, 15, 21, 22–23, 24, 37–38, 40, 43, 48, 59, 60, 235
Bercé, Yves-Marie, 146–47, 233
Berlin, 181
Bienen, Henry, 174
Black Act of 1723, 102